# Teaching the City of God in the City of Man

## Pursuing Salvation Education

Patricia Hershwitzky

En Route Books and Media, LLC
Saint Louis, MO

Make the time

En Route Books and Media, LLC
5705 Rhodes Avenue
St. Louis, MO 63109

Contact us at
contact@enroutebooksandmedia.com

Copyright © 2023 by Patricia Hershwitzky

ISBN: 979-8-88870-062-4
Library of Congress Control Number: 2023942292

Cover Art by Steven Mezzacappa, owner of Mezzart in Las Vegas, Nevada. He has received national acclaim for his many works of art, sculpture, and photography. An art instructor at an urban school for seventeen years, he also has received praise for his encouragement of students in that field.

Edited by Rosemary Vander Weele, M.A., a widely respected Catholic classical educator in the Denver area. She is also an acclaimed Program Leader and Principal Trainer for The Institute for Catholic Liberal Education, dedicated to preserving and renewing K-12 schools in an increasingly post-Christian culture.

All rights reserved. No part of this book may be used or reproduced in any manner whatsoever without written permission except in the case of brief quotations embodied in critical articles or reviews.

# Dedication

*To Our Blessed Virgin Mother and her Most Chaste Virginal Spouse, St. Joseph, who together were the primary earthly teachers of Jesus Christ, Our Lord and Savior and King of the City of God*

In the Light of Mary's Flame of Love, may this work also honor all tireless Catholic educators and St. Elizabeth Ann Seton who lit the way for Catholic schooling in America.

# Testimonials

"Brilliant! How wonderful is it at a time of such crisis in education to have Patricia Hershwitzky's book: *Teaching the City of God in the City of Man*! Just what teachers need to be inspired and taught about vision and problem solving concerning concrete facets of being a Catholic teacher of any subject and any grade. You will absolutely love Patricia Hershwitzky's lively and vibrant style." —**Ronda Chervin, PhD, is a well-known Catholic author, former international speaker and Professor of Philosophy who has authored over seventy books and numerous articles on the Faith.**

"*Teaching the City of God in the City of Man* is a must-read primer for anyone who cares deeply about authentically Catholic education—be they teachers, administrators, clergy, or parents. Hershwitzky marvelously depicts the history of education through a Catholic lens. She offers inspirational tips to help educators grow in personal sanctity, as well as practical tips to help them weave Catholicism throughout their lesson plans. This book reminds each of us that a spiritual battle is at hand and that the souls of young people are at stake. In the midst of a 'woke' and neo-pagan culture that has infiltrated many of our schools (including Catholic ones!), Hershwitzky's primer provides a fresh, encouraging, and much-needed perspective on what it means to truly educate our young people." —**Elizabeth Walker, PhD, Catholic mother of six children and Licensed Clinical Psychologist**

# Table of Contents

I. Introduction and Summary (*Imitation of Christ*, Chapter 43-2) ...... 1

*(NOTE: A synopsis and pull away for readers seeking an immediate overview and of all sections, each of which is intended to be fully flushed into a postgraduate course.)*

II. Teacher in God's Light ................................................................. 47
*To equip Catholic educators with means and tools for daily professional and spiritual self-examination. Ideally taught by a Catholic psychologist or social worker, this course would assist teachers to assess their temperaments, strengths, and vulnerabilities; plan an individualized spiritual and professional journey; and ways to monitor progress or indications of need for assistance in growing in virtue and teacher vitality.*

    A. Teachers As or Under Parental Authority
    B. Signature of Catholic Teachers
    C. Students in that Light
    D. Discerning the Call—Vocation
    E. Knowing Self with Proper Analysis, Self Awareness; Humble yet Confident
    F. Seeking the Guidance of the Master Teacher
    G. Prayer Life; Growing in Knowledge and Practice of Virtue
    H. Trusted Resources and Tools

III. Embedding Catholicism in All Subjects (Fullness of Truth in the Fullness of Education) ................................................................. 101
*To provide Catholic educators with specific and explicit connectivity of Faith to any subject and in cross curriculum ways.*

    A. The Authentic Seamless Garment; Knowledge with a Capital "K" vs. Lower Case "k"
    B. Knowing Students as Persons Destined for Eternal Life

    C. Intentional Cross Curriculum with Faith (Literature, Non-fiction, Grammar, Vocabulary, Written Expression, History, Geography, Government, Civics, Economy including Financial Literacy, Current Events and Issues —negotiable and nonnegotiable), Math, Science, Physical Education, Art, Music, Drama, Technology)
    D. Navigating Secular Influences (See Relating Modern Secularism the Catholic Way)
    E. Determining frameworks: Contemporary vs. Classical; Mix
    F. Ensuring Continuity and Connectivity of the Faith across Courses
    G. Collaboration with Colleagues; Communication with Superiors/Pastor
    H. Trusted Resources and Tools

IV. How to Teach Truth (Forming Eternal Citizens) .................... 135

*To impress the dual objectivity of education in the world: underscoring the primary mission of instilling attributes of heavenly citizenship and being a light to the world, while equipping students to be productive and prosperous citizens in the world.*

    A. Exemplary Catholic Teachers, Past and Present
    B. Seeking and Selecting Strong Peer Mentors
    C. Cultivating Contemporary Popular, Faithful Role Models for Self and Students
    D. Navigating Ignorance, Obstinance, and even Defiance from Parents, Peers, or Pupils
    E. Converts Reverts as Educators
    F. St. Augustine and *Confessions —The City of God*
    G. Tools, Lessons, Resources

V. Unpacking Religions (Belief Systems) of the World.................. 155

*Informing Catholic teachers about some commonalities but also the incompatibility of other religions; exploration of the rise of different beliefs and ways to recognize and respond to the perils of any contemporary supernatural world view apart from Roman Catholicism and often present in such concepts as "mindfulness."*

    A. Knowing Other Belief Systems Prepares Catholic Teachers to be Confident
    B. Deception Within (Heresies and Schisms)
    C. Prominent and Most Common Fallacies and Falsehoods
    D. Globally through Time and Space
    E. Contemporary Apostates
    F. Tools, Lessons, Resources

VI. Understanding Contemporary Catholicism (Building Pathways to Truth and Love) ............................................................................. 185
*To prepare Catholic teachers for today's Catholics who despite well meaning and often charitable and devout parents, colleagues, and even superiors may lack catechetical foundation or were (are) misinformed.*

    A. General Overview
    B. The 19th Century Impact Atop Other Skewed Perspectives
    C. Approaching the Poorly or UnInformed Catholic or Christian in Love
    D. Establishing Boundaries; non negotiable vs. flexibility
    E. Real School Conflicts: Procedures and Preparedness; Tips for Avoiding or Minimizing Contentious Exchanges and Outcomes; Guide for Working with Peers, Superiors; Pastors; Documentation
    F. Tools, Lessons, Resources

VII. Researching for Reliability (Secular and Sacred) ........................ 209
*To guide and arm teachers with timeless faith-based knowledge and honed analytical skills to evaluate and navigate an oppositional (antichrist) world in media, research, and all professional domains. This includes searching through*

*past primary sources that reveal the roots of current crises that threaten the foundations of Faith and governance.*

    A. Crisis of Indoctrination
    B. Developing "Antennae" for Falsehood
    C. The Barometer for Reliability; Checklist
    D. Locating Resources and Advisors
    E. Secular vs. Sacred (Secular not necessarily untrue; not all Christian sources are true)
    E. If a Once Reliable Source Becomes Questionable
    F. Tools, Lessons, Resources

VIII. Wisdom through Salvation History (Church Fathers and Doctors, Saints, Encyclicals) ............................................................. 233
*To provide Catholic teachers with the wealth of teaching, including that found in Sacred Scripture, the early Church Fathers, Doctors, Saints, and Papal insights on social issues and faith related topics. As an entire body of communication, these collectively offer consistent and mutually reinforcing truths over time and space.*

    A. Divine Inspiration in Salvation History: Sacred Scripture; Wisdom Literature; Prophets
    B. Early Church Fathers; Doctors of the Faith (St. Augustine)
    C. Saints and Martyrs
    D. Encyclicals (history of Papal writing; virtually every subject that touches on human experience)
    E. Apologetics and Evangelism to the Present Age
    F. Common Threads and Teaching throughout Church History
    G. Other/Contemporary Writing and Communication
    H. Tools, Lessons, Resources

IX. Eternal Era vs Man Constructed Ages (Impact by and on Catholicism) ...................................................................................... 267
*To provide all Catholic teachers (K-12) a necessary foundation of history, particularly in alignment with Church history, but in contrast with strictly secular history.*

    A. Why All Teachers Should Know History—Church History
    B. Tracing the Rise and Fall; Dispersement and Unity of Mankind through History
    C. Identifying Key Developments from Family to Tribe to Village to City State to Nation
    D. How the Key Components of Civilization Affected and were Effected by God's Plan
    E. The Influence of Innate Knowledge of God's Laws from Egypt, Mesopotamia, Greece, Rome, Western Civilization, to Modern Times
    F. The Impact of Progress: Agriculture, Manufacturing, Industrial, Technology, Digital
    G. The Final Analysis of God's Truth through Time and Space
    H. Tools, Lessons, Resources

X. Government through Time (Impact by and on Catholicism) . 319
*Provides all Catholic teachers (K-12) with needed knowledge, understanding, and perspective of various ideologies and government frameworks that have influenced temporal affairs for better or worse for the World, the Church and salvation of souls.*

    A. Catholic Teacher as Citizen
    B. From the Beginning: Family the Fundamental Government
    C. From Salvation History to the Church: relating to God's Sovereignty
    D. Intersecting Man's Law with Natural Law and Divine Will
    E. The Impact of Culture

G. How to Incorporate the City of God into Classroom "Government"
H. Tools, Lessons, Resources

XI. Relating Modern Secularism the Catholic Way ........................... 361
*Enables Catholic teachers to distinguish between the boundaries of modern secularism and the sacred without compromising Faith (Truth and Love).*

A. Defining Secularism; Tracing its Origin and Historic Influence on Social Order and the Faith
B. Contemporary Interpretation and Impact
C. History Proves Absolute Truths
D. Distinguishing Truth from Fact; God's Laws from Man's Codes
E. Understanding that Truth Always Supersedes and is Superior to Temporal Opinion and Movements
F. Determining When "Secularism" is Harmful, Neutral or Helpful
G. Tools, Lessons, Resources

XII. Summarizing: Temporal Globe Power vs. The Eternal Kingdom
............................................................................................. 375
*To inform and guide Catholic teachers to the reality of leap from nation and national identity to the growing force to globalize the world as one community and how Universal materialism (economics) threatens to overwhelm individual dignity, rights, and the pursuit of the good and God. To instruct on how this impacts teaching and ways to respond faithfully but prudently.*

A. The World Today; United States and Beyond
B. Rising Intolerance; Atheism; False Philosophy (Marxism— Totalitarianism)
C. A Church in Crisis
D. A World At Risk
F. Souls Endangered
G. Salvation and Age of Martyrs
H. Trusted Resources and Tools

# Preface

*Beloved: We receive from him whatever we ask, because we keep his commandments and do what pleases him. And his commandment is this: we should believe in the name of his Son, Jesus Christ, and love one another just as he commanded us. Those who keep his commandments remain in him, and he in them, and the way we know that he remains in us is from the Spirit he gave us.*

*Beloved: Do not trust every spirit but test the spirits to see whether they belong to God because many false prophets have gone out into the world. This is how you can know the Spirit of God: every spirit that acknowledges Jesus Christ one in the flesh belongs to God, and every spirit that does not acknowledge Jesus does not belong to God. This is the spirit of the antichrist who, as you heard, is to come, but in fact is already in the world. You belong to God, children, and you have conquered them, for the one who is in you is greater than the one who is in the world. They belong to the world; accordingly their teaching belongs to the world, and the world listens to them. We belong to God, and anyone who knows God listens to us, while anyone who does not belong to God refuses to hear us. This is how we know the spirit of truth and the spirit of deceit*

1 John 3:22–4:6

# A Word or Few about the Author

Patricia Hershwitzky, Ed.S.

*Readers deserve to know something about an author of any work, including educational background and experience in the topic field. When sharing and encouraging Faith, the author's spiritual health becomes of paramount consideration if not concern.*

*The reader may readily notice the letters behind my name atop of this brief autobiography. They mean to convey a level of education, but, in the overall scheme of being a credible source, they are only one leg of the proverbial three-legged stool and not necessarily the strongest.*

*I have over fifty years active employment experience, thirty years of which directly relate(d) to Catholic or public education, as a teacher and administrator, including homeschooling. I have worked in school systems with varying priorities in California, Maryland, Nevada, Colorado, and Georgia. Subjects included English, social studies, religion, math, reading, and science, but never physics with any degree of competency. (You do not want me near an art or music classroom either.) For twelve years, I served in an urban school in Las Vegas as an English and reading teacher. The goal, no matter where was to maintain a community presence. This was accomplished by taking part in student clubs, parental support programs, and community projects. Along the way, I earned a Masters in Education (Curriculum and Instruction with an emphasis on TESL) and an Education Specialist degree (Administration).*

*Prior to teaching, during, and afterwards, I worked on a travel magazine and then entered public relations and advertising. Concurrently, several ministries beckoned me, several with board positions: I served the developmentally disabled, having had a brother with Down's Syndrome; the National Alliance of the Mentally Ill (NAMI), having a son with emotional challenges; Respect Life Parish Committees and other pro-life work; and Courage-Encourage, as a loved one experiences same sex attraction; and several community based organizations.*

*I have two published books,* The Third Millennium Woman *(CMJ Marian Publisher) and* West Las Vegas *(Arcadia), along with published articles, numerous letters, and other yet unpublished works.*

Yet, regardless of any work I did (or not), when I stand before God—I may be kneeling, actually—He will only permit me to see that person who thought and acted in love and truth, or not. Then, the stark reality of my life will be before me. So...

Take away the book knowledge, any powerful lesson plans, administrative ability, and all the prose and poetry. Who am I? It is this last facet of my personhood that should most propel you to read, reject, or respond to this Primer in any particular manner.

Moreover, I can cry, "Lord, Lord" all day, and we know the end of that story. I can share the following, with heartfelt conviction, but always be on guard with anyone, as it is not how we begin the journey, but how we end it...towards that City of God.

My past is complicated and filled with faithless, even despairing early years. To say I was a fool is supposedly wrong, but I have no other way of perceiving myself until I reached my mid thirties. Then the Lord, Jesus Christ touched my soul, and I soared...then plummeted...soared...and then fell...soared and then bumped a few trees along the way.

Even in my early seventies, I am only now learning more about me. I just recently (nearly) completed Father Chad Ripperger's three volume: "Introduction to the Science of Mental Health," with a "really?" to God. **Now**, you tell me this...now you reveal this about myself?

By temperament, I am likely choleric melancholic. According to one other personality test, I am an "advocate"; by another: "controller." A Strength Finder test had me as community oriented—team player, so to speak. Certainly, you are getting a picture, and it is not always pretty.

So, read the following with all of that in mind, but know this emphatically. God does love me... and you. **Yet, do we love Him?** I desire everyone to be in Heaven, where we will rejoice forever. Yet, that means educators must pursue holiness and lead their students to sainthood. This entails ongoing, non-negotiable growth in virtue! And, I may be a bit choleric and controlling about that in the pages that follow.

# Chapter One

## INTRODUCTION AND SUMMARY

*For the Lord gives wisdom; from his mouth comes knowledge and understanding.*
*(Proverbs 2:6)*

*Education: from the Latin words Educare, Educere, and Educatum. Educare means to nourish, to bring up. The word educate means to lead forth, to draw out. Education is the process of facilitating learning.*

The word "education" is uttered millions of times a year, but how many *ponder* its meaning. Master level students have likely learned about the principles of education and its history through various civilizations and eras. Yet, in a Catholic sense, they should also know that education is more than imparting knowledge, particularly mere facts. Of course, facts are vital to rightful understanding, but rightful reason must be employed to make sense of those facts and how to apply them to living in the temporal world to lead souls to eternal life. These facts are often summed up in "knowledge." Moreover, education is only as beneficial (or not) as it is used for good. St. Thomas Aquinas is the "go to" Saint in that regard.

This Introduction will review the concept and employment of education, as it has been formulated, transmitted, and received through time and around the world. By viewing education through the lens of The City of God, particular emphasis will be placed on why education is eternally valuable only through knowing and living the Faith. For education becomes a powerful tool in the hands of the educator, for better or worse. The knowledge and wisdom of an educator or lack of either may even determine the salvation of souls. Teachers may foster great saints or devils; the pursuit of good or succumbing to evil. Moreover, wise teachers will be keenly aware of those elements in the world that may tend to lead their students astray.

What follows teases at the individual chapters as groundwork for coursework that includes helpful resources and references: 1) Tracing the history of education and its numerous facets and impact on society. However, Sacred Scripture, highlighting the Books of Wisdom, should enable teachers to fully grasp that education without wisdom is likely futile; 2) Examining various religious and nonreligious orientations and identifying the pedagogy of instruction through time and environments for purpose and effectiveness always through the filter of belief systems. This includes the introduction of seditious ideas and concepts from such crafty minds like the atheist and social plotter John Dewey and how certain objectives were achieved in the name of "rights" (Madelyn O'Hair, 1962); 3) Reviewing the history of Catholic schooling, along with its rise and decline. In this section, various saints and Popes will be cited for their keen insights on exemplary Catholic school teaching and why it is infeasible if not ill advised to study history and its components, or any subject, without the guidance of the Magisterial Church; 4) Although covered more extensively in another section, the importance of validating, repudiating, and/or modifying misinformation about the world is critical to the value of education. In short, the city of man has all but cancelled—to use a popular term—the City of God in schools, businesses, social enclaves, and even church.

Then the Introduction will provide a brief overview of course subjects and why each are critical to teaching the City of God in the City of Man. Though some courses overlap and are not exhaustive, each is unique and sharply honed to illuminate the depth to which teachers must dive to truly grasp the challenge of today's Catholic teacher.

## History of Education

This Primer is not to rehash common knowledge but to provide context for major concerns in educational settings, public and private, and even many Catholic schools. By briefly reviewing this background, across time and various groups, from tribes to civilizations, and city-states to nations, an educator should be able to acknowledge the wonderful discoveries of persons from all kinds of backgrounds, but also to pinpoint errors in knowledge and application of that knowledge. Most importantly, students should recognize that **all** good knowledge comes from God, but not all use of knowledge is of God. The former is knowledge with a capital "K"; the latter is knowledge with a lower case "k." The former incorporates the awareness that all knowledge is from God and pursues it wisely; the latter may be utilized for some good, but only as aligned with eternal Truth. Moreover, that God permits evil (or the absence of good) should not be construed as doing the will of God.

From the discovery of stone weapons, the simple machines, and fire to nuclear power and micro genetic research, men (all such reference will assume women) have been exploring and learning about themselves and the world in extraordinary and revolutionary ways. Yet, these discoveries and sharing of them, orally first, have led people to both good and evil. The same stone ax that kills an animal for food can also be used as a weapon. Even fire is not exempt from sinful uses, as in arson. There is no need to cite examples of nuclear power or how genetic research has been subject to evil acts. As an instructor teaching the City of God, the more educated the teacher is with respect to these issues, the better. Most importantly, there are some topics that cannot be debated though educators are fond of robust classroom discussions. More on those in "Embedding Catholicism in All Subjects."

Through time, the concept of education has been an inherent component of human relations for survival and prosperity; for security and conquering; for following the will of God and for self will; for the good or bad. Although the Holy Spirit was present to all, history evidences that a relative few recognized, let alone accepted, the glimmer of Knowledge as God intended. So, by casual or informal education or by organized, classical education, some populations hit the mark on some matters and learned practices like morals, values, and virtues. Others devolved or died due to grave error and pride. For example, some societies, like Sparta hyper focused on military training of young boys though the women learned some basics in economics. Consider studying Socrates, Plato, and Aristotle for more insights on how God reached even pagan minds and civilizations, as natural law is inscribed in the heart, but not always understood as from one, true God. Hillsdale College offers some fantastic free online courses in Greek philosophers, but also early Catholic (Christian) thinkers like Thomas Aquinas. See the Appendix and Bibliography for more information.

Also, the notion of education, in a formal sense, has had numerous influences and influencers. Pagans and animistic populations skewed the most fundamental truth about God, and so many of their lessons tended towards the acceptance of some falsehoods that led to error. Yet, one should hasten to interject that there were still incredible discoveries, often through observation of the environment, nature, like the wheel, the plow, weaponry, mathematical and science concepts. God's creation has always been the subject of observation and imitation.

Then there were the exceptional Egyptian, Greek and Roman minds that brought forth civilizations, populated by great philosophers and sage leaders, as alluded to above. These led to formulated concepts of justice, integrity, governance, economics, civics, as well as the arts and architecture that even today enables masterpieces of reverence towards God.

Earlier education was often geared more towards affluent male youth, but girls could be savvy learners. Subjects were taught by various effective means. We still have the Socratic method of teaching, as one example.

*Today, though, despite enormous leaps in technology, education has never been more at risk for the lower case "k."* We are victims of our own success and advancements, but souls have shriveled as the intellect has egotistically expanded. One could even argue that this is intentional and the aim is not education but indoctrination. It is most doubtful that anyone in such darkness can perceive, let alone acknowledge, any evil intention. Still, the modernistic scheme is diabolical in aim and outcome. All the efforts of past legendary teachers, from all time, and in all places, has been supplanted by manufactured history, the infusion, if not the enforcement of anti-religious beliefs (transgenderism, same sex relations, to name a couple.) Most recently a teacher was cited on social media for complaining that parents might actually hear his "diversity" training—not worthy of the word education—of their children.

In a formerly acclaimed charter school in Las Vegas: The Andre Agassi Preparatory Academy, now the Democracy Preparatory Academy, a student and his mother sued because the student, a bi-racial but white appearing male youth was bullied into denouncing "white, Christian, heterosexual males" as oppressors in an assignment that could make or break his entry into college. (See *Epoch Times* and multiple sources 12.28.2020). All of this seems like child's play now that Satan Clubs are on school grounds!

This leads to a major objective of this Primer and Coursework. One point that will be clear throughout is that parents are the primary educators, and hired teachers are permitted their profession by parental permission. Of course, faithful Catholic teachers can humbly and charitably assist parents who may be misled or ignorant of Truth. Yet, that must be accomplished in the absence of hubris or assumption of some type of superiority in authority.

**Various Religious, Irreligious, and Anti-Religious Orientations**

Before reviewing the history of various religious orientations, the concept of orientation should be clarified. It will also be examined more closely later in relationship to teaching.

The *orientation of education* is more important than the education in one foundational principal: Will it lead the student (learner) towards the City of God or does it keep the student (learner) complacent, yet ambitious, in the city of man, even what Plato might call the city of pigs? Also teachers should not underestimate the pull of other religions, especially those popularized and providing a sense of comfortability with sin and self..

After this course, aspiring educators should not want to pursue teaching unless it is the former they are willing to sacrifice anything to achieve. Not unlike the religious, or any other vocation, occupations are subject to Divine Judgment. Did teachers lead souls to God or away from Him? It will be a no-excuses "final exam." That does not mean that anyone will be entirely faultless or flawless in teaching or that anyone can always control the circumstances of employment. There are times when teachers will have to truly struggle as to how to proceed, ask themselves if a change of school will be necessary, or if the Catholic school they are employed by must be challenged. There are no easy answers sometimes, and this course is not designed to provoke guilt or judgment on any particular hypothetical situation. (The website Cross Curriculum (under development at the time of this writing) will provide a Q+A platform, however, and all students have free access to it and upon completion of this program.)

Educators cannot evade numerous experiences of nagging conscience and serious and some life altering decisions to be made over the span of a career. Family finances may steer some to public education with the rationale they (the parents) could be a good example. Some have been gravely disappointed, though, and have had to make the sacrificial decision that the public domain would not cooperate with best intentions. Other Christian schools may or may not offer a safe haven, especially if you have to forfeit expressing the fullness of Truth. Much may depend on the position, though, and how teachers are expected to present themselves. A Salvation Army tutor may not proclaim his or her Catholicism, but in an after school program designed for student safety, that may not arise. A Quaker Friendship school is not the benign or neutral setting of decades ago. Other Christian or non denominational schools will require a certain muteness about Catholicism. However, these difficult moments can occur in Catholic schools, too. This is raised only to assure teachers that the most important understanding they should have entering education is to always pursue absolute Truth with love and not compromise their Faith. They should pursue those avenues that will best afford them the way to always teach The City of God, but realize that no environment lacks some traits of the city of man.

One other caveat was raised in a *Catholic Thing* article, and this is where solid spiritual guidance is essential. Not all situations, as uncomfortable as they may be, call for an immediate reaction. Also, how one proceeds, even if a response is necessitated to preserve Truth, can do harm rather than help. (See Section "Building Pathways to Truth and Love") which describes real life scenarios with altered details to respect privacy. Still, there will be times that, no matter how one proceeds, with a most loving disposition, Truth will be ignored or rejected.

Furthermore, and this is difficult to assert, public school, with rare exceptions, is most likely not an option, at this time. Prayerfully, that will change. Some charter schools…maybe. However, **before eliminating that wholesale**, candidates should check the curriculum and how the Administration and School Board are comprised and oriented. There are also growing opportunities in charter, pod and hybrid school communities.

So, what have been the various orientations of education? Briefly, they can be summed up in two major perspectives: survival and progress with the latter being where the problems began to ferment and contaminate the spirit of Truth. All forms of education, though, even those that arose for survival, have a basis in some belief about the unknown, supernatural phenomenon, or mystery.

**At this juncture, the view of education springboards into those Faith perspectives starting with Genesis.**

From the beginning, since the Fall and expulsion from the Garden of Eden, man has had to forage in the wilderness to survive. Clothing, food, shelter, combatting beasts and later other tribes, were all new challenges for the couple. Now, before anyone questions: Are people to truly believe there was a first man and woman, who literally ate an apple and were kicked out of Paradise, when it seems evidenced that there were humans or human-like species in multiple places on Earth for tens of thousands of years or more, according to scientists?

Well educated persons need not care a whit about *some* of prehistory. Even those atheist scholars lack full comprehension. There are multiple theories, ongoing "discoveries," and unsolved mysteries. In fact, Catholic educators are better positioned because they accept mystery. That is the Faith…belief in that which is beyond our cognitive and sensory capabilities to prove.

This is THE primary orientation that drove education for thousands of years in the Jewish religion and later Christianity. Even some pagan traditions incorporate some tales with similar themes. And, there is a very important reason, it stands today, and is imperative when teaching the City of God in the city of man.

Yet, not just history is affected by mystery. There is no way of knowing three truths by sheer secular scientific discovery: 1) When was the first human being created in time and space with a soul? 2) Were Adam and Eve expelled for eating a forbidden fruit? And 3) Were all those hominids creatures of tens of thousands of years ago with bodies and souls? To the first point, how long did Adam and Eve reside in the Garden of Eden (believed by some to be in the Mesopotamia area). It could have been hundreds or millions of years in world time. 2) Also, whether they ate an apple is beside the main point of their disobedience not to eat of the tree of the knowledge of good and evil. (Thus, they would become the first teachers of their children about the City of God vs. the city of man though they experienced obstacles with Cain, obviously.) 3) That there were other species of human like creatures with intelligence does not imply they possessed souls though they likely had some infusion of spirit. How all of that plays in God's plan, no one definitively knows. There are many details that will remain undiscovered until we meet God, but there is no need to know for the purpose of healthy, helpful knowledge to live productive lives, earn sainthood, and to be reunited with God forever. However, God's children did not descend from soulless apes.

So, Adam and Eve taught their children. How they took the news may be evident in Abel and Cain. Did Cain harbor a grudge against God? Did the devil dwell in his spirit and ultimately lead to murder? No one but God knows. Still, at some point, mankind took a nosedive in relationship to God which brought them to Noah. (And, no this course will not delve into how the entire world was populated after the Flood, but there is ample secular history to support the telling of a Great Flood from more than Scripture.)

How other tribes and eventually the descendants of Adam and Eve came to animism and paganism is unclear. Yet, people have always wondered about themselves. The Tower of Babel did lead at one point to the scattering of God's children and subsequent wandering and settling. However, no matter where any group landed, they were astute observers of nature, if for no other reason than survival. That curiosity and experimentation would lead to some technology and conjectures. It has been unearthed, literally that the earliest tribes had some inkling about life after death—an acknowledgment of spirit—because of their burial practices. Whether these persons led moral lives or not is not always clear. How God received them at death (and the Resurrection) has not been revealed.

Still, some notion of governance, rules of conduct (civics), economy (hunting and gathering to bartering, then formal commerce, banking, and trade), politics, awareness of the elements (geography), and culture were transmitted from generation to generation, though, again, likely more for survival and some growth than a sense of punishment or reward in the afterlife. Again evidence for that is in early burial rites.

*From Paganism to Neo Paganism to Atheism*

Paganism obviously had its own spin on education. It likely focussed on survival and incorporated oral narratives to "teach" about the deadly forces of nature in climate and wild beasts. Superstitious practices were linked to practical responses in cases of poisoning, illness and diseases, securing or raising food, taming domesticates animals, and so forth. Even pagan groups had reverence for elders, acknowledging their storage of life protecting information and experiences. Multiple gods were "created," imaged, and transmitted. Moreover, as agriculture settled peoples, language was needed, along with a form of communication and other skills, like map making. All early River civilizations also had a religious center, often the rulers of the people. As settlement led to a multiple of occupations, so did the need to pass on facts and skills to survive and thrive.

Yet for the purpose of this coursework, the greater concern is not how people were educated in the past under the umbrella of paganism or animism, but how that orientation has resurfaced with great force in the 21st Century but arguably began centuries earlier but most certainly with prominent anti-Christian schemers like John Dewey, Horace Mann, and other philosophers whose views on knowledge were earth bound, but influenced the course of public education to today's false spiritually. One might even call him the father of progressive education which stressed "cooperation and tolerance" for different viewpoints. Sound familiar?

Dewey had many colleagues in different societal strata and professions promoting like minded goals and supporters for mass public education to shape the minds of all our youth.

The Neo paganism of today has as its gods governors, bureaucrats, judges, and others in positions of power to ensure that the central deity, Earth, is placated and served. Common people of "lesser" esteem are deemed to be servants of this fast growing global regime while the elites though they are provided laxity in self will for basic pleasures. The elites simply serve themselves in the name of Earth. This central tenet has permeated every area of civilization, from the aforementioned governance to religion through social structure, arts and architecture, public works, and language.

Whereas once the pagans of old reverenced fire and wind, among other natural elements, today's neo pagan idolizes solar energy and wind mills. At least the pagan of yesteryear had an excuse in their ignorance of these forces. Today's pagans are prideful lords.

No strand of life is unaffected, and the Faith is deemed not simply wrong or false but dangerous. It is imperative that Catholic teachers realize the full scope and depth of that reality. Nothing that is truly sacred, from Holy Scripture to the Holy Mass, is spared the wrath of the new demigods.

Yet, unlike paganistic naïveté fueled by the absence of Divine knowledge or blinded to it, today's Neo-paganism is a refutation of a known God. He revealed Himself most dominantly 2,000 years ago, but the enemy Satan has succeeded in infiltrating the very souls of persons already darkened by the absence of grace through mortal sin. The evil one's main targets are on two ends of the spectrum, children and elder adults, particularly those in positions of power.

This is why education is on the precipice of doing good or multiplying evil.

This is not stated to scare any potential teacher away from the field, as faithful souls are needed more than ever in this last battle. ***Still, teachers need to be aware that this is warfare.*** The final challenge is arising. *Thus says the Lord God: Because you are haughty of heart, you say, "A god am I. I occupy a godly throne in the heart of the sea—And yet you are a man, and not a god. However you may think yourself like a god....Therefore says the Lord God, Because you have thought yourself to have the mind of a god. therefore, I will bring against you foreigners, the most barbarous of nations. (Ezekiel 28: 1-10 abbreviated)*

Later in the text, how teacher preparation is completed will be more detailed, but know that everything will start with personal humility., including personal weakness. As St. Francis de Sales notes, *"As long as this life lasts, we can never think of living without imperfections. Whether we are teaching or learning, commanding or obeying, we are all weak creatures."* (3) <u>Everyday with St. Francis de Sales, Teaching and Examples from the Life of the Saint</u> (Salesiana Publishers, 1985)

Successful teachers will be strengthened daily—if not hourly—by prayer, starting with Holy Mass and the Rosary if at all possible.

One final point on the difference between ancient paganism — even found in the remote parts of the world today—and contemporary neo paganism is that the former tends towards fear of an unknown power or powers and often leads to behavior that is borne of ignorance. The latter is driven by a force well aware of God but leads masses of people in their own stubborn blindness to self will.

*Classical Education*

As the Church grew in influence and favor following centuries of persecution, Western Civilization realized the flourishing of beneficial education in all strands and subject areas.

*Education: Old is New...*

Education serves many purposes beyond survival and that which brings peace, prosperity, and long life. For hundreds of years in both oral and written transmission of facts and truisms, based on actual experience, tradition, and commonly accepted knowledge, people have embraced either the good, true and beautiful or evil, falsehoods, and ugliness—though the last is rarely perceived as such. Look at some modern art sometime. (A student recalled a high school field trip of a modern art museum where she stared at a fire extinguisher for several seconds before realizing that it was just a fire extinguisher.) Classical Education was also often thought of teaching just the basics like reading, writing, and arithmetic not unlike the Egyptians of yore though most benefactors were male children and wealthy.

Most of the time, though, education is rarely either extreme. This text, coursework, and ongoing website is designed to move the needle of education as close as possible to authentic Truth and genuine love. Like preparing for a long trip with a final destination, our lives must be formed by both to withstand the journey but also travel with joy and confidence. In that, there is everything right about formal education that accomplishes that purpose. Knowing basics about our world, cultivating skills in math, science, and communication; being capable of reasoned arguments that bring souls to Jesus Christ while ensuring the financial support of self and family, and…bluntly…living a good life…are all commendable goals.

Still, it is easy, given our faults, imperfections, and defects, to fall short of the ideal in that regard, Catholic or not. The fundamental difference is in the awareness of those pitfalls for teachers and their students. Moreover, many past non-Christian figures and civilizations incorporated some truths about human nature and a mission to incorporate character traits that demonstrate wisdom and healthy human relations.

In other words, not all forms of education have been or are inherently completely false; even the most pristine Christian educational platform may be delivered with error.

Today's classical education emphasizes history, literature, and language studies that focuses on the best of Western civilization, particularly through the classics. Grammar, logic and rhetoric are pillars of such education. Though "Western" has become the boogey man of the progressive neo pagans, the indisputable fact is that what arose in Western civilization and atop of early scholars and philosophers, as well as rulers, was good in principle. It embodied many truths though the Christian movement was closer to the mark. (Note "closer" only because the delivery of Truth fell short at times.). The goal though was to shape a student to be knowledgeable and think critically. Understanding and then the art of persuasion through acquired wisdom are ultimate objectives. Of course, in Catholicism knowledge of Faith is essential to those end purposes.

Great literature is a standard in such education, and you will hear names like Charlotte Mason, an educator in Victorian England, in this regard and frequently cited.

Again, these approaches will be further explored in the context of fruitful education later.

*Then…*

*Classical Greek*

Mention ancient Greece and education and several names are evoked, including Homer, Socrates (founder of Western philosophy and first moral philosopher), Plato, and Aristotle. Many discoveries flourished in the minds of the Greeks, mostly male. However, the distinction must be made because Greece was comprised of city states, often vastly different such as Athens and Sparta.

Some great teaching techniques arose from the Greek approach including the Socratic Method of open-ended inquiry for deeper understanding of a topic. Effective teaching skills are timeless.

Yet, the primary goal of Greek education was to produce good citizens for peace and war with a more Earth bound emphasis. Given the gods they worshipped, and despite taught morals (Aesop), people would not have been provided anything close to the City of God as an ultimate destination.

It is often that absence that can mislead even well intentioned people to do evil thinking they are doing good.

Regardless, the three A's in early philosophy connect the pagan to the Catholic: Aristotle's works greatly influenced both St. Augustine and St. Thomas Aquinas. It will be fun to learn first hand from God how His masterplan of education threaded through these three minds and souls and beyond with major impact on Catholicism but also government.

*Classical Roman* was based on the Greeks and used Greek slaves but included Roman politics, cosmology, and the ultimate aims of Rome. Like other older civilizations, the notion of education began informally and among families or groups. Many Romans learned to read and write, the bookends of necessary education when language was printed or otherwise recorded. Later tutors arose for the more prosperous, and some believe that the concept of "teacher" evolved by their paid system of tutors.—though many of those were slaves.

One great gift of early Roman education was the language of Latin. This beautiful language of the early Church is still taught in many Catholic home school programs and in some Catholic schools. Its universality still unites believers, and many contemporary converts insist that the beauty of the Latin Mass and its presence in music drew them to the Faith.

The Golden Age of Rome also brought great literature, and drama. Shakespeare was inspired by the Roman Empire.

Overall, Rome influenced many of the ideas we have about schooling, including preschool. That will be addressed later, but there are both good and bad outcomes, depending on who is charged with that curriculum and instruction. It is well known that the current state wants those children under the control of ideas and politically correct "socialization" practices. Still, rightful education must start in the womb for any child.

Yet, what was the orientation of such education in Rome: Primarily, like Greece, it was to ensure good citizens of Rome. In other words, it was Earth bound despite any virtues it may have embedded in its citizens.

*Eastern Education*

Hinduism and Buddhism are two higher levels of thought found in Eastern civilizations from present day India to China and Japan. Again, while the basics were taught, a whole way of perceiving self and the world were also ingrained in youth.

More so, while there were (are) good elements in Hinduism and Buddhism, neither profess the fullness of Truth, and both can lead people astray. Hinduism is all the worst for its belief in reincarnation. Though the term karma is lightly thrown around even in Western countries, the peril is obvious. If one does not have to become perfected while in this life because there is a progression of such growth in the temporal world, such souls are not prepared for Final Judgment. Certainly, no one wants to become a bug in the "next life" because he or she goofed big time and committed evil, for the slothful soul, even this may not be a disincentive to sin. After all, what is the life span of a bug? Of course, this is an exaggeration, but the point needs to be firmly implanted that Hinduism's orientation is deadly.

Buddhists do not even believe in God (any god), so it is not even a religion though still a belief system, and, it too, holds reincarnation as a central tenet. This will be further explored in "Unpacking the Religions (Belief Systems) of the World."

Eastern meditation and the promotion of "mindfulness" permeates our society. Yoga, yoga, yoga, is everywhere, literally. Yet, how few may realize that the postures in Yoga are actually in honor of false deities, not unlike how we fold our hands for prayer, kneel or prostrate ourselves. The ultimate irony is that many in the Trans Meditation community believe themselves intellectually and spiritually superior.

*Agnosticism*

It was only a matter of time before the tentacles developed by the neo educators would choke Faith in the public classroom. At one time, around the famous O'Hair cases that expelled prayer from public schools, one could argue that the Supreme Court threw our nation's system of education to the agnostics. However, it is critical to remember that at that time, most people prayed and studied the Bible at home and attended some church. The devil knew he could bide his time. Those promising safeguards held up only relatively briefly, some would say less than ten years. As neo pagan ideas infiltrated texts and pedagogy, schools began to appear more atheistic and then neo pagan, as we find today. The irony may well be that while God was taken from school, god (the devil) entered.

*Christian. (American)*

Sadly, history may evidence that the earliest American education establishments outside the home were so vehemently Protestant (and anti Catholic), Quaker, and so forth) that by their rigidity, the O'Hair case was inevitable. Note that St. Elizabeth Ann Seton, who founded the first Catholic schools was so pummeled when she was rejected as a teacher solely due to her Catholicism (which one may paraphrase as universal and original Christianity!). Had earlier public endeavors embraced the Commandments, the fullness of Jesus Christ, and the Constitution, as intended, maybe a different scenario would have emerged. However, there are those voices that persist in the need for different schools for different orientations, and that solid Catholic environments should not co-host other beliefs.

Like the wheat and the chaff, people will be commingling as long as we live on this Earth, so the imperative question is not how do to manage different beliefs in a poly religious society, but how to navigate them to remain confidently committed and courageous Catholic while acknowledging other perspectives?

There is no way that Catholic education can accept the shortfall or outright errors of other religions. That is why many of our Catholic schools fell into disrepair.

Still, looking at public education in this country a little closer as it evolved from that largely Protestant orientation to the neo pagan one of today (actually atheistic) may reveal the missteps. Then, we can examine the rise of Catholic education, but how, it too, became an agent of modernity rather than continue in a steadfast Faithful way.

Furthermore, many Protestants of today are no more proponents of the public school system because many of them are now aware that "free and universal" public education was quickly coopted by antichristian forces, some even assert that "the education system was engineered to destroy us." (Mom Delights "Why We Need Education Alternatives" 12/31/2020). More on that in "Relating Modern Secularism the Catholic Way."

## Catholic Education—The Rise of Catholic Schools in the United States

There could be a fair argument that Catholic education is all education. From the origin of discipleship, students of all ages, backgrounds, races, ethnicities, and abilities have been given overarching, global teaching that encompasses all the basics, in one manner or another from the time of earthly Creation. The Church was instrumental in the widespread use of language, particularly Latin, the development of new mediums and forms of arts and architecture , the keepers of history, the expansion of science (any controversy aside), the importance of mathematical concepts, and the art of communication.

The Bible inspired the printing press to spread the Word, and reading became easier and more widespread, along with need for literacy.

Moreover, when we search the Middle Ages, so much flourished in the way of economic and civics advancement.

As we look closer at the Church's existence in various time periods and how the City of God may be integrated, this will become clearer.

For now, though, it is sufficient to examine how Catholic education emerged in the United States and where it is presently. While it followed standards of any formal educational setting, Catholic educators also made distinctions about approaches and strategies that best fit the curriculum.

Socratic inquiry and memorization played and continue to play roles. Despite some crude mechanicals, like bumpy green painted chalkboard and yellow chalk sans computers, the Church has been quite successful with all kinds of populations in transmitting facts and skills. Mother Teresa used a stick and a dirt lot. Catholic schools consistently outpace public schools in math, science, reading, and English scores. Yet, when did all of this more fully appear?

From the 1600s founding colonists valued education, even expecting townships to have such a setting for young minds. While some, like Thomas Jefferson, seemed to be skeptical about the Democracy sustainability, he recognized that education was necessary to cast light on

# Chapter One: Introduction and Summary

future leaders. Moreover, from the beginning, schooling that presented religious beliefs were a lightening rod for controversy. Eventually, many schools ended towards the basics with the presence of the King James Bible. That hardly squelched controversy and resistance. As Catholics were particularly targeted in such town schools, the Church was compelled to form its own niche in educational options.

To this day, though, it is a yo-yo argument. Some might call it a boomerang argument, as it comes full circle every once in a while and hits Catholics on the head. The main difference today is that the secular-minded often strive to destroy the religious schools and actually currently are advancing a most aggressive anti Christian/Jewish curriculum and instruction.

Yet, glancing back for a moment...why Catholic schools? There are numerous articles and some books on the history of Catholic schools. Historian Timothy Walch wrote *Parish School: American Catholic Parochial Education from Colonial Times to the Present*. The author claims that this is a story of heroic commitment and animated by conviction that education is crucially important, one of the most important things we give our children. "It is both a privilege and responsibility of family and of the Church to be good stewards of this gift." The National Catholic Education Association later distributed Walch's work as *Parish School: Revised and Expanded Edition*. Readers may compare the two.

Overall, though, how did this look and evolve?

*Mechanics instead of the Messiah*

The 19th Century brought in over five million immigrant Catholics. The prevailing state driven school setting, which was intended in part to create a homogenous but Protestant society, only further compelled Catholics to build their own, especially affiliated with parishes. This was fueled by Papal and other clergy encouragement, as well (See Encyclicals. Pope Pius IX, Bishop Ireland)

Religious teachers helped tremendously in sealing the deal. By 1900, there were more than 40,000 religious teachers. *History of Catholic schools in America* This was an incredible treasure literally and spiritually. They were so successful, one could argue, they drew demonic attention, and the attack intensified from three fronts: worldly centeredness, outright deceit, and false ecumenicism.

One, public education underwent increasing complexity as presentation, content and purpose also evolved. Two world wars, a Depression, and increasing secularization with growing materialism, hedonism, and immorality was another. Then there was the shift from Church (Parish/Pastor) driven Catholic education to increasing parental control, and what some might even label interference by those not knowledgeable about the Faith. All of this aggravated by rising costs of Catholic education due to the decline of nuns in religious teaching orders led to crisis.

Some might claim that the removal of God from schools also removed the "threat" of Protestant proselytization, so that Catholics could feel more comfortable about the public setting. Others would dispute that by pointing to the increased secularization of Catholic schools, over sixty years. Increasingly, lay administrators and teachers entered who were credentialed with all the "bells and whistles" of strategies and techniques but who also lacked substantial religious education. So, they were also subsequently open to ideas counter to the true Faith.

Two, deceptively, secular branded textbooks and resources that in reality had content that outright scorned Christian history and its values, even subtly, while elevating relativism, were and are recommended through Archdiocesan subcommittees, often comprised of Catholic teachers. However, one hastens to interject that many of these committees based their judgment on others's recommendations and without intense scrutiny. Teachers often volunteer for these committees in addition to regular teaching positions. Moreover, to be just, some of the biases are secreted in the "bells and whistles" of supplementary notes and linked videos. Even so, it is perplexing to know that too many Archdioceses ignore or imprudently marginalize as supplemental such Catholic sources as the Catholic Textbook Project and Phillip Campbells series on world and American history (Tan Books). As a side note, thankfully, there is good news emerging, as with the Archdiocese of Denver Catholic credential program.

Three, the veneer of ecumenism. Cooping with other belief systems muddied the waters and created confusion, especially for students. There have been at least three generations of weakening Catholic schools. Parents, themselves educated in too many CINO (Catholic in Name Only) schools began to abdicate their primary educator role. Moreover, with both mothers and fathers on career paths, understanding of the Faith diminished along with family prayer time. The increase in divorce and other societal transformations only further eroded the Catholic school mission, where parents expected a safe environment more than a sacred one. Separated from sound teachers, whole families lost the Faith.

Ironically, parents of more capable students started fleeing to public charter schools that they deemed academically superior, no longer even considering catechesis as the primary goal. Furthermore, many of these parents considered themselves quite capable of instructing their children in the Faith. They touted personal instruction of the Faith though that was likely compartmentalized into a half hour a day about the love of Jesus Christ and basically the corporeal works of Mercy.

Still consider the absolutely lovely Mom who apologetically pulled a child from a Catholic School and enrolled in a nondenominational school saying, "Well, the Mass there…" referencing that there was regular prayer in a chapel. Hopefully, she understood the gentle correction and suggestion that followed: There is no Mass in that school, but there are some resources for you.

That the parents of those remaining in the Catholic schools, including nonCatholics, also thought they knew best *even in opposition to faithful Pastors* or in compliance with misguided ones, has only further derailed the mission and success of Catholic schooling.

Moreover, while Catholic education boasts many experts in curriculum and instruction in supervisory and developmental capacities, the orientation has tended to be "hit and miss" on always prioritizing the well being of students' souls. Incredibly, one finds almost a mirror of public education with a thin veneer of defense of Faith. Even controversial issues in the public sector, such as abortion and same sex relationships occur in Catholic schools with the Church having to vigorously defend thousands of years of Truth to increasingly wounded families. Bluntly, some do not. Whereas once parents would hardly dare challenge a Catholic school teacher on sending their child to a corner time out, today parents and extended family members are activated to send letters to Archbishops complaining about a matter as simple as distinguishing between sin and a sinner. They no longer want the "s" word even mentioned. Their demands grow, and feeling empowered as the "customer," actually believe they have the right to have their demands met.

The current COVID Virus is only adding challenges to Catholic schools, but the golden blessing may be the awakening of parents and other family members to the value of genuine faith filled education as society weakens morally, and Catholic schools may also need to re emerge as solidly dependable transmitters of Faith and the basics.

The only way is the Catholic way. And the only Catholic way is preparing children for the City of God by living well but faithfully in the city of man.

## The Art and Science of Teaching in Truth: Distinguishing Truth from Man's Rationale

Who is called to teach? Ponder that although it will be covered in *Teacher in God's Light*. At this juncture, this question does not reference parents who have been given the authority and duty to teach their children. They are stuck. However, there are others and parents with grown children looking for fruitful employment of their gifts. Some would make great teachers with the appropriate preparation, and they should not let lack of official work history prevent that consideration. Besides, there are persons credentialed as teachers who are not suited to this profession, temperamentally, organizationally, or otherwise.

High schools of yesteryear often foisted relatively few career choices on young ladies who were compelled to choose an adult occupation—or at least begin on a pathway. Two were most prominent for women: nursing and teaching. Now, some would say how "sexist," and certainly those were not the only two some women chose. They just happened to be the more popular options. Sadly, neither option suited many who only years later discovered their own misery or discontent. On the good news front, some men and women who bucked the system later learned that medicine or education was actually their calling all along, and entered the professions as a second career. Often, they also discovered that previous employment, coupled by maturity, enhanced their delivery.

The major point is that one needs to have done some soul searching, especially if one will be faithful to God in this pursuit. Recall that no one is to be called teacher except the Teacher, Jesus Christ. He will be the headmaster. (See *Teaching like the Master*). Rare is the Catholic who does not have to hone skills for genuinely Catholic learning centers, whether they be schools, homeschool-hybrids, or pods. Pods are becoming neighborhood classrooms whereby several families hire tutors to instruct their children, as an alternative to public school. For seasoned teachers such humility faces another roadblock. Catholic teachers accustomed to public schools, now hostile to Christianity in the fullness of Truth, might be misled and influenced to rationalize the lack of necessity for Truth.

All in season and out must learn the ultimate lesson: Teachers will be called to account for every child's soul over whom they had teaching authority.

*Teaching Requires Wisdom*

Before, approaching that sensitive area of discernment, it would be helpful to glance at the Catholic Churches seven books of Wisdom in the Bible. They are uniquely Catholic, yet, as knowledge is the essence of education, wisdom must be the lead for choosing materials and resources to impart Truth. It should go without stating but it will be stated anyway: This is not meant to insist on only Catholic books or about "spinning" some unpleasant historical facts under the proverbial rug. Truth is the Person of Jesus Christ, but truth in our own fallen human nature must be developmentally and appropriately taught.

Briefly here, but later explored in *How to Teach Truth to Form Universal and Eternal Citizenship,* are the Books and each of their focuses (Very Rev. Peter Kucer, MSA: *Wisdom Literature*). Wise and therefore successful teachers will meditate on the books of Wisdom for insight and steering of knowledge. Reflection is the best precursor to successful teaching. In his *Wisdom Literature,* Father Kucer cities numerous writers in the pithy summary of these books: Job teaches us how to suffer); Psalms teaches us how to pray; Proverbs teaches us how to act; Ecclesiastes teaches us how to enjoy; the Song of Solomon teaches us how to love; and Sirach teaches us how to suffer, pray, act, enjoy and love in fear of God which is the "beginning of wisdom."

*The Art of Teaching*

Some persons are naturals, truly the stereotypical compassionate but firm; orderly but appropriately spontaneous; well prepared but flexible; knowledgeable but open to new discoveries; intelligent but humble; good communicators but also great listeners; and calm but responsive. With experience and professional development, they enhance those natural qualities with outstanding teaching. Who has not been taught by such teachers, had peers who exemplified these wonderful traits, and supervised a few?

Even the ideal teacher will have some fault. Most teachers are truly caring and desire to teach with passion and capably. They will also possess different expertise and confront a difficult subject. So, team or tag teaching is recommended for the benefit of students. A few have serious obstacles like hand printing or writing. However, given our highly technical age and the myriad teaching opportunities, developmentally and subject area, that also should not prevent an otherwise enthusiastic teacher form pursuing teaching. (Do not ask the author to write in cursive.)

Trust, too, that no one escapes that first year! Brief author story because nothing illustrates this fact better: I will always remember one young boy who lived in the nearby projects and was a member of a rather rambunctious first grade class I student taught. One day, Robert (not real name) sat forward, perched on his knees in his desk, attentively watching my reading lesson. "I am reaching him," I gloated to myself. Robert raised his hand after a while, and I eagerly called on him. His remark: "You are new at this aren't you?" Back on Earth, I resolved to continue crafting my teaching skills.

Over several years, teachers will relax, gain in confidence, add to their skills, and simply improve as a teacher. If this is your calling, answer with courage. Good teachers are needed; faithful teachers are vital for the Kingdom of God.

*The Science of Teaching*

Much has been made over the century about how to teach. It is not the intent of this course to rehash all the methodology, strategies, techniques, and programs developed over the years to introduce, instruct, and assess. Some of these developments have assisted and guided teachers, particularly novices. There are studies demonstrating developmental learning and providing some general benchmarks. Assessing can take many forms, and there are both great and horrible measuring tools. Not all tests are equally valuable, and some are very poorly written. Errors have been found in them, as well.

Arguments will be made for and against the Socratic Method, student-directed learning, memorization, direct instruction, group instruction, and so forth. Sadly, behavior issues often the result of poor attention span have required some novel strategies to maximize learning.

Still, all of this is for naught if teachers dismiss or exclude essential knowledge of teaching and students. Each child is truly unique in his or her personality and abilities. That they are seated in a classroom with twenty or more other individuals can lead to canned teaching and less than optimum learning. Even in home school settings, the parent teacher or tutor must become acquainted with the child, and that includes repetition for some, along with different ways to present the information. Finally, some students will not reach their potential until their twenties, thirties, or forties while others who shined as students in a general school setting later dropped out. Regardless of popular opinion to the contrary, there are some basic differences between males and females, as well. Education is lifelong.

So, teachers should review helpful information and some approaches or tips as to how to reach students. They might discover that way that gets across a concept beforehand baffling to a child. Moreover, constructive peer assistance should be humbly sought.

Never forget though, science of teaching has its place, but it can never substitute for the fact that every child is a child of God and deserved respect. Teaching acknowledges tan individual's dignity. Education of the heart and soul takes precedence over education of the brain. Numerous great saints were poor scholars.

## Church Teaching About Teaching

(Sacred Scripture; Sacraments; Catechism; Writings —Encyclicals — Church Fathers; Saints)

Education began and continues with God. He instructed our first parents in sufficient knowledge to be happy for all eternity. Adam was given dominion over the Earth and enabled to name the creatures.

When his mate, Eve was created, he experienced human companionship and community. Of course, we do not know all of what God revealed to them. However, the only forbidden source of knowledge was the Tree of Knowledge that would unleash awareness of good and evil.

This established two truths: God possesses Divine Authority; He is the author of knowledge and therefore its keeper. Secondly, there is evil knowledge. Some would call this the absence of God which results in poor rationalization even given strong intellect. Until Adam and Eve disobeyed God, they had only known the fruits (pun intended) of good knowledge. Upon their expulsion from the Garden of Eden, that evil knowledge would haunt mankind until the end of time.

Even so, God gave Adam and Eve and all subsequent parents authority over their children. This is a primacy command that must be respected by Church and state. Indeed, the state, including the United States, has frequently violated God's authority and natural law in an attempt to proselytize (convert, attempt to convert someone from one religion, belief, or opinion to another) all children. The main target are Christians and specifically orthodox Catholics. That any government representative or employee, professional educator or institution believes itself empowered to do so is actually everyone's fault. Catholics should have asserted our Constitutional rights at the time of the Madelyn O'Hair case that took prayer from school. That no one prayer should be mandated in a school setting is far different than banning all prayer under any circumstances and then to the extreme, excluding the mention of God, at all.

Something was going to fill this vacuum. It should be no surprise that what entered was a "belief" system hyper focused on the terrestrial (St. Augustine) and self gratification—self will— and devoid of Truth and eternal life including the Last Four Things. One popular public school song—in an environment that discouraged Grace before meals—rang out with the lyrics: "Thank you, dirt, thanks a bunch. Thank you, dirt, for our lunch."

It is blatantly unconstitutional, but more importantly the exclusion and now persecution of Christians is also the work of the anti Christ.

On a brighter note, while satan can tempt, his "success" is limited by an all knowing God who permits the evil one's pride to false confidence. TheCOVID Virus (CCP Virus) and the ensuing draconian mandates may well have ushered in myriad opportunities for re establishing God as the Master Teacher and exposing and thwarting the evils of communism and atheism. In other words, God always gleans more good from any evil.

Still, even in a public setting, six key references should be ever present in the classroom *if only within the personality* of the teacher. The most important is frequent participation in the Holy Sacrifice of the Mass and the Sacraments. They are also knowledgeable of Sacred Scripture, Catechism of the Catholic Church, Church Fathers and Church History, Key Encyclicals, and the Saints.

One good article: *The Foundation of Human Society: A Christian Case for Parental Authority,* Public Discourse 8/2020)

*Sacred Scripture:*

The Word of God made Flesh…John I:1 sums up perfect knowledge, identifies the Teacher (Jesus Christ), and leads to the ideal pedagogy. That was not enough for the rabbis and scholars of Jesus' time, following their predecessors of Old Testament. These intellects felt compelled to dissect, analyze, and expound of every aspect of the old law, as to how one should live, including that which was essential education.

Like many educators in contemporary society, these synagogue leaders magnified their self importance and stressed those mannerisms, behaviors, and "letters of the law" that better conformed to the city of man than the City of God.

Holy Scripture itself is most clear that education is highly valued, though scattered throughout the Bible, and especially referenced in the books of Wisdom (Catholic). Proverbs and the Psalms are also particularly familiar. Figurative language indicates a grounded knowledge in the way of life at the time, whether nomadic or settled; agricultural, herding, fishing, tent making, or trade. Parents, though, were the primary educators, with honored priests or other leaders. Examples include Proverbs 4:1-27; 22:6—Colossians 3:21; Ephesians 6:1-4.

The sources are numerous, and teachers are encouraged to participate in Bible Studies that can illuminate education principles that need to be interwoven into every subject throughout the day, all reinforcing by their nature, the desire to seek the City of God, regardless of student aptitude or skill.

With respect to the New Testament, there are also some wonderful Scriptural based resources while teaching the basics. Many may be found in the numerous Catholic homeschooling materials. Others are gems to be unearthed by simple searches or word of mouth.

One word of caution, as there are Protestant based texts and resources. I hasten to interject that many of these, especially when referencing Old Testament passages, may be compatible with Catholicism. Some contain valuable timelines and maps, as well as engaging narratives. Simply watch for bias for Protestantism and cynicism of Catholicism. "Mystery in History" contains a reference to 66 Books in the Bible with the self complimentary notation that the Book of Isaiah contains 66 chapters, somehow to be interpreted as an indication of accepting only 66 Books. A thought: Catholicism embraces seven more Books which is perfection in light of the New Testament Revelation.

In another, a novel with a delightful plot evinced wincing when the author's post commentary discounted some of the articles, sacramentals of the Catholic Faith. Actually, the popular Christian writer was arrogantly dismissive of Catholic practices in an otherwise nicely Christian work.

The bottom line: **Know the Faith** and be confident in the Scriptures, Sacred Tradition, Church Fathers, and Catechism. That will enable greater understanding of the world and distillation of truth helpful to teaching, as well as enhancing evangelization. Students will be confronted by these challenges, anyway, so having a great teacher to guide them may be critical.

A note about a couple of other sources which are in the bibliography: *Twenty-Six Letters to Heaven—A Catholic Preschool Curriculum* by Sarah V Park—is simply delightful and comprehensive. Sarah Park covers the bases with Scripture, Virtue, and Saint of the week.

Another, *99 Ways to Teach Like the Master* by T.J. Burdick (En Route), speaks for itself. In the foreword, Patrick S.J. Carmack, J. D., notes: "Over and again in the history of education, the discovery of some new - and often helpful - pedagogical technique or insight has so captured the imaginations of educators with its possibilities that they have lost sight of the essentials." (6). He notes the decline of scholasticism and the errors by some theologians after the printing press made the Bible more accessible. (Sounds like today!)

Overall, though, T.J. Burdick formats his book heavily on Scripture, describing Jesus Christ in the Gospels as the Master Teacher who demonstrates the most effective teaching training.

*Sacraments*

Exceptional teachers impart knowledge in myriad ways. No comprehensive Catholic education can ignore the reality, though, that there are simply some matters that remain a mystery. So some matters may be identified and described, but elaboration or explanation may be beyond our natural world.

**It is imperative that students be taught that they need not know everything; they will not know everything.** In no small way, the error in the Garden of Eden is being replayed today in modern society where man seeks to be his or her own god. Some simply cannot rest or accept that they will not know and control the world in the way they seek. So, they simply reject that which cannot be evidenced. That is the height of pride.

The Sacraments are an excellent way of imparting the visible and invisible, the natural and supernatural, and the revealed and the hidden. Yet, one may say, "I am a history teacher, and how does that apply to me?" Consider prehistory and all competing theories about the origin of the universe and the controversy about when man first appeared in time and space. Furthermore, modern history is a minefield! The same limitations are found in science. Even mathematics contains mystery. Think about the eternal Pi. Still, when students express disbelief, frustration, or rejection of anything not provable or visible, wise teachers either search for verifying information and expertise , or humbly lead them to prayer and the Sacraments of the Reconciliation, the Eucharist, and visiting with Jesus. While it is not a sin to be baffled or wonder, it can be pride that leads one to scoff at Truth. That is the fine line that is in itself a valuable lesson.

*Catechism of the Catholic Church*

While not all "teaching" is dogma, the Church teachings have dozens of references to education in some way. Interestingly, the education of children is related to procreation signifying that children should arise from Holy Matrimony in union with God and what is then brought forth (education) becomes the responsibility of mother and father. Two recurring themes are: 1) Parents are the primary educators of their children particularly in morals. 2). It is the duty of parents to oversee the rightful education of their children and in a way that instills in them their ultimate end. In other words, parents may delegate other teachers for some substance, but they cannot never abdicate their authority or accountability. They will be held accountable for any neglect of this duty or compromise with evil that misleads their children.

Teachers entrusted by parents have a greater burden, especially in today's world. While educators must respect parents, they can never go against Truth. In public settings, this is a double bind. (Author's note: In one public school class, I did not learn until spring that the majority of students were Catholic. It was my last year in public schools.)

How to break this to teachers gently: They cannot teach in any school or setting that mandates the imparting of lies that lead to the ruination of souls.

Following with some good news. Many families are now seeking tutorial assistance as they are more fully aware and impacted by the utter ruin of public schools on so many levels. These government entities have become the re-education, indoctrination camps of educrats. This includes propaganda about all sorts of evil, primarily sexual in nature, but also revisionists in history to promote selfish behavior that will lead to disorder and chaos requiring totalitarianism to control the unruly. The astonishing scope and depth of depravity can no longer be hidden. Even the once duplicitous no longer even attempt to disguise their deception. They show utter indifference or vile arrogance when challenged.

Teachers: Know the Sacraments…LIVE the Sacraments! Model that life for students, always!

*Church Fathers*

What do the Church Father say about education? Of course, in all their communication, they reference Truth. However, they have plenty to say! Again, we find common themes on the need for parents to take charge; rear them in the Word of the Lord; instructing them to distinguish between helpful and injurious knowledge; and determining teacher(s) with great care and thought. Obviously, St. Augustine, both Church Father and Doctor will be prominent throughout.

Below are some quotes worth citing, but there are many more.

CHURCH FATHERS ON EDUCATION (*See Wisdom through Salvation History*)

"Fathers and mothers, Go and lead your children by the hand into the Church." (St. John Chrysostom)

## Chapter One: Introduction and Summary

"Rear your children in the Lord [...] Teach them from infancy the Word of God. Discipline them when needed, and render them respectful to legitimate authority. Never let them exercise authority over you." (The Apostolic Constitutions)

"With us everything should be secondary compared to our concern with children, and their upbringing in the instruction and teaching of the Lord." (St. John Chrysostom)

"Young people must be made to distinguish between helpful and injurious knowledge, keeping clearly in mind that Christian's purpose in life. So, like an athlete or the musician, they must bend every energy to one task, the winning of the heavenly crown." (St. Basil the Great)

"Seek out with much care and thought, a teacher who will be a safe guide to you in your manner of life; one who knows well how to lead such as are journeying towards God; a teacher who is rich in virtues [...] and wise in the Holy Scriptures." (St. Basil the Great)

"It is not the amount of learning that must be our aim, but the quality of learning. Better to learn two verses with understanding, than a whole page with wandering thoughts." (St. John Cassian)

"The primary lesson for life must be implanted in the soul from the earliest age. The primary lesson for children is to know the eternal God, the One who gives everlasting life." (St. Clement)

"It is good to teach, if he who teaches also acts with good example." (St. Ignatius)

"If a child learns without preconceived and worldly ideas, he has ears to hear the true." (St. Clement)

"A man becomes a Christian with sound teaching; he is not born one." (Tertullian)

"True wisdom is virtue united with knowledge." (Lactantius)

"Let nothing be taught to children except those which nourish the soul and make one a better person." (St. Cyprian)

"The wisdom of the world is foolishness with God, therefore let no one glory simply because of his preeminence in human learning." (St. Clement)

"An important part of a child's education is story-telling, since good stories excite the imagination and strengthen the bond between parent and child. Stories from the Bible are preferred, and the child should repeat them often, to underscore full comprehension." (St. John Chrysostom)

"The human family constitutes the primary and essential element of human society [...] Peace in society will be a direct result of peace in the family; order and harmony in the secular, political realm will be in direct result of the order and harmony which arises out of creative guidance and the giving of real responsibility to children (by assigning specific tasks to the children)." (St. John Chrysostom)

*Encyclicals and Catechetical Writing*

Popes and other Church leaders and notables have written extensively on Catholic education. Note that these are scholarly persons, many with advanced degrees. Yet, they share the common understanding that an education devoid of respect for the family and absent Faith that will lead children to "love, know, and serve God in this world and be united with Him forever in the next" may have only temporary (temporal) benefit and could lead to eternal damnation—separation from God.

A few here but later to be more deeply expanded and explored in "Wisdom Through Salvation History."

Pope Leo XIII (1865) in *Specta Fides* (Look at Faith) noted even then that the tender age of children is threatened by so many and various dangers. He emphasized that there be a union with literary instruction and sound teaching in faith and morals. He further stated that "The wisdom of our forefathers, and the very foundations of the State, are ruined by the destructive error of those who would have children brought up without religious education."

Pope Pius XI (1929) in *Divini illius magistra* (on Christian Education) was all encompassing at a time of grave moral peril. He emphasized the "last end" and that there could be no true education which is not wholly directed to man's last end. He insisted that Catholic education include the "permeation of religion through all subjects and grades of schooling" with Christian piety.

The Pope condemned new methods of instruction based on naturalism, as man is both body and soul with a fallen nature that can be elevated by God's grace.

He touted the important role of teachers who if good teachers are more important than methods.

*Saints—All Teachers*

What saint was not also a teacher by word and or action? Some were more formally engaged in the actual formal process of education like St. John Bosco and St. Elizabeth Ann Seton. Others, like St. Augustine and St. Thomas Aquinas formed Catholic curriculums that embodied truth about many different aspects of living faithfully in the world. Obviously, this very thematic primer is based on St. Augustine's work, The City of God, but also others who espoused similar refrains.

Then, there are the saints of the soul: Two simple yet profound educators were St. Therese of Liseaux and St. Bernadette. Saints Jacinta and Francisco, though children, have taught thousands of Catholic teachers in the past one hundred years, along with Sister Lucia though living as a cloistered Carmelite. As previously mentioned, many Popes were saints who also taught. These were sound thinkers—brilliant thinkers—through history to today—St. John Paul II is an exemplary example. Still living are numerous others like Cardinals Sarah, Arinze, and Burke.

## Summary of Sections

## Education in Eternity — The Priority Objective—Persons will attain Heaven

*Why These Recommended Courses*

To reiterate, from creation, man has known the primary objective is to know God; so all education is God oriented. Yet, by the evil one, the belief in God has been distorted and dismantled. The disfigured image of God has become "self," and even then, the ultimate atrocity is nihilism whereby the recipient of knowledge is led to to reject not just God and moral principles but that life, itself, is meaningless. Under that horrific ruse, the reason we exist is to know self, love self, serve self, but expect nothing upon death. So we have traveled in education from a place of centeredness on our Creator to worshipping the world, even if only temporarily. We have gone from the world was made in seven days (even metaphorically) to we will create our own perfect if briefly lived world…with the Green Deal and End of the Present Age.

In the Garden of Eden—reiterating that the theory is this was in the area of Mesopotamia—yet, the critical truth is that it was a perfect place for Adam and Eve where God provided everything for a period of time unspecified but could have been in the millions of years according to our temporal senses. The only knowledge was of God. There was no need for any other. Then came the Fall, and man had to toil for survival.

The most primitive knowledge of the temporal world was survival oriented. The earliest hunter-gathers had to know where to find food sources, which were feasibly attainable, what may have been poisonous, and how to adapt to climate and terrain. Study of the heavens, stars and the mood may well have guided these journeys, at least eventually. Observing other natural phenomenon like the skins that covered animals, the spark of fire, and the natural protective value of shells and horns added to the most primitive field of education.

The earliest tribes (families) traveled together, and information was passed generationally by oral tradition. These nomadic groups may have communicated with each other, as well, though some hostility likely occurred in a territorial manner and for survival of the fittest. So, weaponry for hunting and combat evolved.

As population grew along with knowledge of the land, settlements were established in the way of villages and towns. To add to the basic survival skills and knowledge, now came more sophisticated and complex principles of land cultivation and animal domestication. Whole cities and eventually civilizations arose along major rivers. Man was learning how to tame the environment instead of being dictated by the environment.

As certain symbols were created and people became more advanced in communication, folk tales arose, along with myths about super powers. Often, these were repeated as much as people needed to be reminded, and elders passed on to children stories that would educate them on the importance of the elements and nature; wild animals and other threats.

When writing was developed, there emerged other lessons, especially related to desirable traits or morals, such as Aesop Fables. Sacred Writing, what is commonly known as the *Old Testament*, and other tales, like Homer's *Iliad* and *Odyssey* would share history, both spiritual and temporal.

When other trades arose, guilds were formed, and master guildsmen would instruct journeymen in a particular domain. Those with a business acumen would impart economic or financial literacy to others, most often within the family. Several areas requiring particular education, such as this and the arts, architecture, and public works, as well as within the area of government, civics, and politics emerged. Even thousands of years ago, there were the bureaucrats, and many would be expected to be well versed in codes.

Then there was a major shift from a predominantly agricultural to industrial environments for the vast majority of people. Even children were being used for factory labor under extremely dangerous conditions, including mining, six days a week for twelve or more hours.

A combination of this and social movements led to the concept of formal education for most children, a free public education. Though Protestant in emphasis, at first, giving rise to the Catholic school system, there were other sects, such as Jewish. Education was perceived to be necessary for the moral development of children, as well as the practical implication.

By the 1960s, and entering into the Technology Age, public education was perceived in pragmatic objectives with an understanding of higher education for many. Emphasis was placed on content; methodology was stressed to optimize understanding. The end purpose became increasingly temporal and even excluded God all together. Students were encouraged to become "book smart" more than "Word smart." The end goal was a career that would maximize advancement and compensation.

Catholic education has gone from the Master teacher calling simple fishermen to become fishers of men to multitudes of teachers having students fish in troubled waters with revisionist history, distortion of biology, embrace of dangerous ideologies, and and an overall contempt for authority, especially Divine authority.

In the ensuing units, the critical aspects of teaching The City of God in The City of Man should be apparent, but it will only be the start of the journey for Catholic teachers. There are ample sources, resources, and trusted person to continuously guide teachers while ensuring their peace of soul and leading them to sanctity.

Yet, teachers should stay focused always on *the* Source, as expounded in one reflection: "What I encountered in that brief but momentous minute was so astonishing I can barely say. Here in this poor, humble, little King I found *all the wisdom that ever was*. Here I somehow knew was the *source of all truth*." (Epiphanies, Through the Eyes of King Melchior, January 2021 Magnificat)

The ultimate goal: To learn to love what we ought to love...and teach others the same.

**Section Themes (Why these?)**

So much has been written, and every faithful Catholic can all celebrate the marvelous myriad articles, books, programs, resource sites, etc. pouring forth by the Holy Spirit. (Author's Note: Even as I was into my second year drafting this Primer, I thought, there is no way I can cover it all. I have dozens of notes and post ems, editing marks, and whole binders filled with wise counsel for educators.) Though living in an oppressed world, no one and nothing can stop Truth! However, herein focus on the main areas educators must incorporate into their teaching and relating with parishes, colleagues, parents, and students. All sections are described in the Table of Contents, but here is the rationale for their inclusion and ranking:

*Teacher in God's Light* is number one. Separate education from God, by any rationalizing, and one invites in the demonic and evil. It may be a slow death, but unheeded or confronted and countered, should anyone take that perilous risk? Now, some people might scream at these words: There is always hope and Divine Mercy. Not only is that dangerous presumption, at the very least, students will have been deprived of numerous opportunities—years for many— to express their love of Jesus Christ and neighbor in ways *in accord with and pleasing* to their Creator. Herein, teachers will better understand this, learn how to know and monitor themselves and obtain tools to grow in virtue.

## Embedding Catholicism in All Subjects (Fullness of Truth in the Fullness of Education)

No subject, no matter how beneficial, will properly serve love—the good of another—and justice if it is tainted by lies. There is not one subject—not one—including math that has not been poisoned by satan. Not one. Contemporary, supposedly benignly secular textbooks, work sheets, "student" media sites, and even in the area of strategies, are replete with overt and subtle end objectives to confuse and indoctrinate young minds towards anti-Christianity. If that seems extreme, well, the devil is not holding back in 2023. Some, (the author included) would contend this has been true at various times in history, but most intensely since the latter 1800s in the United States and other countries. Still, the devolvement seems to be rapidly spiraling downward in the past several years. Who ever thought that the Disney mouse would take off his head mask and reveal a rat underneath? This section will help steer educators to grow in awareness, steer away from the minefields, and navigate towards reliable sources.

## How to Teach Truth to Form Universal and Eternal Citizenship

The "how" is as important as the "what" and after understanding self and rightfully judging teaching materials, teachers will better hone the ultimate objective: Heavenly Citizenship. One crucial prerequisite is the availability of and access to peer models. These are the veteran Catholic teachers who have mapped the road already. The maxim "work smarter not harder" was never more apt. In this area, teachers will be given steps to seeking the right environments (fit), developing mentor relationships, becoming acquainted with great educator saints, and building trusted curriculum materials and approaches.

## Chapter One: Introduction and Summary

### *Unpacking Religions (Belief) Systems in the World*

What teachers do not know can hurt them. If it sounds too good to be true—more importantly — if it seems so fuzzy nice—there should be arched eyebrows. All belief systems promote themselves as "good." Even satanism! All belief systems draw their followers by "ideals" of some sort. Only one, authentic Christianity, requires extreme sacrifice of **self**. Oh, others may allude to self control, fasting, abstaining, and so forth, but none have the Person of Jesus Christ who lived in anonymity for thirty years and was utterly rejected by the world in which He entered into an ignominious death! Educators will be introduced to the appealing elements of other religions, but also that their fatal attraction has duped people for centuries. It is imperative to interject that this chapter is not "religion bashing," as there are and have been many marvelous people throughout history who were not Catholic or Christian—or Jewish—and that includes students who will be in any teacher's classroom but by this focus, teachers will be given the "pointer" to the apex of Faith: True Catholicism.

### *Understanding Contemporary Catholicism (Building Pathways to Truth and Love)*

Preparation is the greatest offense. Three generations, minimally, have passed with ever weakening knowledge and understanding of Catholicism, and this includes administrators, colleagues, and parents of students in even Catholic schools. A well experienced Catholic teacher will "spot" this upon entering any Parish school Mass. These persons: peers, parents, (and grandparents), are lovely people, often most giving. Yet, they have been influenced by the world and may have a tepid attitude towards religion, overall. Or, they are are filled with false self confidence as to the truth. The novice or sheltered teacher entering these school environments may be in for culture shock. How does one respond? Herein real life conflicts are explored, albeit obviously with pseudo names and locations. Educators will need to be prepared for many different types of confrontations, bluntly, even if they teach such seemingly noncontroversial subjects like music, art, or PE. More importantly are the ways to optimally build trusting and mutually loving relationships with those who are in disagreement. However, the caveat is that that may not always be possible, so boundaries will be important, too.

*Researching for Reliability (Secular and Sacred)*

Most teachers may not have control over textbooks and other supplementary resource material, but they can be aware of content and learn how to impart knowledge and judgment to their students. Besides, there will never be a "pure" temporal world in which man produced materials are without flaws, errors, and deficits—including this Primer. As elsewhere, educators must always be students, too. Without being overly suspicious or ready to attack anything that does not carry the imprimatur of one's favorite clergy, educators should be questioners and analysts, especially on important lessons. (Yes, all lessons are important, but some more than others in leaving lifelong impressions.) This also includes being alert even with trusted persons or publishers. It sounds like an arduous task, but consider Martin Luther who was not always a betrayer of the Faith.

*Wisdom through Salvation History (Church Fathers and Doctors; Encyclicals the Saints: The Prophets, Apologists, and Evangelists)*

A wealth of Church teaching is contained in so many sources, including the Encyclicals and educators may be surprised by the range of topics that date back hundreds of years—actually thousands— but cover contemporary cultural issues. Additionally, there are literally hundreds of reliable writings and oral tradition for reliable teaching in any subject. Note that the subject of art, alone, can be explored for its sacredness in non religious commentaries. Additionally, wisdom literature in Scripture, the Prophets (Biblical and Saints), the early Church

Fathers, Church Doctors, and other notable defenders of Truth provide Catholic teachers with a wealth of Reason.

### *The Eternal Age vs. Man Constructed Ages*

This section strikes the chord of the ultimate crescendo of education: knowing and understanding the eternal age. Every teacher should be an astute student of history because persons and events through temporal space and time exhibit a rhythm, even a rhyme. Yet, everything depends on the narrator and narration, both limited in myriad ways even when the spokesperson is virtuous and the publisher above reproach. Furthermore, no other subject can be well taught without the backdrop of history.

### *Government Through Time (Impact on and By Catholicism)*

As with history, all able teachers will understand the concept of government (from the root meaning—to steer) and how God granted man freewill to choose kings from their own ranks and how that corresponded—or not— to His Divine Will in human history. Yes, many wreaks followed that foolish insistence. There are other reasons for all educators to grasp government, civics, and economics, as they all have their origin in the family, headed by a mother and father. Even young pre-school students are most capable of learning virtuous "government." In fact, it could be argued that delaying these fundamental concepts, or not teaching them in the Light of Faith, could leave them open to anti-Christian ideas, at the most developmentally vulnerable period of their lives.

### *Relating Modern Secularism ("Sick"ularism" the Catholic Way)*

This is not the same as simply neutrality of beliefs, as secularism has become a term now more associated with anti-Christianity, gratuitously slapped on anything many regressive thinkers insist is permissible. At one time, mentioning "secular" implied an embrace of different perspectives of the Divine (or not). Mirroring God's "free will," temporal government and culture often recognizes that compelled adherence to one tenet or belief system is not only impossible, it is unjust. However, a purist "separation" of Church and State was always an impossibility given that there is one, absolute, objective Truth. Once the majority agreed upon and adhered to a basic moral code, and regardless of how one described personal belief in God—or not, society bounced along. It is now sinking because predictably — return to that study of history — people increasingly turned to self. So, the basic thesis and development of this section will be that the very term "secular" no longer has a place in discussion. Increasingly, it is the Christian vs. the anti-Christian.

### *Summarizing: Temporal Global Power vs. the Eternal Kingdom*

This is not a conspiracy based thesis. There is an old saying that just because a person is paranoid does not mean the person does not have good cause for paranoia. Satan is global. As the St. Michael prayer so well articulates: ….cast into hell Satan and and all the evil spirits who roam **through the world** seeking the ruin of souls. Regardless, this section is not concerned with the names or entities that may be pursuing evil power but the affirmation that it is occurring and at an increasingly rapid rate given technology. Worse, the smoke of Satan has entered the Church. Now, it is almost comical—yet actually tragic—that some people reject Catholicism because of evil doers. However, that these poor souls have succumbed to temptation is because the Catholic Church is being pummeled constantly and fiercely by a most clever opponent. Compound that by other factors, including the exponential fracturing of Protestantism, the spread of Islam, and the appeal of soft belief systems grounded in Hinduism and Buddhism, and it is little wonder that the conscience is becoming more resistant to the light.

# Chapter One: Introduction and Summary

In fact, the completely worldly among us are literally psychotic which fosters tyranny. Those who do not learn to control themselves will be controlled.

## COURSE WORK

*Eventually this Primer will be the springboard for a masters coursework, but, in the meantime, it is hoped that readers are benefitted and educators learn how to be prudent, just, temperate and courageous and continue to seek wise counsel and sound spiritual direction.*

## TOOLS, LESSON(S) AND GENERAL RESOURCES AND MATERIALS—INTRODUCTION

Following each section will be tools, sample lessons, and some resources and materials pertaining to the respective areas. The tools are those instruments that "nail down, tighten, adjust or shape" ideas. While lessons are developed for adult students, teachers in professional development, or in post graduate work, they may be adapted for students in elementary and high school. For the purposes of this Primer, all lessons will reference students. Resources may be persons, periodicals, publications, podcasts, and have been selected for their credibility over time to confidently and competently build the Faith with integrity but also with hope and compassion.

A caveat: Sometimes sources may fall short or begin to stray from Church teaching. So, it is always vital to know the Faith and build up a cadre of trusted colleagues.

***Primary Lesson for the Introduction***: Analyze the statement: *Education absent the Truth of God is dangerous and sheer folly, may be focused on the material and temporary, leading to spiritual death and eternal separation from our Creator.*

The objective is to identify ways to discern between Truth as revealed in Salvation History and the temptation to seek temporal success.

Read and discuss articles on the Scriptural references.
Resources: *Temptation of Christ: the Trials of Jesus in Holy Writ* (catholic.com); *The Temptations of Jesus* (catholiceducation.org). There are others.
Respond: What are the central temptations of the world; How do they relate to education, especially of children? How can teachers evaluate material and lessons based on this knowledge?

Additional Resources: *The Holy See's Teaching on Catholic Schools* by Rev. Michael Miller; (CERC-Catholic Education Resource Center); St. Augustine—Overview of The City of God; *St. Augustine Confessions*; Bishop John Ireland's volumes on the church in modern times; *Thomas Aquinas in Fifty Pages,* A Quick Layman's Guide to Thomism, Dr. Tylor R. Marshall, 2013; (Search: Greatest Catholic books of all time and see what pops!).

Also, see the Appendix and Biography, but great works are mushrooming.

Special Note: Throughout where there is reference to developmentally developed lessons, Kindergarten, Primary, Intermediate (4th-5th-6th), Middle (Junior) High School, (6th-8th or 7th-8th) High School are the generally identified student blocks. Some schools, especially K-8th, consider 4th-8th Intermediate, forgoing the junior and middle constructs which many educators perceive as misleading with respect to the maturity level of students and introduction of material and ideas prematurely and unnecessarily. At all times, all students in a classroom setting must be considered individually. Whole group instruction must be sensitive to those students with special needs or situations, and teachers are expected to avoid usurping primary parental authority.

So, take the divisions as such and adjust as needed.

# Chapter Two

## TEACHER IN GOD'S LIGHT

### *Parents as Primary Educators (Many Home School); Teachers under Parental Authority*

There is every probability that Catholic educators and those aspiring to teach in Catholic schools will cite the desire to live their Faith in their work, in service to others, particularly children. The overwhelming majority will be sincere in both their aspirations and reasonably self-assured in their qualifications, spiritually and professionally. Odds are that they assume their colleagues, families, and students agree on a Christian vision of education. Moreover, many of these candidates may be parent/educators (home school) or aspire to be. Some will be older, having taught their children and now ready to help other families.

Regardless of background all will experience some "cold splash": Many Catholic educators in classrooms for more than a year note divisiveness and perhaps disillusionment. For parent teachers, this may take the form of having "failed" — that somehow, God having placed parents as the primary authority over their children must surely have equipped them. So what are they doing wrong? Furthermore, the majority of home school parents desire to instill in their children the Truth, but many a day may seem more like Purgatory, at best.

For the hopeful classroom teacher, challenges may appear differently. Most are young and many do not have children. Still, they will expect that Catholic parents, in particular, will have reared their children to be angels, or, at least be responsive and supportive if students misbehave or are oppositional. However, mainstream Catholic schools are not the picture perfect classroom of fifty children sitting quietly with hands folded looking at a nun in habit smiling benignly upon them. Much has changed. *One*, catechetical formation has been weak, at best, for at least three generations. *Two*, the central foundation of society—Catholic or not—has been and is the family, but that has undergone major disintegration. *Three*, other influences from the Pastor, central authority such as the Archdiocese (of Catholic Schools), parents, and textbooks and resources impact instruction in ways that will, at best, puzzle faithful teachers.

The knotty roots are plentiful. Knowledge or understanding of the Faith may be minimalist, distorted, or dismissed. Some of this arises from genuine ignorance, but pride—self will— can deceive persons into thinking they are right and that others may be just aged, ritualistic, or obstinate. There are peers, clergy, Catholic media, and prominent CINOs (Catholic in Name Only) who tend to reinforce false teaching. Catholic education can also be perverted by nonCatholics seeking not truth but comfortability in their own beliefs, from Protestant to Buddhism, to Judaism, to even Islam. Connected to these influences are financial considerations, community popularity, and false notions and narratives about "toleration," "compassion," and "diversity." Then there is modern emphasis on *selective* Scripture, particularly Matthew 25: 31-46 but only the corporeal works and Acts 2: 42-47 which superficially appears to support communism. An even greater scandal is the reduction of the Person of Jesus Christ to that of a man when He is true God and true man. Errors from this perspective play havoc on His Divine Identity while even mocking His humanity. Finally, even the 21st Century Pontificate communication has fostered confusion and by popular media presented as actually anti-Christian. (There is no escaping acknowledging this final concern, regardless of Papal intention or others manipulating messages and actions.)

Still, the most harmed victim in this tsunami of counter Christianity are the children. Their personhood—their identity in Jesus Christ—created in the image of God has been outright abused, spiritually, physically, and psychologically. That a three year old boy may be subject to transgenderism for selecting a girl's toy is appalling, at best. Besides, was it not just in recent decades the mantra of "liberated" minds to encourage children to be nonsexist in their playthings? Fortunately, the *Person and Identify Project* was formed, and there are many other guiding resources for teachers in the Appendix to gain understanding and tools to address these matters.

## *From Disorder to Order*

Much, if not all of this departure from the purity of the Catholic faith can be laid at the footfall of distrust, desertion, and disorder. The only remedy is first a return to trust, fidelity, and order. Three conditions prevail for this to occur: one, is self knowledge with distrust of self; two, disassociation from those who would lead teachers to rely on, or even glorify, self and encourage us to embrace selfishness and the temporal world; and three, incrementally prioritizing the necessary steps for faithful living which always requires the pillars of the theological and cardinal virtues.

The most critical springboard for anyone seeking to teach is that they always seek the Ordaining Will of God, but recognize the Permitting Will of God **which is always perfect justice.** (Heliothropium— 1627, 1862, 1912, TAN Books). This leaves no wrangling of self pity or accusations of unfairness, false combativeness even on behalf of the Faith, or complaints. Witness the undisciplined rageful reactivity to the 2020 election, for just one example. A Catholic, trustful of God's Will will give thanks to God "for He is good and just" at all times, everywhere. He or she knows that only God knows the good that will arise from seemingly catastrophic circumstances, even those that seem to promote sin. A trusting Christian, however, will nevertheless ***still** pray and act* to protect and uphold natural law and Divine authority. He or she will communicate truth and remain faithful even at great sacrifice and support leaders who will keep God's Commandments. Note that the two responses are not mutually exclusive.

Next, or simultaneously, teachers must dispense with the notion that Faith "evolves" with "the times." Truth is not democratic; it is divinely autocratic. God is EVER in the present. With Him, there is no past or future. True, language may seem antiquated; books may reek of storage odors; and persons may appear uncomfortably reserved or stagnate. Yet, teachers must beware of charismatic deceivers who can quote Scripture but have not the Word in their hearts or souls. Any proclamations opposed to **all** Jesus Christ taught, in its entirety, is to be suspect, at best. As elsewhere, St. Augustine concluded that a thorough knowledge and understanding of Scripture was mandatory for anyone teaching the Faith, and as Faith is inherent in all subjects, all Catholic teachers would be well advised to start there.

Third, peers must be sound of soul. St. Francis de Sales, in his *Introduction to a Devout Life*, wonderfully expounds on genuine friendships vs. flirtations or associations that can mislead us. While even Catholic teachers in the most orthodox settings will encounter false companionship, they must be aware of what signals them to be wary and chose only faithful Catholics as true friends. Of course, one is cordial towards the uneducated or ignorant, but thinking one can "play" with those who are actually devilish is to falsely "trust" oneself. Many Catholic teacher has fallen because the faculty lounge "chatter" substituted for the Church.

## <u>What is the signature mark of a Catholic teacher?</u> *(Pursuit of Virtue)*

Of all the definitions for teaching, perhaps, surprisingly, Wiktionary offers one of the best, particularly ***"to point, indicate"*** because there is only one teacher…the Master Teacher, Jesus Christ. Subsequently, all others must point to Him, Truth! It is essential that all knowledge be ever attributed to God with the dual purpose of living a virtuous life well and in accordance with individual talents and gifts and to attain eternal union with God. In short, school, whether at home or in a classroom setting, should be the incubator for forming conscience and community consciousness to serve God and our neighbor. Being a teacher in God's Light also means dispelling the darkness, present in all types of information and communication formats since "the first temptation in the Garden" that enslaves in the guise of making (wo)man gods.

Moreover, absent perfect Love, objective Truth, natural law, Divine authority and revelation, education devolves into a manmade conundrum of facts and opinions often selected, developed, and delivered to advance humanistic ideology towards a utopian or unitarian vision . Even allowing for solid evidence, such as in science, instruction that fails to seek the good of the other and a good end, will likely become constructed to assert (wo)man's dominion over the world in most unhealthy ways. Worse, in a Catholic school, the worldly will be confused with the Godly and appear acceptable to God. At least parents of children in public school can refute "secular" teaching or fill in the spiritual void. Yet, nothing is more horrifying as an adult falling away from the Faith because of what they were explicitly taught in a Catholic school.

Candidly, it will most likely be the teacher who must seek this Truth with reliable advisors and materials. (See Appendix). Even then, prayer must always precede any day and evening respite. As a caveat, there is increasing Catholic educator (administration and faculty) development steering in the right direction. (See Resources/Toolbox and Appendix). The proliferation of programs, classes, resources, and guidance is so ample that this book could be hundreds of pages long just extolling all the faithful voices in authentic Catholic publishing and communication, from clergy to laity.

Also, the mark of a good Catholic educator is not so dissimilar to that of a healthy psychologist. Father Chad Ripperger in his *Introduction to the Science of Mental Health* emphasizes that a good psychologist must be prudent (overall seeking virtuous living), but he underscores that this can be misdirected into carnal prudence with an inordinate weight to worldly reputation and concerns for the psychologist and his or her directee. Furthermore, a healthy psychologist must beware of leaning towards human respect. Teachers need to consider these same fundamental characterizations and intentionally develop in virtue. (More on this in the subtopic on temperament — or disposition.)

In the meantime…solid Catholic educators may possess this knowledge and most willing to share the truth in love, but superiors, not so conscientious, may impose problematic direction or materials, and so they must also know how to intake, filter, and respond to contemporary "professional development," even in a Catholic school. Theoretically these measures boost educator competency but often they result in deflection from the primary mission of education—to become saints and get to heaven—and become top heavy in secular (materialistic) outcomes not infusion of virtue. Having voices of fidelity at the push of a button (to a site or ally) should be in any prudent Catholic teacher's toolbox.

While superintendent of Catholic Schools in Denver, Kevin Kijewski frequently aptly ordered priorities thusly: Heaven first, Harvard second, and (then) Hoops a distant third.[1]

Speaking of a toolbox, this is true from the get go. Generically teacher preparation programs, again, even in Catholic settings, include attention to an educator's self awareness and reflection in several ways: 1) How the teacher evaluates him or herself; 2) How others (administrators, parents, colleagues, and even students) perceive and evaluate him or her; and 3) How someone unknown to the teacher may see him or her. Moreover, this matter is addressed with respect to frequency and intensity of introspection. Various instruments are employed, as well, using personal observation and technology. Depending on overarching expectations, such scrutiny can range from casual to highly formalized.

Yet, what may be paramount are the guides and tools utilized for such personal growth. **These instruments must follow the path of the virtues** which, incidentally also ensures the objectives even most secular programs foster: competency; healthy teacher student relationships; receptivity to learning by students; successful colleague relationships; enriching teacher-parent communication, and so forth.

In recent years, some Catholic school offices have contracted with consultants who administer personality and leadership questionnaires

---

[1] https://denvercatholic.org/growth-innovation-top-priorities-superintendent/

to rank strengths and weaknesses of educators and evaluate administrators using instruments similar to those found in the corporate world: personality indicators, relational patterns; reactivity measurements. While there is nothing wrong with some of these "tools," another foundational "barometer" is critical:

For the Catholic educator, ***the overarching objective should be how one teaches in God's Light.*** This, of course, encapsulates subservient goals with respect to professional delivery of effective instruction. Even here, though, there may be differences because the public domain is ever undergoing some change, allegedly to improve outcomes. So one sees programs emerging like *Springboard*, a particular approach to language arts instruction that candidly, at least at one time incorporated questionable lessons (See Notes), or Kagan, an academic and behavioral approach to maximizing heterogenous teaching while socially acclimating students to work together in a focused and productive manner. Catholic schools often follow suit.

Still, at the same time, numerous Catholic homeschool programs are ever being developed and individualized . (See link) Many have researched and recommend texts and classics from centuries ago. Classical literature is on everyone's radar, but so are some unique resources like Ray's Arithmetic, first published in the 1800s. In fact, Classical education is soaring, as teachers, including Catholic teachers, have discovered that sometimes the "old fashioned" way of introducing children to the world around them is not so passe after all. (See The Eternal Age vs. Man-Constructed Ages). Additionally, along the way, organizations like The Institute for Catholic Liberal Education (.org), Catholic.com, and many others are offering more robust Catholic development. This Primer is intended to usher in a masters program for teachers seeking that appropriate attention to student spiritual development.

So, this particular chapter will also highlight how to ***develop self to teaching in God's Light,*** regardless of other standards, and for the Catholic school teacher, whether a parent in a homeschool setting, a teacher in a non public school or Archdiocesan Catholic school.

Even on the chance that a teacher can be confidently employed in a public domain, these attributes and resources will grow teacher character. These emphases will use language and aspirations that parallel public school but go to the heart and soul of teachers with emphasis on souls.

### *Value vs. Virtue (Also See This Subtopic in Government)*

For example, the public domain uses contemporary standards that mirror social norms like "diversity," "tolerance," "empathy," and "student engagement." Some schools have been known to tout character or name "halls" and student groups by names such as House of Courage, House of Hope, House of Justice, House of Compassion, and House of Respect in a futile attempt to steer young minds in a particular direction. Lacking theological foundation, these aims are difficult to attain and likely to be interpreted in worldly ways. More than one student angrily insisted that teachers had to respect him (her) first. Justice was often understood as racial payback. A sense of hopelessness was witnessed, as the Halls "came tumbling down" after the five year "experiment" with the model.(Edison Schools, 2001)

*The Catholic teacher should be more focused on personal virtue development* and acknowledging the dignity of each student with respect to his or her giftedness or challenges, yet in its original meaning. (Vocabulary has been coopted by the world bound for cultural transformation.) Whereas administrators in public school look at subject competency, variety of strategies to meet individual needs, pacing, classroom management, and standardized student achievement, the Catholic educator *will* incorporate those principles but must be *more intent* on the whole formation of the student, mind, body *and soul.* The teacher's motto will echo St. John Bosco's education maxims: "Without confidence and love, there can be no true education"; "Frequent Communion and daily Mass are the two pillars of education"; "Remember that knowledge without morals is the soul's ruination"; "Religion alone can initiate and achieve a true education."

(Now, in all due respect to St. John Bosco, he also directed teachers to never send negligent students out of the classroom but to be patient with their light mindedness and to take special care of backward pupils. However, that advice is congruent in an educational setting that permits the fullness of religious truth and consequences, albeit in love.)

There are other differences from a public school that may seek empathetic and personable but competent engineers, doctors, lawyers, etc. A Catholic school should be cultivating capable, knowledgeable students striving to be saints and tireless in ensuring both intellectual and spiritual student achievement. The word "should" is important because as previously mentioned, in some ways, Catholic schools have tried too hard to mirror the "professional development" of public schools. These are not necessarily bad, but depending on the environment and circumstances of their employment, the outcomes may or may not be accurate. Contributing factors may be missed, and recommendations then off the mark.

For parents who are also homeschool teachers, the goal should be the same although co-oping can best guarantee that the talents of like minded, like-souled, adults provide that for the children in their family or care. Also, working candidly with other parents can help parent teachers help each other in identifying areas of weaknesses or strengths, especially under spiritual direction. Furthermore, coops can impart to children that Faith transcends their own family nucleus to a larger community of believers.

Regardless of environment, and as will be next explored, individual temperaments, one common virtue must be fortitude or courage. (Father Chad Ripperger would likely say prudence, but that will be the assumed primary virtue, anyway.) In a recent Public Discourse article: "Called to Courage"—Ryan T. Anderson, May 18, 2021—the author asserts that we are all called to a specific path of holiness and service to others and notes that *the only real tragedy in life is not to have been a saint.* He calls for living out our vocation in the public square, courageously bearing witness to Truth in an age of individualism and relativism. He reminds his audience, law students, that universities are the creation of the Church. (Let that sink in because formal education is more heaven derived than world generated, though the worldly would like everyone to think they are the source of knowledge.)

Anderson quotes St. Thomas Aquinas's definition of courage: *That which binds the will firmly to the good of reason in the face of the greatest evils." We fear these evils, by natural inclination, but courage keeps us on course. As alluded to above, of course, other virtues, particularly the other three cardinal ones (prudence, justice, and moderation) are necessary, and educators should view the as the balancing fulcrum between extremes. In the case of courage, for example, one would be neither cowering nor foolhardy. In other ways, educators would be bold but not bombastic.*

As trite as it may sound, even if a teacher achieves this balance, it will be for the love of Jesus Christ and His Truth. More than likely, instead of accolades, the brave, steadfast teacher may spend lunchtimes alone in her or his classroom, hear the distant buzz of mockery, and other quizzical responses to simply behaving faithfully. Other than acknowledging and acting upon reasonable criticism, be that beggar in *The Heliotropium*. All is His Will!

## *Know Self, Know Students*

As will be a continuous refrain, each teacher possesses some gifts from God, but they are each imperfect and exhibit faults. Original sin left the human race with a tendency to sin. So such obstacles like anger, sloth, envy, pride, and so forth can be stumbling blocks, but they need not be twelve-foot walls. Paradoxically, teaching may well lead teachers to perfecting their spiritual life, and certainly God has called persons for that very reason. Again—trust not in self but Him. Be careful about who you trust, but recite the Litany of Humility if needed, as well. One foundational prayer that may help is to beseech God to "block" anything that is not in His Will, and to say "yes" when a roadway is clear.

Then, too, each teacher is *also* blessed with a particular temperament, or disposition, often described in four general classifications although temperaments can and almost always are a mix or overlap. Still, the better a teacher can identify and challenge or accept certain deficits, the better, always acknowledging that he or she does not have to be all wonderful in all areas, subject wise or temperamentally. (See further on for more detail on this self examination with input from other trustworthy observers.) Unless there is a serious impediment cognitively, psychologically, physically, or spiritually, there is no reason that many, if not most, can (and do) teach. One excellent source is *"The Temperament God Gave Me*, by Art and Laraine Bennett which provides ample guidance, yet simply, for knowing, tempering, and relating temperaments.

One essential caveat prior to delving into temperament is the fact that disposition is not set in stone. It would be easy to simply "blame" our dispositions on our innate character. And how many times has any teacher joked about being ADHD or some other debilitating flaw. We can even the playing field of self acknowledged tendencies and work on the virtues that deflate their worst effects while building those that may not be natural to a teacher's being.

However, even if a teacher's temperament is a comfortable fit for any given student, he or she should keep in mind that God gave parents authority over their children in all matters. It the teacher is the parent, great. However, if not, God had His reason. Teachers may use their understanding of a child to serve parents who may not "get" why Suzy is so sensitive, and Peter is also laid back. Regardless, a teacher should not be either falsely emboldened by a popular personality or defeated by impediments. God also trusted some fairly "rough around the edges" disciples to go forth and spread the Good News. Actually He sent all of us, but teachers have a different type of responsibility.

Another note about professionalism is that the credentialed teacher is not necessarily better than a non credentialed teacher; though the licensed teacher may have a larger tool box, know educational law, and understand preparedness and delivery better among other areas of need. Good news, too, is that those with a bachelor's degree can often secure a position as they move through an affordable credential program. They are affordable, online and paced to meet individual needs. Michigan offers such a program for under $300 with another $5,000+ deferred until and if a student is hired in a public, private, or parochial setting. Though it is true that these classes are often associated with secular colleges, Catholic School systems will require catechetical formation aside.

Back to the bottom line: every person has both body and soul, and a teacher's spiritual life will determine success, failure, or simply continuous tensions and struggle. Perseverance is all the more important for teachers. (Author Note: Teaching was a second career after a bustling, highly stressful advertising and public relations position. At first, it appeared that teaching would provide a respite, not just from the secular world, but also an oasis of wonderful experiences imparting knowledge to eager—Catholic—students. Talk about have sold oneself with the good PR of teaching! Nothing proved more wrong.) Another example is Father Ciszak who suffered tremendously in Soviet prisons during World War II—as mentioned elsewhere—was nearly defeated by a false perception of vocation—in his case the priesthood—yet persevered and grew! Teachers often just need to stay the course. They will look back with joy that they did.

How to grow in virtue beyond self awareness? Teachers must be Sacramental. Moreover, the quality of a Sacramental life should be improving over time, albeit everyone trips or falls occasionally. So, teachers should also cultivate self-forgiveness to better forgive students and others. Therefore introspection and balance portend a quality instruction.

*A veteran woman teacher considered herself a good "practicing" Catholic. She attended daily Mass when possible, frequented the Sacraments, and anticipated Confession as a means of cleansing and renewal. Absolutely believing that the confessor was in place of Jesus Christ, the woman spoke openly of her faults. So, she was startled when one priest at the end of her monologue, simply said, "For your penance, say an Our Father slowly. Would that be okay?" Would that be okay? Unnerved the teacher replied, "What ever you direct." Yet, she left the confessional questioning the confidence of the priest. She even asked God, "Was he supposed to ask me...like that?" She "heard Jesus reply, "Yes, because for some I have to be very gentle in how I touch their souls. otherwise they will retract them." Still, not completely certain, she inquired further, "Was that necessary with me?" She "heard" that Jesus allowed him to speak to her as a reminder too her that he invites persons to Himself; he does not impose or force anyone.*

A valuable lesson for a teacher, yes?

## *The Student in that Light*

Equally important is to become a Teacher in God's Light by **envisioning students in God's Light.** Even parents who homeschool can readily identify differences in their children's temperaments and areas of temptation. There may even be a clash of personalities or over identification with a particular child, positively or negatively. If a teacher knows him or herself, he or she can make extra efforts in some areas to meet the children where they are in life.

For example: Five-year-old Susan is very precocious and intelligent. She prefers to rule the learning environment. Her teacher is likeminded but obviously older and the authority in the room. Yet, the teacher should want to cultivate all that is good in Susan's temperament and inclinations so as to capitalize on her strengths, yet not indulge disrespect or disorder. Here is a perfect opportunity for the teacher with a solid spiritual growth plan to model patience, appropriate praise, and (re)direction as the teacher would apply to him or herself. The teacher, in this case, is truly teaching, not just subject matter, but lighting the path for the student.

In *The Catholic Education of Girls*, the author addresses children in general but also highlights the difference in teaching approaches for young ladies. There are some knotty areas with which particularly astute female math and science teachers may disagree, but the text addresses overall differences, not the exceptions. Moreover, in our contemporary, but confused culture, where all persons must be "equal" in all ways, some of these inborn natures are often ignored or rejected. No one need stereotype to observe key differentials between males and females. Again, how sad that public education has veiled the individual person created in God's image.

In all, there are numerous areas that teachers should explore and examine within themselves as persons (children of God) **and** how the children of God in their charge can see them and themselves.

While the eventual actual course, *Teacher in God's Light,* will be hopefully taught by a Catholic psychologist, the following areas will be included in its scope: The Ideal Teacher vs. the Real Teacher vs. the Called Teacher; Identifying Temperament; Examination of Conscience with Spiritual Direction for the purpose of knowing spheres of temptation and vices; Relating to students in a psychologically and spiritually healthy way; Developing a Virtue Plan and Tool Box for Regular Self Reflection, Monitoring Progress, and Tweaking of Personal Goals.

## *VOCATION: The Ideal Teacher vs. The Real Teacher vs. The Called Teacher*

Television in the 50s and 60s always showed the ideal teacher: poised, confident, empathetic, kind, cheerful, and even wise. Of course, there were rarely more than twelve students in the television classroom set and all sat perfectly still—or nearly so, and all seemed to respect with near reverence the teacher sitting at her (usually it was a female) desk with a serene but serious expression. Students always raised their hands before speaking or were quickly admonished and contrite. Some stood by their desks after being called upon. The board boasted word problems and homework assignments. Each episode touted a moral lesson, often with parental (mother and father) support. If the television household was single-parent, widowhood was the most likely cause.

By the 70s and 80s, realism entered and shows like "Welcome Back Kotter" flipped to a rowdier group of students or at least one or more truly troubled students. Still, the lead teacher seemed almost surreal in his or her capability at humorously reaching those youth while still

## Chapter Two: Teacher in God's Light

teaching with great outcomes. One show, set in a fictional Boston public school, promoted a lawyer to an administrator *in one season, and this woman significantly raised test scores that very year.* (See, miracles do happen even in public schools!). *Dangerous Minds,* based on a true story, showed the transformation of a military vet from a frustrated near walk away to someone who used field trips to amusement parks and tossed candy bars to inspire her students. However, she did leave immediately thereafter, so one wonders how much she truly enjoyed the profession. *Freedom Writers* was another success story, and the teacher—at least as portrayed—appeared to be a genuine gem.

Of course, who can forget all the movies with Catholic school settings as well. Loving but firm nuns and pastors always tamed the little ruffians by the closing credits.

That is not to say that there are no "naturals" to the teaching world. There are many wonderful men and women with great temperaments and capabilities. They epitomize the 50s, and most educators, if not all, have met these wonderful souls. Still, they are not perfect, and, sadly, in contemporary times, that very same genteel spirit can also be gravely discouraged by the continuous administrative, student and parent challenges.

The point is that there are literally no perfect teachers, but that does not excuse striving for appropriate perfection. The word appropriate is necessary because one can become mentally ill—literally—trying to be perfect all the time. On the other end of the spectrum, there are some adults who cannot teach for myriad reasons.

It is assumed that educators reading this Primer and taking any related courses, have determined reasonable suitability for the profession, albeit the first year trial is simply unavoidable.

Speaking of, recently a young homeschool Mom coaching a homeschool soccer team turned to another adult and whispered, "I have just learned something." When asked what, the Mom laughed and said, "I do not like children." Actually, she was simply frustrated by a couple of the players' behavior, but this underscores the reality of teaching.

It is highly unlikely that any teacher will like all of his or her students at any given time, including his or her own children.

"Keep it Real" is a good first year motto…and the next year…and the next year. Keeping it real to the extent that you may have an Achilles Heel will be harder. Almost no one becomes a saint overnight. It is most frequently a lifelong endeavor.

## ARE YOU CALLED?

What teacher does not experience "mission" regardless of religion? Teachers do not enter the profession (or vocation) in the absence of seeking to achieve great things for and with students or their children. Some sincerely and eagerly seek to "give back." The distinctions arise with respect to the nature of that mission and whether or not it is one that emphasizes only the city of man or includes the City of God. Catholic teachers with sound catechetical formation, or seeking that, and ongoing immersion in a deeply devout spiritual life are greatly needed in our confused and disordered world.

Despite what the world insists is a rigid, confining, and outdated perspective, history repeatedly demonstrates the nobility and enrichment of formal education with the all-knowing God at its center; Our Lord Jesus Christ as the lead Disciple for prosperous living; and the Holy Spirit to illuminate reasoning by Truth and Love.

Yet, are you called? Only you can answer that in the final analysis, **yet with other professionals' insights and advisably a priest.** However, stressing again, do not allow imperfections block what may be heavenly inspiration to teach. There is no perfect teacher except Jesus Christ. In his book *"99 Ways to Teach Like the Master,"* author T.J. Burdick underscores the reality that it was his rediscovery of the Gospels that all of the educational training he had received was already practiced by Jesus 2,000 years ago. In other words, barring some great impediment and ignoring the hundreds of "bells and whistles," teachers will be just fine if their souls are aligned with God, their hearts are with children and their spirit is drawing them—calling them vocationally— to education.

Moreover, even in the best of circumstances, teachers should balance expectations realistically when envisioning themselves in that role. After establishing that this a true calling for which they are competently suited, there will still be challenges. For example, teachers might ask themselves if they could be directed by someone with less credentials or a highly critical administrator? Can they follow an administrator's directives (obedience) even while vehemently disagreeing (but not about Faith)?

Peter Crawford, founder and headmaster of St. Jerome's Institute in Washington D.C, has developed an in-school school for teachers with frequent classroom observations and feed back meetings, along with a six-week summer course to strengthen teacher ability. While typically teachers shy away or bristle at the sudden appearance of an administrator, teachers at St. Jerome's have acclaimed the frequent interchange and steering towards exemplary teaching. It is all in the attitude, and of course, the virtues of humility and obedience. (CatholicSchoolPlaybook April 2022)

**Here, bold faced, though, the most important aspect is your knowledge of Faith and not being in conflict with any Magisterial teaching. You will never be "called" to enter a Catholic school to counter the Truth regardless of personal experience or perspective.**

Other considerations: Would they be able to withstand with proper humility but charitable gumption a colleague who is always one-upping them? Will sneering or mocking students (this especially occurs in middle school) infuriate them to the point of leaving the classroom after the first month? Or the first day? Submission in any job can be a stumbling block, but teaching multiples those stones.

Teaching requires an exceptional threshold for bearing insult. Yes, teachers may receive some lovely gifts at Christmas time, but there are 180 plus other days in which they may experience disgruntled students, disappointed parents, dismissive colleagues, and dismayed principals.

Their perfect lesson plan may flop; their best intentions to be cheerful may be disrupted by an unexpected incident; meeting with an administrator may have them wanting to scream.

Are you called?

Teaching requires exceptional sacrificial love. As alluded to above yes, teachers will receive those scrapbook worthy notes from students, cards of gratitude from parents and others, and may be an occasional service award. Yet, teachers may find a student note that belittles them; a demanding email from a parent that charges them with horrible indifference, at best; a scornful look from a peer or administrator or an angry exchanges with a student. A virtuous teacher has to love anyway, even ignoring or praying over the slight, knowing that they give joyfully (not to be confused with cheerfully) fifty or more hours a day.

Even with all of that, the answer may well be "yes" because those truly called can embrace the necessary humiliation and brush off insult and move on in charity.

Are you called?

Teaching requires an exceptional abandonment of possessions. Yes, even Catholic dioceses boast step pay, professional development, retirement and health benefits. However, the salary scale is significantly lower, though, and annual contracts are clear in their limitations depending on enrollment and other factors. Teachers can work for a decent retirement, but there may be interruptions. Moreover, Catholic schools lack the fiscal and logistical ability to hold positions for critically injured or ill teachers. Many cannot even afford personal days and must limit sick pay. While many offer mostly unpaid maternity leave, as should be, teachers may have to consider, on their own, what that all entails for them and the school (Church).

If teachers are seeking a pod or hybrid school setting, or are homeschooling, there is even less or no pay. Moreover, they may have to pay school taxes for which they receive no benefit.

So, teachers will likely do fairly well, but there are no guarantees.

Chapter Two: Teacher in God's Light                                    65

## _Called but Then? Seeking the Guidance of the Master Teacher to Grow_

Who are you? Many people do not discover, let alone acknowledge their true selves for many years, sometimes decades. Well known educator and writer, Ronda Chervin self published one of her books, later in life, based on a personal journey with Recovery, Inc.: _Taming the Lion Within: Five Steps from Anger to Peace._ Dr. Chervin candidly admitted her own struggle with anger and how she learned to best confront it. She chose to know and confront herself, and other teachers should as well.

Determining temperament (natural disposition, preferences and tendencies), is relatively easy. One site to access is the catholiccompany.com. There it is argued—although saints and Catholic mental health experts agree— that temperament is not purely secular or irreligious. Moreover, this has been acknowledged as early as 300 B.C. Spiritual directors often desire to know more about a persons behaviors and actions. There are often consistent patterns that indicate an internal disposition, albeit affected by nurture, life experiences. As mentioned previously, Father Chad Ripperger explores disposition quite thoroughly in his book on mental health and how to address a disposition to build virtue.

A special note is that each temperament has certain strengths and weaknesses, both of which can be identified and grown or rooted accordingly. However, there is no reason that any one disposition should dominate! Repeat: With intentional effort in cooperation with the will, any person can moderate disposition, evening out the rough edges and building up the healthy aspects. (See _Introduction to the Science of Mental Health_.)

Here below is just a general overview:

_The Sanguine_ are "airy"—highly talkative, active, and social. Warmhearted and optimistic, they make friends easily. Although flighty and changeable, they have great imaginations and ideas though, on the down side, may not follow through or be tardy in delivering the goods.

The Sanguine may need to overcome superficiality, lust and lack of perseverance. So, he or she will look to seek purity, interior depth, strength, and, obviously perseverance.

However, the Sanguine is also more likely to be cheerful, generous, sincere and sensitive to the sufferings of others.

*The Choleric* tend towards egocentricity, appreciating respect an esteem, and are more extroverted. They may be excitable, impulsive, and restless with reserves of aggression, energy, and/or passion and attempt to instill that in others. Task oriented, the choleric will likely be independent, decisive, goal-oriented, an ambitious. They are often good planners and will desire to get the job done efficiently and in a timely manner. Strong-willed is often an attribute.

The Choleric may struggle with anger, pride, and impatience. So he or she may need God's grace to cultivate gentleness, humility, and patience. (Catholic Company). On the plus side, the Choleric has a strong will, great constancy and energy for carrying out duties.

*The Melancholic* is often a seeker of laws and principles by which man should live. They are analytical, detail-oriented, and deep thinkers, yet introverted and sensitive. Often empathetic, they can arouse profound religious thoughts, but may hold themselves in contempt. Often gifted in areas of art, literature, music and even health care, they strive for a permanent imprint on the world. Yer, they can be perfectionists and may be disappointed in not perceiving their achievements.

The Melancholic will likely struggle with being hypercritical, moody, and despondent and need to grow in joyful acceptance, selflessness, and hope. On the virtuous side, The Melancholic is usually compassionate, long suffering, pious, and contemplative.

*The Phlegmatic* are those with more private and thoughtful temperaments. They tend to be relaxed, peaceful, quiet and easy going. With high tolerance, patience and caring, they appear to be content with themselves and faithful to friends. However, while steadfast, they may be ponderous or clumsy, and they may seem to be hesitant and emotionally flatter. Their emotions are unlikely to show on the outside.

The Phlegmatic should overcome a tendency to laziness (sloth), the inability to control or take initiative and people pleasing. His or her goal will be to build fortitude, holy ambition, and strength of will. Virtues to maintain are a tranquil spirit, fullness of common sense, being assiduous, and near immunity to anger.

Though most are more likely a mix, and teachers may check with trusted friends or advisors for further insights. They should take care to use self analysis tools as guides and not hard and fast determiners of who they are as individuals. By the way the Catholic Company has a quiz though that is only one indicator, and depending on the time of day and other factors, may not be wholly reliable. There is also *the Temperament God Gave You*—see Resources—though that questionnaire is a bit lengthly.)

As a post note: Saint Thomas Aquinas, it is said "possessed the best qualities of the phlegmatic temperament. One example of a Choleric is St. Francis de Sales by some accounts though there is certainly an overlay of Melancholic. St. Therese of Liseaux was believed to have a melancholic temperament, but one wonders if there were not phlegmatic tendencies. As difficult as it may seem, one source identifies St. Teresa of Avila as Sanguine. However, this latter perception may have been effected by a deep spiritual life.

The earlier teachers start, though, the better. However, know that "knowing" oneself and advancing cognitively, psychologically, and spiritually are two separate goals, and the first has the potential to become an escapist hatch. When thoughts or statements like, "Oh, I have never been very patient," or "I often speak impulsively—it is in my DNA—I am ADD, you know," or similar excuses frequently percolate in a response to something said or done, teachers should still realize that they should tackle the obstacle. Will a teacher become the perfectly even tempered, patient, or self restraining person? Likely not, *but all should move towards perfection.*

St. Francis de Sales struggled with the temptation to anger which is why he wrote so powerfully and helpfully about this fault. It has been reported that when he died, St. Francis de Sales had bile stones that indicated that he held a lot inside himself. Now, no one should suggest that you need to interiorly stone yourself, but there are many ways to combat those vices to which we are drawn and cultivate virtue in their stead.

Also, teachers should not permit friends to flatter them in your faults. This is worthy of repeating: Do not be flattered! This has been the downfall of many educators, actually, as the school setting can be a breeding ground for cliques, reminiscent of one's own schools of yesteryear. Also, teacher may congregate or parse in ways that deflect from or shore up their own areas of weaknesses. Some will compliment sarcastic humor or the frankness with which someone counter argues with others. A few might even counsel a colleague to ignore those who criticize them or call them to task. These are not necessarily friends, especially if a teacher can glean a beam in his or her own eye but is too complacent to remove it. *A true friend desires the good of and for another even at personal cost.* These friends of Jesus will want peers perfectly virtuous.

On the other end of this spectrum are the critics who are also foes. They may cruelly nitpick weak spots; gossip among others about these; report to administration, and, worse, parents. Teachers must bear them as well. Yet, know that God knows all. Pray for them, as they do not desire perfection, as they preen themselves and celebrate the wounds they inflict.

Some steps to assure sanctity even amid these challenges is to "beat them to the punch." Teachers should examine their conscience and life even from toddler years. In the *The Introduction to a Devout Life,* St. Francis de Sales, recommends a general self examination of conscience from the age of reason, as a general springboard to laying out a plan for spiritual growth. (Pg 49) They should note what seems to be poor behavioral habits, occasions when they fell into temptation and what caused—triggered—those lapses. Categorize them according to the seven deadly sins and explore further. Was it a particular situations, a certain personality, or something else that caused the stumble or fall?

Teachers may detect a trait about themselves, like being overly and overtly suspicious of others' motives that influences how they relate to them unjustly. Is there a pattern that continues? What, if anything has been tried in the past to overcome these faults? Were they successful and why or why not? As elaborated further on, rotten branches of family trees can contribute to these blind spots.

Finally, teachers should be most careful about jealousy. That perfect teacher who seems so perfectly serene, efficient, and caring may well envy another teacher for his or her spirited lesson activities and ability to think outside the box. Teachers may imitate the best of someone's example and emulate their virtues, but should not try to be someone they are not.

In a three volume tome, Father Chad Ripperger examines the mind, body, and soul in his *Introduction to the Science of Mental Health*. Most may never read this text but hopefully wise superintendents and administrators will resource it for principal teacher development. Understanding the intersect of our bodies, minds, and souls, along with understanding of the will brings educators closer to the Light.

*Individualized Influences*

Also, as alluded to above, aside from our innate temperaments, we have had unique influencers from childhood. Teachers should explore family trees for indications of particular familial impediments and for healing. Often patterns of behavior are generational arising from addictions, abuse, multiple relationships. Too, the faults of one generation can alter the course of the next. Substance abuse in the family may lead to its members being overly assertive, for example, for having to be right in any situation. What do children learn from this…and carry forth?

Were family members of past generations pulled towards the demonic? Were there Free Masons in the family? Our family trees, so to speak may have some rotten branches cultivated by the devil. This may be an area that justifies some uncomfortable but helpful genealogy research. Interestingly, that which ancestors ignore or literally bury may be a clue as to what needs to be closely examined.

Again, family research should not be undergone to cast blame or be merely inquisitive. Certainly relatives of past generations should not undergo unjust speculation as to motives or outcomes. Still, when teachers examine their own temperaments in light of family histories, there may be some "Aha!," moments, greater insights, and then change.

## *Prayer Life as Essential to Maintaining Growth and Staying the Course*

Now, there may be some budding educators who want to simply circumvent these unpleasant facts or sincerely believe they can overcome them by sheer will power. Maybe. Some may fear that if others knew about their family background, they would be excluded for teacher consideration. If an educator is resistant to that "look in the mirror," it does not pretend well for the future when criticism is bound to come his or her way, but the teacher has little or no genuine coping skills. It is hoped that those gravitating towards or showing some affinity for teaching consider counseling with an authentic Catholic perspective or spiritual direction rather than simply give up.

Teachers can seek spiritual direction though this can be difficult due to the dearth of available directors. Yet, so many wonderful books, DVDs, websites, podcasts, and free online courses are available for spiritual growth. It is nearly overwhelming so teachers should narrow their scope. The Avila Institute offers many wonderful courses and speakers. Two text standard recommendations are *"The Imitation of Christ,"* a classic by Thomas Kempis and St. Francis de Sales' *"Introduction to a Devout Life"* both of which teachers may want to daily read brief passages for the remainder of their lives.

The ultimate goal of all of this is foremost to become a saint. Teachers engaged in that process can only be a wonderful bonus!

It *is* a never ending exercise, however, and there may well be times when a teacher thinks, "I will never defeat _____." Teachers need to be gentle with themselves as long as they are not rationalizing. St. Francis counseled this for earnest souls, and teachers may realize that that they may have made progress than imagined. Excessive and intense self criticism is also to be avoided. No one escapes trials and errors. Teachers should make self reflection daily, but include at least one self congratulations. Journal or use tally marks, or whatever works for them in particular. Also, teachers may arrange frequent encounters with someone who has their soul in his or her heart and can help monitor or redirect their thoughts and actions but not someone so close that it may interfere with other aspects of a relationship, personally or professionally (That may be a priest or other spiritual director).

Nothing substitutes for prayer for the discipline of routine prayer, starting upon rising and ending at nightfall. Moreover, nothing can better guide us to fruitful prayer than the Saints and holy persons. As more than one writer has noted, the Saints are now in a perfect place, literally, to assist us without their personal temperaments,—faults, imperfections, and defects—misleading them and us. Also, they have the Divine Presence that is the ultimate determiner of who, what, where, when, and how heavenly graces via the intercession of the saints may come to our aid.

Furthermore, those holy persons will include persons who may not yet be sainted but led incredibly courageous lives and left testimonies to the strength they drew from their Faith. Not all are professional teachers either.

One such example is Father Ciszek who passed away in 1984. His autobiography tells an astounding story of someone who did not seem destined for an exemplary priesthood. In fact, he tried to tell God what he sought, rather than let God lead him. Yet, he found himself as a Soviet prisoner after being convicted of being a Vatican spy in World War II and spent 23 years in Soviet prisons.

In one profound meditative essay, "Put out into deep water" he recalls the temptations to "give up," although not different from many who anticipate a certain outcome, only to have those expectations turn sour. However, he was not addressing the enormous suffering he would one day endure, but the everyday humdrum of a vocation that did bring the dynamics he imagined. Educators often confront these identical feelings in less than five years.

Had not Father Ciszek arrived at the saving grace of God to perceive his vocation from God's will, one wonders would he have survived the Soviet torments. Had he been stuck in resentment and feelings of regret at the time of his arrest, he might well have rebelled or even betrayed his Faith.

Remember the final call for all of us is Heaven.

## TOOLS, LESSON, GENERAL RESOURCES AND MATERIALS —TEACHING IN GOD'S LIGHT

*Not all teachers carry the same burden, so utilizing these "tools" will vary in use, intensity and regularity depending on the individual. However, prayer is non negotiable.*

*Prayer* (boldfaced and in larger font for an obvious reason)—Formal, Informal. Prayer may be highly formalized, as in the Mass or Rosary, or more informal, akin to conversation. However, the ideal is to form the ***habit*** of continuous awareness and relationship with Jesus Christ in the classroom.

Even wise secular teachers behave as though their superiors can hear and see them in the classroom. For Catholic teachers, knowing that God can see and hear all is even more important. Granted that there is likely no teacher, dead or alive, who never gave thanks that someone was not present during a regrettable moment in speech or action, but the overall attitude should be one that invites this scrutiny.

Prayer throughout the day. Morning and evening are essential times of prayer. *Imitation of Christ* by Thomas Kempis—just a small section daily—is worth its weight in platinum. In the morning teachers should prepare for the day, and as St. Francis de Sales advises, anticipate challenges or difficult situations and ponder how to cope with those. (*Introduction to a Devout Life*). **However, there are many others!** Before retiring in the evening, teachers would be wise to examine their conscience and how the day has conformed to planned and personalized spiritual objectives. During the day, teachers may offer brief prayers, from a decade of the Divine Mercy Chaplet to simple but profound "Live, Jesus!" ADAPTION is expected. Better, teachers can journal their own intentions and spiritual references that suit their temperament and need.

—Church and chapel lists with times of Mass, Adoration, and other devotions; Prayer Book which can be simple hand-held photo book with special prayers, important to self: Scripture verses and quotes; holy cards or medals; candles or essential oils, but also blessed oils such as from the Padre Pio Foundation; inspirational CDs (Lighthouse) and classical music; light reading

—Easily accessible (nightstand) books for morning and evening reading: Magnificat, *Imitation of Christ, Introduction to the Devout Life. (Note: The Magnificat* has Scriptural readings, but teachers may also have a Bible nearby. Also, daily reading of the books may be only a paragraph on which to ponder.)

—Foremost in any teacher's "toolbox" are those gifts God imparted to them, and each *is* uniquely gifted. Moreover, humility demands justice towards self and objective recognition of that which God has given to build up the Kingdom of God. Intentional teachers find ways to employ those talents. Perhaps a teacher is especially adept at art or music; some may enjoy mathematics or science. Certainly, many are able communicators and speak and write well. More than a few are able organizers. Also, Catholic teachers have likely—hopefully—already begun their Faith journey and should identify their strengths in the moral virtues, from prudence, to justice, to fortitude, and temperance, from which other virtues flow.

*The Holy Mass*—if at all possible, pray that teachers can attend daily Mass, particularly in the morning. This is a challenge given dwindling priests and dire situations like the recent pandemic, but where there is a will, there is a way. One can tape EWTN Mass if physical presence is not feasible. A subscription to *Magnificat* which has the daily readings and so much more is a virtual treasure chest. Teacher will also discover fantastic lesson ideas, and, in all subjects, as *Magnificat* often features Saints from different professions, special in-depth articles about the beauty of art, including background and history on its cover art; science, math, music, history, and so forth.

The Holy Rosary-After reading *10 Wonders of the Rosary* by Father Donald H. Calloway, MIC. (Marian Press), or *The Secret of the Rosary* by St. Louis de Monfort, it would be difficult to find a Catholic teacher—or any Catholic—who would not return to this prayer of be further inspired to pray it daily. Even given a particularly wearing schedule, a decade prayed well, is highly recommended, especially tuned to the challenges of the day. However, most can recite five decades, in the car or with family, the latter being most efficacious. **(See only one version of the Rosary for Teachers at the end of this Section, but teachers will soon be penning their own intentions.)**

*Consecrations*—best done with colleagues over several weeks, there are numerous great study guides to consecrations to The Sacred Heart of Jesus, Our Blessed Mother, and St. Joseph. Father Gaitley's multiple books and workbooks on these various consecrations have been the basis of many school based groups. Not only does this practice increase personal sanctity, but it tends to bind the community of teachers in common spiritual goals. See again the precaution above, as not all teachers can make this commitment. Still, perhaps an administrator may plan for this as part of a weekly staff meeting or inservice.

*Reading*—Catholic schools should have ample resources for teachers, even a library, filled with insightful and true books, magazines, DVD's, and pamphlets. A Bible, Catholic Catechism, and classics are highly desirable inclusions, along with Papal Encyclicals and Apostolic Letters; timely articles from *The National Catholic Register, Catholic World Report,* or trusted Catholic sites which could be catalogued and available for evaluating in class lessons. (See Appendix Resources)

*Journal*—Teachers often "vent" though that word is emotive more than intellectual. Still, educators have feelings, but it will be how those are processed that makes all the difference. Healthy Catholic teachers will recognize their weak spots: brash temper, insensitive impulsivity, or being hyper critical or overly sensitive, and so forth. These faults may ripple into injustice, injury, complaining, and slander. Better teachers keep a journal and speak to God about their imperfections and seek His guidance about an incident. If the damage has already been done, then, contrition would be the next action.

*Virtuous Mentors*—Even veteran educators benefit by sound mentorship. The teaching environment is not static, even within families. Life events, circumstances beyond someone's control, and myriad factors can upset the best projections and plans. Teachers should have trusted advisors to whom to turn for advice when the unexpected arises or even when undergoing doubts or concerns. Teachers just need to be certain that a listening ear is truly prudent and discreet. Again, it was St. Francis de Sales who warned against confiding in persons (troublemakers) who will only further deepen a complaint (and self righteousness) rather than help the wounded party seek candid self examination healing.

How does one know to whom to turn? Teachers, especially new ones, should develop relationships with patience and prudence, by observing and listening, and prayer. They most certainly can and should ask God, their Guardian Angel and Saints to lead them to wise counsel.

Every staff has such persons, though. If not, the school is likely in crisis anyway.

**TOOLS:** Printable checklists for Examination of Conscience, prayers, novenas, and devotionals abound online geared to school and home. *Hallow* is a recent app, and is a gem. Graceful teaching will also include a goal for amendment or improvement in some area.

Teachers need to take care of themselves physically, too. Wellness Inventory (most appropriate with a physical check up) and Care Package.

**PRIMARY LESSON:** Develop a personalized prayer plan with copies of short prayers and devotions. Include images and Holy cards. Revise as needed or desired for particular occasions, or as others share with you. Include a section for those areas that records some favorite websites to visit occasionally or regularly.

What follows are references and resources for teaching in God's Light. These are also indexed in the Appendix references in alphabetical order. Also, much of the resources can be drawn from and cross referenced to other sections.

## OTHER PROPOSED ACTIVITIES

*The following could be printed, read, and discussed with respect to developing virtue.*

LESSON #1

*Introduction to a Devout Life*: pg 78 First Part:

We Must Purge Ourselves of Our Evil Inclinations. The objective is for teachers (students) to understand the laity's call to holiness.

## Chapter Two: Teacher in God's Light

**LESSON #2. Avila Institute 6/2021. Read and Discuss the following which explores a vice: anger, but puts it in Catholic perspective. First, reflect on a recent experience with anger and journal a response to it.**

It has become apparent to me that I have a hard time welcoming the human experience of anger and figuring out what to do with it. That becomes quite a setup for struggle and heartache – especially during years like this past one! As I look around and observe other humans all around me, I realize that I am not the only one having a hard time here.

Never mind that God created the emotion of anger; never mind that his Son Jesus was truly human and experienced anger without sinning. Many of us Christians feel a major "should" that warns us against anger – and then we find ourselves stuck.

Far too often I have avoided feeling or expressing my anger. It turns out that it doesn't just go away by itself. Anger is experienced interiorly as an urgent call to action; it wants to do things! If we ignore it, much like rushing water, it insists on finding a path. It leaks out on others through sarcastic or shaming comments. It swirls around in resentment, pulling us and those around us down into the muck of self-pity. Or it propels us up to a pedestal of self-righteousness and judgment, from which we eagerly label "those people" as inferior to ourselves and cast blame on them for our misery. It's all their fault! If only, if only, if only…

Resentment is an especially common way of not listening to our anger. As a wise man I know likes to say, we cling to our resentments; we hug them close and snuggle up with them. That sounds strange yet so true. It is easy to stay in a place of resentment because it doesn't take any courage. In my resentments, I can identify myself as a victim. "That guy" or "those people" have caused all my problems, and I am powerless to do anything about it. That feels a whole lot safer to me, because it also means I cannot be held responsible – which in turn means I am entitled. Commiserate and gossip about "those people"?

Don't mind if I do! Think of witty labels for those who are causing all my problems? Sure, that will be fun! Binging on comfort food or sugar? Yes, please! Avoiding important tasks that will actually make the world a better place? Hey, if you were suffering as much as I, you would understand! You get the idea…

Many of us, especially if we have highly empathic hearts, may find that our anger turns inward and erodes us from the inside out. Enter anxiety, depression, or an assortment of bodily illnesses. We can't bear the thought of showing our anger to others, so we allow it to consume us from the inside. For some reason we find it okay to pour contempt onto our own human dignity, telling ourselves we are being kind to others by holding it in. Only our anger leaks out anyway, and others don't much care to be around us in those moments.

What can one do?? Clearly, just putting our anger in the driver seat is not recommended. Aggression and violence cause harm to self and others – whether the overt violence of interrupting, shouting, raging, or assaulting; or the more subtle forms of violence such as the silent treatment, sarcasm, gossip, or passive aggression. They all harm and rupture our relationships. They all result from not truly tending to our anger, not learning to listen to it.

Instead, we can see our anger as a God-given warning signal, an invitation to be curious and pay attention, a call to receive the care we need and to work for the justice and peace that Christ came to bring.

Our anger always has something to tell us – although if we listen deeply and empathically, the full message may surprise us. So often what we think is the problem is not really the problem. The thing we think we are so resentful about is actually just the tip of the iceberg – to borrow an image from Mark & Debbie Laaser. If I am really telling the truth to myself, the thing I feel angry about right now – as frustrating as it may be – is actually so painful because I am feeling the same way I felt way back when – and that causes a strong reaction within me. The anger reaction is a call to action warning me of danger – that if I don't do something, I will feel just as terrified, just as sad, or just as alone and abandoned as I did back then. Instead of "should-ing" away my anger (which never works), I can invite Jesus to join me in listening to it and revealing to me where I most need his love and truth.

In some cases, listening to my anger makes me aware that I am guarding deep and scary places of my heart – reservoirs of unshed tears and grief, tremors of fear or terror, or perhaps even stronger and older anger over harm experienced that was far worse than the injustice presently bothering me. If I allow Jesus to take me into (and back from) those places, my anger becomes the fuel on a journey of retrieving all these broken fragments and becoming a whole person capable of both mercy and justice in the present moment. I begin to know who I truly am and what I deeply desire, and I can be strong in the face of present evils, without needing to "power up" in aggression against others, nor to shrink and hide my true self or let others trample upon me.

Sometimes our anger needs to be expressed. It can be interesting to notice our anger and ask it what it wants to do. Curious asking is quite different from acting out – and if we are in a posture of curiosity and kindness, there is no real risk. Does our anger want to scream? Does it want to smash or break something? Does it want to throw things? Kick or hit or pound? Isn't it interesting how many different nuances our anger can have? Often noticing what our anger wants to do helps us also to get down to its original root and receive the care that we have needed for a long time.

We can also allow our anger to express itself, giving it healthy outlets, allowing it to pass out of our bodies so that we can be released of it. If we think creatively, there are all kinds of ways for our anger to do what it wants to do while honoring human dignity. As long as we are not harming others or self or damaging personal property, pretty much anything goes.

This is all so counter-intuitive for those of us who have been conditioned to view our anger as "bad." Far from causing harm, when we take ownership of our anger, allow ourselves to feel it and acknowledge it, and listen empathically to it, we actually gain the freedom to be released from its grip. Our anger does not actually want to be in the driver's seat – it is crying out for attention and help. When it actually gets heard and taken seriously, it will gladly step out aside and allow the Wisdom of God to take over.

*This post was originally published on abideinlove.com and is reprinted here with permission.*

## RESOURCES Teaching in God's Light

*Introduction to the Science of Mental Health* Father Chad Ripperger (a year long journey at minimum); Return to Order; The Augustine Institute; Avila Institute (coursework); Institute for the Psychological Sciences (course work and sources); St. Thomas Aquinas; St. Augustine; Archbishop Fulton Sheen; Tan books; Sophia Books; St. Ignatius books; Magnificat; Catholic Catechism and Bible Study; *Taming the Lion Within* (Ronda Chervin); *99 Ways to Teach like the Master*, T. J. Burdick, En Route Books; *The Temperament God Gave You* (Art and Laraine Bennett, Sophia Institute Press 2005; Temperament Analysis and Self Check Lists (Catholic sites for analyzing one's temperament); American Society for the Defense of Tradition, Family and Property; Women of Grace; The King's Men; Students for Life; Lepanto Institute; Courage Encourage RC; and others. Novenas are on line through many sites, and daily email highlighting a message from Jesus to Saint Faustina from her Diary uplifts. Daily Catholic Wisdom is another inspiration source.

### *Other Reference Material*

*Books on Saints, Sacred Scripture*

See books that caution against poor direction though they are sometimes found mingled in Catholic references, such as mindfulness (Yoga)—Kathleen Beckman and others have explored these and put them in the Catholic Light.

## THE HOLY ROSARY FOR HEROIC CATHOLIC TEACHERS

**The Joyful Mysteries**

<u>The Annunciation</u>. Humility shrouded in Charity

*Jesus "awaited" the yes...all in the present...only past to us. The first Disciple, Mother Mary would utter her fiat to the entrance of the Master Teacher into the world—the Word made Flesh who would dwell among us. The "future" Apostles were unaware. Even St. Joseph, the chosen earth father for the Messiah would need spiritual guidance.*

Disciples Mary and Joseph depended on God to rear Jesus Christ. Though their trust in the Lord would be tempered at times by human response and tainted by worldly concerns, overall, we can believe that the Infant, Child, and Adolescent Jesus taught them far more than they did Him. Mary would proceed in her discipleship even after the Ascension of Jesus into Heaven having partaken of all the Holy Mysteries of His Life.

Catholic teachers are presented with thousands of opportunities to say yes with love's abandonment. If married, spouses will share in that mission. At times, the teachers "yes" is uncomfortable but not sinful; against personal human judgment but not the superior's authority.

**Pray for discernment; know the faith. Seek trusted counsel. Turn to Mary and Joseph for assistance. Ask God for His Will to be done, to block any action or decision that would contradict His Will; the courage to say "yes" when an avenue seems clear to take, or you are being prompted to do so. Also pray that those around you will cooperate in His Will, too.**

<u>The Visitation</u>. Charity marked by Humility

*Jesus Christ (Body, Blood, Soul and Divinity) accompanies Mary to Elizabeth to encounter the one who will announce Him to the world, St. John the Baptist, a teacher in his own right although intent on instructing souls for eternity rather than minds for earthly concerns. Mary's journey was an act of great love, but as the Lord's handmaid.*

Discipleship in its purest definition emphasizes accepting and assisting in following the Master's lead. It requires authoritative instruction by word and example, and Jesus Christ was the perfect, all knowing Authority. In an instant, He could impart Truth; by His life, He embodied Truth from the womb. Though older than his cousin, John the Baptist knew Jesus, and would teach others that the Kingdom of God was at hand.

Catholic teachers bring Truth to every class and child and are charged with identifying Him across subject domains through time and around the world. Yet, detractors even in Catholic schools have increasingly courted secular research, concepts, and assertions that downplay, at best, the presence of Jesus Christ in even religion! Instead of apologetics, one may well hear apologies ringing through textbooks and resources; other teachers and parents. Attuned teachers "visit" the Faith daily, and know HIS story—history. They spend time with the Church Fathers and holy saints and impeccable witnesses around them.

- **Pray in person with the Blessed Sacrament to recognize Truth and discern ignorance or hostility to the Church.**
- **Imitate the gentleness of Mary and the exuberance of Elizabeth.**
- **Pray for their intercession to be guided to reliable resources and alerted when falsehood creeps in others.**
- **Cultivate knowledge of persons and groups that can be trusted for reliable information but ask also for wisdom to verify.**

Chapter Two: Teacher in God's Light                                    83

<u>The Nativity</u>. Detachment from Earthly Goods (Materialism)

*Jesus Christ, Second Person of the Blessed Trinity, the Word made Flesh, enters the world in a stable on smelly hay in a manger, turned away by people and surrounded by beasts. He possesses no material goods. His Mother Mary likely has only the clothes on her back, maybe swaddling cloth for Jesus, and Joseph is similarity bare of things.*

The early disciples would appear as common shepherds and then the three kings from the East. Neither group would have been the first choice of the teachers, or rabbis, of the day. The shepherds had nothing but their witness—no esteemed "credentials" or wealth. The Magi knelt before the King and left gifts of the greatest value. Indeed, imagine the simple pronouncement of shepherds to others at the great sight they beheld or the Magi returning to their pagan countries with a tale of Wonder entering the world.

Catholic teachers may not feel capable or called. Like the Little Drummer Boy, what gifts are worthy of the King? Yet faith and detachment from the world are two prerequisites. Now, not all teachers are suited to all environments. Some educators may be better suited to a different environment than a classroom. Also, given that Catholic schools parody public schools in pay and other compensation, there is increased temptation to view this position as a job rather than a mission.

- **Pray that you become that teacher in God's Light, seeking a golden retirement with Him. Know yourself enough to prepare daily, after a routine of prayer and Mass if at all possible. St. Francis de Sales advises anticipating what may impede you during the day and be ready to respond in love and truth.**
- **Ask for the intercession of such great saints as St. Elizabeth Ann Seton and St. John Bosco among others.**

<u>The Presentation</u>. Obedience (listening)

*Jesus Christ is carried to the temple along with a couple of turtle doves, though He is the Temple. Mary and Joseph in accordance with the law, follow those precepts with humility, charity, detachment, and obedience. Of course, one could argue about which virtue comes first because listening is essential to be taught and to teach.*

Disciples must have outstanding listening skills, and none surpassed Mary and Joseph in that regard. Also, both spoke little. No words of Joseph are recorded in the Bible. Ears, minds, hearts, and souls were ever attentive to direction and learning more about Truth in Love. Sometimes disciples must carry troublesome news but keep it close to their hearts, as Mary and Joseph did upon hearing Simon's words.

Catholic teachers must embrace authority even when respectfully disagreeing, sometimes openly. There are few places like school environments where there is so much vying for attention, status, and acclaim. Gossip is often rife: teacher against teacher; teachers whispering about administration; parents texting about both teachers and administrators (and even Pastors); and students at times displaying disrespect. Teachers truly must cultivate the minds and hearts of Mother Mary and St. Joseph. Moreover, heeding authority is a nonnegotiable. Only rarely is there a need to seek outside counsel regarding a directive counter to the Faith, though that could arise. Even then, how this is accomplished will make the difference between be perceived as prudent vs. rebellious. Regardless, teachers will feel the sword piercing there own hearts as Jesus was betrayed.

- **Pray for strength in all circumstances even when things are going well. The devil ever roams, and he favors Catholic settings to disrupt and foster dissension. So the St. Michael's prayer is a daily suggestion, as well as the Guardian Angel prayer.**

- **Pray for those in authority over you, your colleagues, the families, and your students.**

<u>The Finding of Jesus in the Temple</u>. Seeking sanctity

*Jesus is right at home, and He presents as the Teacher. Even though He may have received instruction, He already possessed the Truth. He is the Master Teacher, yet, he would still obey his earthly mother and father, return home and await the Call.*

Those in the temple—how many become disciples we do not know. Yet, Jesus's first formal lesson must have impressed some. Mary and Joseph also learned another lesson, this time about God the Father. Also, we see that education takes place in many environments and over a lifetime.

Catholic teachers will not be seasoned, master teachers for many years though some may reach the pinnacle sooner based on God-given attributes and personal determination to hone teaching skills.

- **Pray for wisdom, however, more than skills, though the latter can be directed by the Holy Spirit.**
- **Ask for those opportunities to visit the Blessed Sacrament, daily, if possible even for fifteen minutes. Jesus awaits his disciples in the Temple.**

**The Luminous Mysteries**

<u>Baptism of Jesus</u>. Fidelity, Awareness of Concupiscence

*Jesus was baptized, and the worldly scratch their heads even today. Scores of writings have addressed this phenomenon because obviously Jesus did not have sin in Him. He is Original Love, Original Perfection, Original Truth. Yet, as a sign of the Sacramental necessity of Baptism, the remission of Original Sin and any actual sins committed beforehand, God the Father willed that His Son model this act. More essentially, by the Baptism of Jesus, all the waters of all Sacramental Baptisms are sanctified; Jesus is revealed as the Beloved Son of God, and humility and obedience are demonstrated as necessary for sanctity.*

John the Baptist is the disciple that led baptisms, and one can only conclude that his teacher was the Holy Spirit. This bold desert occupier had a unique role in Salvation History from before his conception and birth, and he leapt in the womb when Mary visited his mother. Later, the Church would know of this Sacrament, likely due to witnesses of the Baptism of Jesus. Then, the Holy Spirit continued to move and inspire before The Third Person's grand entrance at Pentecost, just as Jesus was present from all eternity but was not revealed until His birth.

Catholic teachers need to witness to their Baptism daily, along with other Sacraments of Confession, the Eucharist, and Confirmation. If married, adherence to the Magisterium is critical…a non negotiable. However, if, at any time, if a teacher is living in contradiction of the Faith, it would be his or her duty to seek spiritual counsel, inform an administrator, and leave the classroom. This is not rejection or condemnation but awareness that the person's beliefs no longer serve the mission and the treasury of students' souls are at stake.

- **Pray for that necessary self awareness that each of us must possess to capitalize on the graces of Baptism in both person and occasion. A short daily reading from St. Francis de Sales Introduction to a Devout Life and the Imitation of Christ will assist one's conscience in this regard.**
- **If felled by sin, seek reconciliation.**

The Wedding at Cana. Holy Vocation, Wedded to the Church

*This event in the Life of Jesus Christ is so enriched with meaning—truth, goodness, and beauty, that it would take more than a brief excerpt here. However, in this mystery are the key principles of vocation, trust in Jesus, prefigurement of the Church, and anticipation of miraculous grace.*

Mary is again the central disciple who instructs the stewards to do whatever Jesus asks. Even when He seems to "resist" by saying His time has not yet come. Now, Jesus could have well said anything to the stewards, but he performs that initiating miracle in a way that the guests do not tune in to what has happened.

Catholic teachers may well experience miracles in their daily lives but not recognize them as such. So trust and hope are necessary states of soul for the teacher who desires to work in peace, a peace the world cannot bring. They may, at times, be delightfully startled at how well students progress. Mostly, though, the fruits of their work may remain hidden.

- **Pray to expect miracles, big and small.**
- **Read literature on the lives of saints.**
- **Watch beautifully made movies about the wondrous works of God.**
- **Take a nature walk and simply marvel at that which beforehand you may have overlooked.**
- **Most of all, always be conscious that you are a member of—wedded to the Church, the Mystical Body of Christ. The Bridegroom will do anything to keep His Bride spotless but joyful.**

<u>The Establishment of the Kingdom on Earth</u>. Submission, Thy Kingdom Come

*Jesus is King of Heaven and Earth. As Truth and Love, His reign supersedes all worldly rule and rules. His Divine Authority revealed in natural law cannot be supplanted by any human law, especially that which counters or contradicts God. His Will will prevail; His Kingdom will last forever while the earth passes away.*

God is the Master Teacher; He is the Master Historian; He is the Master Governor; He is the Master Scientist; He is the Master Mathematician; He is the Master Economist; He is the Master Musician,

Dramatist, and Artist; He is the Master Author (from which we perceive authority). All Who hear and embed His Truth are His disciples, including educators.

Catholic teachers, daily, have ample opportunities to establish the Kingdom of God in lessons, classroom, and school. Most powerful will be their presence. A sign of the Cross in front of a church; a nod at the name of Jesus Christ, inclusion of His Presence even on the playground. Hundreds of times in a week, the Kingdom will be pervasive in the minds, hearts, and souls of students taught by faithful teachers.

- **Pray for reminders of God's Presence and Power.**
- **Pray the Our Father with special attention to …thy kingdom come, thy will be done on earth as it is in heaven.**
- **Pray to be in the presence of the Court of God throughout the day and for words of wisdom as you teach.**
- **Prayerfully reflect on the day and modify lessons or communications based on those moments to better build the kingdom of God on earth.**

The Transfiguration. Holy Awe Be transformed

*Jesus appeared as dazzling as the sun with Moses and Elijah as Peter, James and John gazed at this spectacular vision. This confirmed the deity of Jesus Christ but also that time is in the present always but there is eternal reunion with those who remain faithful.*

The disciples seem fixed in the temporal world as Peter suggest building booths. Do they still not get that Jesus is not to be a permanent True Man True God Person in the world? His plan will be so much more spectacular and far reaching through space and time. Yet, it was also a revelation that our permanent joy is not to be found or established in this life.

Catholic teachers may be tempted to over-humanize Jesus, the danger being reducing him to our status, rather than elevating us to be more like Him in His truth and love. Of course, Jesus must be approachable by children, many of whom have been traumatized by our secular, even pagan, world. Yet, it requires a careful balance, so that these children also are amazed at Jesus Christ as true God. They must be also aware that their own well being is predicated on their total abandonment and surrender to all His Being in Truth and Love.

- **Pray that you are transformed to a person of Light who loves God with his or her whole heart, soul, and mind, and neighbor as self in a manner that accords God the highest reverence and holy fear.**
- **Seek wisdom in balancing Jesus Christ's dual nature by avoiding autocratic rigidity and inappropriate familiarity. Jesus Christ is most approachable yet also the most awesome Person through which we were created.**

The Eucharist. Thanksgiving, Union with Jesus Christ

*Jesus gave His very self and continues to do so and also present in all the tabernacles of the world. The Holy Sacrifice of the Mass is a masterful reminder and reunion in the Gift of Self of Jesus Crucified, as well. Though ascended into Heaven, Jesus remains with us, through all time and space, a paradox that will not be understood until we meet Him in Person after death.*

The disciples did not see this coming. There is a good chance they did not understand even at the Last Supper. Certainly though when Jesus was with them those forty days, much more was apparent, more than could be written down in all the books of the world from all time.

Catholic teachers are most blessed to have the Master Teacher within them. If fortunate, and may everyone have an opportunity to attend Mass daily. Truly, there is no better way to start the day than with the nourishment of the Eucharist.

- **Pray for the assignment that affords you daily Mass attendance or at least opportunities to visit the Blessed Sacrament and make a Spiritual Communion.**
- **If that is not feasible, still make frequent acts of spiritual Communion, at least before the first bell rings. As is known from the COVID Virus, one never knows how these precious opportunities may be blocked, but no one can keep Jesus Christ from our souls.**

**The Sorrowful Mysteries**

<u>Agony in the Garden</u>. Contrition. Daily Examination of Conscience

*On the Eve of seeming colossal catastrophe, Jesus enters the Garden of Gethsesame and His Agony. He appears intensely prayerful yet serenely resigned. He asks if the Cup can be removed but fully resigns to the will of the Father.*

Disciples, those who would teach, slumbered in uncertainty and anxiety, troubled and confounded by what loomed as imminent defeat. They believed…yet…why? Once again, Peter would miscue with the sword and later deny, his own sense of abandonment succumbing to mortal fear of the world.

Catholic teachers face such moments as human nature seeks the best of both worlds but also the comfortable realm of human respect. Rationalization may supplant Faith-filled reason. Doubts may be soothed by clergy or a superior's soothing reassurances though that nagging voice calls to you to reject human comfort. Yet, like Jesus, teachers must accept the hinged reality of the cup that will not be removed if it is God's will.

- **Pray to accept that there is only the Cross, and, like Jesus, you must proceed to it even though your most trusted friends and family remain in the courts of earthly kings.**

## Chapter Two: Teacher in God's Light

- **Rejoice because the City of God awaits you, and that no one can take ever.**

<u>The Scourging</u>. Purity

*Without a friend in sight, Jesus underwent a scourging intended to strip away all his flesh. He relinquishes His truly human and truly Sacred flesh to the rage of His tormenters in a message of love to all his disciples through the ages to also forgo the flesh.*

Did the disciples wonder from afar why Jesus Christ did not respond with Almighty Power? How could He permit this blasphemous torture, the ultimate insult to the holiest body. May they not have been not only baffled or perplexed but also horrified?

Catholic teachers may be scourged by malicious gossip, lashed by disrespectful colleagues, and gouged by disrespectful or indifferent students. While they model themselves in modesty and self denial, those around them may actually become incensed by what is perceived to be a judgment on them though may will be a troubled conscience sparking the ire.

- **Pray this decade with yourself in mind for humility but determination to persist in the ways of purity of heart, mind, body, and soul—to be stripped of every earthly attachment.**
- **Offer up any torment you receive in return, knowing that it will save souls.**

<u>The Crowning of Thorns</u>. Meekness

*Surrounded by the most ignorant but brutal of men, Jesus Christ, King of Kings, was mocked in the most debasing fashion. It was not just that soldiers maliciously pressed a crown of incredibly sharp and lengthly thorns into his scalp and forehead.*

*They then chanted insults of His majesty also piercing His Heart worse than any injury to his Head.*

At what point did Peter deny Jesus? Were the other disciples trembling in dark crevices of buildings or hidden away in a locked room? Could they simply not bear another moment of excruciating disappointment that the reign of God was not as they envisioned, or were they so depressed at their own helplessness—powerlessness—that they could not even lift heads?

Catholic teachers will likely be rebuffed and suffer the injustice of sneering fools and grave sinners who belittle their professionalism, their authentic Catholicism, and even their ability to educate. Teachers may experience poorer reviews because of strong Faith or see colleagues with weak or contrary faith rise to power with people heaping awards upon them.

- **Pray a Rosary or at least this decade when tempted to even rightful indignation, having before you the wounded Face of Jesus, His precious Blood dripping from His forehead.**
- **See his sorrowful expression in pity more for his tormenters than Himself. Life is truly short, and in blink we will be meeting Jesus face to Face.**
- **Be prepared to show yourself with your own crown of thorns, the golden spikes ascending in homage to the King.**

Carrying the Cross. Perseverance

*Imagine, even as Jesus picked up His Cross, somewhere, someone was "teaching" and considering himself learned and wise, leading his students to the wonders of truth. Yet, here was Truth teaching the Way. How many times, did Jesus speak the words of life, but He had to demonstrate their veracity. Do as I do, not just as I say.*

Sadly, all the disciples except John missed one of the most important lessons the Master Teacher had prepared. Indeed, it was mostly women who would be graced by that Walk: Mother Mary, Veronica, and even the Weeping Women. Simon would be compelled to help carry the Cross, though, and be converted. In turn, they would be among the witnesses to impart that aspect of determination and allegiance to that Way to Life. Without them, would Scripture have been verified as Sacred Historical Text?

Catholic teachers should look to Mother Mary to imitate her persistence to follow Jesus no matter the cost. (Though St. Joseph was not physically present, he, too, will be a model as he traveled sorrowful paths in the earlier years.). Veronica wiped the Face of Jesus, and teachers will wipe faces, too, of tearful students. Yet, they will also weep as the women did for their children (students), at times. They will be burdened with great tasks that splinter their hearts and souls as they may receive only the press of the beam by cruel godless.

- **Pray earnestly when tempted to give up—and there will likely be days when you may leave the classroom almost hoping someone fires you—pray.**
- **It may be the Rosary or Divine Mercy Chaplet. It may only be a whispered "Live, Jesus," as you clutch a Rosary or mounds of paper, but know that Jesus will come to your rescue.**

<u>The Crucifixion</u>. Every Virtue Exemplified in the Cross (St. Thomas Aquinas)

*Jesus Christ was the Master Teacher even from the Cross! Seven words, a universe of lessons for all time, preplanned from all time. Every single one was perfected selflessness with perfect love for others, first of all those who tortured and crucified Him. Yet, at that time, Jesus appeared to die an ignominious but anonymous death. His teaching was presumed to have died with Him.*

John was the only Disciple present, at the foot of the Cross. He would be blessed with a special mission, including the final chapter in public revelation: The Book of Revelation. The other Disciples would come to understand and embrace the Cross. God, in His infinite wisdom will reach His students, the ones who desire knowledge and the Giver of Knowledge.

Catholic teachers may suffer an anonymous death if they have done their duty fully…perhaps even maligned after death. Daily, they will need to forgive, pray up the contrite offenders, turn to their heavenly mother, plead with God not to forsake them, let known your thirst for appreciation but receive in return vinegar, and finally surrender.

- **Pray to persevere to the end and know that in the end, death awaits us all, and for the most part, we are dying to self daily if we are striving to be saints. You have not chosen an easy vocation though it might seem to be a popular position.**
- **On days when you cannot lift your head, turn upward, and ask for His Divine Grace. He will see you through until that last day when you, too, will be called home to an eternal, well deserved rest.**

**The Glorious Mysteries**

<u>The Resurrection</u>. Faith Right Use of Reason Illuminated by Truth

*Jesus rose in the sealed cavern of a tomb, as He desires to rise up within our walled, darkened souls.*

The disciples hid, fearful and perplexed, and after all they had witnessed. They were still overly bound to the world and the limits of their intellect. Yet, while on the one hand we can question the choice of these Apostles, on the other hand, we should be relieved that Jesus entrusts even the least among us to teach the Good News.

Catholic teachers may be torn at times between utter trust and second guessing. They may know the Truth, but those around them cast shadows of doubt and uncertainty. Others may question the sincerity and effectiveness of colleagues' piety and resolve. Peers, families, and students might viciously accuse them of hypocrisy and self righteousness.

- **Pray always for the fullness of Faith and the wisdom to discern between prideful obstinance and courageous conviction; to embrace authentic charity in corporeal and spiritual acts and prudently balance the two work sets of mercy.**
- **Pray for the insights to detect heresy or misappropriation of short sighted empathy at the risk to souls.**
- **Pray to genuinely forgive those who mischaracterize Jesus.**

<u>The Ascension</u>. Hope, Invest in Heaven as Your Retirement Plan

*Jesus took His rightful place at the right hand of God to judge the living and the dead but also to fulfill the promise of the Holy Spirit, the Advocate, the Third Person of the Holy Trinity. If Jesus had remained on Earth, God's plan would be incomplete. By the Holy Spirit, the all powerful, ever present perfect love could be present everywhere until the "end of time."*

The disciples, again, prefer an earthly presence of God, tangible to the senses. Like children who cling to their parents' legs in the misplaced belief that this secures them, Jesus's followers are reluctant to let go of the Master Teacher in the mistaken assumption that He is necessary in Person to support them and right the world. Yet, they miss the bigger picture and the much grander vision.

Catholic teachers may often flounder and desire assurances, affirmation, and someone to assuage their conscience in the dispatch of duties. There will be times when they second guess professionally and catechetically, and superiors may even question a lesson, statement, or interaction. Too, while mission driven, all the natural concerns about job security and continuity of a position will most certainly intersect with their vocation as a teacher. World needs do not evaporate even when they are not priorities.

- **Pray for wise leadership in your superiors and understanding from colleagues, students, and families.**
- **Of course, ask God to bolster and maintain your position though it will not be heaven on Earth.**
- **Even if your course is altered, through non-renewal of a contract, trust that Jesus has something better for you, body and soul.**
- **Although it may go against the grain of teachers, the St. Ignatius prayer to surrender all to God should be regularly offered.**
- **Remember the saints, particularly those who taught, to intercede for you.**
- **Pray for and trust that God will deeply reward you if you remain faithful and strive for sainthood, as He truly does offer the most perfect retirement plan for all eternity.**

<u>The Descent of the Holy Spirit</u>. Zeal, Receptivity to Wisdom

*The Holy Spirit came like tongues of fire and rested on the multitudes. In a flash, God suspended the language barrier and opened Truth to natives and foreigners alike.*

The Disciples must have literally breathed a sigh of relief, once again astonished but most likely confirmed in Faith and Hope. This would not be the last act of revelation for them, and, in particular, privately, too. Moreover, Holy Scripture evidences a sanctifying boldness in their work thereafter, as their steps are more assured and in the right path. Of course, there would be disputes that arose, differences of outlook, but at each juncture, the Holy Spirit was invoked, and matters resolved. The students were becoming for adept teachers and, in turn, instructing future generations of educators.

Catholic teachers will experience the wonders of the Master Teacher, despite the world, the devil, and personal faults and temptations. That is not to say that they will never experience uncertainty, confusion, self-recrimination, or regret. Yet, God will never abandon any sincere, faithful Catholic teacher, and the Holy Spirit will comfort them even in your darkest times. There may even be some humor thrown in. Teachers should look for that and laugh!

- **Pray to the Holy Spirit daily…Come Holy Spirit, fill the hearts of your faithful and kindle in them the fire of thy love. Send forth thy Spirit and they shall be created. And you will renew the face of the Earth.**
- **And, there are several other wonderful petitions for your repertoire.**

<u>The Assumption</u>. Peaceful Death. Die to Self

*By Faith, we believe that our Mother Mary was assumed into Heaven, body and soul. Yet, it is perfectly acceptable and through ethereal Reason that the Ark of the Covenant would be brought to the glory of God unblemished, unmarred, incorruptible.*

The Disciple John was closest to Mary, and we do not know for certain where the other Apostles were at the time of Mary's Assumption. Still, there has been not any contradiction among the followers then and through the Church including the early Fathers of this supernatural transition, and generations beyond, to today.

Catholic teachers will likely experience illnesses and death among colleagues, students, and families, including both natural causes and tragically, violent means. As this is written, COVID 19 rages across the world and has significantly interrupted education. Never before has so much been placed on teachers. It truly requires a dying to self.

- **Pray for the fortitude and perseverance to educate as many children in all these trying circumstances.**
- **Daily, call on Mother Mary, who is herself a teacher, remembering that the latter part of the Hail Mary was tagged during the Plague, the Black Death.**
- **Invoke the teacher Saints in heaven and the teacher souls in Purgatory to assist you.**
- **St. Joseph, patron of peaceful death, and so also resignation to the reality of death, is ever ready to bring your pleas to His foster son Jesus.**

Coronation of Mary as Queen of Heaven and Earth. Priests, Pro-life. Be protectors of Truth and Life

*There is no public revelation but centuries of evidence, along with reason illuminated by Faith that leads to veracity of this Mystery.*

The early disciples took Mary as their mother which was and is still needed to this day. However, generations afterwards, in the discipleship of Pope Pius XI, there was the proclamation of the last Sunday in the liturgical year being in honor of Christ the King. Jesus Christ is King. Ergo, His mother is the Queen Mother. Her maternal authority is vested by God himself, and she is also, therefore, over our works, including teaching.

Catholic teachers have direct access to that heavenly Court which also includes God's chosen, including the twelve Apostles (excepting Judas Iscariot, of course.). Now, they may feel like the court jester, at times, but as faithful Catholic teachers, they have a unique standing. They should use this access and use it often, without hesitation. They may not receive the expected answer or anticipated direction, but in trust, they will be led.

## Chapter Two: Teacher in God's Light

- Pray often, and have a daily regimen in the morning, during the day, and in the evening.
- A daily Rosary, Divine Mercy Chaplet, and Mass attendance if at all possible, are highly recommended. These are the passwords into the Court.
- Yet, on most difficult days or in case of illness, even short repetitive prayers calling on Mary to intercede with her Son, Jesus Christ for grace will be answered to your optimum benefit.

# Chapter Three

## EMBEDDING CATHOLICISM IN ALL SUBJECTS

*Fullness of Truth in the Fullness of Education*

*The Catholic school student noted in a thank you card her appreciation for having had religion included in a social studies course. Submitted by Puzzled Teacher (2018)*

### <u>The Authentic Seamless Garment: Knowledge with a Capital "K" vs. Lower Case "k"</u>

Absent God, history, government, civics, economy, geography, art, music, and even our concept of community are subject to temporal, worldly transmission of ideas, often corruptly. Moreover, while numerous "secular" books can be useful and objective, and some Catholic/Christian texts and resources contain error or mislead, it is ill advised to depend solely on secularly written and published texts in language arts (literature and written expression), history, civics, economics, science, math, art, and arguably physical education. There are so many examples, but the one that follows is startling in what it tells about human pride.

Absent Christianity, astonishingly time is envisioned only through the prism of human concepts. Today, we see the bewildering acceptance of BCE (Before Common Era) and CE (Common Era) smoothly replacing the longtime BC (Before Christ) and AD (Anno Domini—in the year of the Lord)—in texts used in Christian schools including Catholic ones. Bewildering because what does "common" era mean? Common to whom? One can understand that this separation of time was due to the birth of Jesus Christ, but not everyone is Christian. What one cannot fathom is how altering the truth of this division helps everyone. Reportedly, Abraham Lincoln once asked a crowd: How many legs does a dog have if the tail is called a leg. They answered: five. He responded,: No, it is still four. Just because you call something another thing does not make it so.

It does not require belief in the Presence of God to denote that this is how we have perceived time, at least in the Western world. At the very least, texts and sources should acknowledge the origin and how this arose. According to several sites, Common Era actually refers to the fact that the Gregorian calendar is the "common" reference, and the use of this term, Common Era, may date back hundreds of years. Obviously, though unless specifically referenced most would consider that BCE and CE are the non Christian (and in some cases, anti Christian) a maneuver to eclipse Jesus Christ. Still, it matters not. Time was split by The Incarnation. End of argument.

Another creeping disaster that started with rebranding the study of history, geography, economics, civics, law, philosophy, government, and (ironically) religion: Social Studies. Although the term was reportedly evident in the 60s (though similarly titled works and courses preceded that dateline by a century), those strands were reexamined and redeveloped again under this umbrella in the early 90s. Consider that over a generation has passed whereby students in most public school settings have not a clue about what was touted as the objective of this shift: *to tilt the study of history under the umbrella of worldly endeavors and objectives.* The sad result is a false impression of potentiality in the way of "progressiveness" and civic incompetence. As history fell to the subjective interpretation of social engineers; economics shifted to collectivism; civics is now hinged to Critical Race Theory; philosophy has transformed into odioumosophy (hatred of wisdom); government is propagandized as best driven by the enlightened elites; and religion is viewed through the prism of anti-Christianity. Even the more theoretically objective fields like math and science have fallen prey to racist propaganda and retooling to suit at best, an agnostic society, and at worst, an atheistic one. Oh, and 2+2=4 may be…the solution given by a white supremist long ago.

Most alarming is that the science white lab coat is replacing the clergy's white collar as a sign of authority and truth, and how much

## Chapter Three: Embedding Catholicism in All Subjects

dangerous thinking is espoused and defended through science that actually disguises ideology. Worse, criticism is unquestionably censored with branding of misinformation. The majority of tyrannical acts in recent years has been by the "expertise" of researchers and those who have sacrificed individual integrity for the assurance of acceptability. COVID 19 was only the latest example, but climate change scientists have been elevating themselves for decades. Then, there are the "health care" workers who advance many insidious theories about gender and sexuality in the name of personal well being. (See Researching for Reliability and "Degenerate Moderns."). By the way, the foregoing is not to initiate a debate about any aspect of the Pandemic but to illustrate the extent of worldly influences in the most fundamentally private and individual areas of our lives, including freedom to pursue the good, true, and beautiful.

Not that much of this is "new," especially in recent centuries, but the devil never rests.

That it has returned in use is a red flag for the diminishment of Truth in general education, however. In the 21st Century the "resurrection" of these reference points—BCE and CE— are not likely about clarity or even empathy for the nonChristian. Consider that it was Jesus Christ, true God and true man—the Incarnation— Who "split" time, thusly and to conceal that in contemporary studies is again to nullify or at least greatly diminish the significance of the Word Incarnate entering human history.

Overall, language and what is chosen for inclusion or exclusion in studies — or outright rejected— often conjures the spirit of the Antichrist.

In German, at least decades ago, the article in front of words denoted a feminine (die), masculine (der) , or neuter effect (das). How that is perceived today is not the scope of this work, but the fact that this language goes beyond "the" is somewhat fascinating whether anyone agrees with the concept or how nouns are currently labeled in German. It reveals an important characteristic of what it means to be German and how they communicate. If there is a movement to utilize only "das," the rich heritage of Germany will suffer. All humanity suffers—shudders actually—at what may be next.

Yet, the ultimate test of a solid, well rounded Catholic education is a teacher's firm conviction that he or she is educating persons to become eventual citizens in the City of God after growing to the fullness of their vocation and faith in hope and by charity in the city of man.

## <u>*Intentional Cross Curriculum with Faith (By Subject)*</u>

### History

Back to the case of BC and AD, particularly in Catholic schools, teachers need to embrace that denotation as Truth. To ignore, deny, and submit to the secular manipulation of time is a travesty. Of course, teachers must acknowledge that BCE and CE are now commonly used in any reference to history and time. However, they can impress that ignoring the real roots of this divide is anti-Christian, actually anti-God. Having that discussion, teachers might be surprised that students can accept the shift with the caveat that they know it does not change the actuality of Jesus Christ in human history. One student smartly responded in a class about this that he would think of CE as Christ Era. Good play!

If that was the end all in history texts, and in other subject areas, perhaps this section would be unnecessary. It is not, and the secularism—at times paganistic, agnostic, or atheistic—touts the temporal world, leaders, and ideas, often critical, albeit subtly, of Judeo-Christian history and beliefs. The word "secularism" is everywhere, but it is no longer the definitive word for "separation of church and state," in the vain attempt to accommodate all Christians and recognize non Christian students, but a cover for the spirit of antiChristianity. Now, no one needs to look for the boogey man under every bed and in every closet, but special antenna will be critical as it is nearly impossible not to encounter materials that are not tainted in some way. At times, this is habitual and generational without malice; at other times, it is intentional manipulation and indoctrination. Moreover, one cannot say that it is simply writers and publishers seeking balance because there is too often the acceptance of the worst about Christianity and softly embracing *anything* else.

How can a Catholic teacher accomplish the infusion of Catholicism across subject areas? **There are separate sections in this primer for history and government,** as those are crucial, and within those sections, **the infusion of Faith is detailed**. Yet, other areas require evaluative skills with knowledge of the Faith. Here are some suggestions and rejoice! See the Appendix for the "smart and inspired" responses and avenues of instruction to navigate around the lies:

**Language Arts (generally covers reading, grammar, and written expression, but should include logic, classical literature, and rhetoric)**

Language Arts instruction leads into myriad minefields, and it has the potential of outright abuse of developing student minds. What do children read, when, and how? How is nonfiction selected, what subjects, and most importantly in ways presented by teachers? Grammar may seem like a safe area, but resources can contain what may be referred to as background propagandist messaging. In learning to develop writing skills, beyond the approaches and mechanics, what topics are chosen and for which age group. Is objective research explicitly taught? If debates are included, is care taken to ensure there is no *debating* abortion and other resolved issues by the Church? In other words, there can be no "pro" position for abortion, so it should not be a debate topic. (A debate about how best to serve a woman in a crisis pregnancy would be acceptable for a mature group.) However, breaking this down:

**Literature**—what do children read? The maxim "Always better to be safe than sorry" should apply. Once certain material is imprinted on a child's brain, there is no washing it away. *Readers should stop here, and spend at least thirty seconds rereading this and pondering its implication.* Teachers cannot rescind what has been impressed. This is why pornography is so insidious. The brain will retain! Now, it is impossible not to have some matter cross that boundary as we live in a pluralistic world, and even homeschooled children will be exposed to stories and play acting that might counter their Christian upbringing or be questionably interpreted. So, another maxim should be "Forewarned is forearmed." Teachers should know what is out there and plan to address it calmly but truthfully should the questions arise.

For a universal example: Harry Potter. This popular fictional series has generated more controversy than almost any other work in memory. The polar responses include the admonishment to never let your children read these novels or watch the movies. On the other side, including clergy and some Catholic resources, this is being overblown, and the series can be accepted with Catholic explanations and addressing where the author deviates from truth.

Here is the dilemma for teachers, especially in a classroom of two or more dozen students. Students will bring the books from home for free reading despite administrative or teacher discouragement. One could fairly argue that explicitly and publicly arguing this might lead to inappropriate inquisitiveness and aggravate the situation. Parents may assert their parental authority, ironically, or chime in that at least their children are reading, and that so thrills them. Of course, finicky eaters might eat junk food all day long, too, but that analogy will be likely dismissed as condescending and arouse resentment. So, what to do? Hopefully, the school will have a policy that clearly states standards of how books and other reading or viewing material are selected for the classroom, along with strong recommendations for at home reading. Moreover, of course, the parent is the primary authority, but that does not mean they may override or alter the authority of an entire school or even classroom. If strong disagreement arises, the parent has the right to withdraw their children without "faculty lounge chatter" but with prayers for every success in the future.

### Chapter Three: Embedding Catholicism in All Subjects 107

Homeschool teachers, or in a pod or hybrid setting, already have a philosophy about acceptable fiction reading material. New publications can be discussed as needed, but classics are likely the prominent choices, anyway. Of course, what to read is also contingent on individual children, their abilities, temperaments, and personalities taken into account.

Prayerfully, a school or district has a recommended book list that emphasizes the classics and warns about some questionable options. Do not depend on this, though. Within the public domain, incredibly the most egregious reading is being actually promoted by whole school boards. (Loudon County, Virginia) and not just opposed to dissenting parents but unleashing federal investigations against them!

Cana Academy recommends: Classic Books List, The Educational Plan of St. Jerome Academy; 1,000 Great Books List (1000goodbooks.com. CatholicSchoolPlaybook also boosted a K-8th book list in a recent article: "The 27 Books Every Child Should Read from Kindergarten to Eighth Grade." Also, there are many more such pieces erupting on the Internet daily!

Others within the Catholic school system include: The National Catholic Education Association has recommendations although there are a few questionable ones. The Dominican Sisters of St. Rosa Lima (2014) published a terrific list, according to grade level, and their preface provides wonderful criteria for other selections. Michael O'Brien published *A Landscape with Dragons" The Battle for Your Child's Mind* some years ago, and he, too, provides guidance and suggestions. Another recent release, touted by Michael O'Brien is Cheri Blomquist's *Before Austen Comes Aesop: The Children's Great Books and How to Experience Them*. Search and teachers will discover. There is a plethora of sites and faithful Catholic experts. Educators may share these with colleagues and parents, too.

With respect to public book reviewer sites, teachers explore carefully, as many sound "good" like Goodreads, but may or may not be reliable. Certainly teachers should reference these but with the reservation that reviews and reviewers must be scrutinized. Though many are well intended and highly educated, they lack discretion. A few are truly in a dark place. Once a Catholic educator responded to a person recommending a Neil Gaiman book, anticipating at least an acknowledgment of disturbing (auto) biographical facts about Gaiman the commentator may not have known. Instead of showing appreciation, the person scorched the Catholic educator and basically told that person to mind (his/her) own business. Speaking of comments, the comment sections often reveal more about the books than the actual site hosts.

However, most teachers may well enter a school with the year's curriculum already established. If this is a Catholic school, there will likely be some choices but new books are being written every day. The classroom may even have a library, and teachers may note some books that cause some wincing. Again, educators cannot change everything, but they must think proactively and focus on what is "good, true, and beautiful." That should be the standard at all times, in choices and how to teach the stories or novels. (Astonishingly, as this section was drafted, news was that even some of Dr. Suess's books were being yanked from shelves.) Another note of caution, as schools host book fairs. Teachers have no control over these hosts, but they can certainly express opinion. There are Christian based book vendors. Fortunately, even some more "open-minded" Catholic administrators are shying away from Scholastic, for one.

Finally, after collaborating with administration and trusted peers, teachers need those parent and student discussions to enable them to select wholesome but engaging reading. Parents are the primary educators, though, and teachers may be in some uncomfortable spots at times. Nonetheless, educators should be confident in the reality that a school has many students with varying backgrounds and home situations, and classroom novel study must recognize those differences and potentially negative outcomes from a popular novel that could do harm *even to one child*. What parents allow in their own home, particularly if they are having those necessary conversations with their children is their responsibility and for which they accept accountability. Teachers

Chapter Three: Embedding Catholicism in All Subjects        109

cannot put out all the fires, and should not try. Keeping one's own "fire" lit for active, engaging reading uplifts all.

**Nonfiction** (allegedly based on fact)—presents unique challenges. For one thing, most define "nonfiction" as true or factual. Saying so does not make it so. (A dog has only four legs.) For example, some years ago, a language arts text included examples of opinion and fact pieces about a controversial topic. The irony? The so-called factual article on student cell phone accessibility read more like an opinion piece supporting students having a cell phone in class, and the "opine" letter to the editor, that opposed this notion, included cited research. Fortunately, following explicit instruction of opinion vs. fact, students were able to make the distinction. Appropriately guiding students to "study" a situation is most often rewarding and hones their skills to detect misinformation or "position pushing" in presentations. (See Researching for Reliability)

In one 1990s current events class, students were taught how to read for bias in news reporting, contrasting two major urban papers with opposite political affiliation. By the end of the year, seventh grade students could often identify either newspaper fairly often by the headline, topic, and led. The slanting was often evident in the opening and reporters' choice of language.

In another middle school course, students read a legislative bill that aroused much interest as it pertained to the issue of equality. Among other factors taught was that one word could change the interpretation of a law, that just because something was proposed in legislation did not make it morally acceptable, and politics drives many of these laws. (NOTE: In 2023, this format of reading and interpretation will require prudence in selection, as proposed legislation has become increasingly anti natural law.)

This only proves that teachers should not fear "content"—to a certain extent— but teach students ways to examine and evaluate text, especially in the light of the Catholic Faith. It will be part of their job to know what students are being exposed to and by whom. Unfortunately, though, it is only getting worse with so much changing within 24-hours. Witness the Merriam-Webster sudden inclusion of the offensive "sexual preference" based on a single Senate hearing. Even a dictionary can be used for establishing questionable facts. As an aside, teachers would be best to instruct word meaning *within etymology* whenever possible but underscore our rapidly changing world and the myriad opportunities to skew information. Wikipedia is another example. One noted reference is a *First Things* article by by Carl Trueman: "Clinging to God and Grammar" (September 23, 2021)

Also, teachers should be certain to assess any source—or insist students do so—by identifying its publication date, publisher, and author. This will help them always to place a source in context. Teachers should impress upon them that credentials may or may not support the author's position. Having Ph.D behind a name does not ensure objectivity, let alone adherence to Truth, as Catholics know it to be and as revealed by Divine Authority.

Then, primary sources should be included but with appropriate caveats. Just because something is "old" or was published in a particular era does not mean it is comprehensive or reliable. The devil has been around throughout history. Still, some of what was written in the past supports the stability and reliability of Magisterial teaching . Tan Publishers will offer Catholic writing of "yesteryear" that demonstrates that truth does not change, only people expressing truth can skew it. Conversely, "new" is not bad, as there are some marvelous endeavors to update those history studies, as well as ensure integrity in other fields of study. These are in the appendix, but be on the lookout for others, as the Holy Spirit seems to be on the move these days!

*Grammar*

Now one would think that a grammar book would be just that, but not always. Decades ago, one English text publisher included the typical student activities for various components of grammar. In this case,

Chapter Three: Embedding Catholicism in All Subjects       111

it was an exercise whereby students needed to determine the correct subject-verb agreement. In isolation, the individual sentences were rather benign and about King Henry VIII. Collectively, they portrayed him in a positive light. Now, it was not an end-of-the-world exercise, and the compilers likely thought there was no harm in it. Yet, that is not the point. Well-intended persons can still lean towards material that is at best, not helpful, and at worst, ingraining attitudes.

Speaking of grammar, it is essential that Catholics learn the skills of language, In recent decades there has been criticism of "dumbing down" students whereby the tools of communication including the mechanics such as spelling have been minimized. In one after school program, populated primarily by at-risk students, one particularly bright first grader submitted his sentences to the tutor for review. When the tutor insisted he correct misspellings, he tartly replied—in so many words— that correct spelling was unnecessary according to his teacher. And that was thirty years ago.

Now, one should not conclude that this is deliberate or malicious, at least not on the part of any individual teacher, but there is a tragic decline in expectation and what society should hope is a well educated populous. It also enables mental sloth, as students lazily speak poorly or use language inappropriately. Obviously, it spills into written expression if that is required to any sufficient degree!

*Writing*

Aside from the concerns about the basics, teaching writing may seem otherwise like an area in which teachers have total control on topics and research. Not so, not even in Catholic environments. Also, at times the Archdiocese or various organizations may provide an essay contest with problematic themes. One can imagine that this will intensify in the George Floyd era and Critical Race Theory. Yet, the biases were and are already present in public school, and in reading and short answer portions of standardized tests. Even the Catholic Academic Decathlon (California) competition raised eyebrows when it included leading, politically charged questions several years ago. Here, too, parents or other family members may coax research and writing in a direction that demonstrates the family attitude on a subject more than the student's. However, students often mirror their parent's opinions. Teachers should use care in what is assigned and be clear on acceptable and varied resources. This cannot be it too open-ended or narrow and should be reviewed early in the research. This is where topic is critical, and here are a couple of dos and don'ts (the second person voice is intentional:

Teachers:

- Do share appropriate examples and trace "arguments."
- Do make certain the subject is developmentally appropriate.
- Do clarify the topic, but here for older students. Make certain it is not a topic open to "argument" for or against, unless it is opinion based, but that requires extra care, so that students are compelled to be thorough in their research. Teachers who overgeneralize topics, like "climate change," should be prepared for some political speechwriting. Better might be: "Climate change—real or not?" Or "How Can One Person Make a Difference? A provable case."
- Do prepare how the student should compose the essay with a thesis. Show examples that demonstrate students understand a thesis, and that it contains an assertion and possible opposition to a claim.
- Do provide strategies for support of a thesis: examples, elaboration, explanation, expertise, experience.
- Do have a discussion (or cross curriculum with a math teacher) on the use of statistics.
- Do provide a list of balanced resources for students to investigate. Avoid the Internet and social media. Students should submit their references early, preferably with parental oversight. Do not rely on library personnel filtering.

Chapter Three: Embedding Catholicism in All Subjects 113

- Do introduce critical analysis of source material.
- Do have students prepare their essay in stages knowing the thesis statement sets the course for their work.
- Do not generalize or leave too much to student options, as they lack the knowledge to discern questionable sources.
- Do not intentionally limit resources though a class on how to determine reliable resources is certainly helpful. However, steer them in the direction of reliable Catholic books, magazines, and printed, audio, or video materials. The Catholic Church has boasted some of the greatest philosophers, historians, scientists, mathematicians, and artists.
- Do not tell the students which position is "acceptable" by tone or direct teacher opinion, no matter how knowledgeable you may be on the subject. Remember this is about teaching skills not indoctrinating. ***Magisterial teaching is the exception. Then, intervention may be necessary.***
- Do not express disappointment in student work only because it counters personal knowledge or experience. Again, topic choice is critical, and do confer with other teachers or administration of your ideas. Chances are, too, that certain types of writing will be explored throughout a year: narrative, (auto) biographical, fact-based, opinion.

Finally, written expression is just that. Teachers should take care that technology often captures this writing…forever…unlike the olden days when fountain pen to composition paper most likely landed in the garbage can by year's end. Instill in students the need for prudence, fortitude, temperance, and justice in all of their studies and expression.

This is especially true for expression in social media, a particular topic to address, explore, and direct, as it will likely be the most frequently used medium. In this vein, teachers should be developmentally preparing students for a lifetime of future communication not yet envisioned. However, when they are taught the basics, including forethought, planning and organization, students will be more specific, objective, and effective.

**Math**

*Mathematics is the language in which God wrote the universe. Galileo*

The world is replete with the wonders of nature in number and shape; phenomenon like Pi and the imaginary zillions of points. In geometry, the sacred is evident from cell to galaxy. Teaching a hexagon? Show the bumble bee's honeycomb. Others found in nature include pentagons, spirals, waves, and, of course, lines. Architecture also reflects nature in myriad ways. Measurement and weights: Explore the Bible. Teachers will compare contemporary manmade tools today with the natural physical reference points like fingers, hands, and arms thousands of years ago. Unites of comparable measurement include bath—six gallons; cubit—length from elbow to hand (about 18 inches)fathom - six feet; finger span (digit) 3/4 inch; mite—1/8th cent. Teachers should have fun converting Biblical measurements, 38 verses by one source. The ark appears then to be 540 feet long, 37.5 feet high and 75 feet wide

They should reference history for the Greek, Phoenicians, and others' contributions. Saints related to mathematics include: Archbishop Thomas Bradwardine (1290-1349) whose studies were a precursor to the Theory of Gravity; Bishop Johannes Muller von Konigsberg (1436-1476) known as the Father of Modern Astronomy and among the first to use symbolic algebra; Roger Bacon (1214-1294, Father of the Scientific Method; Francois d'Aguilon (1546-1619)and J, laid the foundation for projective geometry; and Johannes Widmann (1460—1498) who created the plus and negative sign, just to name a handful.

*The Magnificat*, as previously stated, is a marvelous publication that surprises readers in many different areas including the sciences and

Chapter Three: Embedding Catholicism in All Subjects                                115

math. If possible, explore past publications online. For just one example in July 2021 edition are the saints who were known for their love of nature.

However, in math, chances are that secular texts will be used, often splashed with "Common Core" for their wider audiences, as Catholic administrators also seek to stay current. However, these math books may include pictures, illustrations, and word problem scenarios that pose problematic social and political scenarios. Increasingly, acceptance of same sex "couples," obviously conflicted youth about their gender, and other abnormal presentations of personal identity is exponentially exploding across many visually impactful environments, and schools are included—one may even say specifically selected—for that "push."

It can be expected that they will integrate those cultural values (or deviation) in many ways. One is by posing word problems that also incorporate contemporary norms in relationships and political correctness. Included as examples may be studies and various graph types that favor certain popular opinions about race, sexuality, and politics. This could be accomplished overtly or subtly. Workbook and activities may also pose challenges.

Even twenty years, ago this would have received "hoots" if not "boos" from the majority, even those more liberal.

Educators must realize that textbook publishers are not necessarily the noble professionals they present themselves to be. They seek profits, and they will cater to the audience. Common Core may seem benign compared to accommodating the current (cancel) culture. Educators should conscientiously look for some extremism as various entities vie for the attention and dollars of thousands of schools across the country. Moreover, with newer versions of societal extremism, school systems will purchase more frequently. What is a few billions with the multi-trillion dollar legislative packages coming from Washington D.C.?

How might a Catholic math teacher do likewise but with faith related truths or cross curriculum exercises? Administrators and teachers need to seek those experts who report truth. Catholic Vote offers surveys that could be analyzed, critiqued and compared to similar polls from other sites. *JusttheFacts* provides ample content for all types of scenarios involving mathematical skills, as they, too, report numbers. (*JusttheFacts* is a generally reliable source for civics and government.)

Yet, even with caution and absent obvious indoctrination, teachers are at risk for cleverly designed sample polls or graphs. The teacher may or may not be aware of these practices, including skewing. One popular approach is to present a scenario such as ninety percent of all students surveyed said they prefer pizza to other food. Then it must be revealed that only ten students were surveyed; they were all at the same pizza restaurant; and the question was: Tonight, which food do you prefer to all others?

Bar graphs may show the "tip" of results that tend to exaggerate or minimize one response area. In other words, depiction of the spread of percentages or numbers may be skewed pictorially.

So, teachers should not hesitate to "go back in time." Sounds retro, but at least it is not spiritually regressive, and there are many splendid teaching books of a hundred years ago. Math books, like Ray's Arithmetic and others, demonstrate proven principles in teaching but were inexplicably tossed for the "new and improved" approaches. In one section, of a Ray's book, students are shown how to use prime factorization to determine both greatest common factor and least common multiple. Once mastered, the technique is quick and reliable; enhances number sense; and imprints prime factorization for other computations like division.

Teachers may even assign family games as homework! Monopoly is a fun way for students to practice math skills as a banker. Even young children may employ skills such as counting as they move around the board. Dominos require adding; Pictionary increases art skills and humor; Yahtzee provides practice with counting, patterns, and sorting. The list goes on, and the added benefit is fostering family time together.

In all cases, teachers should avoid the calculator except for higher levels of math and only after students have mastered counting and multiplication tables; understand operations and concepts like variables. Nothing is sadder than seeing a high school student in an evening program struggling to determine 6x7 using a calculator except for her response that a teacher told her to use a calculator for such work.

Math will be significantly related to economics and science, too, so teachers can and should incorporate these disciplines as illustrative and appropriate. The more natural contexts are the best by which to practice and appreciate mastery of math.

Again, the goal of Catholic (any really) teacher is to gather the best in a myriad of sources over time and develop thinking students, not just passive audiences that may incorporate faulty reasoning instead of problem solving.

**Technology**

In A Public Discourse article, *Technology and the Soul: The Spiritual Lessons of Digital Distraction*, (3/18/2022), Joshua Hochschild asserts upfront, in reference to social media, "the age of digital media has unleashed a profoundly threatening human experiment." And that such media "seduces us to waste our souls." Yet, more insightfully, Hochschild both extols and critiques broader technology as helpful to our human achievements but impactful on patterns of behavior, relationships, family dynamics, child development, political authority and even sense of self.

So, this elective practically demanded in Catholic schools, is fraught with possible abuse and requires its own purposeful, explicit unit on using technology for the good of another and the common good. Depending on the student's age, issues ranging from privacy to warnings about particular sites; the deception of the ill intended; and legal concerns should be included in any course.

However, technology has also been used wisely and for the advancement of the good, true, and beautiful. St. Pope John Paul II extorted the use of technology in good ways to be used to benefit people and spread the Faith ( cite source). Today, many videos and websites tout all that is the best in the Church and help evangelize and convert thousands, if not millions. Intriguing is that Blessed Ramon Llull (1232-1315) is known as the "Father of Computer Science" having invented the first analog computer. (National Catholic Register)

Starting with the earliest inventors, the subject of technology can be fascinating and inspiring. Strictly speaking, technology is the human development of *any* tool used by people, and even those in prehistoric times demonstrated keen insights into the use of materials in nature, coupled with understanding of certain patterns, and, of course, observing nature. Making fires was among the first advances, likely following the effects of lightning and regular forest fires. One archeological source in Boston University claims to have found evidence in South Africa of a man made fire dating back 1.2 million years. Likely, at first, once assured that they could tame fire and capture it, early man kept a fire going somehow. Later, people learned that friction between certain objects could make sparks and fire, and that critical technology advanced further, enabled migration and changed the course of how people lived.

It was the ability to create fire that helped people stay in one location during colder weather and initiated settlement: towns, cities, and then whole civilizations.

Myriad other discoveries and developments built upon each other to provide food, clothing and shelter. In the study of history, students will appreciate the early Sumerians, Egyptians, and, of course, Greeks and Romans. Other cultures, including the Incas and Indus inhabitants, Chinese and Japanese, add dimension to their understanding, grasp, and utilization of technology in all its simplicity and complexity.

A look at how the simple machines, like the invention of the wheel, led to more complex machinery fosters appreciation for early observation of nature. Watching animals, including insects, provided early man with ample clues and examples of what and how they could build.

Always though, there is a First Cause that students must recognize and acknowledge. All our inventions and development are possible only by God's Will and in His time and space. As with any gift, technology, as it is understood in the 21st century requires prudent and judicial use in moderation. It must be judged by its intended purpose for good or the absence of good—evil. Also, like literature, what parents permit at home is out of any teacher's knowledge and permission. However, most Catholic schools have written policies and expectations in student handbooks, and a technology teacher should have an approved classroom policy.

## Science

From a recent *Catholic Thing article, "The physicist believes in miracles."*

One example is *"The Science of Eucharistic Miracles"* (Catholic 365). Miracles encompass both the natural and supernatural worlds, but the "miracle" is so because there is only a supernatural explanation for a particular natural phenomenon. It is literally the Divine Hand moving something in the natural world. The only surprise is that we should be surprised. Sadly, the world, especially the "secular" world dismisses miracles and worse, advances abominable concepts.

Science is becoming increasingly fascinating and problematic for unsuspecting students. Even Catholic students can be mired in conflicting messages about basics like sex, climate change, the universe, health and medicine, and scores of other topics. Dissecting worms once made students squirm, but now, the secular world is more focused on "dissecting" personal identity. The old times when the greatest controversy was evolution has given way to revolutionary perceptions of the human being, and it is often a step or more below the animal and plant kingdom. There was a recent legislative proposal in a Western state to grant vegetation a bill of rights, akin to the one for people in the Bill of Rights, at least to the extent of their "right to life." How ironic is that?

Still if teachers will focus on the grand beauty of creation and how it reflects and reveals truth and goodness, some of this other "noise" need not enter the classroom. As mentioned above, nature is abundantly revealing about God, the Creator, and Catholics have always appreciated the truths in science despite some ugly rumors to the contrary. Teachers can always integrate the faith in some way, however. It is mandatory to know the magisterial teaching.

Biology in collaboration with the Theology of the Body; earth science related to dominion and stewardship; physics as once thought the power of the gods; chemistry as the wonder of atoms, molecules, and matter.

Father Gaglia wrote about the Periodic Table in relationship to virtues. As a priest and a biologist, Fr. Fred Gaglia found the periodic chart of elements a wonderful expression of the order and adaptability of nature at the chemical level. After many years of teaching the beauty and order of God's creation, he began to see a relationship between the periodic table-this order of the elements into groups and functions-and the order and functions of humans for their spiritual growth. He took the symbols of the elements of nature and applied them to another pattern of order, in our lives as children of God. These can be used, by metaphor or analogy, as symbols of the way we can live ordered, virtuous lives. Fr. Gaglia shares his message eloquently, bringing the beauty of science and spirit into one enlightening book. **"Periodic Chart of Virtuous Living for Teens - One Element at a Time,** by Fr. Fred Gaglia has provided a way for young people to have a spiritual and moral parallel to their study of science and technology. It is a way to enkindle and motivate their search for the virtuous life, by relating concepts of the periodic chart with their growth in the spiritual life." - Bishop James D. Conley. The subject of light alone, in reference to the rainbow, is worth emphasizing.

Students should also learn about the Catholic or Christian scientists (not to be confused with the sect Christian Science), most of whom disavowed atheism based on discovery; the saints who studied science, and Popes who wrote encyclicals about God's creation. (See Section on Wisdom through Church History) Teachers should also not neglect the Jewish or other non-christian scientists, like Einstein, who concluded there had to be a God. However, the Catholic Church got a bad rap for being anti-science, and that branding still rattles the flasks in school labs. However, saints like Gregor Mendel, founder of modern science of genetics, another famous Catholics should be prominently featured in the classroom. Mendel is ideal for a science class on genetic traits, especially given the DNA bending social engineers who demand science can be altered by surgery and chemicals. *Epic Pew* cites some top notch Catholic scientists, including Copernicus (1473-1543) most known for his knowledge of astronomy; Albertus Magnus, O.P. (1200-1280, patron saint of natural science who was also superlative in physics, logic, and biology; Nicholas Steno (1638-1686) who excelled in anatomy and geology, and has body parts named after him (Stensen). Father Stanley Jaki (1924-2009), a Hungarian Benedictine priest was known for his expertise in physics, but also for bridging Catholicism and science, teaching that science developed out of Christianity.

Nor should teachers avoid controversy, though, so students are prepared to defend the Faith and truth despite the falsehoods of the Church regarding science. Being developmental about the matter and always including administration and parents when in doubt is "an ounce of prevention." Also, note that Catholicism does not shield a scientist from making errors. That is to be expected and teachers need to discuss some of that in history. (Book on myths written by a secular professor.)

**Geography**

Geography can be as flat as the two-dimensional plats depicting different land forms, or it can be exciting, interwoven into the tapestry of history and that includes Sacred History in Scripture. God, the Creator magnificently embellished our fallen world with all types of shapes and materials; water bodies vary but each has a particular role to play in world history, seen and unseen. After all, the first four civilizations prospered by major rivers. However, none of these pagan features were enabled in the life of Jesus Christ. The Scriptural land forms (literal and figurative) are plentiful though.

The Bible offers dozens of potential lessons about geography in the story of God and mankind. The symbolism, alone, associated with Scripture, is worth the journey: mountains, rivers, soil, lakes, seas, valleys.

Fact based sources can enliven the role these geographic features played thousands of years ago. *Walking the Bible* by Bruce Feller traces the physically logistical theories related to the first five books of the Bible. While it has its worldly (and skeptical) aspects, what he discovered should bolster faith. The author carefully studied many geographical features prominent in the Old Testament in his 10,000 mile trek to the reality of the Israelites who wandered in the desert for forty years.

Mountains and mountain ranges evoke the trials and triumphs of explorers and settlers, and most notably in Judeo-Christian history, the height of God's awesome power. Mount Ararat, Mount.Sinai/Mount Horeb, Mount of Olives, Mount Tabor, Mount Carmel, and Mount Zion would be excellent material for a geography/religion unit.

Bodies of water to be studied include: The Tigris and Euphrates, believed to be near the Garden of Eden; the Red Sea; the Sea of Galilee featured in Scripture (teaching); and the Jordan River (where Jesus was baptized). Of course the desert and vegetation underscore God's lessons and through Jesus Christ.

Fiction, though based on research, can also illuminate the role of geography. One example is in the Clive Cussler novel: **Flood Tide**. Chapter 22: *Of the major rivers of the world, the Nile casts a romantic spell from and ancient past, the Amazon conjures up images of adventure and danger, while the Yangtze entwines the soul with mysteries of the Orient.* The author then turns to the Mississippi, and teachers certainly understand that significance. Scholars also are then reminded of other such important waterways like the Tigris and Euphrates and later, the Jordan River. Other literature sources figurative and literal application; Mark Twain's Mississippi River threaded through much of his work. One special note: Some students have never seen a river or major body of water, like those in arid climates. Teachers should plan to bring those alive at least through video presentations.

Teachers should highlight geographic influences in history, science, and the arts too.

The fact is that geography has shaped and been shaped by people: their lives and livelihoods; their help and hinderance; their imprint on art and even architecture, their imagination in engineering feats.

Every part of the world, on every continent, geography narrates history as an echo of the past and a trumpet for the future. All manner of spiritual life has found its external fulfillment in geography, from the Sacrament of Baptism to the rock of the Church; from the richness of the vineyard to the penitential desert; from the tempest sea to the jagged shorelines.

So, while the basics may be a necessary exercise that produces some student frustration, once those are mastered, the exploration of the world comes alive in more than the the actual subject, also in literature and poetry, in math and the sciences, in religion, art, and even music.

## Economics

What is economics? How did economics develop? What is its relationship to governance and politics? Is there one superior paradigm of economics? How does Capitalism breed corporate (and individual) greed. Why is Communism so spiritually deadly and actually diminish economic opportunity? Do teachers (and therefore students) understand the relationship between the rise of Islam and pursuit of economic gain and dominance? Can the basic tenets of Christianity, if fully practiced, end the imbalance of goods and services among people? What is the role of government in overseeing the economics of a particular locale, state, or country? What part, if any, does government play in ensuring the rights of all participants in an economy? How does the Catholic Church perceive its role and in relationship to government? For example, what did Pope St. John Paul II mean when discussing subsidiary assistance (involvement) in his communications, including encyclicals and other Popes and church leaders in discussing the wealthy and poor; Christian economics and the like? Will there ever be a proper balance between "solidarity" and "subsidiary" help?

All of these questions will arise during the study of government and politics, but they can and should be addressed in children as young as Kindergarten although in much simpler terms.

Many virtues are related to economics, but the understanding should start with knowledge about economics. Most basically stated, economics is the production, distribution and consumption of goods and services, individually and collectively. It involves buying, selling, and trading. It can be viewed as something as simple as two children trading toys to much more complex and global economic systems with many layers and players. It may entail tangible items like manufactured products and intangible ones like stocks and bonds. At the core is how people use resources, readily available, literally in or on the ground, or farmed or manufactured. In any economy, services based on education and experience have worth in exchange for currency or bartered goods. Furthermore, the vocabulary of economics is vast and not covered in this particular Primer, but from the pre K teacher who may have an in class store for rewards to the high school teacher who may actually engage students in stock exchanging of creating an imaginary business, those terms will obviously be needed, more or less.

As economics has its root in household affairs, there are numerous examples of work, trade, cost, expense, reward, and renumeration in the home. These opportunities are especially true for homeschool teachers. Certainly, on daily basis, parents could easily reference a concept of economics impacting or being affected by all members of the family. For one example, many paper products are now being produced with cheaper material, in smaller sizes, for more money. Even a third grader can grasp that the paper roll stand no longer covers the entire length of a roll of paper towels. Allowing capable children to assist in self check out, on a weekly basis can lead them to conclude that prices are going up. From, there concepts of inflation and conservation may be dinner hour discussion.

Of course allowances have always been a parent favored economics lesson, and teachers often have treasures for students to select with their earned "bucks."

In other ways, teachers may extend textbook lessons that involve word problems about the cost of purchasing items to comparing the ultimate cost of difference if paid with a credit card. Negative integers in math are always better understood if a student has a "checkbook." Overextend, do the math incorrectly, and the "check" is going to bounce with money owing the bank, usually Bank of Mom and Dad. Again, Monopoly also teaches these realities in a "safe" environment.

Yet, as children develop, other more complex economic realities, such as supply and demand, fairness in business, and taxes will be incorporated into lessons. Furthermore, parents (easy if they are already homeschooling) have myriad opportunities to increase acumen in the area of economics. Shopping, filling up the tank, helping in researching a replacement of a broken appliance all offer real life ways for students to learn.

For the Catholic teacher, however, what is most critical, *is the imparting of individual responsibility and accountability* when relating to family and neighbors, near and far. Most importantly, given the broad appeal of contemporary socialistic proposals and policies, Catholic teachers will need to examine their consciences for biases towards any particular economic theory and beware, when teaching, of those prejudices.

However for the purposes of this Primer, a couple of prominent ideals should be first explored. (See Economic Lesson Plan for Teachers.) Both capitalism and communism have their allies and for particular reasons. So, first, is the survey of teacher understanding about these models.

Chances are that Catholics have been taught of the attractiveness of socialism (communism), and those tenets certainly are most appealing. Some teachers (parents included) may be staunch capitalists believing that all individuals are solely responsible for the outcome of their endeavors via hard work and determination. Most, though will likely fall in between with a romantic attachment to the notion of a governmental utopia but realization with reason that such a state is unlikely to be attempted except by totalitarianism or achieved in a fallen world, where even the best intentions fail to rouse some people. In the latter case, the outstretched hand (out) may be grabbed, but then as soon as there is expectation of reform, just as abruptly slapped away.

Teachers should study individual results of the survey and consult the Catholic Catechism and other writing with respect to economic approaches to understand their understanding of these models. They should return to the statements and compose some thoughts for each assertion in light of Church teaching.

The third part of this lesson is identifying your most preferred model, understanding any misunderstandings about each model and finally determining what area is needed for further study. The appendix has some resources for additional understanding, especially for Catholics.

Again, teachers should be mindful that even at a very young age, children can detect by word choice, tone, and other expression what they should incorporate into their understanding about work, responsibility, sharing (charity), materialism (and detachment), healthy self interest vs. selfishness, and gratitude.

As a hint, effective Catholic teachers will see the attributes or appeal and flaws in Capitalism and Communism and work towards building a cache of resources to developmentally teach economy, objectively but lovingly to impart a Catholic model of economy that includes a stewardship model for entrepreneurs and business developers. Students should glean that the way economy works (or not) is not strictly in adherence to one of these concepts, but that they should strive to understand their responsibility as Catholics to be industrious and just. Still, this needs to be imparted developmentally though a Primary student can certainly understand the concept of tithing. By high school, students should be able to also discern how "giving" is not always charitable, depending on the cause.

**Physical Education**

One would think that physical activity is a rather neutral environment but not so. There are many lessons from the nature of eligible participants to basic concepts like teamwork and sportsmanship to discussions about Yoga that is apparent in many Catholic environments including Catholic schools. Our society is imbued with false notions regarding equitable competition, self esteem, and the mind vs. the body vs. the soul with a heavy emphasis on self empowerment often found in Eastern spirituality.

Yoga is based on Eastern meditation and paganism. The very physical gestures are a form of tribute to false gods. The crossed leg position with forefinger and thumb touching, palm upward reflects one of those goddesses. It invites a spirituality that contradicts Catholicism in a subtle but real way. Moreover, many Christians are unaware of that and quite innocently embrace yoga and mindfulness, thinking it will bring them power over their weakened selves and restful healing. (See Kathleen Beckman's book on mindfulness.) Therein is the core dilemma. Of course, we should take care of our minds and bodies, but never at the expense of our souls. Nor should we depend on only our inner resources instead of or more than God.

It might seem picky, unkind, or excessive to focus on this, but it is a way of life prevalent in all corners of society, including the Church (and schools), that it is almost unavoidable. In a recent *Weakest Link* episode, one contestant spoke in an alien language imbued with references to positive energy and when eliminated, needing to shed the negative energy before returning home. What public community center does not offer exercise based on this spirituality although if asked, they would not immediately make that connection.

Thousands — millions — are daily inundated with Yoga, from women's magazines to health kiosks in medical settings. Cancer patients are among the most targeted. However, to interject quickly, this is not demonstrative of some "plot" to deChristianize society as much as it is a practice most often viewed as benign and mostly exercise. Its danger is in its *hidden* origin. If we are what we eat, we are also what we chant or dwell upon mentally. One cancer patient had to awkwardly communicate to a Christian physical therapist what Yoga really entailed. The therapist had no idea, but together, the patient and therapist remixed and re-imaged the exercises to reflect worship of the one, true God and with associated prayer and music.

In *A Lightbook of Soulfulness*, this contrast is explored and offers a Catholic perspective, as well as prayers and resources, and the biographies of many Saints over the ages who suffered with cancer. By the way, one most notable one besides the classic St. Pelegrine is St. Zelie Martin (Mother of St. Therese of Liseauex) who died of breast cancer when St. Therese was only four years old, and there are numerous other examples.

Now, there may well be faithful Catholics reading the aforementioned and being somewhat baffled or even irritated. They will claim that these matters never entered into their exercise practices, and they are quite fine. Others in the past have also said the same for the Ouija Board and Dungeons and Dragons. A dive into some of Father Chad Ripperger's study of the occult might illuminate the spiritual risks better. Moreover, people are in the presence of evil in myriad unintentional ways, why intentionally invite it in?

Also, in many ways, physical education should be taught with the rigor of any other subject in that Catholics should take care of their gift of body and in relationship with and respect for others bodies.

Incidentally, this includes modesty in sports wear. Obviously, in certain competitions, shorts and Tees are often the dress code, but even then, care should be taken to foster correct fit with nothing unnecessarily exposed.

Students should understand the body systems, one of the most important ones receiving attention lately being the lymph system. Of course, all of this baffles thinking persons even more, when considering the hyper focus on "health" issues like sexuality, gender identity, contraception, and abortion. Instruction is so skewed as to be sorrowful. This is not to discount addressing sexuality, but that should be accomplished by a teacher who has been especially trained in a Catholic approach and the Theology of the Body.

In sports, whether in friendly PE class activities or formal programs, opportunities abound to build virtue, a sense of responsibility to others, and fair play, along with a cheerful attitude (humility) when losing a game or competition. Humility entails choosing a sport that complements the persons natural ability; justice is more than be a good sport; fortitude (perseverance) may test a child's temperament, but everyone is needed in team sports. Again, there are many saints upon which to draw for these lessons.

Teachers should respect their colleagues who teach PE, too. In many schools, they are the subject of snide comments or joking. For the capable PE teacher who had to pass coursework for this subject, which most often includes health matters, as well as extracurricular responsibilities, this is not only uncharitable but unjust.

## Art

It can be established that no other religion surpasses the early Christian Catholic Church in art of all mediums, across time and cultures. Most Catholics know about Michelangelo and Leonardo da Vinci; others may be familiar with Renaissance sculptor Donatello and Post Impressionist Paul Cezanne, among others. Yet, there are hundreds of noted artists and some are most intriguing if obscure. One atypical example relates a convert story is Wu Li (featured in Magnificat) who was one of six masters of 17th Century Chinese painting from that time period and around the time of the Ming Dynasty collapse. Jesuit missionaries greatly influenced Wu Li though he initially pursued Confucianism and Buddhism. He was also known for outstanding Chinese Christian poetry

Then studies may include those who write about art. James Patrick Reid in a 2021 article in *The Catholic Thing* wrote beautifully about painting being transformational "of materials, of vision, and of consciousness—which is also a Catholic concern." (March 20, "A Transforming Vision.). Reid explores the techniques and perspectives that illuminate the eye often to a marvelous three dimensional depiction of famous works like "The Last Supper" with special emphasis on certain elements. There are numerous other resources, including regular features on art in the Epoch Times.

There are numerous children's book of art and ample activities. Even Lego got "into the game" with different religious models to build and figurine figures for various Gospel scenes. *How Catholic Art Saved the Faith: The Triumph of Beauty and Truth in Counter Reformation Art* by Elizabeth Lev is another. (Sophia Institute). Critics note her keen ability to reconnect contemporary readers to a time when such creativity lifted up a wounded world (Post Reformation) and brought many to the splendor of the true Church. In most of Church history, nothing compares to the magnificence of its majestic artists and sculptures, monthly featured in *Magnificat* with historical and stylistic explanations. Moreover, young children can appreciate simple symbols such as water and other natural features; study the expressions of art subjects; note the environmental features and what tone they set, and curriculums like *The Good and The Beautiful* intersect the 'reading' of artwork in its language arts program.

## Music

Nothing uplifts, inspires, and instructs the soul like good music. In addition to Sacred compositions in various languages, including Latin, classical music has been studied for its positive impact on the mind, body, and we know, souls of listeners. If anyone has ever watched a child work with the background of such classic singing or just listening to great symphonies, it is quite clear that this tunes the mind and beautifully.

True that many Christian hymns are acceptable in Catholic circles, and that is fine to a point, but not at the intentional exclusion of those Sacred hymns and Gregorian chants, especially if they are deemed "outdated."

Also, it is truly a blessed child who learns how to play a musical instrument. So many skills and virtues are involved, including focussing, diligence, attention to detail, perseverance, instrument maintenance, practice, and so forth. Too, rightfully teaching music inclines children to tune out the clash and clang of modern songs which are most often attention getting covers for mind altering lyrics that rob youth of all that is good, true, and beautiful.

Many years ago there was a song about how God made a man out of fifty pounds of clay. A father watching his daughter quietly move and hum to the music prompted him to ask, "Do you even hear the lyrics?" She had not been paying any attention, but those words were being seeded in her imagination and memory.

In addition to providing music and instrumental instruction, as with art, it will be to the students' advantage to learn the great creators of music, both from long ago and contemporary artists. Furthermore, many saints have been Divinely inspired to compose that music.

The stories of composers and singers can be inspiring by themselves. Blessed Cripple the Hermit (1013-1054 AD) was born so terribly deformed that he was placed in an abbey at seven and remained there for life. God had plans, and his scholarly fame spread years later.

He also wrote hymns, including Salve Regina and Alma Redemptoris. That was not his limit as he also wrote a treatise in that subject.

Here, cross curriculum plays a role with art and history—even math—considering that music is associated with that. Integrate the Psalms, as well, working with the religion teacher or consulting books and articles on them. Increase student awareness of these during Mass. There is reason for jubilance. David was known to dance before the Lord!

Of course, schools and churches provide ample attention to music, sometimes instrumentally or in a choir. Regardless if this leads to long-term participation, the study of music notes, alone, is an important literacy to embrace.

Teachers would be wise to incorporate this regardless of subjects they teach. Middle school students particularly show increased buoyancy entering a classroom with music already in the background. In short, music uplifts and motivates everyone within earshot.

**Dance and Drama**

Teachers can well incorporate dance and drama into numerous subjects. A play using an oversized decimal point or acting out sentences or passages from literature. Excerpts from Shakespearean plays can be fun. Some teachers create their own puppet theatre using PVC piping. Older students in one class many years ago were directed to write and act out a history story or government concept, and one group demonstrated the evil of communism with some dressed in black while the other democratic half celebrated in white costume. The homeschool curriculum of Schola Rosa includes Great Works from classic literature and poetry. Children learn and memorize better with physical gestures that bring these readings more to life. Their timelines lend themselves to movement and pantomime.

Everything from the Greek tragedy to Shakespeare to Aesop's Fables can be acted. Presentations may have many adaptions including

Chapter Three: Embedding Catholicism in All Subjects        133

dialogue, cultural dance, history re-enactments, to name a few. Students can write short plays based on famous persons or saints. The variations are limited only by truth, dependent on the teacher (or students), and as they adhere to a sound lesson.

## TOOLS, LESSON(S) AND GENERAL RESOURCES AND MATERIALS—EMBEDDING CATHOLICISM

### TOOLS:

Catholic barometer for all subjects- lessons: 1) Is it truthful or free of even subtle error?; 2) Is it age appropriate?; 3) Does it honor God's and His creation in some way?; Are there any aspects that need reinforcement in the areas of good, true, and beautiful? 4) Is there a way to link it to faith? 5) Are there any components that will lead to the need for anticipated responses, and is there preparation for that?

### LESSONS:

***Primary Lesson***: Truth vs. Unreality; the Natural vs. the Supernatural. From K-adulthood, there is evidence for timeless Truth; Unreality has "markers" as well. Simplistic exploration of the world around us and then that which is unseen. (Story of the little child who noted that he could look at the crucifix and know that it was not really Jesus; he could accept that he could not "see" Jesus in the Eucharist, but knew He was truly present. However, there is always the supernatural which is a challenge to the worldly.

- Create a template with four columns headed: Fact/Fiction and Natural / Supernatural.
- Read *The Weight of the Mass: A Tale of Faith* Josephine Nobisso (based on a story told as true). Identify the characters and main story points and classify them under one of the headings. Discuss.

Lesson #1: *Music Soothes the Savage Beast or Disturbs the Soul*

This activity is designed for introspection while listening to two different types of music when completing an essay prompt. The the first ten minutes will be listening to harsh rock and roll; the second ten minutes to classical music.

Self evaluation in completing a topic sentence, ideas for supporting paragraphs, organization, and mechanics

Lesson#2: Double Lesson on Music and Disability

Listen to a selection from a Renee Bondi CD. Describe the person singing. How do you "see" her?
Compare responses to Renee Bondi's bio
 Other possibilities include art analysis, evaluating a contemporary textbooks; sharing a favorite subject and why

**RESOURCES:**

Too numerous to list here, but see the Appendix and Bibliography and some below.

**BOOKS:**

Father Gaglia's book. (The Periodic Table of Virtues)
Michael O'Brien's *A Landscape with Dragons*
Cheri Bloomquist's *Before Austen Comes Aesop*
Stacy Trasancos *Science Was Born of Christianity*
*The Weight of the Mass: A Tale of Faith* by Josephine Nobisso

ALSO SEE THE APPENDIX.

# Chapter Four

## *HOW* TO TEACH TRUTH

### FORMING ETERNAL CITIZENS

Catholic teachers must be equipped with more than knowledge about Truth. They need to learn and grow in *how* they teach that Truth if the ultimate goal is preparation for citizenship in Heaven. This is where knowing one's self and what is Truth converge and intersect to steer educators to their optimum "classroom" and students, even if those are a teacher's own children. As asserted elsewhere, no teacher is the ideal teacher for all personalities, age groups, and subjects. A healthy teacher can successfully identify strengths and weaknesses and demonstrate humility to seek assistance for the latter.

Just examine the first Apostles, each unique and destined for certain demographics and regions (cultures). Consider St. John who was likely the most peaceful among the twelve and capable of sharing in the excruciating suffering of Jesus Christ, yet he was not martyred. Others came to that point of ultimate self sacrifice after numerous trials, like St. Peter. St. Paul seemed hardly the candidate to share the Good News with a group of children, but St. Luke or Matthew might have had just such a disposition. Some of this is speculation, obviously, but one point is clear. Jesus calls many people to their vocation for a particular reason, and that includes those who conclude their calling is teaching.

Then there is the challenge of providing basic knowledge because there is still the world to navigate. Catholic teachers must do more than point to Heaven; they must instill reasonable productivity and a rightful spirit of prosperity in their students. Recognizing their students; strengths and weaknesses, honing their particular gifted areas, and balancing their quest for success with virtuous boundaries is a huge undertaking.

How?

Pedagogy, the manner in which teaching is conducted has been subject to numerous perspectives, advisements, and revisions over the centuries. Yet, there are "tried and true" methods—approaches—that are universal. It all begins with God's Word and His Story — Revelation. Conscientious, contemporary Catholic educators, including those outside the classroom, provide advice, structure, and resources, are guided by central principles in how they teach. One is having exemplary role models; another is choosing peer mentors with prudent discernment (This must include the lives and guidance of the Saints); a third is being appropriately flexible; a fourth is being in "student" mode and open to reliable direction in introducing concepts, pacing, and strategies. The latter includes individualizing instruction even within one classroom to meet foremost the spiritual growth of students and then their course work. Finally, education has undergone many critics and revisionists over the centuries, and while not advocating for one approach or another—i.e. lecture. vs. group engagement—it is sufficient to establish that "one size does not fit all or all the time."

### *Exemplary Teachers*

A popular but somewhat banal saying is "What would Jesus do?" Well, when it comes to teaching, we already know. In his book, 99 Ways to *Teach Like the Master,* T.J. Burdick makes the point that Jesus did show HOW to teach. Among Our Lord's approaches were narration, but with an emphasis on parables. At other times, He referenced Scripture. Occasionally, he admonished with His "lessons." Our Lord used figurative language—metaphors. Always, he taught people "where they were" in life without forcing the listener to accept truth. At times, He taught along with physical healing. Almost always outdoors, Jesus taught using environmental elements, like mountains, the sea, trees, and so forth. In one passage, He wrote in the sand. Also, Jesus Christ taught by example, starting as an Infant, He led the Way towards eternal life. He demonstrated the way, the truth, and the life by carrying His Cross and dying for love.

It may be common to forget in the everyday frenzy of mastering the "daily objectives" and ensuring all children are grasping what is considered the basics, in a preconceived sequential order.

Even excellent teachers sometimes become caught up with world and how children must be prepared to survive and thrive here, sometimes forgetting that "vocation" is all. Some will grow to be great persons. The majority will live relatively obscure lives but can still accomplish great things in the way of evangelizing, just by their humble but virtuous lives. Always, teachers should strive to "see" their students in the Light of God (See "Teaching in God Light").

A disciplined prayer life is critical although with the caveat that it cannot be so rigid as to dominate other priorities. There are days that seem to be overloaded, and may require numerous pleas to Heaven for help throughout. An early morning emergency at home may halt that quiet time. A Rosary may be left unfinished as the computer crashed with the day's lessons vanished, or the printer jammed. An ill teacher may mean no planning period when some prayer time is included. Teaching is filled with the unexpected.

Still, spending some time with Jesus Christ every morning, even for a brief period while helping prepare the family breakfast, can relax that mind in turmoil and help foster a peaceful and productive day that is pleasing to Jesus Christ, not the principal, the superintendent, and so forth, although teachers will be obedient to them. If docility (the willingness to be taught) is expected in students, it must begin with the teacher' docility in the presence of God.

A teacher who declares him or herself too busy for prayer, he or she is too "busy." One may recall the story about filling a jar with sand and pebbles. When the sand is poured in first (daily life occupations), the pebbles (prayer) does not fit. Yet when the pebbles are placed first, the sand snugly fills to but not beyond the brim.

## *Mary and Joseph as Teachers*

The Holy Family's daily home life was hidden for the most part, so how Mary and Joseph taught Our Lord is shrouded in mystery yet not understanding. Inferences can be confidently made. The home atmosphere was prayerful with references to Scripture and holy practice of the Jewish faith (God's Word and Covenant that preceded the Incarnation). Virtue is pronounced throughout, and that is the most essential foundation for any sound education. Mary and Joseph were humble, charitable, chaste, obedient, and faithful. They detached themselves from material goods, but trusted. They were docile and ready to listen. Their very existence "proclaimed" every needed knowledge and understanding to live well but walk toward God and eternity.

Together, it can be assumed that they were quite the team, from everyday delineation of chores to how the days were structured. They promptly went to Bethlehem for the census, the stable for Jesus' birth, and the temple for the Presentation. Even when Jesus could not be found for three days, no temper was displayed but an acceptance of their son's unfolding detachment from them. Scripture does not record anything Joseph said, so his method of teaching was likely more by example, such as in carpentry, and quietly leading the family in faith. When speech was necessitated, as in overseeing Jewish customs and rites, one can almost imagine him moving with purpose more than speaking. Teachers are encouraged to read Cardinal Sarah's incredible, *The Power of Silence*. It is not a quick read, but even a bit a day, or during school breaks, will emphasize that silence speaks louder than words.

Mary and Joseph laid the perfect blueprint for what should be transmitted in fact to all God's children but with few words and peacefully.

When Joseph departed this earth, Mary continued in that practice but as our mother. She showed us the way to share Truth by pointing to Truth more than verbalizing it, which makes Mary's Magnificat all the more resounding! Still, she could identify a productive "lesson" when necessary, like the Miracle at Cana. Yet, like her holy spouse, when that "hour" had come, she taught us how to live the Truth by her surrender to suffering but still be ever present before God.

Likewise, smart veteran teachers will share that they do not use many words, as much as *demonstrate* how to read, write, solve math problems, or explore the world. This is often accomplished kinesthetically. There is time for the "lecture" portion of instruction but that needs to focus on the main points. Thus, the Socratic method of teaching, the Charlotte Mason openness to natural settings, and guided teaching and practice are all calming but effective ways to impart knowledge and understanding.

*The Apostles*

By grace…by the Holy Spirit…the Apostles were enabled to carry Truth. However, it is fascinating that Jesus Christ chose an almost motley crew to accomplish the spread of the Word, the essential facts and, as we know such, opinions, so to speak. They represented different backgrounds although most were not necessarily formally or highly educated like the Scribes or Pharisees. They knew Jewish law and history, though.

Notice how Jesus Christ "sent" them to different areas, various people, and so forth. In other words, He knew the right "fit" for each. Teachers, therefore, may be guided by this in that everyone has special talents or gifts. For example, it does not matter how well a teacher may know art, artists, masterpieces, and so forth. If he or she cannot teach the techniques of art, that may not be a good fit. So, humility on limitations is essential with the "how" of teaching, well beyond the knowledge itself.

*Early Teachers: Church Fathers (See below for philosophers)*

It could be generally known and accepted that the Church Fathers saved the Church by their teaching, passing along the truth at a time it was most necessary. Note that how this was accomplished varied although their writings are perservered for the most part. Still, how they imparted knowledge depended on their geographical location, audience, and means. (See Wisdom through Church History.)

Today, teachers will most likely learn from them by text, however. On a brighter note, some have been portrayed in film, represented in live seminars and presentations, or brought to life by inventive teachers with a flare for drama. As long as what they shared is not misinterpreted or translated poorly, the how is open to various modes. Teachers are encouraged to explore Avila Institute for a deeper dive, and several Catholic publishers offer in-depth biographies and commentaries on early Church teaching.

## *Special Orders and Religious*

Through the centuries, different teaching orders and religious sisters have received approval. These educators have honed pedagogy — curriculum and instruction — though again in varied ways. However, not all teaching orders are a good fit for all students. St. John Bosco's Salesian order was especially adept at reaching young boys. St. Elizabeth Ann Seton was able to launch the concept of Catholic schools but her influence was noted more as the Church grew in the United States. The Ursaline and Notre Dame Sisters are two others. The Christian Brothers order may be well suited to those students (male) who require a tighter methodology that leaves little room for individual mischief. The Dominican sisters are marvelous for their temperament and ability to impart knowledge, particular virtues. As previously mentioned, one order in Tennessee developed a beautiful, well organized — by subject and growth —literature document with an outstanding introduction as to what constitutes a good book. Two orders produced exceptional virtue programs with the Dominicans of Mary, Mother of the Holy Eucharist (Detroit Michigan), showing how to live those virtues.

Teachers may study and employ all the successful approaches and strategies well developed and timeless, as fits their environment, including home school parents. Of course, and thankfully, some schools do have teaching orders as members of their faculty.

There is an abundance of assistance, but one needs a caveat. St. Ignatius Loyola and Father John Hardon, S.J. must be storming about in heaven as they witness the deterioration of that teaching order here on earth. Certainly there are still good Jesuit priests and schools, but caution is needed before subscribing to any of their curriculum or resources. Tragically, too many now even advance same sex relationships as normalized. Recently one infamous Jesuit priest blasted pro lifers.

*Philosophers*

St. Augustine was one of the most influential philosophers in Church history, and his "City of God" propelled this Primer. His work will be explored as an extended unit at the end of this chapter. In the meantime, it is helpful to know that St. Augustine for all his success in rhetoric and imparting what he thought was outstanding knowledge. At one time a follower of Manichaeism, he humbly and wisely accepted that in order to teach catechumens, he would have to be taught by Holy Scripture. Indeed, he saw no pathway to successfully teaching the Faith except by deep knowledge of Salvation History.

Another giant and likely the most famous education philosopher is St. Thomas Aquinas. Note the present tense, as his writing touches every facet of *how to teach*. A brilliant mind that so well explored the human person, he illuminated all the facilities of the person in order to teach and be taught. There is literally nothing that cannot be gleaned from St. Thomas Aquinas for the well being of the classroom. He was foremost faithful, yet humble; knowledgeable, yet understanding; incredibly organized, yet open to inquiry; thorough, yet accepting that he had produced virtually nothing in the reality of God's Knowledge. (It was straw.)

Teachers must accept limitations, that they will confuse and be confused, that they can only give a bit of the totality of knowledge, and, most importantly, in the end, it is truly all in God's providence. Moreover, any prayerful teacher who has struggled to brainstorm a strategy, technique, approach, and so forth, can likely share a story when the "lightbulb" turned on. The Holy Spirit was present.

The prime message from all these early teachers is that they can only do so much, but if they do so in love with an earnest desire to impart Truth, God will show them the way.

<u>Popes as Teachers (See Wisdom of Church History)</u>

Popes and their Encyclicals are explored in *Wisdom Through Church History* but suffice to say that the Holy Spirit is ever present, and the Encyclicals are only one way they have communicated. Some have done better than others, however. Candidly, a few taught poorly or contrary to Truth. Still, overall there is a wealth of teaching and the ***how*** of it in many papacies.

Perhaps, one most recent example is St. Pope John Paul II who was a master teacher! There is a regrettable adage, "Those who can't, teach." Pope John Paul II proved that good teachers "do" in myriad ways. He traveled the globe, specified young audiences, illustrated the truth in many ways but mostly by how he lived, and gently, yet with extraordinary confidence shared all that anyone needs to succeed in this world and achieve the next. He modeled the ideal pupil of Jesus Christ.

Contrasted with another memorable Pope—Pope Benedict XVI— though, one detects different approaches. Pope Benedict is also a great teacher but with a different style. His "how" is more formalized. As for Pope Francis, there is the back brain buzz his words sometimes evokes. There has been considerable commentary about his "style" which is not the specific aim of this book. Suffice to mention that the cross of Franciscan and Jesuit brings about a challenging understanding at times. Still, a gentleness is perceived, along with a longing for good will. Always, though, we must pray for our Pope and that prudent and charitable voices will help clarify immutable Church teaching. God always raises up such persons for these times.

## SEEKING AND SELECTING STRONG PEER MENTORS (TRUSTWORTHY CONTEMPORARY ROLE MODELS)

After learning about themselves (Teacher in God's Light), educators should actively be on the watch for those persons who can fill in the "gaps". This may relate to both teaching skills and inculturating virtue. Moreover, this mentor might or might not share the same weaknesses. An AA meeting gathers those who experience alcoholism with the goal of assisting each other through temptation. Certainly, someone showing at a meeting bragging about never having a drinking problem may strike a sour chord. Yet, if there is someone who appears patient under any circumstance, it might be helpful for the reactive teacher to observe him or her as to any techniques or responses they have cultivated. Of course, some are simply, by nature, less anxious than others. Opposite dispositions offers opportunity for growth. If one's temperament is phlegmatic, seeking peers who are diligent in their daily structures and lesson planning might be advisable. However, envy and overcompensation should be avoided.

Hopefully, administrators and Catholic School offices will construct "professional development" in a way that best matches a particular faculty and staff. He, she, or they will know well what mentoring will be most helpful and not subscribe to "cookie cutter" presentations and activities for whole schools. Catholic school offices are actually in the best position of those special days to offer a wide variety of Diocesan day development according to what their administrators know about their particular faculty.

Some teachers may need to move from lecture mode to structured but student engaging activities. Others may be too "loose" with foundational concepts and directions. A few may simply need guidance and materials to build resources that offer the best variety of presentation of information or concepts; practice of skills; and authentic assessments.

It should not be assumed that teachers have even been taught well in the way of delivery and assessment. An education degree is one metric of competency, but veteran teachers often bring to the novice better understanding of the practical approaches by sheer experience. One such area teachers may inquire of mentors is in homework—now known more as independent practice. This is often a major impediment to ensuring understanding. How such assignments are determined and developed can "make or break" an otherwise healthy learning environment.

As a sidebar, "homework passes" are typically not a wise way to impart the importance of any independent practice, unless they are tied to a student's comprehension of a concept or skill. For example, if a student has demonstrated proficiency by diligent focus in class on—say—subtraction of two digit values—is homework necessary for that student? Maybe that particular student needs to work on paragraph writing, spelling, or something else. That also individualizes students; they are not members of a group or mass. Also teachers *must* review submitted homework in a way that determines understanding and facilitates forward moving. Moreover, if only the evens or odds will be assessed, just assign those. Better, provide independent practice on critical concepts only.

There are so many ways genuine role models can assist and save teachers unneeded angst.

In domains outside the classroom, Catholic teacher sites are now offering guidance and even lesson plans. The Institute for Catholic Liberal Education (ICLE) and Catholic School Playbook are two such sources for professional development and resources. A proliferation of solid Catholic teachers have written books and produced videos that will be a gold mine for even the seasoned teacher. In fact, it would be an injustice to name just a couple and limited teacher scope on the matter. A list is included at the close of this section, but teachers are advised to be on the alert for additional ones.

Chapter Four: *HOW* to Teach Truth  145

*FLEXIBILITY: A special note*

It is important for children to see that all faithful Catholics teach in some capacity though not always formally in a class setting. In that regard all are teachers and all are students throughout life. (Quote from Epoch Times about ceasing learning.)

As none are yet perfected, how one teaches is not always neatly packaged or in one or a few persons. Cultivation of teaching practices that incorporate the ultimate aim of a solid Catholic education is ongoing, and teachers may locate role models even outside the mainstream of an educational environment. A neighbor may be a fantastic cook and a faithful Catholic. A family member may display a knack for teaching the growing of a family garden. A parent might make an excellent speaker on law or medicine and serve as an ongoing adviser in these areas. Perhaps a teacher knows someone in accounting to teach a class on record keeping; another may be married to a banker to teach the value of savings. The options are endless and often these noncredentialed teachers are so passionate about their livelihood or hobby, the students are charged by the enthusiasm. As long as they are not anti-Catholic and their presentation is known to administration and approved, their religious affiliation may not be a concern.

Here are some real life examples although names have been changed in some incidents. Mrs. Q quilted well, and she initiated an annual course on teaching middle school students how make baby blankets which were then donated to families in need. A parent, alarmed at poor manners among students proposed and developed an etiquette class. One staff member at a school had some knowledge of hens, and soon there was a chicken coop and eventually fresh eggs. An artistic father volunteered at a homeschool setting to teach some techniques to the children. One African mother descended from royalty in her native country contributed rich background in the study of the continent overall. In some cases, these experiences have motivated people to enter teaching.

## NAVIGATING IGNORANCE, OBSTINANCE, AND DEFIANCE (parents, peers, and pupils)

There are days when even the best plans go awry due to poor student responses. The teacher has tried everything in how to present a concept or skill, but disruption of some type is blocking receptivity. The notion that this does not occur in homeschool is false, as families have varying personalities, in conflict, at times. In these cases, the problem is not how but maybe when, or, if how, what other ways may reach the student(s) who want(s) to learn. Hopefully administrators can be savvy enough to realize it is not always the teacher, and, if a particular student resists all types of approaches, something has to change in order for the teacher to reach most or all of the other students. If it is a home issue, counseling, attempting a different schedule, adding a snack period, or other approaches may resolve the clashes.

Then there is another snag in the "how" as even experienced teachers can share difficult moments when the "perfect lesson" has been pounced upon by a parent, peer, or student. Whether it is in the teacher approach, selection of instruction; materials (especially ancillary ones); or a dispute about what the child said the teacher said, even the best teachers will face opposition from parents or students.

How to respond? That depends on the "snag." Of course, administrators should review lesson planning to assist teachers in avoiding some unexpected resistance or counter reaction. Moreover, the administrator may "know" something that the teacher does not due to confidentiality. As previously mentioned, the Faith cannot be compromised, but the Truth can be conveyed in myriad ways. A teacher need not construct a compare and contrast Venn diagram exercise on sin (mortal vs. venial) by using examples that may be reflected in a class family. And teachers, especially novice teachers, may be stunned at the backgrounds of some of the students sitting in the class.

Yet, it is not necessarily the teacher, and many have been sadly discouraged from the profession by administrators who fail to recognize that even a novice or struggling teacher may not be at fault for a particular difficulty.

Many years ago, a mother met with the principal to complain about a writing assignment. She claimed that her son could not complete the outline, and the instructions were too complicated. The teacher was called in to explain how this project had been introduced and explained. The surprised teacher looked at the student and reminded him that it was *his* personally chosen topic that had been used for a whole class outline—just to demonstrate how an outline could be developed. It was an awkward moment for all.

On the opposite end of this spectrum were twins in a sixth grade classroom who both submitted research papers that looked as though a college professor had produced them. How coincidental that the mother was in the field the children researched. Now, the students had been appropriately taught all the steps of research to produce a five-page final paper. These were at least twelve pages and included elaborate citations in the twins' final. What had the students learned? The mother insisted that her daughters had done the work independently with some guidance.

In both of the aforementioned examples, the greater concern was the lack of ethics or virtues. In the first case, a child had lied to his mother; in the second, the parent may have been deceptive. A teacher can do only so much in outlier situations. Of course, it would behoove a teacher to also commend that work which has obviously been accomplished by the student and without complaint. If fact, having bonus points or classroom recognition for healthy work habits might be incorporated into long term assignments.

## BUILDING CURRICULUM AND INSTRUCTION DEVELOPMENTALLY

Teacher preparation is essential for units and lessons, along with anticipating student reception, especially readiness for questions and answers, as they may pertain to Faith. Off the cuff responses may be incorrect or misunderstood. A book, *Did Adam and Eve Have Bellybuttons* foretells the type of questions that may arise. Students should be able to reiterate what has been taught and paraphrase orally or in writing. Many misconceptions have been discovered that way even after a carefully prepared lesson and delivery.

Student's ages and abilities impact HOW an educator imparts knowledge and skills. For homeschool, hybrid, or pod environments ages may vary considerably which will necessitate some appropriate discrimination and varying approaches. Students vary in their learning aptitude and style of learning. Some youth are more active, easily distracted, or tend to process information only partially or incorrectly.

How does a teacher impart the mystery of the Sacraments to a five year old or a teenager? How should a teacher discuss different forms of government to a child with special needs? Is it ever appropriate to share explicit details of abhorrent science experiments that misuse the human body? Does secular or generic Christian music have a place in classic education? When and how does one discuss Critical Race Theory or gender identity, or does the teacher? Incidentally on these last two, Brave Books does introduce the concepts in story book format for ages 4-10.

While there are some humorous anecdotes about teaching gone wrong, once an error is made, undoing it takes double or triple the effort. There are typical techniques for all teachers, regardless of setting to ensure that students have received the knowledge as intended and can apply that knowledge with competence and fidelity. As these are most typically shared in teacher education courses, it is unnecessary to cover them here. However, a few reminders.

Teacher preparation and anticipation are necessary. They need to be ready for questions and answers, especially as they may pertain to Faith. St. Francis de Sales noted the benefit of anticipation for the spiritual life. It helps to consider what may occur and how to provide maximum benefit rather than confusion or ill feelings. Also, off the cuff responses may be incorrect or misunderstood.

Also, the teacher should be docile—docility being a virtue—and be willing to be taught him or herself. This can become necessary in a couple of ways. A middle school teacher by background will likely approach all students in similar fashion or at least fall into that comfortable "zone." Others may note that. Teachers should accept other teachers who have more experience with this age group or have done research. It is important to listen and ensure what they are conveying is understood.

This cuts both ways and across various temperaments.

Sometimes, though, students need to be challenged, so teachers should ascertain the source of difficulty in learning. Just because some concept may be too complex does not mean the student is incapable of learning it or cannot be suitably introduced to it. Truly amazing stories have emerged at the incredible capacity for even young students to grasp more complex ideas. Still, if all else checks, then the teacher should seek peer or administrator assistance.

Under all circumstances, though, teachers should be aware of developmental stages and stepping stones that they do not become stumbling blocks or ill conceived skipping stones.

Many years ago, a young child with Downs Syndrome began to stand and walk by one year old. The family was ecstatic. However, he had missed a vital area of hip development by skipping crawling. He received physical therapy and was fine, but it was a trying and frustrating period for the young child. Teaching…again…is about how (and when).

## *Converts and Reverts as Educators*

A final note on "how" to teach truth is that those Catholics faithful from birth are marvelous. Yet, converts—even reverts—offer fresh perspectives. Moreover, many of them come from a public domain, some having been agnostic or atheistic. As the saying goes, "It takes one to know one," and teachers who have lived in a pit or been singed by the demonic can bring perspective to those educators who may never have been challenged.

In even the best Catholic schools, there will be parents, family members, and students who are sincerely ignorant or woefully and willfully oppositional. Sometimes, this occurs in a family or student by a traumatic event or unexpected life change or obstacle. At all times, teachers must be aware that the devil never rests, and there is no complete comfort zone for teaching.

Still, with those who have been tested, failed, but rose again, different strategies may be employed, or, even some subjects circumvented for a time until they may be re introduced successfully. Consult those educators who have been in the trenches either through free will or by coercion. Surprising statements and odd behaviors may be unexpected, so forewarned is forearmed.

For example, one teacher many years ago had a student who suddenly took an interest in satanism. The parents seemed genuinely surprised if not shocked. The situation was ill handled because the teacher had no idea how to approach this student and was even intimidated by him. How different this may have been handled had a peer had some idea about that "world" and how he or she escaped it. Now, no one is suggesting to hire ex-satanists in Catholic schools, but there may be a wealth of insight that is kept hidden by shame or fear. So, if a solid Catholic teacher who happened to dabble with the Ouji board until his or her return to the Church is advised that some middle schoolers are playing the board on weekends, that teacher may know how to reach these young minds about the danger of this practice more than others.

Also, spiritual sources are available for the laity to appropriately combat demonic influences.

Converts are a treasure because they bring in the best of more than one world view. Often these are former Protestants, but they may be Jewish or Muslim. Ronda Chervin is an excellent example of a Jewish woman who brought her rich background to writing and teaching for over fifty years.

Former Calvinists, Pentecostal, Presbyterians, Assembly of God...the list goes on can best defend the Faith because they once likely "attacked" Catholicism. As noted elsewhere but worth repeating, many years ago, Tim Staples explained that he had great success getting Catholics to leave the Church because they did not know Scripture. Then he met a Catholic who did and taught him. Staples then spent much time trying to track down the ones he had pushed away to get them back into the Church. A Pastor in Florida is a most dynamic preacher, and he attributes his Pentecostal upbringing for that persuasive style. Yet, his often riotous sermons show keen fidelity, and he does not mince words. How he moves his parishioners is vital. He smiles, and, oddly, he is a bit docile, as when one of his members asked for a talk on God's mercy. (She taught him a bit.)

Still, this all illustrates how style, even pacing, choice of words and topics—when and where—all contribute to successful teaching.

## *St. Augustine and Confessions to the City of God*

Perhaps there is no greater example of the "how" than St. Augustine of Hippo. This brilliant early Church Father and Doctor, who had the excellent insight to know that teaching is different from other skills and often requires a particular grasp of the subject to reach students. Moreover, there is a foundation and order to teacher preparation that accompanies familiarity with content. (*The Deposit of Faith: What the Catholic Church* **Really** *Believes* — *Jesus Teaching Divine Revelation in His Body, the Church,* Msgr. Eugene Kevane, 2004, Authorhouse).

In other words, yes, a business executive may be an excellent math teacher; a published author a great language arts teacher; a musician, a captivating music teacher. Still. In each of these areas, it may well be that a return to basics is necessary to fully comprehend the scope of what must be taught and how it should be presented. St. Augustine, who accepted the Truth, had explored Church teachings, and been promoted by holy persons still determined that he was deficit in a foundational area: Sacred Scripture. His big "how" was to support teaching with the Word. This required humility but also prudence (wisdom) and justice (for the students). Even seasoned teachers can learn novel ways to reach students, and that often requires expertise of others and experience.

He knew about developmental curriculum and instruction hundreds of years before it was coined in modern educational practices.

## PRAYING, KNOWING AND CALLING ON SAINTS

As is applicable to all sections and all teachers, at all times, there is no substitute for prayer. It may well be that teachers may never know if their children attain Heaven, but there is no excuse for a teacher not to use challenges and trials for their own salvation. Then, the Saints are always standing by like St. John Bosco and St. Elizabeth Ann Seton. Trust that they had their share of suffering while pushing errant students to learn while growing in virtue. Teachers will be more reassured, confident, and maybe amused after they read their bios and timeless but successful approaches, albeit with those "snags

## TOOLS, LESSON(S) AND GENERAL RESOURCES AND MATERIALS—HOW TO TEACH...

**TOOLS:** The best tool for being proficient in how to teach is honing observation skills and seeking role models. Plan observations in other teacher's classrooms or view some lessons on line. Even watching public school teachers can sharpen how you would teach a concept differently, perhaps with language that underscores temporal considerations but in the context of Catholicism. (Ex: Viewing a teacher on a lesson about recycling.)

## LESSONS:

**Lesson Plan #1:**
(Interview a non teacher Catholic who is specially gifted in a particular area. How did she or he learn that skill; what lessons did they learn along the way about which resources or persons to trust for information? Which temperament or virtues did he or she believe were most advantageous to success in their endeavor? How does their particular giftedness contribute to their spiritual growth?)

It is important for children to see that all faithful Catholics teach in some capacity though not always formally in a class setting. In that regard everyone is a teacher and all are students throughout life.

As none are yet perfected, how one teaches is not always neatly packaged or in one or a few persons. Cultivation of teaching practices that incorporate the ultimate aim of a solid Catholic education is ongoing, and teachers may locate role models even outside the mainstream of an educational environment. A neighbor may be a fantastic cook and a faithful Catholic. A family member may display a knack for teaching the growing of a family garden. A parent might make an excellent speaking on law or medicine and serve as an ongoing adviser in these areas.

**Lesson Plan #2**
Examples of virtuous entrepreneurs, finance experts, bankers, should be researched, especially for articles about their Catholic Faith and how they apply that faith to their occupation and being contributory citizens. Of particular interest would be how they cultivate virtue, maybe by a hard lesson they learned about following God's will, not their own.

**Lesson Plan/Activity #3**

The best way for a teacher to learn HOW to teach is by teaching. Yet, ahead of that opportunity would be observation, unit or lesson development, introspection (See *Teacher in God's Light*), an a small environment practicum. Volunteering for teaching catechism or Vacation Bible School are also great avenues. Fortunately, prospective teachers may be able to watch Catholic teachers online, especially as COVID brought forth Zoom classrooms.

However a word of caution. Catholic teachers should research Catholic schools (and parishes) to ascertain the degree of fidelity to an authentic Catholic education. This is not to disparage any school or church, but some are more intuned to the integration of Fatih—the necessity of Faith—than others. A few are master schools at Catholic identity across subjects and campus. The Institute for Catholic Liberal Education would be a great start to steer prospective teachers.

Other than a "hands on" approach, teachers would do well to start their personal libraries, even digitally and have ample resources before entering a classroom. Daily emails bring forth a wealth of information and guidance, and the real challenge might be how to parse and store them.

**RESOURCES:**

See resources for connections with faithful Catholic teachers and access to models of virtue in each of these subject areas. This will include scientists, researchers, musicians, singers, artists, sports figures, authors, and historians.

CERC, Institute for Catholic Liberal Education; School Playbook, Pontifex University Masters for Catholic Administrators

Hal Plummer's (former Superintendent of Schools Atlanta Archdiocese) Presentation on St. John Bosco

# Chapter Five

## UNPACKING THE RELIGIONS (BELIEF SYSTEMS) OF THE WORLD

### *Knowing Other Belief Systems Prepares Catholic Teachers to Be Confident*

*Ever wonder why Pontius Pilate and his infamous line:* **What is truth?** *reverberates still?*

It is **the** classic question that has led (wo)man astray since Adam and Eve. In fact, Adam and Eve's Original Sin was the prideful attempt to be self empowered by truth, to become all knowing. So, one of the effects is that this question still haunts our relationship with the one true God and the one, holy, Catholic and Apostolic Church. Certainly for those who seek Truth, Jesus Christ already gave Himself, but too many were and are dissatisfied with that.

Moreover, contemporary communication has only aggravated the confusion, and "religions" are increasing exponentially by the century! All but one seeks to "explain" away the need for genuine reliance of Truth, at the cost of self.

According to sources, there are over four thousand religions in the world. (reference.com). Within the largest, Christianity, there is likely a denominations for every 65 people with some claiming about 34,000 denominations in all, while others claim much higher denomination figures. (The completepilgrim.com). The site humanreligions.info asserts "…it is simply impossible to list all varieties of religion, as we as a species have created an almost infinite variety of religious and transcendental ideas." That stated, it cites eighty-one entries, from agnosticism to obscure sects in various regions of the world with information on origin, heritage, founder, holy texts, and reference to concepts like the afterlife.

Essentially, then, there are religious beliefs that are almost as individualistic as fingerprints, and if one could read the thoughts of others, it would likely reveal that everyone has such distinct impressions beyond overall acceptance of dogma. Even among the most orthodox Catholics, one can perceive nuances in the expression of their faith, various questions and challenges, and opinions that may or may not perfectly complement the teaching. Even holy persons differ in tone, deliverance, and practice of faith and virtues.

However, there can be only ONE TRUTH.

So, the following maxim may seem oxymoronic, but it is not upon close examination:

*Have confidence in Truth; Do not trust yourself.*

Moreover, *at any given time*, some new "religion" may emerge as the truth (See The Eternal Kingdom vs. Global Power), so it is optimum to rely on Truth through the Magisterium of the Catholic Church, and as espoused by numerous credible clergy and laity (Saints) through time and around the world. The early Church Fathers (and early Church history) are reliable constants. St. Thomas Aquinas is always a steady and solid foundation.

So, while providing many of the mainstay religions, it would be far more productive and helpful for Catholic teachers to be able to detect fallacy and falsehood, no matter how well intended , spoken, or written, the believer, by commission or omission.

Of course, it is helpful to note that none of the falsehoods are new; they are merely repackaged and redelivered by charismatic or powerful people in any age. They can be numerated and summed up rather neatly, as well, though do not underestimate the cleverness of the evil one in disguising evil as good. Evil is always wrapped in "good" which is why there is so much contention over these beliefs.

It helps to restate that Catholic educators MUST know the Faith; be prepared for colleagues, parents, and students who do not; and learn how to best navigate to evangelize without repelling those in ignorance. Moreover, educators (whose nature may be prone to intellectu-

Chapter Five: Unpacking the Religions (Belief Systems) of the World    157

alizing), should approach the truth like children. Knowing is not equivalent to understanding, and not everything needs to be explained. Much *is* mystery.

In belief about the supernatural, what is true…what is false?

According to John Cassian, a mid fourth-century monk, from whom much of St. Benedict's rule is drawn, an analogical precious coin is the "test" for discerning truth, thereby "sifting out false religious teaching." ("John Cassian's Rules for Discernment" Father Dwight Longenecker, The Imaginative Conservative March 19, 2022)

Cassian outlines four principles: 1) Is the coin truly gold; 2) If gold, is it counterfeit; 3) Does the coin bear the proper image of the king; and 4) Is the coin of true weight (a possible alloy intermixed or shaved a bit?). Father Longenecker extends this analogy to corresponding quality, authenticity, authority, and quantity.

Easily while exploring different beliefs, from animism to pantheism; from multiple gods with human qualities to the one, true God; from simple wonderment to rejection by agnosticism or atheism, most will fail this "test" on all four levels, some on most, and a few on at least one.

However, there will be some who will reject truth no matter how well it is pondered and gifted in a manner deemed charitable and nonjudgmental. Furthermore, Catholic educators would be best prepared to be calumniated even by faithful Catholics as being insufficiently Catholic or too tolerant of those struggling with tenets of the Faith. It can seem like a lose-lose proposition, but every faithful Catholic has confronted the same challenge in every age, everywhere.

Smile…Catholic teachers do not always win…sometimes, there will be those situations, environments, and, at least, days when they are truly confounded and bewildered about what to do. That is where prayer and fasting enter.

Finally, Catholic educators MUST know Church history, as it will provide them with the assurance that there is nothing new under the sun; become acquainted with great apologists and sources for defending the Faith; and maybe even laugh at the repetitiveness. However, it is prudent to mention one new wrinkle. As much as history "repeats" itself, our present age is confronting evil in at least one unique way. The "progressiveness" of the 19th century and "new progressiveness" of the 20th and 21st centuries veil disguise evil uniquely. Whereas previously, the good guys were distinct from the bad guys, today many bad guys perceive themselves as good as like never in history. Nero never acted other than the diabolical character he was. He did not prance in a priestly robe and assert he was acting with any noble intent. He did not proclaim himself devout or behaving for the betterment of mankind. He was just a vicious, evil madman. Today, the clever rogue folds his and her hands piously and insists that he or she is devout and wants only equality, justice, tolerance, and even charity, even while breaking natural laws left and right.

### *However, still genuinely understanding other beliefs can act as guardrails*

Moreover, this is more than just knowing and having skim information. (Is there any teacher who is unaware of other religions in the world?) Unlikely… in this globally "diverse" culture that leans heavily towards softer belief systems, if any at all. Moreover, educators, having taken other classes or through personal research or experience, know that Catholicism is often marginalized as just another way of believing in a "higher power." Some are converts from one of those religions.

Regardless of past knowledge and life practices, hopefully this section through the religions of the world—through time and space—will add to one's knowledge and relate it in away particularly helpful as a teacher. This holds for any teacher, including cradle Catholic homeschoolers because children will encounter different beliefs through the course of their education that may at the very least puzzle them, and, at the worst, challenge their Faith. It is not uncommon that children even from the most orthodox, Faith filled families later question or become attracted to falsehoods. The devil is seductive and often appeals to what appears to be "fair" and "loving." Yet his is an empty hope that relies on excessive presumption and wishful thinking.

Also, being a Catholic school teacher does not preclude similar challenges in the classroom through literature and religion, but also science. Current events definitely raise questions from the most sincere students about the seeming rigidity or paradoxes of the Faith. Personal experiences shape families as well and can cause dilution of Faith. Again, any core family may be surrounded by other extended members who are fallen away Catholics or have joined a different denomination. At the very least, neighborhood children will raise questions in children's minds and sometimes ones that stomp parents.

Then, the overwhelming majority of Catholic schools invite nonCatholics. Even at fairly solidly Catholic schools, students of many different family backgrounds may be be registered. Catholic schools have educated Protestants, Jews, Muslims, and Buddhists. Many students have come from fractured families, by divorce, battery, substance abuse, and even suicide. Again, welcoming, not as a welcome mat. Some of this is a genuine outreach with the intent of providing a loving educational environment. Occasionally it is in the hopes of evangelization opportunities. Too often, it is more questionable interpretation of "tolerance" shaded by financial concerns. That last claim seems harsh, but it is a reality for what some incorrectly perceive as a way of "saving" Catholic schools. Too often, again, in cases of acknowledging even subtly the "legitimacy" of other beliefs—not here addressing the dignity of the believer—can only serve to undermine the authenticity of Truth. It is neither honest nor loving. Furthermore, in a wishy-washing environment, neither the nonCatholic nor the Catholic student is convicted in Catholicism by the time they transition from 8th grade to high school.

One anecdotal experience illustrates this. Several years ago, a lovely nondenominational Christian requested a principal conference. She was concerned that the Catholic school was not sufficiently welcoming of nonCatholics. Everywhere there were signs of Catholicism and in various endeavors. She entreated the principal to visit the Catholic school website where her child had attended previously. She said it would inform the principal of a "welcoming" Catholic School. The principal obliged, and on the opening page was a testimony by a Buddhist parent who warmly recommended the school. *He said that the school had always made him feel comfortable (about his beliefs).* Catholic educators should take a moment and consider the ramifications of this testimony and make distinctions. For example, a caring environment that would never permit an obese person to be taunted or tormented, but it would not feed that person fattening cafeteria junk food. The former is commendable; the latter condemnable.

Yet, Truth be told, Truth must be told.

While "sin and damnation" should not be compelling students to hide in closets from the horror of eternal flames, especially belonging to a different faith, the truth *will* make some uncomfortable. Returning to the obese person, even there, certainly in any health class, the subject of nutrition and proper weight would be appropriate objectives no matter who was sitting in the room!

So, how was it that this Buddhist (who did not believe in God) felt so "comfortable" (being Buddhist)? More to the point, how could any Catholic education risk someone's salvation for a few brief years on Earth. Now, this is not to judge any nonCatholic, but not everyone is "ok" in their present relationship with God.

*The primary mission of being a Catholic teacher is to teach objective, authentic Truth that will carry students into a wise life in the city of man and then the City of God.* Certainly that entails a solid education, professionally delivered in the basics of language, literature, math, sciences, and the arts. However, it never requires a surrender of one thread of truth about the Faith.

Still, teachers cannot escape colleagues, administrators, parents and students, who may rock their world with other religions, insisting they are truthful, and that Catholic education must be nonjudgmental, "spiritually embracing" over "religiously dogmatic" with the ultimate objective to develop civic minded, compassionate world citizens to change the world for the better, not themselves for eternal life. *That is how poorly Catholics have been catechized over multiple generations.*

Now, studies could be cited to this effect, but the personal experience of many teachers in recent decades can attest to this overriding infusion of the temporal world into Catholic education over fifty years. It is obvious in public education, but there, socialism is increasingly inculturating atheism. Many are stunned at times by the audacity of parents who insist that the school must accommodate for the _____ (insert religious belief) of their children, as though they did not know they were enrolling in a Catholic school? Well, maybe it was not so Catholic or it gained the reputation of being "flexible," "tolerant, " or even flirtatious with other beliefs.

21st Century Catholic teachers will have no easy road. They should take real comfort, though, that it has likely never been without challenges. It just seems that when the unchallenged religious orders took charge through the fifties, and pastors ruled the schools, the Faith was far better transmitted and defended. Even so, great erosion has occurred. Calm, confident, courageous, committed will be required attributes of a successful Catholic teacher.

Oh, one more thing: Successful Catholic teachers will be forewarned and armed to respond. Once they know the belief systems through history and of the world today, they will be much better prepared. Hopefully this chapter will assist in that direction and provide tools and resources to stay the course. (Also see Embedding Catholicism, Sickularism or Secularism, and Catholicism Today.)

## **PROMINENT AND MOST COMMON FALLACIES AND FALSEHOOD DISGUISED IN GOOD**

*Along with belief systems associated with them*

*Heresy, Apostasy, and Schism*
*The Ghosts of the Past Haunt Still*

Ardent students of Catholic Church history will be quick to note that all slings against the one, holy, Catholic, and apostolic church mirror world religions in some way. There are numerous ways to package assertions about Truth: What—better Who—it is; what are the essential beliefs; what may be "negotiable" or non negotiable. Yet, in the finality of analysis, through time, the image of the one, true God has been evaded, distorted, or maligned in some way, but all those lies tend to deny the omnipotence, omnipresence, and omniscience of God. Moreover, looking closer one of four skewed outlooks emerge regardless of source: 1) adoration of the Earth and material being; 2) self determined and empowered destiny; 3) the reduction of God to human limitations; and 4) the elevation of man's power over God's.

**Deception from Within**

Any cradle Catholic who knows any converts can likely attest to embarrassment about their own ignorance of the Faith. On the one hand, born and reared Catholics often just accept the practices of Catholicism; on the other hand, they can be incredible naive and susceptible to other influences, even those with "good" intentions.

About thirty years ago, Tim Staples, well known Catholic convert, humorist, and Scripture scholar, noted that he had successfully pulled Catholics from the Church because they did not know their Faith, let alone Sacred Scripture. More than one former Protestant convert has boasted the same.

Yet, not all such deception occurs from other Biblical Christians. Those trusted Catholics, especially the clergy, can inflict real harm on ignorantly trusting souls. Always the two bookends of knowledge and trust must be implanted in every soul.

Setting aside the "other" world religions for the time being, it is imperative to study the different belief systems *within* the Catholic Church. *No, there are not really different belief systems within the Catholic Church* but millions of Catholics believe that it is so. So being Catholic might place Catholics in the most perilous situation with respect to

## Chapter Five: Unpacking the Religions (Belief Systems) of the World    163

knowing and understanding Truth. (Later, the evolution of man's understanding of supernatural power will be delineated historically and geographically, although many similar refrains will be noted with respect to the skewed outlooks above. Whether Martin Luther who was adamant about his intentions to challenge what he considered serious offenses by Church leaders, or a Buddhist priest who extols followers to be peaceful, charitable, and tolerant, the denial of Truth is present in both.)

Most critically, there is a better than even chance that if a Catholic educator is misinformed, that was a result of poor internal instruction and guidance. For just one example: How many Catholics do not blink an eye at Yoga and Mindfulness — not necessarily in that order —but most often twin associative thoughts and behaviors are typical?

Before Jesus Christ was buried, the detractors tried to bury Truth by quoting His previous followers! Catholics need to know, first, what were (and are) the heresies and schisms of record that continue to attack the Mystical Body of Christ. They should examine other belief systems, and the defenses of Truth that challenge them, primarily found in Church's first four general councils: Nicaea in 325; Constantinople in 381, Ephesus in 431, Chalcedon in 451 set the Creed and declared all other statements heretical (pathos.com). Aside from the Magisterium there are also the Church Fathers and many wonderful apologists over the centuries. All of that still fails to stop perpetuating lies!

Heretics did not always know they were heretics until Christian authorities defined doctrine in the 4th and 5th centuries. Also, some heretical ideas arose that reappeared occasionally until the Middle Ages, including the emphasis on the "chosen few" and necessity of full knowledge (gnosis). Today, the same could be said.

However, for the purposes of this section, twelve major heresies will be explored, and they cover the majority of error regardless and still prevail today. (History of the Catholic Church, Father Peter Kucer and other)

***Gnosticism***—In essence, this is the rejection of the material world which appears to be aligned with teaching that has us focused on Heaven. That is the deception, however. We are both body and soul, and what God has created (from all time) is good, and we are saved through the material world! (Pg 108) As the old saying goes, God does not make junk. Moreover, Gnosticism defames the Savior who is relegated to an importer of "secret" knowledge. Yet, we are beings of far more than "knowledge," and Jesus Christ is the Person of Love and Truth. Also, we do not perish just by "lack of knowledge" but sin which is the antithesis of love. Some sects of Gnosticism even dabble in secrecy and magic. It's literally a diabolical twist on that which God fulfilled in Creation and Redemption.

Another way to summarize this heresy is that it appeals to the intellect and those striving to become pure "spiritual beings." It sounds like an imagery right up the alleyway of Lucifer, a spirit that detests God's creation and most of all the creation of male and female.

***Docetism*** claimed that Jesus only appeared to be human but was actually pure divinity, and this again, is that evil jab at the Word made flesh…and all flesh. Note that this emphasis on the spiritual is also prevalent in many eastern philosophies.

***Marcionism*** was named after Marcion (85-160 AD), who erred by completely rejecting the Old Testament, believing that the New Testament superseded that "angry God" with a merciful one. What might Jesus Christ say, ironically? "You are thinking not like God, but like man." How ironic—or idiotic—that this heresy should arise when Jesus Christ quoted (knew) Old Testament truths. This shows that when people try to figure out God on their own terms, these are the types of errors made. However, we see this continuing today! People may not outrightly reject the Old Testament, but they excuse or rationalize it as though it is old news, not an integral prefiguration of the Gospel.

## Chapter Five: Unpacking the Religions (Belief Systems) of the World

***Montanism*** This heresy was aided by two women, Priscilla and Maximilla, who were cited as inspired prophets by Montanus who rejected Church authority (135 or so AD). He claimed that the Holy Spirit working through persons like them were all that was needed for Church order and harmony. And, here everyone thought the women's movement of the 1960s first brought about such pronouncements.

***Manichism*** was dualism in that there was a good God who created spirit and a bad God who created matter (re appeared in the 12th century). The notion that for the world to be redeemed, the good spiritual principle that is intertwined with evil matter needs to be released from its imprisonment. Yet, good and evil are not so evident and distinct in that sense.

***Donatism*** developed around 300 AD insisted on the holiness of ministers to validly administer the Sacraments. That some clergy may not have been courageous during the Diocletian persecution did not negate the sacramental action. Note that this is still s point of concern raised periodically by Catholics concerned that their priest may not be faithful, so how does this impact the forgiveness of sins or the consecration of the Eucharist?

***Arianism*** made the claim that Jesus is fully human but not fully divine—from this Adoptism. It was held that Jesus was not fully equal to God the Father which is noted in other heresies. Also, note how often the contemporary Catholic "reduces" Jesus to just a "teacher," a "healer," or "advocate" for social justice? That is a form of Arianism. Note that all of these heresies are extremes in one or the other perception of Jesus Christ. Poor mortals who cannot accept the dual nature of Jesus, who insist he must be all human or all God.

***Pelagianism*** held that human beings can imitate Jesus Christ sufficiently and successfully in the absence of grace. Again, we see strains of this in persons who believe themselves "saved" by mere declaration and good works in their own estimation. These persons, even well intended, reject the Sacraments as a needed source of grace.

***Apollinarism*** advanced the idea that Jesus Christ, the second Person of the Holy Trinity, did take on a human form, but had only a Divine Mind. Obviously that would not make Him true God and true man, and erodes confidence in us as persons who need to imitate Jesus Christ. This goes to the heart of those who simply can not or will not accept that they must pick up that cross and follow Him.

***Nestorianism*** contended that Mary was the mother of the human Jesus but not the mother of God (Theotokos), and that the human and Divine nature of Jeus Christ was not united in one person.

***Monophysitism*** held that Jesus divine nature overcame his human nature, and the latter was absorbed into His Divine nature. Humans simply cannot seem to grasp the unique but mysterious nature of Jesus Christ. So, as it typical, like an old radio, it needs to be taken apart again and again to attempt an explanation which is not ours to know fully.

***Monothelitism*** asserted that Jesus Christ had only one will, the Divine will. (See Quiz 6 Activity in Catholic Church History)

### *SCHISM—When differences cause a literal split.*

Schism is often brandied about when it appears that opposing internal factions cannot resolve differences in teaching or agree on authority. Three major schisms are detailed a bit below, and it becomes evident that they area about the same matters that still rattle the Church in different quarters today. Knowing what impelled the schisms helps Catholic educators to focus on that with which they must retain fidelity without getting distracted by minor differences.

For one simple example: Many years ago, there was a misunderstanding about fasting, especially not eating meat on Friday. Typical of media, the issue was distorted. Never did the Church dissolve the desirability or need for "fasting." Moreover, the focus on meat is an entire subject by itself, as there are so many vegetarians and fish lovers to make such "sacrifice" potentially a moot point. Similarly when certain Saints were removed from the Catholic roster, critics gleefully pointed to the Church's errors in ever having named them at all.

This is nitpicking, not schismatic fodder.

Schism entails major dogma.

The first major split entailed the Greek east and Latin west, largely over matters of papal authority and liturgical differences. There were differences in discipline (I.e. married or celibate clergy, liturgy (leavened or unleavened bread), and doctrine (whether the spirit proceeded fro the Father alone or from the Father and the Son.

The second major one was the Great Western Schism (1378-1417)—there rival papacies—pope in Rome and Avignon—there had been antipopes before, this was first time in history that the same college of cardinals gathered in conclave —elected one man and then months later repudiated their choice and chose another. (Council of Pisa only made it worse. Schism resolved at the council of Constance in 1414.

The third major schism was Protestantism, and the one that most still divides Christians. Though Martin Luther was excommunicated in 1520, the damage was and continues to be devastating and widespread. This was obviously huge and still plagues the world. Sadly, the premise of the schism revealed cracks in the holiness of the the institutional Church at that time, so it had real causation, but Luther and others permitted their own pride to carry away their faith to the ruination of millions of others.

## What do all fallacies have in common?

There are some common attributes of all heresies, apostasy, and schisms. One, they arise from persons thinking intellectually about the world, its origin and end; its order, and what it means to be fully human. Two, doubt develops as the human mind can only comprehend so much in the absence of Divine revelation and grace. In other words, people rely on their senses, their mind's grasp of reality, and even emotions and limited memory, to determine that which is credible with regard to their surroundings, God (or not), and life after death. Three, most frequently, faith is diminished by "self." In extreme cases, often highly intellectual and learned persons will develop concepts that make the most sense to them, personally, and will also then contort everything to fit their world view. Sometimes this results in a stringent literal interpretation of religious history and Sacred Scripture; other times, the consequential belief system broadens to be mistakenly inclusive. Four, when (and if) the self becomes the center of a belief system, "all hell breaks loose" literally. From this extreme comes such social orders like Nazism and Communism, whereby the focus is shifted to the world in a utopian fantasy. Frequently, even if followers do not believe in sin or God, they will likely delude themselves with some wonderful eternal life after death or nihilism (which makes them more prone to reap great wealth and power while they physically live.) Some beliefs like Buddhism or Hinduism recognize that there are good and evil persons, so they have grasped onto the notion that a person can gradually work his or her way to a higher, moral state but through reincarnation.

Note that in all the belief systems that defy the Magisterium of the Catholic Church—and even within certain sects of that faith!—most often there is manmade systems of forgiveness and penance almost always absent the concept of eternal hell. Thus, one hears statements like, "I have to work on myself," not in the context of grace by the Sacrament of Confession and Penance, but by gazing at a mirror and giving oneself a real talking to, or visiting a likely modernistic mental health provider.

Even if hell is acknowledged, some belief systems like Islam define and denounce sin according to human precepts, albeit ostensibly, by believed revelation of a higher power.

In other words, for millions, if not billions, hell is a myth designed to keep people in check behaviorally or for the perceived enemies of modernism and materialism (utopia).

Hell is candidly not understood even when well explained. Many simply cannot embrace the truth that there can be permanent separation from God. In all (human) fairness, it is an incredible reality to grasp. Most simply cannot perceive that Hell is a person's rejection of God, not the other way around.

Yet, imagine that someone is so in love with another, he or she would do anything, including giving up his or her life for that person. The person jilts that lover, may be even scorns, rebuffs, and maligns that ardent admirer. Then the object of that love learns that the admirer has moved away and not left any forwarding information. Is that departure mourned? Perhaps not, but imagine that the person left behind might fall on horridly hard times and never know what he or she missed. Imagine that for an eternity.

## WHAT IS REQUIRED OF THE FAITHFUL

### The Magisterium

What is the Magisterium? Definitively, the Magisterium is the two thousand year legacy of authentic and objective truth from the time of Jesus Christ, and as prefigured four thousand and more years previously. Cut away all else, everyone else, and if the world was nearly destroyed and the only viable remnant was a man, a woman, a well translated Bible, and the Magisterium dogmas, and Catholicism, the one, holy, Catholic, and Apostolic Church that would rise again.

Note then that just "knowing" a teaching is Magisterial may be insufficient. Even the Magisterium has been attacked, frequently quite cleverly. It will require a healthy balance of reliable resources to maintain balance as will be clearer at this chapter's end. Even very solid Christians (Catholics) have been misled. Christian convert Constantine the Great was instrumental in the Council of Nicaea that countered

Arianism, but there is still some questions about the depths of his deathbed beliefs today.

Given contemporary media and rapid communication (or miscommunication), confusion can reign over the most noble of our clergy.

Catholic educators need to remain steadfast and avoid pitfalls that may simply drag them into faculty lounge disputes that resolve nothing or parental conferences that devolve into debates. Simple but sound are the keynotes.

## WHAT IS NOT REQUIRED OF THE FAITHFUL

First, contrary to popular criticism, Catholics (or any Christians for that matter) do not need live in an isolated prayer cell awaiting the kingdom of God…The Apocalypse Individuals were created to find joy in this world, grow in knowledge, love, and understanding of Truth, and utilize all the gifts received intellectually, as well as spiritually. In short, it is perfectly expected to prosper. However, how Catholics live is critical to the ending. Recall how the master entrusted his coins, and how each either helped that investment grow or buried it. (Scripture)

Those destined to be leaders cannot cower; those called to contemplative prayer still must be educated in that practice; those with keen skills have an obligation to employ them for the good of all. And so forth. Teaching (and living) the City of God in the City of Man does not mean that the temporal world is disdained. It means bringing the City of God into souls and elevating them to higher aims.

Along with knowing and being capable of responding to falsehoods about the Catholic Church, Catholic educators also need to recognize those areas that do not require belief or following, practically everything beyond public revelation with the exception of declared dogma, like the Immaculate Conception of Mary. This is stated because so many hope for the imminence of the Second Coming, but children still need the teacher's aid, intent on Sacred Scripture, Tradition, and imparting Truth, not the Rapture.

Believers are not mandated to accept, for example, Marian apparitions, regardless of how evidenced. However, that is **not** to say that Our Blessed Virgin Mother's appearances—and her most Chaste and Virginal Spouse, St. Joseph, are to be denied. The Church encourages its members to accept that such miracles and God's continuing presence is quite probable, and Faith, by definition, impresses this upon the soul. The Church has recognized many as genuine, and there are many graces that flow from these devotions. Moreover, most certainly, knowing these and the miracles the Church as recognized attributed to them is most edifying. Fatima is one very much proven apparition. Nonetheless, while skepticism of the most prominent apparitions, like Fatima, is saddening and deprives the soul and mind of God's wonderful intercessions, a Catholic can still attain Heaven in the absence of grasping that reality.

This is mentioned, as recent turmoil has led to some unproven events; several persons claim to have visions or a share in a prophecy doom. The End Times are cited with greater frequency, as fears of the Great Reset rule passions. (See The Eternal Kingdom vs. Global Power.) Now, there is reason for concern, but not panic. Catholic teachers must be the calm, reflective and reasoned persons in the room.

The Faithful do not have to pray in the manner of their neighbor (Holy Mass and the Sacraments) aside. They are free to be involved in various ministries of the Church. They may disagree in politics unless the disagreement is about a nonnegotiable Commandment or law of the Church. Many wonderful Catholics bring an array of suggestions, based on their personal and professional experience that others may not be so inclined to pursue.

Furthermore, many saints, including the Apostles, have tussled with one another, experienced disagreements, and some quite extensive, since the origin of the Church. Yet, they remained faithful to the central tenets.

As for various religions, many books have been written, but this section will focus on reliable Catholic Church references and historians. Major sects will be identified historically and by region. Some will be grouped together as they are very similar in their main teachings. None will be maligned, but Catholic teachers should be able sufficiently knowledgeable to spot the errors in each and be forearmed, not to create disputes or oppose other adults in their educational environments but confident in their own evangelization.

**Globally—through time and space.** *See Christopher Dawson's The Age of The Gods and Progress & Religion*

ANIMISM and PANTHEISM

When addressing "man" this is intended to encompass woman and all creatures, including those scientifically identified as hominids. However, it is not the objective here to discern every nuance of human existence, as previously addressed, but to better grasp the many factions of beliefs about the extraordinary and the supernatural. Now, there is only speculation about Adam and Eve and their descendants to some extent. We assume they were aware of God, but having been expelled from Paradise, it is most likely their intellect was darkened and their conscientiousness of the Father dulled. They endured concupiscence. To what degree is difficult to pinpoint though God did speak to them, and even when the murderous Cain complained to God that he was not his brother's keeper, Cain was assured that he would still be marked by God's protective seal.

Still, was this true for all human-like beings? Was there a point when very early descendants of Adam and Eve (especially from Cain) grew even more distant from the one, true God. At that juncture, it can be assumed that ever since such men walked the Earth, they sensed startling phenomenon over which they had no or little control. Numerous aspects of life must have puzzled him, yet with an (increasing) intellect, he attempted to resolve their origins and how to master the elements. By his senses and passions, coupled by imagination, it is not difficult to understand that "some" entity—some "power"— had to be attributed to a might force or forces. Nature, itself, became the source of deification. The sun was a major one, along with the sky's offerings of the moon and stars, constellations. Interactive dynamism such as thunder and lightening, tidal waves, and earthquakes all brought about a primitive respect for environmental phenomenon.

From that point, the "gods" were born, first presenting themselves in the objects themselves and then brought to distant, aloof, plateaus or places like the mountains, skies, and even bodies of water. A dominant spirit lived in (all) nature and inanimate objects.

Again, this is not about figuring the minds of beings who lived tens of thousands of years ago, but to understand that in the absence of the illumination of Truth itself, man would have conjured up his own sensibility about the environment in which he lived, starting with the elements of wind and fire.

**Man like Deities —Early Myths East and West**

The next progressive step would have been to ascribe human like attributes to the "unknown." This is seen in both eastern and western civilizations, some cultures imitating each other in these endeavors. What may be most quizzical is the aversion to one, true God and so the devil was in the works for sure. As Father Ripperger so intricately relates in *The Introduction to the Science of Mental Health*, the human person is a complex being with sensory receptors, imagination, memory, and intellect. So man, depending on his knowledge and understanding and to what degree, will rely on those senses, memory, and imagination to think about his surroundings and make conclusions about even its mysteries and self.

In our limited knowledge of tens of thousands of years past, ironically, we can only imagine how man perceived the world, its origins, and its destination. There are some artifacts and anthropologists and archeologists have confirmed some of what people used to belief, including an afterlife of some sort. Yet, most of what we have to study are myths.

Father Peter Kucer explores these in his books on civilizations but also in his church history, and to sum up:

It is natural for man to seek "order" out of "disorder." Something inherent in us acknowledges that there is order. Moreover, even pagans who pondered life extensively, like Aristotle, had to conclude there was a "first cause"—something or someone (Prime Mover) who created all ensuing life. So, major cultures have had theories about Creation.

Jewish people believed according to Genesis; Christians embrace that story of Creation yet augment it with other Truth, including the Triune God (Three Persons in One God), and that the design was to be peaceful and harmonious prior to the Fall.

Any deviations or contradictions had their source in satan. Again, satan is the disrupter, to whom our first parents listened with tragic results, but that is not how God desired our lives, and it is not how eternal life will be. However, the impasse for many persons is what is required to gain that eternal life. Many either in ignorance (lack of knowledge and grace) or by self will, insisting against all reason to the contrary, cling to a false perception of not only this world's origin but what will follow death, having one's cake and eating it, too.

Yet, to the myths, some showed startling similarities to the Catholic Christian belief.

## Man Denies One True God and Eternity

In some way, and from the beginning, man has denied or opposed God and Eternity. Put differently, people want to know all and have power over their own lives, including the storyline and main characters. If they can control the narrative, three objectives are met. One, they can act according to their own will. Two, they can act godlike. Three, they can change the "ending" to one that suits their fantasy. That some of this is a consequence of having been deprived of sound teaching is beside the point.

Then there are persons who are "good." Good is impressed on everyone's soul, so that even without encounters with Christianity from the first, some people will be…good, of sound temperament and oriented towards love and truth. One can perceive that in some persons of all creeds.

Thus, stated differently, some people are more Catholic than some Catholics.

So, when examining different beliefs, teachers can look and acknowledge that which conforms to Truth, but also knowing that which does not by its absence of good, commonly known as evil. This is most evident in the dogmas of any faith system, so there may be similar teaching but with fatal flaws.

With predominantly Eastern civilizations, religion began to mirror a denial of life after death or at least as all three monotheistic (Jewish, Christian, Islam) religions know it. These include Hinduism, Buddhism, Zen, and other Eastern schools of thought about divinity.

The Japanese creation myth (Father Kucer) notes order out of chaos and three divine beings called the Three creating Deities.

The Norse imaging of creation is far more convoluted but encompasses all types of bizarre figures but also a first male and female. Yet, there is a succession of powerful figures, often attacking one another and metaphorical references to the physical features of Earth. However, it at least proves that there are expansive boundaries to human imagination.

The Greeks also noted that the universe was originally chaotic. A tale of night and day with the light of day bringing forth earth, Gaea, is described. Still night played havoc, producing doom, fate, death, sleep, dreams. A multiple of gods wrestled with each other, as earth went through upheaval at the start. Yet, like the Norse and other myths, these powerful figures were all too human, and faith, hope, and charity were absent.

The Babylonians boasted seven tablets of Creation, some of which reflects the Christian belief in God the Father and Son, but in the case of the Babylonians, it was only one god, Anshar who made his eldest son into his own image.

Aside from myths about creation, there is acknowledgment of good and evil attributes, but none are comprehensive or completely compatible with the Catholic Church, and none emphasize virtue grown by free will in cooperation with grace, let alone the path to salvation.

(Again, it is not the intent of this Primer to delve deeply into these other beliefs but to highlight some similarities and differences based on previously mentioned effects. For more in-depth information, Father Kucers "History of the Catholic Church" and his books on Eastern and Western Civilizations pour forth more detailed information.

He includes the Catholic understanding of history, though, and there are numerous other references in the Resources and Bibliography for teachers to explore.)

**Man Becomes God-like**

While one can at least understand various civilizations and cultures taking the wrong road to the fullness of Truth, it should be emphasized that this most occurs due to man's weaknesses and vices. For anyone genuinely seeking Truth will find it. (Scripture)

From 1 Kings, 12-13, Jeroboam, first king of the northern Kingdom of Israel, (922-901 BC) had no excuse. His was a decline into evil, turning his people back to the bullocks to preserve his own rule. He knew better or should have but chose his own self deification.

Still, less leeway should be granted those who detour or denounce Truth for self empowerment. See the sections on history and government. Also, many belief systems, including Christianity have been "used" to justify or at least excuse prejudice, hatred, theft, injury and murder. This only proves that all the "i's" can be dotted and all the "t's' crossed, but evil under any other umbrella is still evil.

This is likely the biggest stumbling blocks for highly intelligent and influential persons who have the power to change the course of history. They would be like gods, and it matters not their background — Hitler was baptized Catholic—nor their geological location, Xi Jinping in China, nor their era, as it is happening today. Those who seek deification are driven to ignore and bury their consciences and ruthlessly demand thrones. So darkened are their minds that they truly do not grasp that the temporal world is passing away, and those in hell will be forever forgotten, left to their eternal torment.

*Freemasonry*

Freemasonry is a prime example of a movement that has darkened Faith for centuries and continues today. This self empowering organization crosses time, nations, and demographics with members that would surprise many Catholics. It is absolutely anti-Catholic, materialistic, and self worshipping. Incredibly, many Catholics (and not a few Jews) have clamored to be members, as though they could mix "oil and water." Catholic teachers would be wise to check their family tree for the spirit of Freemasonry and participate in a Family Tree Healing. One anecdote: Recently a Catholic revert was approaching death from cancer. He had been a Freemason but never sought "deliverance" from its evil effects thinking it was unnecessary. He received the Anointing of the Sick, but his family noted that it required incessant prayer, and being interiorly compelled to turn away—not to watch him face to face— during his last hour, while they heard horrible growling sounds. Prayers intensified. Then the room calmed and the man passed as short time later, but obviously satan considered this man's membership in the Freemasons to be an eternal bond. Had he not turned back to the Church (and St. Padre Pio) and been favored by a very spiritually alert and prayerful family, who knows?

When in doubt or if in ignorance, teachers must learn Holy Scripture, the Catechism, and the Magisterium of the Church, the latter being the immovable cornerstone of Catholic education.

## *In the Contemporary World:* The presumably harmless or helpful religious beliefs

Though the one true faith has been demonstrated and evidenced despite controversy and conflicts over the past 2,000 plus years, the world persists in advancing Eastern spirituality, Islam, Judaism, many sects of Protestantism, numerous offbeat strands of ideology regarding the supernatural, and even agnosticism and atheism. It is typical that proponents of religious freedom will even insist (and judges concur) that satanism—the antithesis of what has always been defined as religion—be legally accepted as a "religion."

Most of these alternatives are defended as harmless, at worst, and helpful, at best. So, it is worthwhile to examine these in the 21st Century.

### *Eastern*

Note that Eastern religions have infiltrated the West in astounding ways. Transcendental meditation abounds in every sphere, as a means for relieving stress and anxiety. Mindfulness, and other aspects of Eastern belief systems, seem gently empowering of spirit, but they ignore the one true God and tend to instill in persons that they possess abilities to cure themselves and become healthy, spiritually as well as physically by sheer will power, not His Will Power.

*Buddhism* which is actually a multi stranded group of beliefs that are common in the denial of God, too, appears peaceful and loving. Many modern Buddhists have drawn world praise for their serenity of spirit and adherence to benevolent attitudes towards their neighbors. Catholic school teachers may well have a student in their classroom at some point whose parents are Buddhist. Unless there is direct contradiction to their beliefs, the outcome may be rather comfortable for the teacher and school. However, if the Catholic teacher, especially a religion teacher or teaching religion, mentions certain Catholic truths, especially older Buddhist students may balk or angrily contradict the teacher.

*Hinduism* is often confused with Buddhism, but there are stark differences. The idea of reincarnation sounds appealing but it lacks any basis in reality and leads millions to presumption and eternal death.

*Protestantism* There are so many denominations and non denominations that it is impossible to review all in light of the Catholic school teacher. Suffice to say that the most challenging tend to view Christian life as that which focuses on material well-being with the assumption that anyone with "good" intentions will be saved. The current media, including movies and other entertainment reinforce this. Beware of a Catholic school that boasts a "Christian" mission. While it is true that not all Christians are Catholic, but all Catholics are Christian is not to be misinterpreted that Catholicism is just another Christian sect. It is the fulfillment of Truth with apologetics, no apologies. Unfortunately, many Christians, albeit well intentioned, absolutely believe that Catholic schools should accommodate their teachings—not just be welcoming. To provide pure solace to a partial believer, one who does not possess all that is true is selfish and often a sign of a school that focuses on the bottom line rather than the end of the line. That does not mean that these schools explicitly and overtly strive to do this, but there is considerable rationalization. Moreover, many Catholics actually believe more in generic Christianity than authentic Catholicism.

One plus is the historical compatibility with Protestantism in most of Scripture. Catholics boast seven more Sacred books and have since the Council of Nicea (AD 325). Too bad that Protestants simply discarded that which did not meet their modern standards including the books of Wisdom (See Wisdom through Church History).

William Bennett's *Tried by Fire* recalls the story of pre-Reformation Christianity's first thousand years, and it is a valuable resource for religion and history teachers, as that is pre-Reformation. It underscores the shared beliefs if all Christians, and such stark realties as the Blood of Martyrs seeding the Church (3rd Century Tertullian)

Bennett describes the immense global impact of Christianity on the world and the manner in which it dethroned kings and toppled false gods, forever changing the dynamics of political thought and civic conduct, raised virtue over vice. He covers the major figures of those eras from the early Christians to the Church Fathers and even the ensuing councils.

Like with other beliefs, the older the student, the more there may be in class confrontations and follow ups by parents.

*Jewish* At one Visitation school in the 90s, a Jewish student would enjoy a visit by the Rabbi once or twice a week for instruction. He lived across the street and was a wonderful soul. His young charge otherwise attended all the classes and daily Mass.

There were students of other beliefs at the school as well, and for the most part, the authentic Faith was taught with few hiccups. One Protestant student asserted that she was going to wipe off the ashes on her forehead on Ash Wednesday, but after being advised to simply remain in the pew, she changed her mind. Furthermore, no student who did not believe in the Real Presence of Jesus Christ was compelled to genuflect.

*Islam*

The Muslim influence has become increasingly difficult to navigate, as Islam is more likely to be publicly accepted than Catholicism. Indeed, not just a few Catholics consider Islam to be actually a heresy. Again, though, there are attributes of this faith that are congruent with Christianity, and, ironically tenets more aligned with Catholicism (abortion, same sex, transgender issues) than with Protestants or Reformed Jews. Also, there are many what some would describe as moderate Muslims who are aligned with the softer, more community oriented, and "charitable" aspects of Islam.

Still, those commonalities cannot disguise the incompatibility between Catholicism and Islam or Islam's history. While Christians often exceeded the boundaries of appropriate conversion, Islam was always, at its core, about compelled conversion. Even when it permitted nonbelievers, those were taxed heavily and then eventually persecuted, imprisoned, or killed.

The tenets of Christianity never espoused such extreme measures; it was individuals or groups that either misinterpreted or exceeded their authority in such matters.

Also, Islam, like some other religions is economic based despite its promise of Paradise

## *The Ultimate Heresy; the Final Schism*

With the rise of Industrialism, the move from an agrarian to an urban society, and the so-called "progressives" that determined that man could reach utopia by scientific and intellectual pursuits, faith, as we know it was increasingly engined by the notion that man was inherently good as a cumulative directed and driven mass. Of course, this required some persons in controlling power, oxymoronically absent God.

Christopher Dawson in *Judgment of the Nations* succinctly notes that unlike other dark periods of history, our current age is not distinctly good vs. evil. It used to be that despite all the hardships man could bring upon his fellows, the presence of authentic good was clearly identified. What has evolved over the past nearly two hundred years now is the blurring of evil and good. Worse, vice is hailed as good!

The media praises the bold politician who preens herself; looting and arson are acts of justice; defunding police is equalizing; being wealthy (even among some mega churches) is a sought after and reportedly worthy objective; gluttony is excused as genetically induced; envy is a sign of healthy emotionalism; being embittered is cathartic.

Even hundred years ago, abortion would have appalled most believers regardless of denomination. Today, abortion is even celebrated as heroic? One group claims that they have spoken with their unborn children and that these children have agreed to be aborted for the mother's sake. Some hold signs explicitly calling for killing children in the womb.

Marriage even in primitive cultures was between a man and a woman. Pagans may have explored same sex relationships, but not presented themselves as family. The most ignorant knew it required a male and female to procreate.

Vocabulary itself—language—the basis for all civilized education is maligned, distorted, and disfigured. Viability means life without any dependency; vaccinations are simple gene therapy; gender is whatever the individual deems him or herself to be.

Catholic teachers need to be well read but also guided by trusted Pastors, Deacons, and others in the Church who know and have experienced the fallacies, many appealing. Sadly, Christianity itself can present pitfalls, as so many claim to be Christian, even Catholic, but their words and actions belie that they hold fast to Faith. Moreover, there are very "nice" people who perplex the faithful by notable charity, yet concurrently hold anti Christian opinions on abortion, marriage, and other critical issues of the day. The difficulty is in being kind while not capitulating. Or being overly demure.

During a controversial situation at one Catholic school, one very wonderful teacher followed the principals direction on teaching about the anti-Christian content of a novel that had been introduced in error, the principal's lack of oversight. She was cooperative but admitted that she was conflicted about the matter because it appeared to be a negative appraisal of one of her peers. No amount of assurance completely erased her ambivalence, and it may have been likely that the students picked up her hesitancy. To paraphrase a popular movie, it often seems like this is "No Country (or World) for seasoned Catholics."

It will take very strong Catholic educators to stay the course during their tenure and for life.

## TOOLS, LESSON(S) AND GENERAL RESOURCES AND MATERIALS—UNPACKING RELIGIONS OF THE WORLD

**TOOLS**: Again reading, listening, observation. Yet, most important will be knowledge of the Catholic Faith via Magisterial teaching and trusted commentary. Prayer is essential along with trusted colleagues. A "cheat sheet" checklist with the Apostles Creed would be a tool idea.

**LESSONS:**

*Primary Lesson*: Fulfillment of Truth vs. Shards of Truth vs. Absence of Truth

Create a table; across the top show categories for every major belief system in the world, including atheism. Down the left list all the characteristics, tenets, teachings on the one, holy, Catholic and Apostolic Church. Use subsets of beliefs. For example, Islam will show a recognition of and devotion to Our Blessed Mother, but not that she was the Mother of God. Place a green check or a red negative on each tenet. If the particular belief system actually opposes a belief, fill the category with a black mark.

From this table, all types of activities can be created like Jeopardy, Bingo, and Matching

*Secondary Lesson:* Create a double bubble or Venn diagram comparing Catholicism with another religion. Use the Apostles Creed for the compared attributes

What are some similarities; what are some differences?

**RESOURCES**: A Catholic Bible; Copy of the Apostle's Creed always handy when the subject of religion may arise. This needs to be studied. *Catholic World Report* (current reporting on departures from the Truth)

Books by the Very Rev. Peter Kucer (Western and Eastern Civilization and Church History); Other Church History (The Brothers of Mary); Avila Institute; Catholic Textbook Project; Phillip Campbells's four-part series, *The Story of Civilization*, Brant Pitre's wonderful works that bridge the Old Testament with the New Testament.

Writings of well known converts: Scott and Kimberly Hahn; Tim Staples; Ronda Chervin; Dr. Paul Thigpen; Dietrich and Alice von Hildebrand; Cardinal Arinze, Dorothy Day, and of course, the Saints.

Other well known Catholic Converts (See *50 Catholic Converts* by Matthew Bunson (Catholic Education Resource Center—CERC)

# Chapter Six

## UNDERSTANDING CONTEMPORARY CATHOLICISM

*Building Pathways to Truth and Love*

This primer includes addressing teaching in a deficiently catechized age and how to research for authentic Catholicism as well as relating secularism to Catholicism. All of these topics are intertwined in some way but also differ.

For the Catholic teacher who was reared in the Magisterium of the Church and may feel even patronized by a course that focuses on how to teach in a wounded Catholic world, this particular topic may seem redundant as well as unnecessary.

Yet, "Catholicism Today" moves beyond the reality of a significant number of Catholics who believe themselves faithful but are, in fact, not well formed. Moreover, it transcends the concept of secularism but being fully aware of it and its impact on Catholicism and the world. Finally, the balance of authority has shifted. Now, acknowledging that parents are the primary authority in their children's lives, and should be respected in that role, what is happening today in many Catholic schools is not so much the exertion of authority, as much as opposition to the Church on one or more fundamental issues. Moreover, instead of parents advocating for their children's thorough education, and pursuing how they may help, they often literally voice themselves as "consumers" and become enmeshed in complaining about non academics or the absence of specials, and the like.

*In the late 1950's, a WWII survivor Catholic teacher would stand in front of an incoming class and announce, "Your parents can go to the Pastor; they can go to the Bishop; they can go to the Pope, but I am in charge of this classroom." (Or words to that effect.)* In those days, the Parish often subsidized Catholic schools that were well staffed with nuns who often lived at a nearby convent. $50 per family annually was reasonable tuition, even given the time period. It was understood that the Pastor was the ultimate "principal." The Baltimore Catechism was often the textbook for religion; prayers were said frequently throughout the day, and the reverence for the Sacraments was impressed regularly.

Fast forward to the 21st Century and Catholic schools are most often overseen by an Archdiocesan Office of Catholic Schools, operated similar to public in policies and procedures, and even teachers now receive a step pay contract although lower than public school. Parents pay thousands of dollars, often well above $7,000 annually per child, nuns are rare and likely out of habit. The Principal is the laity, and maybe the Pastor has a genuine say in the school, but most likely will often be invited for prayer or to deliver some religious instruction. Still, neither parents nor the teachers may necessarily respect, let alone, like the Pastor. Furthermore when there is dissatisfaction, it may well be in a letter to the Archdiocese.

Whereas in the 1950s, Pastors could lock their church doors on late comers or bar them for immodest dress, today, they are advised to be understanding and "tolerant." How ironic that it took the COVID 19 Pandemic to lock the church doors, but complaints were nonexistent from many. Homilies? The Pastor decades ago might openly rail against sin, but today, especially if it is a school Mass, the advice is to focus on "good neighborliness," nonviolence, and filling the food pantry. There are exceptions, of course, but more often than not, the celebration of the Mass almost completely obliterates the Sacrifice of the Holy Mass.

Put a different way, teaching truth can be a stand alone exercise, but it will never be fully successful without understanding why today's Catholic Church is not only fragmented but, as some claim, already schismatic, if not schizophrenic. Also, contemporary Catholicism baffles the mind and soul beyond just the explanation that we live in a pluralistic world and therefore we must be secular in our governance. In the regard, Reilly's *America on Trial* with the prerequisite of philosophy can help illuminate the extensive and myriad tentacles that have choked the Church—always meaning the Mystical Body of Christ—

within the institutional, human driven meaning of Church. Hillsdale College offers a wonderful array of courses to provide philosophical background, as well, to help Catholic teachers understand how we arrived at the troublesome juncture in which we find ourselves.

On the one hand, the explanation is quite simple; on the other hand, the effects and their origin are identifiable but for complex reasoning (or lack thereof), almost inexplicable. After all, history and its repetitive rises and falls of civilizations and fidelity to Truth to guide, yes? However, as it will become evident, multiple factors can contort reality via means of the transmission of culture and education.

To illustrate this dramatically, visit the enormous 2004 tsunami that killed over 200,000 in fourteen countries along the Indian Ocean coast. Some speculated why a warning was not issued, based on the significant regression of that coast line waters preceding the tsunami. Picture of people casually wandering the extensively deep shoreline seemed not have aroused concerns. Yet, if one studies folktales and the like, we see how lessons of nature are passed along generationally. In this case, experiencing the dramatic pull back of ocean should have alarmed locals and sent many sounding the call to flee to higher ground. So what happened here? Was there a "generation gap"—did people assume understanding of these phenomenon through public education or that such common knowledge no longer needed formal instruction? Now, that is not to make a claim that this would not have been a catastrophic event anyway, but how many more lives may have been saved?

This is like *any* teaching. Unless some matters are *explicitly* taught, almost tirelessly and persistently, our descendants will fall for clever ancient ruses in the name of whatever.

Most importantly, if a Catholic teacher does not understand Catholicism today, he or she will not be an effective evangelizer. This is not promoting dilution of the Faith in any way, but the acknowledgment that there are millions of Catholics comfortable in their understanding of "truth" not in any small part due to supposed authorities on the Faith from educated laity to high ranking clergy since at least the mid 1900s

Who is today's Catholic?

The 2020 election certainly throws easy identification into a quandary though confident Catholics well catechized would deny that. The argument, though, could be made that it does not matter what anyone thinks or even knows if many do not know or reason. That a knowledgeable Catholic may want to tear out his or her hair at the incredible acceptance of a tinsel form of faith also does not matter. This is the reality of our world.

Catholicism is no longer "universal."

Furthermore, the claim that misinformed or miseducated Catholics really know better is simply irrational. The truth is inscribed in the hearts and souls of every person, but their spirit may be blinded or even darkened. Nor is it just to assert that these perspectives are a ruse by people who are merely seeking the easy way or power may also miss the mark. That may be true, and for some a convenient cover, but that is not necessarily apparent for many. Oh, at some very deep level, there is a churning of that embedded knowledge, but they do not recognize it as such, and they experience that nudging as the assaults of rigid Christianity. That is why there is so much rage, too.

How many are simply baffled that very powerful persons like Pelosi and Biden, just to name two, are absolutely convinced they are devout Catholics—not just Catholic—but devout and still promote—not just remain neutral—promote abortion that has claimed 63,000,000 in this nation alone in the past fifty years. Yet, it does not stop there, and they and other Catholics in office insist that marriage can be between two men or women? They shrug at disorder and lawlessness unless it hits their front door, literally.

Consider, as well, the students in a Catholic school who return home daily to a different faith world than the one you present in class. They may challenge you or, even worse, simply ignore you. Their parents may describe some teachers to their children as fanatic. In the worst cases, a principal or other superior may ask a teacher to explain a parent complaint about a particular session on the Faith although most often, sin. This occurs in the most orthodox schools, by the way, and there is really no escaping from today's Catholic who … is not orthodox.

Here is a look at today's multi faceted Catholic in different ways and from different perspectives.

## *The 19<sup>th</sup>-century Impact atop Other Skewed Perspectives*

In the beginning…although we hold that there is no real beginning as God always was and will always be, a mystery that throws folks off through history. Still, at the start of humankind, though this particular primer will not delve into evolution and the like, man with any intelligence and reason determined that there were powerful forces beyond their comprehension that had the potentiality for help, hinderance, and harm. Over much time, humans moved from a world bound orientation to acknowledgment of gods to the revelation of one God and the Holy Trinity.

One would think, and this is where people always get into trouble though, that it would be a grand progression of illumination and that a grand society would evolve along with the understanding of Truth, and all would live happily ever after…on Earth…at least until death…and went to another much more wonderful Heaven, authentic progression.

In some ways, that is exactly what people think should be, but they are ever grasping at the earth bound utopia though the true meaning of utopia was not for temporal existence. Still, could people not have all found some common shared life in the meantime?

Three reasons they continue to aspire and then destroy what they have made here in a continuous cycle of achievement to devolvement and finally collapse—whether in what Reilly calls the pre philosophy age (America on Trial) or in 2020. One is Original Sin; the second, concupiscence; and, three, Satan and his minions. Compound that by significant materialism, a false gravity towards the temporal world, and a skewed sense of empowerment.

Original sin is removed by baptism, but each is in a weakened state, subject to temptation, illness and death, and corruption. For Catholics who fail to recognize this or believe themselves to be "saved" in a post Protestant-Catholicism or think themselves good Catholics because they live in accordance with Acts 4 or Mathew 25: 31-46, this is not even much of a thought. Quickly, it must be interjected that even faithful Catholics, the daily Mass attendees and frequent communicants can deceive themselves into a self satisfied bubble. The latter often think themselves good, and do good, but are weak in evangelization and may even discourage conversion by condescension or subtle scorn. The Litany of Humility is a recommended daily recitation.

Concupiscence impacts all Catholics, from the most ignorant to the greatly knowledgeable, and the delusion that can arise from those extremes again tend to destabilize even orthodox parishes and communities. Again, it must be stressed that this does not mean that the Truth can ever be diluted. However, the manner in which we present ourselves and that Truth can either renew or destroy whatever remnants of Faith may be present in a soul. Catholic teachers must reflect on those times when they may have been ignorant, truly or by obstinate self will. None has lived perfect lives; many are reverts having lived in blindness even for decades. Exploring those times in one's life and asking, what would have impressed or persuaded oneself to think differently about Catholicism, can open understanding. Teachers may ask close genuinely Catholic relatives how they perceived them when away from the Church, That might produce some "ouch" moments, but they will be worth their weight in gold if it helps steer a teacher in approaching parents, peers, or students clasping wrong directed ideas.

### Chapter Six: Understanding Contemporary Catholicism

Satan is on the prowl—has been since the dawn of mankind and will be until the end of this temporal world. He does not rest. C.S. Lewis in *The Screwtape Letters* illustrates the perpetual cunning of the devil and his minions. Teachers may want to pause here and think about that vice or bad habit that they are attempting to overcome and replace with a virtue. How many times had anyone said, "I did it again!" With the world, ones self, and the devil, all have much to overcome. Now, teachers should show mercy to the Catholic who is a lukewarm or confused but not in a way that compromises truth. As an aside, having a St. Benedict medal and other sacramentals nearby and for prayer reference may be advisable.

Also, reexamine history since the dawn of God's revelation to and Covenant with the Jews. (See The Eternal Age vs. Man Constructed Ages.). Record impressions with each deception or downfall. Which factors were at work, knowing that pride is a given? Strive to detect that the challenges of the temporal world invite human solutions though that is not in itself a bad thing. Note individuals who rose to power for themselves not the good of the other or the common good. What devilish details were in the minds of those who eventually brought division, war, and the attacks on the Church? Always, the vices are present—the seven deadly sins—always—though also always packaged as some rationale for an end utopia, appealing to often marginalized persons and populations.

Yet, in every age, the engineers of change somehow always think themselves the first cause of utopia. In America, the unraveling of morals and subsequently natural law did not have its origins in the 1960's "sexual revolution," but in the preceding century. By some accounts, the decline began by the 1830's, but certainly as Americans advanced industrially and urbanization significantly outpaced ruralization, the die was cast. Although secular, *The Scarlett Sisters, Sex, Suffrage and Scandal in the Gilded Age* explores the radical lives of two such figures, Victoria Woodhull born in 1838 and her sister, Tennie Claflin born in 1845. Their family was atypical to be kind, and the author notes that Tennie "would never know a normal childhood." (Myra MacPherson, Twelve Hachette Book Group, 2016) Regardless, they had followers and imitators, and "progressive" women revere them, as classical models of womanhood.

INDUSTRIAL AND TECHNOLOGICAL AGE IMPACT — The fracturing of family and community; from family and extended community to self and isolation

Rapid transformation of America following the Industrial Revolution, coupled with an enticement to seek "riches and fame" in urban areas led to many societal ills that were already present in various civilizations across the world even before the Birth of Jesus Christ. However, the rapid rise of cities and some disenchantment with agricultural life resulted in the multiplicity of temptations and fallen souls.

Students of urban history are most likely to discover that city life, from the mid 1800s, publicized exaggerated opportunities while breaking up families and incentivizing malicious politicians. Tens of thousands of immigrants, fleeing persecution, illness, and death in their European homelands, aggravated all the ills of that time period.

There are many resources for a teacher to read for full understanding of the negative impact of rapid urbanization, but it is not the objective of this text to go in-depth. Suffice to say that the Church was very much challenged by all the affected Catholics, and the early 20th century movies that depicted idyllic parishes with wise pastors and capable mother superiors seriously glosses over what was occurring underneath in the belly of any city. Of course, one can lose his or her soul in any environment, and that has been demonstrated, but just note the topics of encyclicals since the mid 1800s, and the issues that arose with anti Christian solutions become apparent. Today's Catholic is likely a descendent of those early major city dwellers. Generationally, their wounds have passed along, sometimes buried in family secrets, but damaging all the same. Unresolved, unreconciled, unhealed family trees have produced rotten fruit, even unwittingly.

Today, we are living in the Technological Age, and that has had both blessings and curses. As background, realize that teacher families—even homeschool teachers—likely will contribute to unique circumstances requiring continuous monitoring and healthy responses. Few families are cohesive on how and when technology is acceptable or beneficial. Yet, even in families that significantly limit television, computer use, or other cell phones, those around them will somehow present frustrating scenarios. Digital is more invasive and deadly than COVID-19.

How to address these requires advance knowledge and skill. Teachers should check out helpful resources, assist schools to subscribe to regular workshops for teachers and parents, and never assume that any child under their care cannot reach the forbidden sites. Also, dispel the assumption that Catholic adults will always agree with faculty. Contemporary Catholics who have been misled can be tougher to convince than others. Just recently, a controversial Netflix movie, "Cuties" brought accusations of censorship against protesters. Incredibly in the face of what could only be described as child pornography, that such a position dared to be advanced should shake everyone. And one can bet, there are some Catholics who defend the film.

They are victims of the creepy-crawly but soft footfalls of the devil. Mary Cuff in an insightful *Crisis Magazine* article "Disney Has Been Corrupting Kids for Decades" traces the diabolical decline of Disney. The scariest conclusion is that there will be still many Catholics who will roll their eyes and assert that Disney is just playing the politically correct corporation, and *their* children will not be adversely affected. How ironic in that Cuff's piece underscores the eventual demise of the "toad in the heated pot."

Thus, generational patterns are set and intensify with passing time. However, one might just as easily point to Adam and Eve, albeit acknowledging the respite periods following God's Covenant with Israel and then the establishment of the Kingdom on earth and the rise of Christianity.

## THE CONTORTION OF PHILOSOPHY AND ITS EFFECTS

Early philosophers like Socrates, Plato, and Aristotle brought forth knowledge about the unknown in unprecedented ways and how we can think about God that latter supported monotheism and the great government experiment known as the United States of America. Even Cicero of Rome, who significantly and positively influenced St. Augustine, was pagan but knew of God.

Yet, man is prone to the trappings of the intellect that cloud the soul. Others emerged and led to unraveling of some sound principles previously established. There are numerous such agents though one is hesitant to crown them with the title of philosopher as that implies a lover of wisdom. They include but are not limited to Nietzsche, Camus, Engels/Marx and Foucault Hume, and Descartes. Others followed suit, and the thinking about who we are as persons—if personhood is even acknowledged—and any supernatural being or origin—was tossed on stormy seas.

Not all was lost, as other great minds have rescued us since from the disorder, confusion, and doubt. Still, millions of souls have been misled, countless perspectives of truth and faith proposed, and the insidious pursuit of utopia on Earth continues.

Hillsdale College offers engaging online courses, their Introduction to Western Philosophy among other great options. They are not Catholic, but they host Catholics and are not hostile to Catholicism. While a donation would be advised if at all possible, the courses are free. Most importantly, they are well organized and presentable even to those who may not have a background in philosophy. (Explore other courses, too, such as history.). There are also many Catholic thinkers who are themselves genuine philosophers or write brilliantly on that topic. (See the Appendix for notable authors and publishers.)

Chapter Six: Understanding Contemporary Catholicism 195

## *APPROACHING THE POORLY OR UNINFORMED CATHOLIC OR CHRISTIAN IN LOVE*

### GOOD INTENTIONS; POOR OUTCOMES

One would think that by 2023, we would know all the devils tricks and masks. Repeatedly though, either through ignorance or excessive reliance on one's own power, we misidentify, ignore, or reject the threats. Like always, they have emerged and evolved gradually until what is "good" appears "evil," and what is "evil" appears "good." Still, there are ways and signs for astute teachers to recognize, avoid, and counterbalance the ruse.

First, know that the average Catholic today has likely never been taught not just the Faith but with right reason. Laity taught them religion, often from a textbook with a teacher's guide. There is nothing inherently wrong in that, but two concerns. One, the teacher, him or herself. Was he or she well formed in the Faith; did they live and defend the truth of the Faith in all ways; were they even perhaps angry or bitter against the Church for what they are convinced? Furthermore, the kind, patient temperament of a teacher does not necessarily indicate a solid inner core or sufficient knowledge and Faith development.

Now some think that teachers of younger children may not do much harm in this regard because lessons are rather simple Truths, and a teacher's private life is not subject to student scrutiny. The thinking is that teachers can successfully navigate away from that which may confuse students. On that latter point, many years ago, a ten year old student was in a class where his teacher introduced her boyfriend. The young lad promptly went home and scoured the phone book and discovered that both the teacher and boyfriend shared the same address. Imagine what children could do with the Internet today.

Moreover, there are those precious Sacramental classes of First Reconciliation and Communion. If those are misrepresented, the effects can be lifelong. A teacher who is struggling with conscience may not be able to hide that as well as he or she thinks. Also, a conflicted or falsely thinking Catholic parent who, likewise, has issues, may attempt to manipulate these Sacraments and teachings, diluting their reverence.

The second consideration is that religious texts vary in their orthodoxy. Again, some are not "bad" per se, but they fail to ignite reverence and sanctity in recipients of the Holy Eucharist and Confession. Today's Catholic, from administrator, to teacher, to parent, may not know this. An educator's obligation with respect to today's Catholic is to ensure that the fullness of Truth is taught. Yet, this is no easy task, so anticipation is a healthy reflection. Knowing the truth and foreseeing potential situations are key. (This is covered in a separate section "How to Teach Teach Truth—Forming Eternal Citizenship.")

The problem goes deeper, as deception is widely known but now excused or diminished in value. This is not new, as Socrates (469-399 BC) died for the same darkness. What was his crime? He was accused of corrupting the youth of Athens with…truth. Basically, that was it. Socrates challenged the notion of the gods, strived to instill morality…virtue…and for this he was condemned to death. If there is a difference or twist today it is that people, including self professed Catholics rank the importance and nature of behavior to fit a comfortable suit.

However, this is where one has to be so cautious. People, for the most part, truly believe they are pursuing good; they believe themselves to be good…and right (not to be confused with the political meaning). Catholic teachers, regardless of frustration and eagerness to set matters on the path to Truth, know that for many Catholics today, they are convinced they are on the right path. Moreover, they are equally convinced that orthodox Catholics care more for their rituals and rules and towing some imaginary line of faithfulness—but indifferently— towards their imagined eternal reward. They may be sure that the person crawling on knees towards the Tabernacle is for show. They may think that women who wear veils to Mass certainly are doing so to demonstrate outward piety. They demand, incessantly, where are those strong

Catholics to help the woman in a crisis pregnancy or ensure that the immigrant is welcomed. (Screwtape loves it!)

However, we *do* have some Pharisees in the Church, but not all who strongly espouse abortion as a foundational issue or cite Thomas Aquinas on immigration are such. The real challenge is to convey that to those who, at their core, are experiencing a tug of conscience—whether they identify it as such—that a wholesome Catholic can and must be both a minister of corporeal works of mercy *and* spiritual works of mercy.

Too, it is essential that the poor outcomes of an imbalanced faith life—whether primarily stressing Matthew 25: 31-46 or Mark 7:6-8 be shared with students. The Church is not part and parcel believers; they must embrace the Word and Sacred Scripture in its cohesive entirety. However, humbly admitting that poor motive and self interest can enter the heart on the most controversial issues among all Catholics is necessary, as is the reality of the devil and the world.

Incidentally, though not popular to mention, the poor are not without sin, and the wealthy can be most generous servants and saintly stewards.

It would be helpful to have those noble examples, such as the kings, (persons of royalty and wealth who gave away their belongings) available for student reading regardless of your subject area.

## THE PERILS OF GENERALIZATIONS AND THE FAILURE TO DISTINGUISH AUTHENTIC DIFFERENCES OF GOOD AND EVIL

Today's Catholic may also be so global as to miss the beam in his or her own eye. Teachers will most likely encounter Catholics who demand that their children participate in all types of good will events, like food drives and purchasing water wells in Africa. They tend to heed general "good," but overlook or miss the subtle nuances in the details which may well be seedling for evil.

Now, it is not the purpose of this text to call out anyone or judge anyone's heart and soul, but there are glaring examples that cannot be referenced vaguely or opaquely to illustrate that the general good can never justify sin. They include prominent people and organizations and authors and publications. Sadly it includes clergy. (See Appendix) Their motivation may mitigate the culpability, but I am not God, so this text will adhere to that overriding principle that no good can come from evil. The following is not exhaustive but describes some of the most egregious false alliances with Catholicism. Here are two basic generalizations that fail to discern that good cannot arise from evil.

*Generalization: If one is helping the poor, all other considerations are secondary.*

The Gates Foundation is one such organization. In the misleading Jesuit magazine *America*, August 5, 2019, Melinda Gates' struggles with the Catholic Church are reviewed, especially with the conflict between seemingly charitable acts and Church teaching. In 2012 the Bill and Melinda Gates Foundation pledged $560 million to increase access to contraceptives. Melinda Gates defended this action as "following her conscience" and "putting her faith into action." Parenthetically, educators will be likely challenged similarly.

Teachers will hear "but the group does so much good, " "or it is impossible not to have some differences of faith working with various organizations serving the poor." False! There are numerous organizations that help the poor and remain faithful to the Magisterium of the Church. There is never an excuse to *knowingly* compromise with grave evil; there is no reason to do so.

As a postscript on the Gates Foundation, natives in those countries they provide contraception and abortion are often appalled at the audacity of an American enterprise to disrupt their way of life in such an intrusive and counter culture manner. They have even been accused of being colonists.

## Chapter Six: Understanding Contemporary Catholicism

*Generalization: _____ is so bad, any means of eradicating _____ is justified. (Fill in the blank with racism, sexism, xenophobia, homophobia, and even capitalism.)*

Politicians, academia, and non profits are likely the most famous for this line of thinking, and there are many Catholics in those ranks. Of course, there are degrees of this rationale, and one could respectfully agree that some discomfort, as long as it was not evil, may be necessary for a greater good. Many laws have been added to the books to bolster this argument. One example that comes to mind immediately is that no one can drink and then sit in our vehicle with the key in the ignition but sleeping at the wheel. If caught, the person faces face criminal charges, fair or not, whether our intention was to become sober before driving home. That point was comically made in an "Everybody Loves Raymond" show.

Yet, others are extreme to the bad and hurt innocent people or those whose religious conviction strongly compels them to appear discriminatory when, in fact, that is not their intention. Today's Catholic may or may not sympathize with this type of rebel. The baker in Colorado comes to mind. Here was a man who simply wanted to bake with a clear conscience. He had never turned away anyone for their sexual orientation, but he held that marriage was between a man and woman. Furthermore, he could not contribute to such ceremonies in any way…to be complicit by his very labor. This does not even take into consideration that while making such a cake, he would have to decorate it against his will. Imagine forcing a photographer to take pictures of nude couples. (Oh, wait, there may well be such a case pending!)

Yet, unbelievable, this man was attacked even by some Catholics.

These matters will arise regardless of teaching environment, if not in person, through books, texts, and other media, with colleagues who seem to be orthodox but will surprise teachers when you least expected.

*It is a mantra but educators must Know—capital "K"— the Faith...pray for that discernment that either closes the argument or leaves some openness. Teachers: stock that library and have plenty of resources and faithful Catholics along your journey.*

## THE COMPARTMENTALIZATION OF FAITH AND SELF ILLUSION

This may seem like the previous topic, but it differs in one major way. These are the Catholics who deep down sense something askew but will evade or mask that discomfort to live in the absence of conflict or delude themselves that they are being "peacemakers." This latter group of misguided Catholics can be the most problematic, as they are most likely quite loving and faithful for the most part. Still, they will hold back or even attack if associated with Catholics who have definitely split their faith and prioritized the corporeal works of mercy in a pluralistic, temporal world. The worst of these may well be those who scorn the piety of orthodox Catholics and even charge them with hypocrisy and rigidity. These mixes can be quite explosive.

Finally, teachers in God's Light will need frequent, lifelong examinations of conscience. This will be lifelong.

Again, prayer is the foundation of any Catholic teacher's life. Nurturing Faith is a never ending process, and trust.

## *ESTABLISHING BOUNDARIES: NON NEGOTIABLE VS. FLEXIBILE*

*When Truth is Attacked in the Catholic Classroom*

Step back forty or so years, and the most serious challenge in Catholic schools was likely the single parent. At one time not necessarily uncommon, there was still a stigma associated with a divorced Mom or Dad. There may have been other matters to navigate like substance abuse or psychological issues, but chances were that the majority of

## Chapter Six: Understanding Contemporary Catholicism 201

schools were affiliated with the Parish, boasted teaching nuns and classrooms with mostly intact Catholic families. Fast forward to 2023, and Catholic schools must walk a lethal minefield of same sex couples, transgenderized children, pro abortion parents and teachers, and anti-religion sentiment. Now, COVID 19 has struck at the heart of education everywhere, and Catholic schools are not exempt although many did and continue to offer safe, sane refuge. Moreover, schools will be bombarded from both sides. Too, it is not unusual for the parents to go straight to the Bishop!

So, it is virtually impossible to avoid challenges to Catholic teaching regardless of environment, and whether it is considered modern or orthodox. In the former case, modernism, teachers will encounter parents who may have chosen a Catholic school for its academic excellence, security, and stability—ironically—but disagree with some aspect of the religious instruction. Many have been steeped in the "sick"ularized world from childhood and honestly may be so conditioned to certain rights that they have a difficult time discerning truth. That so many in public life: elected officials, judges, and government employees claim to be "Catholic" only complicates their reasoning and confounds them. In the latter case, orthodoxy, parents may expect a monarchial administration that oversees every aspect of the classroom, and in ways that may seem genuinely archaic. By the way, similar types of friction can develop between pastor and administration, administration and faculty, and among faculty. Daily, teachers may be perplexed about how and when to speak or act.

Generally, these complex challenges appear in one of six ways (excluding the Archdiocese): Pastor vs. School; Administrator vs. Teacher; Administrator vs. Parent; Teacher vs. Teacher; Teacher vs. Parent; Teacher vs. Student. *See scenarios at the close of this section, along with some example situations to work through after reading accounts based on real life events.*

However, these scenarios will illustrate that there are no quick, easy solutions—sometimes there is no resolution. Why? Typically, there are few straightforward responses and resolutions. **While Truth must be**

**upheld always with conviction, confidence, and courage,** there are may wounded persons in our midst from all walks of life and in all professions. Their children are being reared in homes that could benefit by spiritual guidance but also compassionate charity. It is likely that family understanding of the Catholic Faith has been influenced by Freemasonry, Marxism, and superstitious spirituality, or ignorant about needed filter systems in the way of multi media devices. Still, the Church must be the overseer, and given a solid catechetical program, excellent curriculum, and instructions, parents should be cooperative (or leave), and students should be docile (willing to learn). With respect to Truth, failing to maintain the red line in the sand may topple a school for all the wrong reasons.

Catholic educators while stuck in the controversy, confusion, and disorder, must nonetheless temper zeal with love. Reactivity can actually do more harm than good, as that is often sourced in fear, anxiety, and occasionally righteousness. (*As a special author's note: Lived that and hopefully learned by it.*) Again, this must be stressed: No compromise with the Truth, but also no conditions on Love. Compassion means to suffer with, and there will be times that fidelity requires faith that God will assist to resolve knots in our Catholic schools. Our Lady, Undoer of Knots, will be at the forefront, too.

Just to be clear, though, teachers should know, though, that not every encounter will end well. Life is not a two hour Movie of the Week where the crisis is resolved in that time frame, and the villain is always defeated. Sometimes, no matter the kindness, patience, spiritual support, and flexibility on negotiable areas given a family, they will leave furious and disgruntled and perhaps leave a trail of destruction.

One gnarly area is the admission of nonCatholics to Catholic schools. This is covered elsewhere, but it bears repeating. Anyone should be invited into a Catholic school **if** that family and student(s) understand that the Faith permeates all subject areas, and there will not be any compromise on any Magisterial teaching. Furthermore, combativeness, counter-reactionary behavior, and actions that undermine, if not threaten to destroy, the integrity of the school will not be tolerated. It is prudent to meet with those parents and share the curriculum, if not have them sign their acceptance of it, especially in religion and liturgies.

Three final points: One: teachers should not over anticipate difficult situations or pick quarrels. On one occasion, cupcakes were sprinkled in multiple colors, like a rainbow, and, of course, the temptation was to muse if the activity was "pro gay" rights. Sometimes, a horse is just a horse, and a rainbow is just a rainbow. Unless there is something truly nefarious, as revealed otherwise, it is best to assume the best. Two: there is the reality of authority. Teachers are responsible to God for what they impart to students, and must be knowledgeable, in a developmental way, as to what they teach even about social issues and current events. If their superiors (pastor, principal, superintendent) directs imprudent instruction that falls into the non negotiable spectrum, they may have to risk their position. In areas of negotiables, such as what must be included on all prayer tables, hopefully, those can be resolved with a candid but respectful conversation. Teachers will "meet"many saints (if not already) who suffered questionable directives from superiors but could submit without compromising the Faith. Three: teachers are not responsible for the actions of others. God did not call teachers to judge colleagues but to live in truth and love. A prayerful teacher will ride the wave.

## *Real School Conflicts*

SCENARIO ONE: When a Catholic School is not faithful to Church teaching as presented in the teacher interview

*An excited applicant asked her primary question: Was the school supportive of the Pope (who was considered orthodox)? "Oh, yes," was the response, and there was evidence of that in the choice of religion textbooks and overall environment. Yet, within a couple of years, administration was leaning towards more relaxed teaching, including the distribution of contraceptive literature to "share" with the youth who were reportedly sexually active.*

The teacher was in a quandary. The brochure was not directed to be given to students but quietly handed by the principal to the teacher for that possibility. Then the educational culture changed more with even faculty of two different religious orders being openly critical of clergy and more traditional Catholicism. A student identified as likely "gay" evinces some faculty lounge snickers, and overall, the sterling spirituality plummeted.

<u>What could the teacher do? What should the teacher do if staying the course fails?</u>

In the above scenario, the teacher quietly stored the brochure in a desk drawer and continued to teach the Faith. She responded to challenges with a spirit of fidelity, but in one other episode knew she was risking her contract. That was a disagreement with the Pastor over the students' right to a veiled confession, rather than face to face. Eventually she departed the school for other family reasons. Though in one way relieved, she reasoned that she had done her best to "stay the course" and teach and promote the Faith, and unless compelled to act against conscience, she would have remained.

And that last conclusion is KEY. Catholic teachers will not always be in optimum positions although it is hoped they will intentionally seek to teach in schools that adhere to the Magisterium of the Church. However, as stated more than once, a perfect world is not terrestrial but heavenly. Unless, ordered to disobey the Church, the discomfort teachers experience with a wobbly administration and peers, may still bring witness to students who would not otherwise have the fullness of truth.

Chapter Six: Understanding Contemporary Catholicism

SCENARIO TWO: When a Pastor contradicts School Administration

*A popular Pastor engaged the intermediate grade students with wonderful humor, answering questions with quick quips that had them excited to eagerly raise their hands. He was considered to be a faithful priest and known for many solid homilies on various contemporary issues. Then one student inquired about Harry Potter, and to the principal's shock and dismay, he admitted that it was one of his favorite series. He even recommended them though the principal personally discouraged them in the school.*

What could the principal do? What should the principal do?

There are few more contentious areas than literature and popular entertainment for educators to navigate. To further complicate the matter is those who favor "open book" schools may well be well-reasoned, faithful Catholics. Yet, they bristle at what they consider censorship. Also parents, in particular, will insist they have authority over that matter and love that their children are reading. That teen sons would read Playboy with even greater enthusiasm does not phase them. That stated, there was little the principal should have said in the moment for several reasons. One, the students either already had permission for that series, or not, given the particular climate of that school. Two, this was a Pastor for many of the students, and the timing for challenging his enthusiasm would have backfired, anyway. Moreover, addressing it later, given his unreserved endorsement would not likely have had any impact but to create an unnecessary chasm. Three, there was the possibility that the question was a loaded one from the start. (Harry Potter has received mixed reviews from many good Catholics, so it was an easy bone to pick.)

What the principal could do and did was create an approved book list for whole class reading, utilizing the Dominican Sisters of St. Rose of Lima in Tennessee. She also buttoned down how books were to be selected and approved for any classroom. Her explanation was simple and true: What parents allowed at home or for private reading was their responsibility, but a Catholic school had the moral and theological duty to offer literature that would enrich students and assist them on their life journey in search of the true, good, and beautiful. Furthermore, not all students are sufficiently mature or well formed in their Faith to filter novels that might entice them to false dogma and even, candidly, the demonic. It is the duty of a Catholic school to be the gatekeepers in these incidents.

Regardless, teachers should be prepared for ongoing, heated discussions and surprising acceptance of the most egregious fiction and nonfiction, some actually atheistic. They should not be surprised to find such even on an Archdiocesan book list.

SCENARIO THREE: When Teachers Group Together to Oust a Faithful Teacher

*The eccentric teacher struggled with classroom management and organization, but was otherwise an outstanding Catholic who loved his subject. Yet, the other teachers quietly mocked him, and, individually, several approached the principal to relate his inefficiency and consider not renewing a contract.*

What could the principal do? What should the principal do?

First, this does happen, especially in school sites that have had an imbalanced understanding of authority and boundaries over an extended period of time. Certainly, if a teacher poses a danger, a prudent peer would quietly but conscientiously report it to his or her superiors. The principal may be open to that which is provided in confidence and charity. Yet, regrettably having to communicate a significant concern is one thing; to "gang up" on another teacher and advise outcomes is quite another. Furthermore, there are many laws and Office of Catholic School policies in place that protect everyone on school sites, including teachers. Unless a serious offense has occurred, and despite no guarantee of a contract, certain steps must be taken to correct an erring teacher. Besides, it is the just course of action. Moreover, the reporting teachers were hardly faultless themselves.

In the above scenario, everything was done to help guide the teacher, and he admirably attempted to correct his faults. Sadly, though, the "bad press" and increased gossip that moved to parent circles proved to too much. He graciously resigned at the end of the school year and pursued working with a different population of adults in need of assistance. However, the residual impression only further damaged the school's cohesiveness and camaraderie. For in such an environment, it is often, "Who is next?"

The principal should take concrete steps in internal policy to discourage such inappropriate collaborating to remove a teacher. Ironically, more than one of the teachers who instigated the negativity were no longer at the school a year later.

## TOOLS, LESSON(S) AND GENERAL RESOURCES AND MATERIALS—UNDERSTANDING CONTEMPORARY CATHOLICISM

### TOOLS:

Build a library, especially with short articles on matters that may arise in a classroom with parents, administrators, peers, and students. Develop a "general plan" of response in the case of a controversial issue or confrontation: identify the issue; clarify understanding of what what said or understood; inform administrator; arrange student and or parent meeting depending on the nature and severity of the conflict. An administrator may develop a school wide "response."

### LESSONS:

*Primarily Lesson*: The Derailment of Faith—timeline 150 years ago and recent 60 years. Compared to Old Testament; Renaissance, Enlightenment. Identify similar patterns of dissent and compare to today;

person or persons who clarified and resolved conflict...or not...and why not? How do contemporary apologists address history and how it may be "repeating" in our time? Role play with a peer on an "argument" by a student or parent that would require explanation or response. Practice demeanor and, based on individual temperament, how and what to anticipate. A choleric teacher disputing a choleric parent may lead to some firecrackers.

LESSON PLAN ACTIVITY. (Discuss and record what the participants could or should have done. It would be helpful to have administrator input in the way of school policies and regulations.)

Some more scenarios to those above:

SCENARIO FOUR: A parent insists that a religion teacher not teach about sin.

SCENARIO FIVE: A student is spreading disinformation about a teacher based on overhearing his mother talk with another parent.

SCENARIO SIX: It is openly acknowledged that a teacher who professes Catholicism is living with her fiancé.

(THERE ARE MANY MORE)

**RESOURCES:** *The Catholic Thing;* The Catholic Catechism; Scripture; Lepanto Institute; Religious Institute; *Voice of the Family;* Women of Grace; Catholic Answers; First Things; Crisis Magazine

Catholic School Playbook; Institute for Catholic Liberal Education; Holy See's Teaching on Catholic Schools—The Seven Marks of Catholic Schools (for researching potential employment sites)

# Chapter Seven

## RESARCHING FOR RELIABILITY
## (SECULAR AND SACRED)

**A teacher—whether in the crucial role of parent or in a classroom setting—will be ever searching and researching for reliable information and insights on living the fullness of Faith authentically in Truth and Love. However, that will not be his or her only challenge. All information *in every subject area* has been tainted by cultural revolutionary content and language. Even grammar texts do not escape as vehicles of indoctrination.**

That was boldfaced because there are no perfectly complete, perfectly compiled, or perfectly comprehensive sources of information. Time and space limit the scope of any communication or record. Human error and prejudices, shortcomings, and (candidly) ignorance taint even the best intentioned persons. By "ignorance," it is meant that any person's knowledge is limited—no one "knows" it all though some are better informed in some areas that others. Moreover, for some, certain aspects of governance, history, culture, or the branches of science or math appeal to their sense of "mission" or expertise. Like feeling the proverbial elephant, educators must navigate their instruction with questions and qualifiers. Even Holy Scripture can be humanly distorted, edited, or misinterpreted though often with "good" intentions. History informs us of treachery in imparting the Faith.

Then there are intentional maligners! Most recently Critical Race Theory, itself theorized to be massive bunk topped by a grain of truth about racism, is actually foisted on students, in addition to all the falsehoods—no—evils of "sex education" that was the trial run for this latter movement. It makes sense that fostering an environment that coaches rebellion against the sanctity of the body and entices youth to seek physical pleasure without consequences would also darken the intellect in other matters.

It is an arduous journey and one fraught with difficulties at times. Rarely are the lines between worldly truth and falsehood so clearly distinct. A teacher may trust a source but then be bombarded by another source, *also trusted*, discrediting the former. Teachers will be challenged by concerns in "tone" or rigidity, or, the opposite, some one or article being overly compromising and falsely tolerant. A credible voice might devolve; a formerly trustworthy publication, blog, or website may veer off course (or conversely straighten up).

How do teachers navigate in a world filled with millions—billions—of loving Christians convinced of their own perspective on Faith and how to live it? What can a teacher do with secular materials now even overtly imbued with anti-Christian "messaging" or relativistic selectivity in what is included? "Elevator music" and buried indoctrination can be missed in our harried world of education.

## *The Crisis of Indoctrination—inside and Outside the Church— Need for Vigilance*

There was *never* a time a teacher could "rest" from the threat of misinformation. Textbooks have never been perfect; newspapers and other periodicals often sacrificed objectivity for sensationalism; politicians have always been self-interested even if they were inspired to "serve the public interest." Catholics have been frequently at odds with one another even at the Parish level. In other words, communication has always been subject to manipulation, deceit, and most recently censorship in someone's best interests, usually for the benefit of the ego or the wallet.

The Church has experienced the same, and it lead to the great schisms in history between East and West and Protestantism. Today, there are grave concerns that an impending chasm is growing between the orthodox and "liberal" Catholics, and that the Church will be a mere remnant of itself in the near future…if Jesus Christ does not come back in His Glory before then.

Chapter Seven: Researching for Reliability (Secular and Sacred)    211

On that last point, as previously stated, Catholic teachers—prospective teachers—are cautioned not to focus or dwell. The end of the world has been predicted since the beginning of the world. The Apostles during Jesus's lifetime fully expected His imminent return at one point. Periodically, visionaries and astute Catholics have heralded the end as well. Often, there are convincing arguments, drawing from Scripture and other private revelations. It does not matter.

God is in the Present. Catholic educators must be there with Him. So, that means being wholly aware and informed about who is saying what, where and when, and why? This is no easy task, as trusted Catholic news organizations have been questioned, and there is no shortage of critics about any major issue facing the Church. Who does one trust, and is that in every situation? What are the hallmarks of questionable communication? From where is it most likely to arise and when? How is the communication developed? In other words, does it leave more questions than it answers? Why is something communicated and to whom? All of these are critical questions and require a checklist of sorts.

Yet, the primary indicator will be the content. Does it advance vice or value or virtue?

*The Hallmark of Vice*

Social media giants like Facebook, TikTok, Instagram, Twitter all advance vice. Oh, they disguise themselves in a friendly mission statement. They insist that they strive for accuracy and the good of humanity. Furthermore, they often support "worthy causes." Yet, looking into the background of the founders and CEOs, and one finds an underlying advocacy for abortion, same sex relations, trans gender transformation, and a dirty laundry list of other evils. All of these sites are quick to cancel accounts, remove postings, and otherwise intimidate the naive users if they stray from the path of false liberation. Openly Catholic posters may be especially targeted although Catholics are becoming savvy about how they post certain material so as not to be tracked. (Politics are aside, but these same sites will often harass anyone who espouses conservative views.). Still, the question remains, why support these enterprises at all? Should not all good Catholics log off and close accounts?

Some will argue, and it isn't entirely wrong, that their accounts are a good presence on an otherwise dismal site, and that they can share some solid teaching and healthy stories. Many Catholic enterprises, including outstanding parishes utilize Facebook for live streaming Mass and other events. They would be hard pressed to find an alternative. It is not the purpose of this Primer to debate the absoluteness of any one source of exchange or news, but to forewarn teachers that this can be a minefield.

*Value vs. Virtue*

Some other sites and publishers may not quite hit the mark. They are frequently conservative and espouse healthy values, but they are not necessarily virtuous.

Virtue, virtue, virtue should be the overall objective of all education. Teachers will succeed if they emphasize virtue in all subjects. It may seem that some, like math or science escape this oversight, but without math skills, economic principles cannot be applied; technological aptitude declines, and even the simple appreciation of beautiful geometric design goes unattended. Science may devolve into mere investigations of how man has discovered and mastered (or attempted to master) the forces of nature, the composition and operations of the body, or climate control. Absent virtue, vocations in these fields risk becoming temporally oriented.

One wonderful resource is *Good and True Media* who define themselves as "a family media company dedicated to inspiring children to live virtuously." Numerous authors, including Catholics contribute their books to this site. Of course "values" are imbued throughout healthy children's literature.

## Chapter Seven: Researching for Reliability (Secular and Sacred)

Still, there is is some caution about those venues that only emphasize value, as they may be a mixed bag literally that lean into political persuasion. Values and virtues are somewhat similar, but if one creates a double-bubble map or Venn diagram (See Lesson at the Chapter end), and teachers will readily understand the distinctions. The virtues uphold healthy values, but not all values uphold virtue.

For one example is the newly minted *Brave Books*. While presenting a series "dedicated to bringing real American values that endure," this endeavor is confined to "conservative" culture values. It is useful for story time and some discussions about individualism and community, but some of the noted topics (on the back cover) may not be for "innocent" eyes. Savvy children, as young a five may ask, "What is gender identity"? "Cancel Culture"? "Critical Race Theory"? "The right to bear arms"? A children's book should be just that with accompanying material for the teacher or parent.

Now to their credit, *Brave Books*, a rather new endeavor launched by a sincerely concerned father, founder Trent Talbot posted an informational YouTube on how to teach concept topics that brought in more of a virtuous emphasis and cautioned against introducing high level concepts "out of the gate."

The benchmark that should be used for all material is: Does it boast, pinpoint, and uphold virtue or not? Even bad news history has the potential to impart lessons, but virtue must be the standard by which these sad episodes are taught.

By the way, not all that is old is good, and not all that is new is bad. Not every gesture of the contemporary Church requires extinguishing, and traditional practices still need to be taught in understandable and appealing ways. As just one example although the course will delve into numerous other ones over time and geographically, is the narrative about General Custer. In *Our Pioneers and Patriots,* a 1940 text about our nation, and republished by Tan in 1994, General George A. Custer is portrayed as "our best Indian fighter" against the Sioux who were "well armed and they were wild with rage." The connotation is obvious even if not entirely inaccurate. Likely this was not a deliberate attempt to cover Custer's prideful character, as much as it was the prevailing conclusion at the time and without all the modern research tools at hand today.

Fast forward to the Catholic Textbook Project's excerpt "Slaughter on the Little Big Horn": June 25, 1876, and the student learns a more objective account, one that portrays the General is a less favorable light having disobeyed orders and the Sioux as having had their reasons for rejecting a land deal. (*Land of Hope and Promise: A History of North America*). This just demonstrates that any historical account, especially one popularized by the majority at the time, deserves re-examination. Also, the fact that Custer was not the daring darling fighting savagery does not alter the fact that a number of Native American tribes were brutal. Early missionary saints in the "new land" were martyred despite simply seeking the good for Native Americans. Some were tortured, even after successfully living with a tribe for awhile.

Also, as was foretold two thousand years ago, by Jesus Christ, Himself, there are wolves among us. Church history, accompanying secular history needs to be taught developmentally but accurately. Some will gloss over the grave betrayals; others relish in exposing the sins of the Church and Church leaders. However, the tendency today is to hammer the Church, from all sides and from inside. What intensifies the situation today is that there are overt attempts to denounce, if not destroy, the Church's Magisterial influence. So, knowing both current events and history, as mentioned in another chapter is vital for every teacher, regardless of instruction level and subject.

### *Barometer for Reliability*

On the most practical level, all educators would serve their students best by establishing certain baseline expectations, a checklist of sorts:

1. The five W's and H, basics of journalism: What was the information published; who published it? When was the source published and why? Where was it shared and how? All of these provide

insights as to the background of an historian and his or her motive, especially if that goes beyond the state of informational. How sad that just recently major media outlets are jostling about what constitutes "news" and what that should not only entail but how it should look to readers and listeners.

One most illustrative example of this exploration for truth is in *Degenerate Moderns* by E. Michael Jones who exposes the fallacies and evil of the infamous Alfred Charles Kinsey, "the collector of 4,000,000 gall wasps and compiler of 18,000 sex histories,' who "liberated the conscience on all matters sexual in the latter 20th century. ("The Case Against Kinsey," pg 83). Jones painstakingly roots sources of misinformation fostered by the Kinsey Institute and its promoters, verifying or disputing various claims. His is a prime example of not simply accepting what is published but unpacking the myriad layers that often accompany an accepted "fact" after years of repeated deception, sometimes done without ill intent, but likely sympathetic allegiance.

2. Has the information been verified by at least two other credible sources? Better if at least one source is not "content friendly." Those without strong bias or even opposing viewpoints are more trustworthy. Agreed that this double checking can be time consuming and irritating. Why can't there not be ONE source upon which to depend. If it is any consolation for teachers, there has never been ONE, outside of God, but he does not run a social media site. More frustrating, Catholics must often wait for someone to pick up the ball and correct misinformation.

Some years ago, Rodney Stark wrote *Bearing False Witness—Debunking Centuries of Anti-Catholic History*. Non Catholic Stark wrote from deep frustration as an historian. His work serves as both a beacon and sign of hope in today's highly anti-Christian propagandist environ. However, those examples are few and far between, likely because many people want to think the worst of Catholics.

This is not "personal" but by attacking Catholicism, opponents strive to discredit them on the most important issues of the day.

A trickier task is to check footnotes. The Coalition for African American Pastors, now Coalition of Americans for Action and Principles (CAAP), published a book, *A Dream Derailed*. A critic pointed out an article that disputed some of what was claimed in the book and with footnotes. Yet, taking a deep dive into those footnotes revealed that the critic was unwittingly skewing the book's statistics. Furthermore, when investigating footnotes in *A Dream Derailed* by Rev. Bill Owens, the respondent detected authentic verification. So, sometimes, a fact is accepted by citation, but footnotes by themselves do not necessarily "endorse" a perspective. One also suspects that footnotes often add attractive cover to alleged facts…or falsehoods.

Speaking of…

*Just Facts* is a non profit institute dedicated to publishing comprehensive and rigorously documented facts about public policy issues. One of its "standards of credibility" is the use of primary sources, including the investigation of footnotes to determine if the citation matches that declared in the body of work.

Also, by expanding to that which is stated directly and explicitly by any source, teachers may discern that "interpreters" tend to either exaggerate or hyperlink certain positions by those they quote. Mining can be time consuming and arduous, but how trends begin are often the fault of "philosophers" documenting history. Moreover, there are few areas in our modern world that are not subject to conclusions built upon personal opinions. Even the most conscientious among us have tendencies to become not merely reporters but "movers" of public attitude and policy.

Catholic education has been one of those areas most impacted. There has been tension in America between the public domain and the

Catholic since Catholics first set foot here. (In the 20th century, matters worsened with the O'Hair related cases that removed any prayer from public schools.) Despite this stark difference, it is still a struggle to steer Catholic parents to authentically Catholic education, and many actually embrace the entire secularized ("sick"ularized?) — no, antichristian—environment in the "name" of toleration and understanding. Yet, leading Catholic educators may be at part to blame, as the more "liberal" history—not classical liberal—of Catholic education has been advanced over time. Even the name of the overarching organization: National Catholic Education Association (NCEA) mimics the public counterpart: National Educational Association (NEA) in more than title. It is as if Catholic educators sense the need to exert their expertise and delivery of a comprehensive educational system that includes all the necessary principles of language arts, "social studies", science, math, music, and the arts. Thus its own history is subject to closer scrutiny.

In *Parish School: American Catholic Parochial Education from Colonial Times to the Present*, a National Catholic Education Association (NCEA) Centennial publication, Archbishop John Ireland is portrayed as a most liberal bishop who was adamant about the unification of public and Catholic education on some level. He thought that the best approach to public education was to acknowledge its contributions to society—free education—and noted it had a praiseworthy place in American culture. Yet, in Ireland's "The Church and Modern Society" Volume 1 (1896), while acknowledging he has "no quarrel with the educational work of the State. (Pg 247), further admits that the schools and colleges of the State, "however, give no place to religion in their programs; and my ideal school is the in which secular knowledge and religion truth blend together in inseparable union." He sympathetically notes the demand for public schools to be nonsectarian. In short, Archbishop Ireland found himself in that familiar double bind of the State being bound yet accessible to all, but he would also build up the Christian school and Christian college. He also said "All knowledge is deficient which does not lead men back to God, the Author of all being; that does not show how all things fit into the general workings of a Supreme Providence." And: "So important is religion in the formation of character, in the cultivation of morals, in the preparation for the life of eternity, that, when possible, it ought to be taught as a daily lesson, and with all the force and diligence which the most skilled masters possess. It ought to be taught so as to be indissolubly connected with other affairs in life, and be sunk so deeply into the souls of pupils as to be made part of their very nature." (Pg 250)

Contrasting Archbishop Irelands exact words with his quotations in *Parish School* provides needed depth as to this Archbishops's thinking on education. He is no way diminishes the essential necessity of religious education. Nor does he conclude that a public education is sufficient by any stretch, but that some benefit is to be found for those students who have no other access to general education.

Research, especially beyond others' research, no matter how well documented, can make all the difference in facts and understanding of a person, event, or circumstance.

3. What is the nature of the information in scope and detail? Even, what information was used? "The Imaginative Conservative" published an article on the late Dr. Walter Nugent (November 2021). In it the author Bradley Birzer praised this historian's exceptional scholarly aptitude. Dr. Nugent employed economics and political theory and incorporated social science and literary tools. Most importantly, he taught Birzer that research is a fine art that extends beyond books, magazines, journals, newsletters and newspapers. Dr. Nugent brought in census and insurance records and instructed in how to locate the most obscure statistics.

So often there is insufficient time to explore, but just having the awareness that much may be omitted, often unintentionally, or added, perhaps intentionally to the scope of knowledge may be sufficient in most cases. At least, teachers may pose questions, like: Do you think this person (event) is fully explained. What other

Chapter Seven: Researching for Reliability (Secular and Sacred)  219

questions or points would you like to pose? How would you expand on your knowledge of this person (or event)?

4. Is the information and how it is described subject to change, or updated, with new discoveries or changes in cultural mores and language? As noted with just one former folk lore hero, General Custer, glossy tales can blur a multitude of sins. However, one can go too far, as poor Christoper Columbus and even St. Juniper Serra have discovered from beyond. Balance, knowing that human beings all have imperfections, faults, and defects and subject to their temperaments, is crucial. (Obviously, Jesus Christ and Mary aside, though even they have been contorted in history!)

Those who explore family genealogy may all be nodding heads at this juncture. That docile great grandmother may have had five husbands; the adventuresome uncle popped up in a news article relating a murderous brawl. One of the funniest shows featured sibling psychiatrists who boasted their belief of royal despondency based on a valuable artifact. Later, as the plot developed, it was discovered that their ancestor was actually a chambermaid who stole the piece in her flight to America.

Modern technology—the Internet—instantaneous news—"fake" news—maligning news should all contribute to the increasing desirability to pause, reflect, and check, and then double check.

Even a small word can affect meaning to an entire story. Recently, the term "bully" was discovered as a 1920s news article descriptor about a man who otherwise was well-liked and widely respected. Puzzled, the reader investigated the etymology and learned that "bully" in the 1800s carried a positive connotation and could refer to the superiority of something or formidable size of an individual. These startling encounters could apply to many words. Teachers should use care in dictionary searches, as well as reading for meaning when exploring history. Etymology is one of a teacher's best allies!

***Still, the greatest checkpoint for truth and accuracy is our Faith.*** Those who are ignorant will even lose faith.

First, knowing the Faith is a non-negotiable, albeit a lifelong study. Particularly crucial is knowing the magisterial tenets. The Magisterium is the inflexible, immutable "brain" of the Church. Numerous resources detail the horrible consequences that follow a man's brain that attempts to circumvent or otherwise distort thinking with real reason illuminated by Faith.

Second, there is the "heart" of the Church which admonishes individuals who attempt to impose the Truth in a way that can unnecessarily, imprudently, or unjustly kill wayward children. This can be in the form of personal judgment, most often arising from personal pride and assumption of one's own superior state of grace.

Third, there is the "body" of the Church which moves in compassionate charity with persons willing to sacrifice their own creature comforts and truly walk with the poor, the ill, and marginalized.

All of these are attended by myriad individuals and organizations; fostered by edifying communications and movements; administered by doctors of the Faith; and monitored by knowledgeable philosophers (lovers of wisdom). None are perfect, some are better than others, and all are limited by space and ability to cover all needs.

Still, some, despite grand names and glossy mission statements, and some good, are dangerous to souls. There are others that mask devious agendas under the guise of furnishing water wells or animal breeding and the like. (Who would think that *Save Our Children* would actually promote deadly policies that kill children?). Their temporal (even atheistic) affiliations compromise Truth to the detriment of those they strive to assist. (Catholic Relief Services remains embroiled in controversy, and millions are confused by conflicting perceptions of the organization that still remains on the rolls of many Catholic Archdioceses and parishes.)

Then, there are those who start well but are later persuaded by false doctrines, even into heresy. The converse can happen, as well, but due diligence is required to discern reliability.

# Chapter Seven: Researching for Reliability (Secular and Sacred)

## *Growing antennae*

Yet, how do you know? Experience and knowledge are the antennae that need to be cultivated. Grow and use that pair of antennae for Truth and Love! The more educators know the Truth of the Faith, the better they will be at distilling information for good, separating anything that contaminates it. Of course, one can always depend on the Sacred Scripture, interpretation of which aligns with the Catechism of the Catholic Church (revised edition); Sacred Tradition; the Saints; and others who have passed away in the ardor of sanctity or sanctified works.

The classical thinkers and writers should be explored: St. Augustine, St. Thomas Aquinas, St. Francis de Sales. However, numerous contemporary apologists like the Popes of the 19th and 20th Century, most notably Pope Leo XIII and the Pope Pius's, St. Pope John Paul II, and Pope Benedict XVI (See Wisdom through Church History), Archbishop, Archbishop Fulton Sheen, Father John Hardon and many others today at the Augustine Institute, Tan Publishing, Sophia Institute and so forth. It is no exaggeration to say in 2023 that teachers (parent and classroom) could spend the day just reading, watching, or listening to healthy sources.

*Truly, the Holy Spirit is abundantly pouring out His Spirit on an ill world!*

What will follow are numerous sites, periodicals, organizations, and e-communicators, along with brief descriptors, that have demonstrated fidelity to the Faith. This is followed by those that have led to confusion about the Faith, at best, and wounded the Church, at worst. Teachers should keep in mind some reservations.

Even the most trusted organization can have "sleeper agents" for heresy. Notably, the Communist Party infiltrated the Church's most precious and devotional groups in the 20th Century. (*The Devil and Karl Marx*). Ironically, or oxymoronically, the most notorious groups may lead some of its members to the Truth, so that they become greats spokespersons. Our spiritual lives are fluid, and those not advancing will fall behind. Not all who start well will end well. Slow but steady is best, and the tortoise is the proof.

Then, one must receive information in accordance with its content, despite the delivery. Candidly, the glib, soft-spoken, and even humorous spiritual leaders of our day receive the most positive attention. They craftily wrap their messaging in easily digestible and desirable wrapping. On the other hand, there are Faith spokespersons, reporters, and commentators who turn off their audiences with palpable outrage and outright condemnation. Moreover, the media gleefully thrives on highlighting only harshness and elements of judgment. Some may be simply "dry" communicators with "nuggets" buried deeply and dug out only with patience.

Also, there may be areas within any of these guiding resources that may not appeal to a teacher objective or course, and no teacher should fear questioning the so-called experts. Thankfully, great teachers are great students, eager to know…it is hoped.

These resources are not exhaustive, as new ones are sprouting—like *Catholic Sprouts!*— all the time. However, teachers will be able to sort any new ones and evaluate them for truth and Catholicism in ways that may be helpful. They should look to sources interspersed in different areas of the Primer, and these are all compiled in the Appendix besides. The ones in this chapter are included as they send updates electronically. However, teachers do not need them all, and learning how to choose pertinent ones, while storing the rest will become easier over time. However, while there is no personal endorsement for any of these, per se, there would be no deliberate inclusion of knowingly dangerous sources.

Also, teachers should compile sources from friends, colleagues and trusted mentors to whom they can turn if in doubt or realizing some subjects require others better versed in a particular area. For example, although not a Catholic issue per se, but the Russian attack on Ukraine (2022) startled many Americans. Suddenly there was a plethora of "opinions" about Putin, Russia, Zelenskyy and the Ukrainians. In the background, however, were the steady military historians and tacticians

## Chapter Seven: Researching for Reliability (Secular and Sacred) 223

who had watched Russia and the region for decades. They became the voices of reason about what to expect; they were more likely the ones not scouting social media but turning to those closest to the military operations. Also, they were the ones to discount disingenuous gossip or plain wrong interpretations of what Putin intended or how sanctions would work or not.

Teachers should know the trusted and faithful Catholics on Church doctrine, and create a database of sorts in other areas, like health, science, history, and so forth.

Finally, and this is critical. ***Teachers should not fear reading those who are ignorant of or who have abandoned the Truth*** because knowing them will also strengthen teachers' ability to address falsehoods and understand their students and why they (or their parents) fall prey to lies. Note that it is not declared that knowing this will change hearts and minds, but that understanding and guide teaching and communication, albeit without compromise.

For convenience of follow up, the list is in alphabetical order. This will be followed by some main issues and how reliable sources address them and compared and contrasted with questionable - at best- persons or communicators do so. (Note: These are also included in the larger Appendix and Bibliography) Not all of these are Catholic or even Christian by self description, and this is by no means an exhaustive list. However, they are good sources for history and current events. Finally, none of these lack critics for one reason or another. Use those antennae. Some notes on each follow.

As a postscript and outstanding example of an educator's finely tuned antenna, note this great Palm Sunday, 2022 message from homeschooling Mom, Mrs. Jennifer Husmann:

My Friends---

I wanted to share an example of how our Catholic faith has formed so many aspects of our culture and history, far beyond St.

Nicholas, Easter eggs and the St. Patrick's Day parade, even here in present-day Florida.

Florida public school children hear in fourth or fifth grade, if not before, that in 1513, Ponce de Leon stumbled upon St. Augustine, Florida and immediately noticed the flowers, and thus decided to name the new land: Florida. This, we are told, is where our state first got its name.

But if you take an honest look at the Florida landscape, you will notice that a first-time visitor would not really be impressed with an abundance of flowers in Florida, especially coastal Florida. Pristine white sand, swaying palm trees, seashells of every shape and color, shimmery green waves crowned in white foam-- no denying the palette of beauty here in the Sunshine State. But once a new explorer penetrated the wilderness, beyond the beautiful beaches, he would encounter, well, a swamp. That is the interior of Florida, prior to draining and development which ensued later. I don't know if Ponce de Leon and his men would have immediately thought of "Land of Flowers" much less simply "Flowers" to identify their discovery of this new peninsula-- it just doesn't make sense.

Today's feast reveals the truth, which the public school textbooks hide from view. Ponce de Leon landed on St. Augustine, not far from the Georgia border, on Palm Sunday of 1513. Palm Sunday is the first of the eight days prior to Easter, and according to the old liturgical books, the lay faithful could fulfill their Easter obligation of making a good Confession and then receiving Holy Communion, beginning on Palm Sunday, and have it still "count" for the Easter obligation. Thus, our forefathers referred to Palm Sunday as the **Flowering of Easter**, or *Pascha Floridum*. The first budding of the Easter celebration emerged on this day; we taste a brief joy this Sunday, which will pick back up again in one week at that greatest Feast of the liturgical year.

So Ponce de Leon and his men named that mysterious and swampy land "Florida," not because it was laden with lillies and roses (Roses actually bloom in Florida in December, not April). The **piety of practicing Catholics, at a time when our Faith shaped and directed all of actions, even secular actions and experiences;** this is where we find the key to the naming of our great state. (The public school text books could not deny the significance of naming that first settlement "St. Augustine"- the mental gymnastics required to brush away the piety behind that part is too daunting for even the most adamant secularists!).

I hope you enjoyed this brief history lesson-- its a great hobby of mine to study these hidden gems of our rich Catholic faith.

(Signed Jennifer Husmann)

NOTE: Three takeaways here. One, the realization and acceptance that public history is often devoid of Church history or misconstrues it. Two, a passion for truth will lead to discoveries like hers. Three, she shares that with others. It is fervently hoped that all Catholic teachers do likewise.

## TOOLS, LESSON(S) AND GENERAL RESOURCES AND MATERIALS—RESEARCHING FOR RELIABILITY

**TOOLS:** Students (Teachers) will learn trusted sources and should definitely build up local faithful Catholic contacts. This is an area that simply requires time and experience though some teachers have well tuned antennae already. Some are natural sleuths.

*Primary Lesson*: Defining and Describing Reliable Research; Identifying the Tools. Each participant chooses a contemporary article that captures his or her attention. Periodicals and Newspapers are the best sources for this activity. They should respond to the following:
1. What drew their attention?
2. Were they intrigued for personal, political reasons, as a teacher, or as a Catholic?

3. Did the headline relate to the content, or were there surprises? (Note: Many article headlines are composed by those other than the author and often to grab reader attention. They may also be worded to instill a bias on a particular person or event.
4. Were quotes, statistics, and other "evidence" supporting the thesis of the article verified, and what did the analyzer discover?
5. Provide one other article on the same person or event and describe its content in relation to the first one. (Choose a source that is published by someone in disagreement with the conclusions of the first, if possible.)
6. Was there any content that would relate to the Catholic Faith—challenging or supporting it?
7. Summarize what was learned by this exercise.

Lesson #1. Read various articles on how to conduct reliable research: its origin, perspective, context, audience and motive. There are degrees of reliability as well.

Lesson #2. Choose one of the sites below and select an article. Verify its content with other information. Some comparison and contrast may evolve, but then doublecheck the veracity of any contradictory presentations. Write an analytical critique and why you agree or disagree with the site article. Include any questions you still have that you would like answered.

Lesson #3. (What do value and virtue have to do with researching for authentic Catholicism?)
*Motive is a driving force for any communication, and if the intent is skewed, the content will be likewise slanted, incomplete, or hyped. This frequently occurs in history, but also science, whereby evolution is the overarching theory on human development. How "reliable" is a source if it is developed by the mere temporal minded or even anti-Christian writers?*

## Chapter Seven: Researching for Reliability (Secular and Sacred)

*Related to this is the notion of value vs. virtue. Even atheists share "values," but if they have no respect or little regard for virtuous living, their intent will show through the selection of topics, content, and final analysis.*

*This lesson will explore how one history event may be presented depending on its selection and intended audience. Those two aspects will determine its development.*

**RESOURCES:** The Catholic Catechism; Scripture; The Truth Meter; Sammons, Eric, *The Brainwashing of the Catholic Mind, Crisis Magazine*, March 28, 2022

This insightful article reminds readers that The Current Narrative whether it is COVID, Racism (Black Lives Matter), Ukraine, all have common denominators with respect to messaging, often propagandized: It activates strong emotions; It simplifies information (that contains a kernel of fact); It appeals to the hopes, fears, and dreams of a targeted audience; and It attacks opponents. The end result is often submission to group think.

Sammons advises that Catholics can resist the hook, line and sinker, as the person formed by Sacred Scripture that sees the Narrative in balanced and reasoned context of the Catholic Faith and recognizes and resists warped efforts of world leaders often opposed to God. After all, as Sammons concludes, we should be focused on the Eternal Narrative.

***Aleteia*** — a wide band coverage of those current events and other Catholic subjects of interest to today's Catholic.

***The American TFP***— (American Society for the Defense of Tradition, Family, and Property) These emails are often coupled with petitions for action. However, they also highlight some situations not reported elsewhere.

*Augustine Institute*—an exemplary organization that provides very fruitful publications and speakers. Edward Sri is one more popular presenters.

*Avila Institute*—For depth of spirituality and course offerings, the Avila Institute is unique in its overarching materials but also for those who want a richer spiritual life.

*Catholic Answers*—As the name implies, many solid and succinct answers about the Faith and the history of the Catholic Church.

*CatholicCulture.org*—boasts itself as the "World's Catholic Library." Like other sites, many of these understandably rely on private donations, but you can still access information.

*Catholic League*—This vigilant organization has been in the forefront of issues affecting Catholicism for decades.

*The Catholic Thing*—A daily source of wonderful articles and editorials on many of the contemporary issues confronting and challenging Catholics and their understanding of what is occurring at home and abroad, within and outside of the Church.

*Catholic World Report*—Always faithful and informative on a wide range of issues, persons, and events.

*The Catholic Vote*—Although this is a political organization, it is a great resource for facts in that arena and verifying what swirls in other more secular sites.

**Church Militant**. (This organization has received criticism for extremity of reporting and narrowing focusing on just a few topics and clergy and almost always negatively. The Primer's author has been associated with CM almost since its inception and understands the background of its founder, Michael Voris. That established, there is solid research and investigation that spurs stories. Advice: An adult site and proceed through the minefield carefully and focus on verifiable and objective facts.)

*Courage/Encourage* The history of same sex attraction; how the rise of "rights" erodes male-female family relationship; and other corresponding matters are sourced in numerous DVDs talks, and books. However, this is a teacher and parent site only, as this international group does not impede on parental authority even for well intended minors. Of course, anyone with a computer may explore the resources, but Courage-Encourage respects the integrity of family authority and also desires that interested minors inquire upon adulthood. Chock full of great testimony and facts.

*Crisis*—A regular periodical with substantive articles for reference and issues.

*First Things*—Richly developed articles for reference.

*Human Life International (special comment of Father Paul Marx)*—one of the forerunners in the battle for life, its founder the late Father Paul Marx was also a social scientist of the highest caliber and exposed treacherous cultural encroachments around the world even back in the 80s and 90s.

*Just Facts* is generally a dependable site. Its standards are superior. However, the author was engaged is some debate about a survey posted that she believed to be slanted. As it had a military component, she consulted with a military historian and expert who took exception to some of Just Fact's contention. Again, it cannot be sufficiently emphasized that teachers candidly critique even those who appear to present indisputable information.

***Lepanto Institute***—As the name suggests, this site focuses on the power of the Catholic Church in world events.

***Lifesite News***—Reports on issues related to life, as its name suggests. It often provides frequent news updates on legislation, the Church, and other articles of interest

***The Loop***—Sponsored by CatholicVote, this site scours the airwaves and other sources for current events that have an impact of daily lives of Catholic citizens.

***Priests for Life***—For decades, Father Frank Pavone has led clergy and laity in numerous issues devaluing life from conception to natural death. It often analyses current events with facts and quotable experts.

***Population Research Institute***—Its founder, Father Paul Marx, enlisted Steven Mosher, a well known and highly dependable researcher and analyst with respect to world issues, most notably related to China. While population is a primary issue, those persons and events that influence populations are also covered, globally. Most reliable for facts and trends.

***Return to Order.org***—As the name suggests, this group focuses on those issues that threaten disorder, chaos, deceit, and so forth although with an emphasis on America's socio-economic decline.

***The Ruth Institute***—Jennifer Morse has been at the helm of disclosing lies about sexuality, family, and marriage for over forty years. Great info on all matters related to the sexual depravity of current society and how marriage and family have been attacked. Information, experts, and testimony abound.

***Veritas Current Events***— A relatively new site, with good intentions to be faithful.

*Women of Grace*—A long time refuge for the Catholic woman, in particular, and also with many dependable resources and experts in myriad areas of Catholic life and education.

There are also secular publications and news sources, but those will be included in the Appendix with the caveat that they are often non Christian

# Chapter Eight

## WISDOM THROUGH SALVATION HISTORY

(Early Church Fathers, Doctors of the Church, Saints, Encyclicals and Other)

*Wisdom is ageless, eternal. From the beginning God is wisdom and that wisdom was imparted from the very earliest time of man. Adam and Eve turned from wisdom, and when ousted from Paradise, roamed the Earth now fraught with the spirit of foolishness and death. Yet God ensured that His Word would be communicated to anyone with ears to hear, eyes to see, and hands to act. Thus, we see from the earliest accounts that wisdom was recognized and acknowledged though not always in its fullness or at all times.*

### *Divine Inspiration in Salvation History (Sacred Scriptures and the Seven Books of Wisdom)*

*The teacher appeared flustered. The Baptist student in her Catholic school religion class just raised her hand and challenged the teacher's Scriptural quotation. Defensively, the teacher retorted, "Well, you are Protestant, so you likely do not have the right Bible." Later in the faculty lounge, she complained about the same student who was always so quick to point out the teacher's lack of knowledge about the Bible. "Why should I know ever chapter and verse?" she lamented. Had St. Augustine been in the room, he might have gently (or not so gently) interjected that lack of Scriptural knowledge thwarts education.*

In the above scenario, one can sympathize with the teacher. Likely the vast majority of Catholics, teacher or not, have listened to Scripture all their lives and likely more than their Protestant peers in Mass alone, especially if they are daily attendees or meditate on the daily readings. However, the difference is that Catholics rarely memorize Scripture, often alluding to special Gospel stories or lessons but without citation. Still, the more a Catholic teacher truly studies Scripture, the more likely he or she will relate it to God's history and Church history as affecting or impacted by human behavior through time and space. Literally nothing is contained in Scripture that does not correspond to those persons and events regardless of century or location.

One excellent source among many is Father Eugene Kevane's *The Deposit of Faith: What the Catholic Church Really Believes (Jesus Teaching Divine Revelation in his Body, the Church,)* which studies both origin of the catechumenate of the teaching Church and the "teaching program" of the Apostles by Jesus. "Deposit" is the key word, and one can think of all the priceless wisdom being secured in the vault of the Church under the umbrella of Magisterium. However, like any truly valuable account, it took authentic leadership and much time and many appointed to secure it. Moreover, because of its great worth, thieves are ever attempting to "rob the vault" and replace the content with counterfeit ideas. In this case, in modern times, that false currency has been described as "philosophical discovery" theoretically fashioned and "perfected" by human ingenuity. (The author prefers to call such philosophy odiumosophy (hatred of wisdom, just as secularism has become "sick"ularism.)

From other sections, it should be clear that this has always been a real threat, but in recent times increasingly more intensely, at least over the past nearly two hundred years. Still, in the flow that follows, it will become clearer that Wisdom (with a capital W) has always be present, offered, explained, and possessed by those genuinely seeking Truth. Yet, time and again, people have rejected God.

First, a solid discussion of the meaning of wisdom is necessary before presenting it in context of God's relationship with man.

Wisdom is one of those words that have lost their primary and original meanings through time, misuse, and even abuse. Overall, language can and is used as a tool, even a weapon. As to how one interprets communication is more impactful of intent, unless that intent is explicitly expressed. Ownership of words can alter understanding. Those who claim authority over language can change meaning. Worse,

### Chapter Eight: Wisdom through Salvation History 235

when once trusted publishers like Merriam Webster co-conspire in distorting historic definition, those who fail to question will be propagandized.

Because it is so much in the limelight, the word "gay" can no longer be comfortably used as something jovial or fun. Recently Merriam Webster dictionary, almost whimsically determined that the phrase "sexual preference" was an offensive term. No discussion, just momentary emotional and prejudicial reactivity. Preference, by the way, according to its etymology means "place or set before, carry in front." Arguably given that we are clearly and by DNA created male or female (with very rare exceptions), any deviation of that core identity would have to be consciously and deliberately "moved to the rear," while a psychologically induced identity is placed in front.

Wisdom has also undergone shifts, as strictly temporal or wobbly religious understanding has warped its meaning. What is it not? It is not intelligence. It is not empathy. It is not shrewdness or cleverness. It is not articulation. It is not ability in any field. It is not achievement. It is not a religion or religious person, per se.

So, what is it? Let us start with the ideal. Then, there may be further exploration of the imperfect and finally, the evil spin.

***Perfect Wisdom is Perfect Love perfectly merged with Perfect Truth.*** In other words, wisdom is God, and we most often reference its presence in the Holy Spirit although it is universal in the Father and embodied in Jesus Christ.

This wisdom can, has been, and is shared with persons throughout history, depending on the person's openness to sanctity and capacity for that knowledge and love. As God's creation, though, with the exception of the Blessed Virgin Mother and others we may speculate, that perfect wisdom will not be achieved in this temporal world. Moreover, even if Adam and Eve had the opportunity to possess that perfect wisdom, at some point, they permitted their human nature to fall into temptation.

Even so, thanks to Perfect Wisdom, people still have ample ways to maximize the fruit of wisdom in their lives if they live faithfully and intentionally seek it, albeit in humility and obedience. That sounds oxymoronic, but wisdom cannot be attained without those virtues.

So this section hyper focuses on the truth, goodness, and beauty of supernaturally inspired Church heroes, encyclicals, based on knowledge and understanding of wisdom found in Holy Scripture, the Church (Mystical Body of Christ), Saints and holy persons who were exceptional prophets, evangelists and apologists.

## *The Bible*

The Truth of the Bible, the written word of God inspired by the Holy Spirit, can only be found in the Catholic Church.

Catholic teachers must believe this with their entire being, for if anything comes from the outside, or if any humanistic leeway or false insight permeates the Church's interpretation and teaching, it is from the evil one, albeit the "messenger" may be naive, ignorant, or him or herself of evil intent. This warning extends to those who would "cut and paste" Scripture to achieve human goals discussed elsewhere in the book. However, one other example: When Jesus was in the Garden, at one point in His excruciating agony, he uttered, "Father, if you are willing, remove this chalice from me; nevertheless, not my will but yours be done." (Luke 62: 42). Many false ministers have focused only on the first part of that verse to suggest that "even" God avoided suffering. Yet, this verse is *hinged*, and if someone has ever seen a doorway with a hinge but no door, he or she knows something is missing. Furthermore, read John 17, and it becomes abundantly clear that Jesus, even in His most difficult time, was thinking of *us*. If anyone has ever experienced a person thinking aloud to "teach," this is easily understood. For example, a parent who want to instruct a small child in how to dress, might go through the steps of self dressing aloud. First, I…Then I…Next I… and so forth. Jesus spoke aloud those words for us to indicate that He was most certainly suffering, and the true man in Him naturally sought relief. Also, it is not a sin to ask God for an intervention. Still, always Divine Will must be desired and accepted.

Chapter Eight: Wisdom through Salvation History 237

Back to Catholicism...the Bible is not owned by the Church, but no other religion can boast a continuous stream of trustworthy understanding from the time of Jesus Christ to now. Some of the greatest minds and souls ever to be created attest to the the integrity of Church interpretation and application in everyone's life. The last note is critical. It must apply it to *daily* life.. Furthermore, the Old Testament beautifully prefigures the New Testament. Brant Pitre is an author and scholar of Judaism who has splendidly brought together the two.

Now, what part of the Bible should Catholic teachers know? All of it, although it is a lifelong journey, from Genesis, through Exodus, Leviticus, Numbers and Deuteronomy (The Pentateuch) to The Historical Books: Joshua, Judges, Ruth, 1 Samuel (1 Kings), 2 Samuel (2 Kings), 1 and 2 Chronicles, Ezra, Nehemiah, Tobit, Judith, Esther, 1 and 2 Macabees. The Wisdom Books follow: Job, Pslams, Proverbs, Ecclesiastes, Song of Solomon, Wisdom, and Sirach.

The Eighteen Prophetic Books follow and precede the New Testament, perhaps even thinking of them as ushering in the Incarnation, though Isiah lived about seven hundred years before Jesus Christ entered the world. (The Great Adventure Bible, Ascension Press)

### *Wisdom Literature*

As a precept, wisdom of philosophy should not be confused with wisdom found in Divine revelation, as the former is bound by nature and the world, and the latter pertains to the supernatural. Now, the best of both complementary worlds are those thinkers and communicators who have developed proficiency in both, and the Church boasts of thousands of such through temporal history. Moreover, it is either God's sense of humor or simply that people misunderstand how the Holy Spirit operates, but even pagan philosophers like Socrates, Plato, Aristotle, and Cicero deduced the presence of (the one) God though in a very limited way lacked Divine revelation about the true nature of God. One might even insist that their awareness was due to an all natural but keen observation of the world through their senses and then reason with some heavenly "spark." Still, they influenced great later Saints like St. Augustine in his conversion, so the Divine Will was most certainly influential.

Wisdom has been explained as starting with "the fear of God" though in the sense of awe, not terror. Those who are genuinely wise, ironically, do not rely on their intellect to guide their thoughts, words, and actions, yet utilize their intellect in cooperation with holy respect for Divine Will, as revealed in the Word and through the holy, Catholic Church. In fact, all of our difficulties in history have been rooted in excessive "familiarity" with God, coupled with an exaggerated sense of self empowerment. Just the opposite needs to develop: appropriate humiliation and obedience, along with the highest reverence for the Creator of all.

How does one recognize wisdom, aside from obvious markers? One fundamental way is to know and understand Holy Scripture. While wisdom is threaded throughout the Bible—Old and New Testaments—one section, solely possessed by Catholics—provides a terrific blueprint.

The Very Rev. Peter Samuel Kucer, MSA wrote a timely tome, *Wisdom Literature*, in which he also touted *A Catholic Introduction to the Bible, Vol. 1* by John Bergsma and Brant Pitre. Parenthetically, Brant Pitre, as previously mentioned, is an outstanding scholar on the Old Testament. Studying the Books of Wisdom is also required to best grasp Salvation history.

Succinctly, *Wisdom Literature* flushes out the seven books of Wisdom in an understandable and most helpful manner. These Books impress upon readers and "hearers of the Word" wisdom as a practical type of knowledge reflected in right living. Through the Books, the world can be rationally understood. What follows is a true synopsis, but Catholic educators are strongly encouraged to explore all seven Books of Wisdom with the aid of the Very Rev. Kucer and others' keen focus on the priceless content. Catholic Bible studies, videos, special programs, and so forth can add to that understanding.

## Chapter Eight: Wisdom through Salvation History

The seven books are Job, Psalms, Proverbs, Ecclesiastes, Song of Solomon, Wisdom, and Sirach. Now, a person may wonder why read all those books when there is already a book titled "wisdom", but read on. Too, these are presented chronologically, as to help readers grasp the historical significance as each Book was written but later classified as a Book of Wisdom. Note that the Bible was written in parts at different times, and so our present configuration is man organized under the holy inspiration of the Church.

Job is believed to have been written sometime after Noah, as there is reference to the Flood, but prior to Moses. It chronicles the worst days of one of God's faithful servants and is briefly described as a guide as to "how to suffer." Why would this be classified as wisdom? As one can read in "Knowing the Religions of the World," heresies are often rooted in the rejection of suffering in one way or another. Because man often cannot reconcile suffering with an all mighty and loving God, he or she will reject God, hate God, or transform the image of God to an all too human being.

Job's response was none of those. He accepted that he did not understand God, and there is that awe and intense reverence for God. Job could not know all and realized it was not his place to know all though he felt appropriately confident to wonder. It is ok to ask; it is even ok to be angry with God when misfortune cannot be phanthomed. However, if a person cannot reconnoiter those ambivalent feelings and arrive at acceptance and hope, chances are he or she will fall prey to a false understanding of God and Jesus Christ, and therefore, the Catholic Church.

Psalms are sung at every Mass, but it may be likely that many sing the words in the absence of depth. Yet, Psalms can teach Catholics how to pray. Catholic teachers would find many moments of silent retreats just reflecting on the daily psalm. The other advantage is that the flow and rhythm of Psalms helps balance people emotionally. Note how the Rosary, based on the number of Psalms may have a similar effect even while reinforcing Scripture and virtues.

Proverbs direct readers and ponderers in actions—how to think and behave. Within the Proverbs are particular *timeless* warnings, such as against false freedom. The proverbial (literally) Lady Wisdom and Lady Folly provide distinct pathways. Seriously, it is almost inconceivable how modernists have been able to contort Scripture to evade fundamental truth. One may blame the devil, but humans rationalize rather than reason when they want to act a certain way, thinking falsely that "God cannot see" them, not unlike the child who covers his eyes and insists on the same about people around him or her.

The Book of Ecclesiastes made famous by the song, "Turn, Turn, Turn," puts the temporal world in its place. All is vanity. Yet, while the juxtaposition of vice and virtue is evident, there is also a certain sense of how to enjoy life rightfully.

Song of Solomon focuses on Divine Love and how to love. It is a special wisdom to be able to love perfectly or at least strive to love God perfectly.

The Book of Wisdom touches on Salvation History and how to determine goodness and avoid evil. It presents the complementary nature of justice and mercy. As St. Thomas Aquinas remarked: Justice without mercy is cruelty while mercy without justice is the mother of destruction. Pope Francis also expressed similar understanding in a Bull of Indiction of the Extraordinary Jubilee of Mercy noting that justice and mercy are two dimensions of a single reality. The Book of Wisdom also impresses with the immortality of the soul, reflecting the image of the Divine God, which contests numerous beliefs that deny this or attempt to layer afterlife in the realm of the temporal world with such dangerous ideas as cows being deities. (Hinduism)

Sirach heightens the awe of God and moves from vertical to horizontal relationships. As always, since Adam and Eve, the tribes, the cities, the nations and civilizations, human traits have been a constant. The Fall by sin may be projected against different backdrops but persons have alway succumbed to vices and have had to strive for virtue. Sirach provides much insight with respect to successfully navigating difficult people and circumstances from the neighbor to those in power.

However, as indicated in *Wisdom Literature*, there are a couple of gnarly areas that have been misinterpreted, especially concerning women. Careful reading should clarify that women have equal dignity with men.

## *The Prophets, Evangelists, Doctors, and Apologists*

All loyal sons and daughters of the Catholic Church over 2,000 years concur that cultivation and maturity of all the virtues are necessary for sainthood. Actually if Catholic educators read, accepted, and pursued a genuinely virtuous life no other direction would be necessary, Wisdom begins with holy fear (awe) of God, but the person must then be transformed by the cardinal virtues of prudence, justice, fortitude, and temperance. From these all the other virtues flow. Fortunately, ample sources abound in this area, and the Dominican Sisters have wonderful print and video materials in virtue development for students.

### *Prophets*

Not all prophets were equally virtuous, but they all grew in truth and love. Even Jonah! Yet, there is some misunderstanding about prophecy which is not "seeing the future" by some mystical means although some saints have forewarned about future events. A prophet is a person who speaks the truth, often in environments that fail to grasp truth, distort it, or ignore or reject it. They also have keen insights to human behavior and can discern good from evil with the natural consequences that will follow poor decisions.

Now, the Bible includes major and minor prophets of particular importance in salvation history. As these words are being typed, it is Lent, and Isaiah is the most prominent voice for the coming of the Messiah. Yet, each prophet was a particularly important trumpeter of his era.

It is not necessarily in the scope of this Primer to review all the prophets, per se, but Catholic educators should know them, their message, and how they relate to the revelation of truth over time and in a timeless way, regardless of geography.

## Early Fathers of the Church (who are also evangelists and apologists)

It must also be impressed that the written—printed Bible as we know today in several translations and emphasis—did NOT exist in the early centuries of the Church with any widespread awareness of individual possession.

Much of the Church's credibility rests with the Early Fathers of the Church, from that first few hundred years of the newbie Church until present day. Father Kevane points out that the Church Fathers were not theologians but catechists. Their mission was to preserve that rich deposit of Faith and share (teach) it to others, especially in the newborn stage of the Church that which was under frequent attack. They prevented the contamination of paganism even as persecution and barriers were raised. This entailed a rigorous, three-year initiation and catechesis to ensure that the early Christians knew and accepted the fullness of Faith before being baptized. The Apostles Creed was foundational.

These giants include: St. Clement of Rome, St. Ignatius of Antioch, St. Justin Martyr, St. Irenaeus, Origen, Hippolytus, Tertullian, St. Gregory, St. Cyprian of Carthage, St. Clement of Alexandria, St. Athanasius, St. John Chrysostom, St. Jerome, and St. Augustine . As Church Fathers embraced the fundamental wisdom of Truth in Love, having been so close to the early Apostles by close generation, they were able to "generate" (or father) the Faith with integrity to actual events, testimonies (witnesses), and primary sources. They communicated on so many wonderful aspects of the Faith that Catholic teachers are encouraged to pursue their works on the Sacraments, the Mass, and even problematic challenges almost two thousand years ago that we assume are "modern" developments. Scholarly, yet, always humbly and obediently honoring the Sacred, the Church Fathers solidified the foundation of the Church.

(The foundational Councils that were convened, based on contention but also the intervention of wisdom, were largely successful in solidifying understanding and the catechetical Church because of the Early Church Fathers. Catholic educators will likely study them in their careers, but they can always be referenced if some pertinent questions arise. Having a resource of those would be beneficial.)

## Church Doctors

Though this designation did not emerge until AD 300s, the essence of being a Church doctor existed from all time. Its official designation is bestowed by the Pope in recognition of outstanding understanding and interpretation of sacred Scriptures and the development of Christian doctrine. (Dr. Marcellio D'Ambrosio crossroadsinitiative.com 8/2021). However, we can certainly accept that in the Old Testament, key figures like David and Solomon merited outstanding holiness, doctrinal insight, and extensive writing (for the time) on these matters. Also, there are likely many more wonderful Catholics who provided keen insights and persuasive treatises on any number of issues who were not so recognized.

However, let us look at the thirty-six men and women so designated from the birth of the Church and their place in history. What was occurring at the time of their intense outreach; why did they feel compelled to highlight certain matters or spiritual wisdom? Two of great importance to this work are St. Augustine and St. Thomas Aquinas.

Church Doctors are often misunderstood, but certainly the Church Fathers were also that. Recipients of this honorarium exhibit an outstanding holiness and are often great communicators, most often with a body of writings that pour forth the authentic teaching, and they are known for an in-depth grasp of the one, holy, Catholic and Apostolic

Church. Their articulation of the fullness of the Faith has both defended the Church and converted souls. Particularly these exemplary minds and souls have risen in times of Church turbulence to infuse persons with genuine wisdom about truth.

However, and this is an important distinction, some Doctors of the Church have been more hidden than public. For example, of the thirty-six so titled, as of 2021, one is St. Therese of Lisieux who is the youngest of the Doctors and died at age of 24. However, she packed so much into that brief life, and her "Story of a Soul" has touched millions over the decades.

Catholic educators, especially history teachers, should know the Church Fathers and Doctors intimately and correspond their lives and influence in their respective time periods. Their impact is "timeless" and without geographical boundaries.

(Crossroads initiative.com)

## *Saints and Martyrs*

How "wise" is it for someone to sacrifice all and die for one's Faith? One only need look at Jesus Christ, True God and True Man, on the Cross—the Holiest of Pulpits—for the answer to that. All who listened became saints, both declared and unknown to us at this time. Catholic teachers should study the Saints lives to better know how to "die to self" and emulate Jesus Christ. There are numerous saints, literally for every temperament, life situation, and person. Teacher candidates reared in Churches barren of statues (and maybe with only the Resurrected Jesus on a Cross), should be even more prompted to learn the history of saints. More so, though, is the illumination of Faith by the lives of martyrs. There are excellent examples in the past two centuries, as well as in our recent history, from St. Marie Goretti to Blessed Frassetti. Still, two "musts" are the timeless models of Mary, Our Heavenly Mother, and her most chaste spouse, St. Joseph. Moreover, in the words of St. Francis de Sales (Every Day With St. Francis de Sales): *The lives of saints are nothing but the Gospel put into action.*

Chapter Eight: Wisdom through Salvation History            245

*The Wisdom of the Encyclicals*

Some popes have been wiser than others, living virtuous lives, even to the point of martyrdom, or brilliantly communicating and compassionately interacting with the world . Sadly, some popes have been tools of the powerful or themselves despoilers of grace who have ignited controversy, confusion, and contention. To further baffle the laity, "bad" popes have been advanced by the ambitious and worldly, while "good" popes have been undermined by calumny. Throw in the political mix modifiers of "liberal" and "conservative," and how can any of us know for certain whose influence we should respect and whose directives we should honor? Therefore, a few precursors before delving into encyclicals, those precious, timeless and often prophetic letters from the Holy See. While not in themselves dogma, they are most often insightful commentaries on the immutable truths of the Magisterium.

One, all popes are fallible. No pope is without fault or imperfection. Many confessed sins daily. Moreover, those critiqued almost always succeed(ed) in some virtue. Yet, *all times*, popes are chosen by God's will, sometimes, by His permission, for whatever good end we likely fail to envision. Thus, calls for Popes or any clergy to "resign" can displace authentic evangelization and mislead, albeit unintentionally, sincere catechumens. Of course, there are situations that scream for removal of clerical authority, but secular remedies will not resolve root causes. It is akin to weeding by pulling off only the visible plant.

Two, even when popes write or otherwise communicate the Faith, particularly in those special letters known as Encyclicals, there are ample theologians and other clergy, including Cardinals and Bishops, to critique or clarify. Remember that an Encyclical addresses important teachings on significant topics, but others do weigh in. In other words, it is insufficient to wonder about a particular pope—and one that comes to mind immediately is Pope Francis—and why he said or wrote this or that, or acted in some questionable way. We must seek Truth in charity and trust. Also, beware the media, some of which sows dissent as *its* primary mission. Prayers for discernment are helpful, but Catholics, including educators, must still respect the *Papacy* instituted by Jesus Christ Himself. For those sincerely seeking the truth, especially in Encyclicals, God will not fail, but quick responses may not be forthcoming.

Three, educators need to avoid the trap of "time" to devalue any particular message. The very earliest encyclicals still emphasize eternal truths, and the specter of Communism was rejected almost before the term was coined. *Humane Vitae* was roundly denounced by millions a mere nearly sixty years ago, as not being with the "times" and science, but we now know it was prophetic. If educators have the opportunity, they can scour the popular periodicals of that age, including Life, and other popular mediums. It was not unusual for Catholic doctor, scientists, theologians and the like to popularly quote to support the contraceptive agenda.

Sadly, as is human nature, past writings have been ignored as "out of touch" or no longer relevant because (wo)man fails to be impressed by God's Omnipresence. He is always "in the present and has always been in the present." Styles of language and idioms may change, but the core message never does.

Four, lifting convenient excerpts to substantiate a position, especially as a Catholic teacher who is also a citizen of a secularized country, may be tempting but rarely prudent or judicial. This occurred with *Rerum Novarum (1891)* (Rights and Duties of Capital and Labor), often cited to solely support one or the other. However, the "Progressives" tend to focus on references to the rights of Labor almost exclusively. Capitalists love the admonishment to workers to basically be honest and respect their employers. Educators must read and know the entire body of any encyclical, along with tempered responses, to better live the principles contained in the letter and inform students.

Five, the Encyclicals are often sorted by subject and publication date, but often letters contain more than one theme. For example many encyclicals have touched on the dangers of socialism—even moderate socialism—as being incompatible with Catholicism, but other topics

Chapter Eight: Wisdom through Salvation History                247

are may be covered. Indeed socialism — always the precursor to atheistic communism — may not even be the main topic of a particular Encyclical. Also, Encyclical libraries organize differently, so some perusal is necessary. Still, note: Encyclicals may be accessed on several sites, including ewtn.com. One tip: Some sites show more recent encyclicals or highlight particular topics. Teachers need to have at their disposal a resource list of all. (See Tools and Resources at the end of this section.)

*Why is it vital that Catholic educators know the Encyclicals?*

Our human response, in conjunction with the Faith, often provides keen insights into both the platforms and pitfalls of living the Truth. Some errors confound with their repetition. Not to overstate the threat of communism, but it is rearing its monstrous head again in 2023. However, the threat is more insidious as generationally consciences have fallen into greater darkness and more hearts have been hardened.

Related to history and human nature, the knowledge of the Encyclicals can make better sense of how we are to live in the world on our way to The City of God. Even those Letters that seem to be bent more on accommodating the world reveal to us our responsibilities in some way, as well as our limitations. Idealism, such as ensuring a pristine environment, may not be objectively achievable, especially depending on global—often anti Christian— efforts. Climate change is one minefield issue. However, that is not to dismiss the ideal, but place it in perspective. We are stewards of the Earth

In addressing worldly issues with balance and reason, the Church, in many quarters, has been drawn to materialism and a greater emphasis on the state of the world rather than the state of souls. Moreover, in a vain attempt at "inviting" persons and groups of different belief systems towards the Light of the Church, even the best intended have succeeded in only bowing (sometimes literally) to false gods and smothering the authentic mission of the Church to save souls.

Regardless, Encyclicals enrich knowledge and put a human face and real events on living that Faith. They spark deep dives into Faith. Scripture was truth 2,000 years ago and is truth today. The setting and cast of characters are more often foreign to contemporary readers. With letters, one can study current events in light of previous similar ones, albeit often several generations removed.

Finally, but not least important, teachers can make connections to Scripture, the Catechism, history—sacred and secular—including areas like science and literature; music and the arts. The Encyclicals and other Papal communications should offer guardrails for that journey.

## *How to Study Encyclicals*

There are some great commentaries and even books written about Encyclicals, so teachers should plan and create an expanding library. Fortunately, the digital world offers many opportunities to do so "in the cloud" although some paper backup is advised.

In the last almost 300, years, nearly 300 encyclicals have been written—for a reference. The first one noted was by Pope Benedict XIV in 1740, yet they became more popular in the latter 1800s, likely as the populace became more literate and the world more geographically expansive. As previously mentioned, how Encyclicals are read and studied is critical to how their content will be imparted. Depending on the subject being taught, teachers may take advantage of the summer or breaks to build those cross references. In addition to Encyclicals are Apostolic Letters and Papal Bulls, the latter being described as dramatic declarations.

Cross reference is likely in more than one topic. Too, teachers should study the time period in which the Encyclical was written; trace other Popes who addressed similar issues and compare and contrast content. Often Popes will reiterate, clarify, or bring fresh support for a previously written Encyclical. Pope Pius XI did this with *Quadragesimo Anno (On Reconstructionn of the Social Order)* reviewing Pope Leo XIII's *On the Condition of Workers*. Within the latter given in Rome on May 15,

# Chapter Eight: Wisdom through Salvation History

1931, Pope Pius XI reiterated the just cause of workers and the right to their associations, but reinforced opposition to socialism that could arise from a skewed interpretation of the right, especially by forces who would then "direct" workers into collectivism. Pope Pius echoed Pope Leo XIII in that private property was an inalienable right (within reason), and that to destroy that concept would actually hurt the average worker in the long run.

That brings up the fact that research of commentary will elicit questions or challenges to any particular letter, as the Catholic Church has often been the source of rationalization for government overreach in the name of "charity" and "equal rights." Yet, armed with the Faith, those may be addressed accordingly by ignoring, acknowledging with reservation, or presenting with sources of truth, depending on the age and developmental level of students.

## *How to Educate with Encyclicals*

There are Bible studies which are indispensable and assist in building Catholic communities. Still , an Encyclical Club would help enlighten Catholics to the immutable truths of our faith regardless of the period in which we live. As Jesus said, "It is not for you to know times or seasons which the Father has fixed by his own authority" (Acts 1:7). Yet, concurrently, "You hypocrites! You know how to interpret the appearance of earth and sky; but why do you not know how to interpret the present times." (Luke 12:56). EffectiveCatholic educators need to read the sign of the times! It will take every tool in the Catholic Church toolbox to do so with insight, and forecast. Teachers will have to begin by self education in many cases.

In a traditional setting or at home, some classes may entail actually studying an Encyclical, particularly those related to history and government. The public, and that includes Catholics, are so bound by a limited view of what the Church teaches. Yes, all that we learn should enable us to freely pursue the good to attain heaven. However, we are to live our temporal lives well, and that requires all the subjects of worldly matter. As mentioned above, name a topic, and you will discover that the Church has addressed it and more than once. Certain concepts contained within an Encyclical can be taught with simple references to the letter.

Of course, religion classes are another environment ripe for reviewing these Letters, and this would be a great opportunity for cross curriculum activities between teachers. Then there is application of basic principles found in the Letters. For example, in the classroom community, certain duties are often assigned to students, such as helping with distributing or collecting material, erasing the white board, cleaning desk tops, being line leader, and so forth. What an ideal setting to discuss the authority of the teacher (boss) and duties of students (workers). Although no money changes hands, these are often opportunities students relish for the prestige and praise at having done a good job. A simple class lesson is on the duties and responsibilities of the teacher and students in this environment. (See Section Lesson at the end of this section for details.)

**Encyclicals—An Important Sampling**

*Spoiler Alert: Primer Author's Bias for several Pope Pius's*
Other Popes have written Encyclicals on Modernism, and most frequently Popes will cite encyclicals by their peers, building upon, contextualizing, or updating current concerns but most often with the same theme and doctrines guiding their thesis:

Pope Pius IX (1792-1878) *Pontificate from 1846-1878)*. Quanta Cura (Condemning Current Errors)

Pope Pius X (1835-1914) *Pontificate from 1903-1914* "On the Doctrine of the Modernists" (September 8, 1907) and "Lamentabili Sane" (Syllabus Condemning the Errors of the Modernists), July 3, 1907 are **MUST** reads.

Chapter Eight: Wisdom through Salvation History                                251

Pope Pius XI (1857-1939), *Pontificate was from 1922 to his death, seventeen years during one of the most crucial periods in modern history:* <u>The Church and the Reconstruction of the Modern World: The Social Encyclicals of Pius XI</u> *(Image Books, 1957)*

However, absent the ability to obtain this book or a reprint, read and study for a full understanding of this Pope's observations of and advisement about the "modern" world, as follows:

*On the Peace of Christ in the Reign of Christ; On the Kingship of Christ; On the Christian Education of Youth (NOTE: As previously mentioned, topics often intersect); On Christian Marriage; On the Catholic Priesthood; On reconstructing the Social Order; On the Present Distress of the Human Race; On the Apostolate of the Laity; On the Church in Germany; On Atheistic Communism; On the Religious Situation in Mexico.*

Pope Paul VI (1897-1978) *Pontificate 1963-1978*. On Evanglization in the Modern World

There are others and most recently St. Pope John Paul II and Pope Benedict XVI wrote on the ills of modern society and how to best faithfully address them in hope and charity.

OTHER ENCYCLICALS

Of course, there are numerous Encyclicals on the Faith, natural law, reason, Catholic education, the priesthood, devotions, saints, and other religions. False and dangerous movements like Freemasonry have been topics. However, most importantly the Church is quite cognizant of those areas that interface all societies and require wise observation, interpretation of events and developments, and truthful perspectives in the area of marriage and family, government, politics, economics, history, civics, philosophy, education, science (including evolution), music, entertainment and the arts.

Often an Encyclical will focus on a particular country like Ireland, Italy, Germany, Belgium, Hungry, the United States and so forth, or regions like Central Europe. And less people think that the Church is merely reactionary, Communism in China was a topic in a 1954 Encyclical about the plight of the Church in Communist China, Pope Pius XII "On the Supranationality of the Church." Then in 1958 anther Encyclical by Pope Pius XII: Ad Apostolorum Principis (Communism and the Church in China)

More specific topics like justice, slavery, poverty, materialism, environment, taxation, immigration, persecution, peace, missions, communication, labor, and life have received special attention and often ahead of worldly insight.

## A Special Note on Evangelism and Apologetics

Many people throughout history have proclaimed themselves "evangelists," but herein the title belongs to those who have always proclaimed the fullness of Truth. St. John the Evangelist immediately comes to mind. Care should be taken not to confuse dynamic oratory or writing skills with knowing and understanding truth. Unfortunately, many have been swayed by the apparent giftedness and even knowledge of self proclaimed evangelists. Yet, a glib tongue and crafty pen can be deceiving even from people within the Church who claim to be Catholic but obviously sow confusion and disorder, if not evil.

How is a Catholic to know? The definition of the word is "zealous preaching" (and the like), but the root meaning is "the preaching of the gospel"—to spread or preach the Gospel" with the Greek root "euangelizesthal or "bring good news." Note the difference in inflection and connotation. The former evokes imagery of the tent revivals of the 19th Century; the latter a sense of sharing that which will benefit persons eternally. It could be in a whispered voice.

That requires some prerequisites. Going back to the need to know Scripture and in relationship to the Tradition of the Catholic Church will help Catholic teachers distinguish between a great homily (and teaching style) that is delivered with zeal and simple zest empty of truth or misguiding. Teachers need to know the Faith from reliable teachers and spokespersons, regardless of style and to know how to detect the authentic "preacher" from the simply dramatic one who can quote some Scripture.

Candidly, anyone who hems and haws on core issues like life and sexuality is most likely to be cause for wariness. So are the "evangelists" who hyper focus on materialism, the evil of only one particular political party, and seek donations for prayer. Catholic teachers should be especially alert for those who appear to "like the sound of their own voices" in matters of Faith.

There are scores of credible voices who may not even be great speakers. Some very faithful evangelists may be quieter, more subdued, and even dry in their presentation are sadly dismissed or ignored. Catholic educators would be best to examine the content of any messaging and employ prudence to heeding or heaving what is communicated. Gentleness is a gift, and wise presenters with this attribute "move mountains." Dr. Paul Thigpen and Anthony Lilles are two who come to mind, the former a convert and extraordinary speaker on Scripture.

Like Evangelization, Catholic Apologetics has been present from the beginning. It is a matter of gifts, and some faithful can stir people's hearts and souls; some may provide a solid defense of truth; a few can accomplish both. However, Apologetics requires a very deep and ongoing understanding and study of articles of Faith. There are also some trademarks of genuine Apologetics as outlined in Father Peter Samuel Kucer's *Catholic Apologetics—Witnessing to and Defending the Faith,* Enroute 2018. Encapsulating the main features of an Apologist, one needs the ability to identify virtue vs. vice. The defense of Truth should not be evoked with quarrelsomeness or anger. Genuine apologetics is absent vainglory as well. Furthermore, responses are thoughtful and based on a thorough knowledge of the Faith. There is no substitute for honesty, and a rash or thoughtless answer to appear knowledgeable can do real harm. Also humor is another trait of a genuine apologist, yet never in a mocking way towards others.

By the way, Father Kucer also emphasizes loving Christ, knowing Scripture Chapter and Verse and what the Church *actually* teaches. He further advises recognizing virtue in nonCatholics and anticipating difficult topics like the Eucharist. Of course, prayer is the antecedent of all such efforts, and likely even while speaking or otherwise communicating . Then, too all the attributes of a good listener take precedence over advancing opinion. It could be added that one never knows when a "seed" is planted or where or when it will grow and blossom. So patience is helpful. Fortunately, there are great models in our Church history.

St. Francis de Sales is an excellent role model for apologetics, as is Thomas Kempis (*Imitation of Christ*). A more modern example might be Patrick Madrid, Scott Hahn, or Edward Sri. Cardinal Sarah comes to mind, and his *Power of Silence* speaks volumes about Truth and underscores that words are not always necessary, and how a life is lived will be more powerful testimony than speaking.

Hopefully more and better educated Catholic teachers will be among the voices of today that are rising in defense of the fullness and truth of the Faith. Some are listed in the Resources, along with or inclusive of titles of Church Father, Doctor, or Evangelist, but the key point is that more come forward every day. The Holy Spirit is truly pouring His Spirit on Earth, so much so that there will be no excuse for anyone at the end of their lives to claim they did not have those advisers.

More to the point is that every Catholic teacher should be ultimately an "expert" apologist for the fullness of the Faith. Their names may never be known to the world; their contributions may be revealed only in the life to come; and, in the worst circumstances, they may even be calumniated during their life time. Yet, truth will prevail, and the souls they save will be known to them forever in joy.

Chapter Eight: Wisdom through Salvation History 255

## *Common Threads and Teaching Throughout Church History*

The history of the Catholic Church is replete with difficult moments as previously mentioned. There have been numerous heresies, along with today's heresy of Modernism. Judas the Iscariot betrayed Jesus Christ after years of closeness to the fullness of truth in Person. Tragically, many have fallen away since, and one can only continuously pray the Divine Mercy Chaplet in atonement for their sins (and ours). Still, the core of the Church has remained steady and sturdy.

St. Augustine explains the dichotomy of the City of God vs. the Terrestrial City (of man) in the life of Jesus Christ and the fate of Rome, the former being one of peaceful surrender to grave violence and the other a grave source of violence even to the peaceful. And, that, in one short sentence sums up the Catholic Church teaching: "Pick up your cross and follow Me."

Still, the Catholic teacher should study Church history and may do so along side of human history. See the close of this section for an example of what that may look like. Understanding how the Church intersects with human endeavors brings to life, literally, the intervention of Divine will into history. Always noteworthy is how Our Lord Jesus Christ rules from Heaven. While not disturbing the free will of anyone, He nonetheless has raised up Saints and Martyrs; powerfully persuasive and holy Apologists; circumstances to move (wo)man's souls towards salvation; and brought forward keen theologians, dynamic presenters, gifted writers, and superior minds in all fields of drama, art, music, science and math. His timing is perfect even if the world and those in the Church are not.

Among the distinctions to be made are how different people viewed the Creation of the world rather than the Creator; how persons of different faith perceive the meaning of life and being human vs. the Catholic view; how civilization grew but stumbled and fell while the City of God shines upon the hill still; how heresy was met and defeated by truth; and how the Church overcame the trials of schisms like the East-West Divide and the Protestant Reformation.

Moreover, the Church grew and expanded around the world. Missionaries brought the Gospel even at the cost of their lives.

Furthermore, the Church has survived opposing forces like Islam, vicious and discredited accusations about the Crusades and Inquisition, world ages like the Enlightenment Era, and numerous enemies of the Church in every age. The French Revolution threatened the faith there, but many eventually returned. The Papacy, the Holy Mother of God, and the Eucharist are among the subjects of vile, blasphemous assaults today, but all emerge triumphantly. As these words are being typed, Pope Francis will consecrate Russia to the Immaculate Heart of Mary on March 25th, the Feast of the Annunciation. How is that for durability?

Even so, perhaps the most saddening, but not surprising has been the modern day betrayals from those inside the Church. Still.

history continues until the end of the world, and as long as people live, there will be those who succumb to temptation of the world, the devil or themselves and fall into mortal vices to their own perdition. (However, we always pray for all such souls). It is not the intent of this Primer to delve into specific individuals or groups of which the Catholic teacher must be wary. Candidly, even a great soul today may turn tomorrow. So it cannot be sufficiently emphasized that there can be no substitute for knowing the Faith.

Yet know history, too!

## TOOLS, LESSON(S) AND GENERAL RESOURCES AND MATERIALS—WISDOM THROUGH HISTORY

**TOOLS:** Create a binder with materials including Encyclicals although many are in short booklet format; the more tech savvy may create a spread sheet or special organized docs to retrieve as needed.

Chapter Eight: Wisdom through Salvation History 257

**LESSONS:**

**SAMPLE LESSON ON TEACHING ENCYCLICAL CONCEPTS TO YOUNGER STUDENTS**

**Rerum Novarum**
*Grade Level: Primary*

*(Note: There may have been a previous lesson on jobs, overall: types and differences between the authority figure (boss) and workers.)*

*Objective: Students will define "authority," "justice," "duty," and "compensation"; describe a just work environment; and distinguish between the role of the person in charge and the persons doing the work; they will be able to explain their duty to follow directions, use the materials wisely, and maybe even help with collecting and displaying work and then cleaning up; they will explain that the supervising person has the greater responsibility and accountability for jobs well done and has a bigger burden.*

*Materials Needed: Simple Power Point on the Outline of Duties and Responsibilities*

*Procedure:*

*Warm up: Display a picture of a classroom set up for an art lesson and ask students what do they observe. (They may respond that they see a piece of paper on every desk; a corner with supplies — or a cup for each student with colored pencils, paintbrush, etc.; they may see an enlarged series of drawings on the board, showing the steps to a final picture.).*

*Questions: Who did all of this? (Students will likely say or point to the teacher.). In response, he or she may acknowledge that and explain that this is part of her job as a teacher to be sure that the classroom is set for a lesson. He or she is following the authority of the principal and school officials. However, did the teacher obtain*

all the supplies, including the tables on which the students will work. (Admittedly, this may be tricky as many teachers do purchase supplies!)
Ideally, the students will answer and the teacher affirm that the principal makes sure there are ample materials.

Direct Instruction: (no more than five minutes). In every work situation there is someone in "authority" and that person has a "duty" to perform. He or she must use that authority justly and ensure that workers are "compensated." (In this case with a piece of art that may be brought home and displayed on the refrigerator.) However, those under that authority must contribute their part and be mindful of the "investment" in materials, and be respectful of the desired outcome. They are expected to work diligently and in an orderly manner, respectful of those around them.

Power Point on the specific lesson and how it will proceed. First slides should be an overview of vocabulary and roles of the teacher and students. The final slide might be the expectation for students to clean up the classroom and submit their work carefully.

Follow-up: How did the art lesson proceed? Did everyone do their part? Did everyone work well together? Answers may vary.

**RESOURCES:**

A library of printed Encyclicals organized by topic and time. Many are printed in booklet form, but all are available on the Internet.
*salvemariaregina.info*
*catholicqanda.com*
*papalencyclicals.net*
*vatican.va*

**Holy Scripture**
**Imitation of Christ**
**Introduction to the Devout Life**

## Chapter Eight: Wisdom through Salvation History

**Magnificat**
**St. Augustine**
**St. Thomas Aquinas**
**Encyclicals: (EWTN—though Library has changed format)**

**Popes of special interest: for modern times**
**St. Leo XIII**
**St. Pius (all)**
**St. Pope John Paul 11**
**Pope Benedict XVI**
**See general bibliography for contemporary authors and commentators**
**Very Rev Kucer—Wisdom Literature and Prophets**

Other Resources: Encyclicals by subject/topic; early philosophers Aristotle, Augustine, Aquinas — those markedly temporal oriented; contemporary philosophers Dietrich Von Hildebrand, Popes, Father John Hardon (*Wisdom of the Catholic Church*); Hillsdale College courses; *The Deposit of the Faith*, Father Eugene Kevane, Ph.D.

Aquilina, Mike, *How The Fathers Read The Bible—Scripture, Liturgy, and the Early Church,* Angelus Press, 2022 (Explores the encounters with Liturgy, and as teaching was heard and interpreted by those closest to Jesus Christ, THE Primary Source.)

Primary Lesson: Defining Wisdom (Early philosophers to church Fathers; distinguishing between "love of wisdom: and "hatred of wisdom"—after the spirit of the antichrist. Philosophy vs. Odiumsophy

**(TOOL AND RESOURCE)**

AUTHORS NOTE: This Timetable could have followed The Eternal Age vs. Man-Constructed Age, but Faith denotes Wisdom which transcend time placement but cedes to it in some way.

## SIDE BY SIDE FAITH VS SECULAR HISTORY

| FAITH | SECULAR |
|---|---|
| Prehistory—Creation<br>Evolution (God's Plan) | Big Bang<br>Evolution (survival of fittest)<br>Millions of years.... |
| 4000 BC<br>Adam, Abel, Cain.... | |
| 3,804-3604 BC<br>Seth/Enos<br>Enoch Irad | |
| 3604-2348 BC<br>(See above descendance from Seth and Cain) | 3000-2000 BC Pyramid Age of Egypt<br><br>Phoenecia founded cities |
| 2348-2004 BC<br>Noah and descendents | Elam and Asshur—Assyria<br><br>(See Egypt) |
| Nations of Ham (Gibeonites, Hittites, Jebusites, Perezites, Cush)<br><br>Tower of Babel | King Menes, Memphis capital<br>King Snefru<br>Japan mystery surrounds early history, Culture largely Chinese<br>China took title from Earth color, yellow<br>Fu Hi (Leizu, founder of silk industry)<br><br>Peruvian ceremonial centers, 2000 BC<br>Early colonies to America |
| 2004 BC-1754 BC<br>Noah 950 yrs.<br>Shem<br>Abraham 175 years—lived during the life of Shem<br>Hagar and Ishmael cast out<br>1879 BC God's Covenant with Abraham | Astronomy Astrology cuneiform<br>Babylon Kingdom<br>(Horses come from Iran)<br>Egypt 12th Dynasty, Great Pyramid<br>Indo German Tribes<br>Doctrine of Zoroaster (2200 BC)<br><br>Syria<br>Phoenicia (Baal, Astarte, Moloch) |

# Chapter Eight: Wisdom through Salvation History

| | |
|---|---|
| | Rise of Assyrian Power |
| | Egypt (Joseph) |
| | Victory of Hyksos |
| 1754-1504 BC | Pharoah's death-Israel—1604 about) |
| 12 sons of Jacob | Greece The Pelasgi |
| Ishmaelites buy Joseph | Persia about 1579 BC |
| | Japan history begins about 660 BC |
| | China Tang-Shang Dynasty 1704 BC |
| | Ancient Chinese great astronomer |
| | |
| | Syria ruled by Egypt |
| | Phoenecia first trading nation seaport; Citidal of Thebes |
| | Egypt –greatest power |
| | Greece-Lydians take Mycenea; Argos |
| | |
| 1504 BC -1254 BC | Persia a branch of Aryan stock |
| Moses | |
| Exodus (Ark of the Covenant erected) | China animals for sacrifice – high degree of civilization; pension for old Lyric poety; export silk; burial of dead |
| Generations of Ishmael | |
| Nations of Ham | |
| | |
| See Japan | Phoenecia trade German/British coasts |
| | |
| | David and Goliath |
| Indo-German Tribes | |
| | Egyptian Dynasties Rames; time of decay: 1129-1004 BC |
| | Rome: (see notes) |
| 1254 BC-1004 BC | Greece: Trojan War about 1184 BC-Cidadal of Athens |
| | Persia |
| Time of Judges—1104 BC; First three kings—1004 BC on | Indo German tribes-Sanskrit language |
| Saul/David/Solomon born about 1029 BC | China: Eunuch system; Zhou Dynasty 1179-1154 BC—polygamy-brick stone |
| Twelve Tribes of Israel (10 north Canaan; 2 south, Judah) | |
| Assyrian power increases | Mound Builders in Illinois, 1000 BC |
| Philistines rule Israel (1129-1104 BC) | |
| Nimrod (native kings) | Arab Nations |

| | |
|---|---|
| 1004 BC--754 BC<br>FAITH<br>Solomon Temple<br><br>Time of Kings<br>Prophets (Assyria N; Babylon S) | War with Israel<br><br>Phoenecia -king Solomon's friend; Carthage founded 814 BC<br>Assyrian great power 879 BC on<br>Egypt Dynasties; decay of royal power<br>Many foreign rulers 905-305 BC<br>Rome-Etcrusan War 779 BC<br>Greece Ionian and Dorian colonies;<br>Homeric poems 929 BC; First Olympics 775 BC<br>China: Age of vigorous thinking<br><br>Carthage Naval Power |
| 754 BC-504 BC<br><br>Many tribes in NE South America are strikingly Semetic in appearance<br><br>Nebuchadnezzar invades Judea, 629 BC<br>Ezekiel | End of Assyrian Empire 602 BC<br>Nineveh destroyed<br>Greece (Hippeus 552 BC)<br>Persia |

## AD

*NOTE: OTHER IMPORTANT STRANDS MAY BE INCORPORATED INCLUDING CHURCH FATHERS; POPES AND ENCYCLICALS; PERIOD SAINTS OF GREAT INFLUENCE; CITIZENS OF INFLUENCE*

| FAITH | SECULAR |
|---|---|
| 1 AD to 250 AD<br><br>The Life of Jesus Christ-33AD<br>Saul's conversion 34 AD<br>Jerusalem taken by Titus 70 AD<br>John banished 90 AD<br>Apostles slain except John 100 AD | Classic period Mayan 225 AD<br>Bolivia 200-375 AD<br>Monte Alban Mexico 100-200 AD<br><br>MIGRATION OF NATIONS<br><br>Germans defeat Romans 25-5 AD |

| | |
|---|---|
| Beginning of Apostasy 100 AD<br>Jews in great number exterminated 135 AD<br>Flavius/Josephus to 150 AD<br>Jews scattered among nations 175 AD<br>Infant Baptizing 175 AD<br>Transubstantiation Mass 200-225 AD<br>Martyr Worship intro at Rome to 200 AD<br><br>250 AD-500 AD<br><br>Constantinople conversion 325-350 AD<br>Sunday worship<br>Christianity becomes state religion 330 AD<br>Constantinople becomes the capitol 330 AD<br>Arianism condemned 325 AD<br>Council of Nicaea; Nicene Creed 325-350 AD<br>Christianity spreads 450-500 AD<br>St. Patrick in Ireland 450 AD | The Julians to 50 AD<br>Britain becomes a Roman prov 50 AD<br>The Flavians to 100 AD<br>Nero burns Rome 100 AD<br>Persecution of Jews and Christians 100-150 AD<br><br>Buddhism spreads China, Indo China, Tibet, Japan<br>China Han Dynasty 202 BC to 220 AD<br>Beginning of Roman decline 170 AD<br>Aztec calendar 275 AD<br>Mayan early classic 250-600 AD; Civilization, 300-1300 AD<br>Native Americans believed in supreme deity; feared spirit of evil<br>Huns in Europe 325 AD (Attila the Hun 434-453 AD)<br>Vandals in Spain 407-429 AD; Vandals in France 425-534 AD)<br>Egypt under Roman control 350 AD<br>End of Empire 395 AD<br>Japan-Arrival of Sushen 325 AD<br>Buddhism prospers 325 AD<br>Chinese: Wu Hu Period 304-439 AD |

MIDDLE AGES (MEDIEVAL) APPROXIMATELY 400s (5th Century) TO 1400's (15th Century) Yet, Three Traditional Divisions of Western History are timed a bit differently. This era is on a separate complementary comparison, events may appear on both.

| FAITH | SECULAR |
|---|---|
| 500 AD – 750 AD | |
| Catholicism set up by Justinian, 538 | Mississippi Moundbuilders, 575 |
| England converted, 597 | Mayan early classic -to 600 |
| (See Islam in Secular Column) | Pinnacle, 625 |
| Portions of the Bible translated into Anglo Saxon | Mexico trade center, 650 |
| Sale of Indulgences, 700 | Tikal becomes the largest city-state in MesoAmerica with 500 K inhabitants |
| Justinian 527-565; Code | Rise of Mississippi culture 700s |
| Japan Christianity introduced, 627 | Pueblo in Az above ground homes |
| | Mohammad born Mecca 572 |
| | Chronology begins 522, Koran revised |
| | Mohammad flees Mecca d622 |
| | Persia, Syria, and N Africa become Mohammedan 630-711 AD |
| | Arabs in Spain (711-722) |
| | Arabs fail in siege of Constantinople 715 AD |
| | Arabs in France in 720 AD |
| | Visgoths in Gaul and Spain 415-711 AD |
| | Rome conquers N. Africa 300-600 AD |
| | Arab slave trade begins in 700 AD |
| | (Note N. Africa converts to Islam) |
| | Moors (Islamic Africans conquer Spain 740 AD |
| | Japan Buddhism state religion 500 AD |
| | China--Foot binding; Sui Dynasty (589-618) Tang Dynasty 618-907 AD; |
| | Christianity introduced 627 AD |
| | Mayan Civilization 300-1300 AD |
| | Bagdad founded 762; caliphate 850 AD |
| 750-1000 AD | Architecture and Science flourish (See *Politically Incorrect Guide to Islam*) |
| Worship of images restored 787 AD | Kingdom of England est 827 AD |

# Chapter Eight: Wisdom through Salvation History

| | |
|---|---|
| Separation of Greek Church from Rome 867 AD | Germany 843 |
| | Japan—classical age of literature influenced by China |
| | Forms of mass and indulgence introduced into Buddhism |
| | China Golden Age-three forms of religion Confucian, Buddhist; Taoist |
| | Tang Dynasty 618-907 AD |
| | Invention of block printing (abt 925 AD) |
| | Five Dynasties and Ten Kingdoms 907-960 AD |
| 1000 AD-1250 AD | |
| Decree of election of Popes 1025 AD | Song Dynasty 960-1234 AD |
| | |
| | Leif Ericson reach N. America 1000 |
| Order of Dominicans 1150 AD | Pueblo inhabitants build circular mounds |
| Council of Toulouse 1229 AD | |
| Inquisition formally established 1233 AD | 900-1100 AD |
| | Mayan Civilization, 300-1300 AD |
| | Mohammedans take India 1030 AD |
| First Crusade 1096 AD | Seeds of Rebellion in Europe nations materialism and Pantheism (1200 AD) |
| Second Crusade 1140 AD | |
| Third Crusade 1189 AD | |
| Fourth Crusade 1203 AD | China-Political Reform; gun powder (1140) |
| Fifth Crusade 1222 AD | |
| Sixth Crusade 1248 AD | Yuan Dynasty (Kubla Kahn-Mongol) ruled |
| | China 1234-1305 AD |

# Chapter Nine

## THE ETERNAL AGE VS MAN-CONSTRUCTED AGES

What is God's Kingdom?

*What was God's Plan for (Wo)man from all eternity?*

Before embarking on God's "vision," it must be clearly understood that there is NO time nor space with God in the way we think. God is of all eternity and is endless. We perceive time and space because of Original Sin whereby we (and as descendants of Adam and Eve it is "we") attempted to expand our ego to understand and "be like God."

Yet, such a feat is impossible! (Author's Note: As an illustration, I recall my Dad telling a childhood story of when he and his brother were walking across the top of a wall in direct disobedience as to how they were to venture outdoors. His brother thought he could turn the corner of the wall and somehow land on it "across too distant a way." Physics taught him a very painful lesson about "space.")

When our parents opposed the will of God and ate of the forbidden fruit, their perception of life was about to be changed as they were thrust from the Garden of Eden into the wilderness. In the absence of God and all of His supernatural grace, they had to then grasp at life starkly. The concept of time became a reality, as did space, as they no longer had the intimacy of God in eternity and expanse. Ever since, man is compelled to think of past, present, and future and limitations on where he can reside, work, and thrive.

It was not meant to be that way.

Even with the expulsion, God was ever ready with perfect love and justice to establish His kingdom; His rule; His way to the maximum potential of life.

Obviously, though, that that was not to be the case.

However, all are still a temporal people, and most are accustomed to viewing such matters in a certain order and way, this book will continue in that conventional manner. It will start with Prehistory and then History through the prism of God's Plan. It will explore major periods of transformation through man's actions and how it could—should—have been; how revelation vs. realism, and close with the hope of changing perception of knowledge to embrace unchanging Truth. It will include the various government models, belief systems, society types, and economies. (See Government Through the Ages.) God's interventions will be interspersed whether recognized by historians or not. Most importantly, it will acknowledge and document the reality of the City of God and all of its inhabitants, now truly in a "utopia" that man could never fully envision. (Also, reference the preceding sections side-by-side Faith-Secular history.)

HISTORY IS...

Mention the word "history," and most people would immediately think of school, textbooks, different "eras" (or civilizations), along with popular words and phrases like "prehistory,""ancient," "past," "eyewitnesses," "documents," and "those who do not know history are doomed to repeat it."

The history of the word history is varied with different origins cited along with varied interpretations. Still the "story" in the word history is evident in all, except that history is theoretically factual. Pre-history is determined to mean that which has passed along from generation to generation verbally or in pictures and art; artifacts and remains. It is that period of the human "story" prior to formal written language which then formally recorded and documented events.

Regardless, the "Story of Mankind"—and here it is understood that this includes "woman" by the root of "man"— is ultimately only one true story with one reliable Author. Moreover, those who understand that there are two realms—man (temporal) and God (eternal) also know by reason and Faith that there are also two "cities"—that of

Chapter Nine: The Eternal Age vs Man-Constructed Ages

man and that of God. In that regard, God is the Master Historian and the only reliable source of that by which we should learn our lessons. He sees all, knows all, and is immortal and eternal. Yet, in this world, everyday events and figures have been and are observed and written (now video taped) for over five thousand years by many different personalities, citizens of various nations and times, and shared in multitudes of languages. More frequently than not, God is not included in perceptions and realities about what has transpired in humanity. Even when God and religion are integrated into motives for behavior—even conflict—it is too often accomplished with a disdainful tone that borders on disapproval or disbelief. So, what passes for man's history is ultimately subject to human nature with all its distortions, biases, and even manipulations. In short, most of recorded history is man-oriented with full blown ego on the part of those who act (or react) upon its script.

Worst of all, human initiated history leaves a trail that invites speculation, commentary, and even opinion that translates into political, economic, and social action often with blinders. People earnestly study the past, seeking ways to understand human behavior, including response and reaction; interrelations between various groups by gender, race, ethnicity, and religion; and ceaselessly "experimenting" with form and function. The final goal is always the same, though, with the inextinguishable belief that with the right persons, the model systems, and education, progress can be made, and utopia eventually achieved. Again, God is not in this equation, or if He enters into consideration, He is "used" as a means to the end of human conception of an ideal society.

Finally, how ironic that in the 21st century, we have re-entered the city-state division of ancient Greece and Rome; the tatters of post 20th century socialism; and the pagan rituals of the Aztecs (among other innocent slaughtering civilizations).

This section will attempt to establish that there was only one route for mankind from the beginning, starting with Adam and Eve, despite all the naysayers and even hardened, jeering critics that claim such an origin and such a Plan are both naïve and the product of fanatical minds. Furthermore, the plan for man and woman (family) was never desired by God to be outside Paradise—the Garden of Eden. It was their free will—which still is given to all today—to counter the Will of God, and that led to the consequences we still experience today.

However, even if man and woman were to fully embrace God's Kingdom as a guide to living with Him and others, this would still be a temporal world with all its disorders from Original Sin. The ultimate question and challenge before us, then, is can we accept that, knowing that by such surrender, at least we can live the very best lives (history) while awaiting our reunion with God for eternity in Heaven.

Robert Cardinal Sarah may have penned the most succinct summary of the historical nature of man. In *The Day is Now Far Spent*, he noted when responding to a question about consequences of post humanity, that 17th century philosopher Blaise Pascal wrote: "The whole series of men, over the course of many centuries, must be considered one and the same man who always exists and learns continuously." Cardinal Sarah adds, "The idea that one man should be surpassed by another is arrogant and stupid. There is no difference between Adam and the man of today, ontologically speaking, and in their ability to sin, to rebel against God; the only insignificant difference is that the man of today wears expensive clothing and has a mobile phone, while Adam and Eve discovered they were naked." (The Day is Now Far Spent, pg 209)

An extended thought might well be that Adam and Eve's "nakedness" was material; yet modern man's "nakedness" is wholly spiritual. One could also humorously add that apples still play a central fixture in the consistency of man to fall prey to temptation, complete with Apple's "bitten apple" logo.

At the core: *Letter to the Hebrews 4:1-5, 11. Let us be on our guard while his rest remains, that none of you seem to have failed. For in fact, we have received the Good News, just as our ancestors did. But the word they heard did not profit them, for they were not united in faith with those who listened. For we who believed enter into that rest, just as he has said. "As I swore in my wrath, They shall not*

# Chapter Nine: The Eternal Age vs Man-Constructed Ages

*enter into my rest," and yet his works were accomplished at the foundation of the world.*

History was already accomplished from the origin! It is the fallen world that is stuck in a timeline, seemingly in a cruel cyclic repetition of allegiance to truth and faithfulness to God, but then rebellion and self reliance. Complicating how we adhere to Divine Will while relating to each other and the world is the tendency to challenge free will. The faithful have often sought temporal behavioral control, as though man can smother sin by the instrument of governance and punitive consequences. The atheist still exerts dominion over all materialism, through collectivism, as though man can master suffering and equalize worldly existence by sheer totalitarian force.

Indeed, change the time period, location, and other identifying features of history, and people are still impressed with familiar patterns of human behavior, how those are influenced by environment—physically and socially—and how man affects the environment through virtue or vice. Moreover, when vice reaches a crescendo and overcomes humility and obedience to God, the ending is always the same, albeit with some different details and people. However, all the time a mixture of good and evil are evident but at different proportions in different places.

The moral: Man is alternatively bowing with mea culpas before God and then, forgetting the shame and consequences, being crushed by consequences of pride and rebellion. It is within these wavelengths that we can detect the red flags and self correct or choose to remain blind and pursue self gratification.

*What is history?*

Pope Leo XIII (Pontificate from 1878-1903) was a most prolific voice against the dangers of modernism and masterful at what one might deem the "theology of history." His *Annum ingressi (1902)*, regrettably largely ignored, extorted the reader to have a clear understanding of history to understand the social and political events of the time. Moreover, the document urged Catholics to stand on solid doctrine and in sync with the Magisterium of the Church. Yet, more enlightening was how Pope Leo XIII connected the dots in this Apostolic Letter from the Middle Ages to the French Revolution in the latter 1700's to the start of the 20th Century. Pope Leo XIII placed the Middle Ages, when the philosophy of the Gospel governed the state, against the present age, where chaos reigns.

He explained the egalitarian devolvement in three stages but one denial, beginning with Martin Luther who denied the Papacy, Our Lady's centrality in salvation history, and the Holy Eucharist thus dismissing holy regality in Christianity. Then the French Revolution further advanced this egregious principle societally by denying that there were or should be any variance in the status of people. (Off with the Queen's head!). Worse, as the monarchy represented the Catholic Church, Catholicism was targeted and silenced with thin acceptance of private worship, prohibited religion in governing. Sound familiar?

Communism then applied falsified "equality" to the economic and political spheres. Yet, Pope Leo XIII saw these progressive stages as war against the Church—against God and spoke against a "backward society" that proclaims absolute equality among people, including sexes, attire, and even Catholic religion and pagan sects. ("*Understanding the Theology of History in the Teaching of Leo XIII and the Thought of Plinio Correa de Oliveira,* Nelson Ribeiro Fragelli, The American Society for the Defense of Tradition, Family, and Property, March 1, 2022)

One wonders that Pope Leo XIII was prophetic, and today, what would he say? This corrupt egalitarianism has finally led to the ultimate denial, that of the sovereignty of the individual, and nihilism. However, God is the Master Historian. It is His Story. We know the ending, and Catholic teachers can be among the protagonists!

Teachers know…KNOW history to understand and be able to guide souls.

Even so, basic truisms do not capture exactly what *is* history. In *History Forgotten and Remembered, author* Andrew Zwerneman identifies thirteen features of history. Briefly paraphrasing, they are: Past events

## Chapter Nine: The Eternal Age vs Man-Constructed Ages 273

though familiar are unrepeatable. Or, as noted military historian Brian Sobel often quips (Quoting Mark Twain), "History does not repeat, but it rhymes." This speaks to the wonderfully captivating and unique narrative characteristics of history. Two, there are extraordinary events that intersect with the flow of ordinary times. This also reminds us that not all is under people's control, as a whole, even in more virtuous states. Three, the past is different but it informs us today. Again, we may return to setting, that basic premise that people's nature does not change but the circumstances around them.

In "The Virtue of Obedience" (CERC—Catholic Education Resource Center— Weekly Update August 4, 2021), reprinting *First Things*, July 23, 2021), Archbishop Charles Chaput notes: *History, of course, doesn't repeat itself. History is a creation of unique and unrepeatable people. So the gulf between Europe 1521 (various Reformations) and our circumstances today, in 2021, is huge. But patterns of human thought and behavior do repeat themselves.*

Four, history provides us memory, by which we can view our condition sympathetically. One could add…or critically. The notion of memory though does strike at the heart of spiritual and mental health, however. As mentioned elsewhere, Father Chad Ripperger's *Introduction to the Science of Mental Health* and many other tomes, explore the role of memory in human behavior, including self image, perception of others, and circumstances. Also, intersecting is one's passions (appetites), temperaments, cognitive powers, and then will. For example, if someone sees a knife in another person's hand, and associates a memory of being assaulted by a knife, how might he or she respond? Of course, other "memories" and associations may arise; reaction may be related to the familiarity of the person holding the knife; and also, the tendency of either to be aroused to impulsivity or anger could direct action. Hopefully, the will through virtue will have tempered rash defensiveness. Also, memories encoded in historical summaries may be "false memories," sometimes devised for emotional self protection or springing from wounded pride.

Magnify that single episode by an entire group or even nation, and one can readily understand how "memory"—including collective memory may impact the future course of relationships within a country or with other countries.(Critical Race Theory comes to mind.)

Five, history gives us observational opportunities that together with memory, form understanding of the past. A caveat should be interjected here. Often, this can be accomplished inappropriately or off mark, as a person living today, even when related to figures of the past, can fall into the trap of interposing his or her own experiences or personality into motive and rationale. (See above.)

Formative events require observation to the fullest extend of context. In other words, not all events can be practically studied and educational content should focus on key ones. However, better fewer with total review than several with selected detail or perceptions. Teachers may think of that proverbial elephant as described by the three blind men. What would be worse would be blind persons feeling a hundred animals and describing creatures.

The seventh feature: Only people have history. Perhaps a different way to look at this is that only people reason with memory.

History is not a judgmental agent. Ages are descriptive not defining. When "How to study history" is explored, this will be expanded. It is helpful to add here, though, that Ages are manmade benchmarks, can be alternatively named, and, in some ways, fluid, according to newly discovered information and as time passes.

*So, the intent of this Primer is not to teach history but direct educators to study history wisely, so as to impart to students that which is critical to their understanding of past human behavior alongside salvation history, and how to support students in their understanding while promoting virtue. However, in "Tools," some editable sources will provide standard timetables with respect to Eras and Ages, prominent persons (including Saints), and resources such as the Prophets, Church Fathers, and Encyclicals that better form a pattern of God's Presence and Authority in history.*

A ninth feature is looking at history as a concept of unity. It grasps the movement, chronological and qualitative, of the whole of our existence in time. As a narrative genre, history is meaningful, purposeful, and expressive of who and why we are. Combined with setting and context, history is best served to the audience.

Another aspect of history is that it provides an occasion for hope if we orient towards the good inherited.

Another but prominent feature: "Human existence originates from within and from beyond ourselves." History is snippets of eternity, at least temporal world history. All persons were perceived and conceived in an eternal framework. This temporal world and history as it is known will cease, and that eternal kingdom will need no recording. It will just …be.

Beyond features though, it should be impressed that history is quite extensive. What is studied can make a critical difference in how students perceive the world around them and even how they navigate that world. It can make all the difference to their eternal destination. That is how vital a healthy but wholesome curriculum is developed and presented in appropriate ways to children at different ages.

This is why **all** teachers need to have a good handle on history, correct any faults of earlier instruction, be open to modification and clarification with trusted resources, and pursue the subject even after formal education. (See Researching for Reliability.)

*Why study history?*

So, why study history? What is the point if people already know the plot, characters motivation, conflict and resolution? Could teachers not just sum up with a sentence or paragraph, develop a blueprint of how to proceed; and vow to sin no more? Also problematic are those who cherry pick history or prune it in a way to either elevate or degrade individuals or groups. Optimally we pursue knowledge and understanding of the past to live better in the present and ensure a future eternity with God. (Ok…who does not like stories, too?) People want and need understanding, inspiration, warning or assurance, purpose, order, and direction. At a point beyond formal schooling, everyone will be challenged in their families, neighborhoods, work, and performance of civic duties. Still, studying history goes beyond the obviously basic lessons of living a moral—value inclusive— life.

The critical "Why" of studying history is to attain Heaven. So, in particular, Church history,, inclusive of Scripture, alongside of world history noticeably distinguishes why living virtuously is mandatory. The juxtaposition of these two— ethereal and earthly—provides stark contrast and boldfaces the times and places people have fallen from grace and into ruin.

*How to study history*

So, particularly history teachers must not only know history but understand any given curriculum regardless if they are homeschooling or standing in front of a whole class. They need to know enough to ask pertinent questions and the ability to modify, add resources, or challenge textbook content. They need to be inquisitors, as well. Just the simple, "Why is _____ an objective in the _____ grade course on American history?" can be illuminating and a jumping point for further discussion, lessons modification, and better clarity for students. The good news is that in 2023, there is a plethora of wonderful curriculums and approaches to history instruction though planning ahead is essential. Here, shared colleague units and cross curriculum sites can enormously assist teachers. More is available online, all the time. As the adage goes, "Work smarter, not harder."

There are myriad curriculum guides and approaches to studying history, some more inclined to narrative like the excellent Catholic Textbook Project, but other worthwhile structuring like Phillip Campbell's four-part series and Tan Publishing materials. In fact, a combination of resources is the history teacher's best support, and there are good arguments against using any one textbook to cover a particular event or time period. Always, though, an appropriate, developmental progression of study is key and in conjunction with other subjects or current events. Of course Faith—Salvation history (Holy Scripture in companionship with Church history)— from the time of the Fathers through the last 2,000 years, must be interwoven and applied.

A special note to Catholic school administrators: Homeschooling programs often provide that progression through the year and by grade level. Of course, Catholic schools may vary, as Archdioceses generally map different subjects with non negotiable objectives and recommended resources and texts. Still, if there is some openness for discussion and enhancing a more robust history curriculum, most Archdiocesan curriculum leaders are open to input.

A general course outline at the end of this section is *just* one example. However, there are several ways by which to explore history, but these thoughts should assist teachers in approaching this subject, even those who are compelled to follow prescriptive objectives. More importantly, and worth repeating, Holy Scripture must precede and thread instruction. It is mandatory to have a genuine relationship between Truth and History, and as it pertains to Scripture and Sacred Tradition that resulted in the Magisterium.

To start...

*Catholic teachers must dispel the idea that man's written history is superior to God's Word as inspired in authentic Bible text, or that Biblical accounts are merely figurative or the product of exaggerated human imagination.* A Great Flood that destroyed the world is in historical accounts other than the Bible, as just one glaring example. In this regard, teachers must reject the incessant anti-Christian spirit that ridicules the Bible and believers. Throughout history, most intensely in the modern era, the devil's propagandists have managed to marginalize Holy Scripture and cast it as "among equally acceptable beliefs and tenets." Simultaneously, certain mere human figures, albeit some brilliant, have been elevated as experts and thoroughly scholarly on matters on historic events and time periods. These include scientists, mathematicians, researchers, as well as philosophers.

Now, those persons are to be respected but always in context of their limitations and possible propensity towards pride and other sins. Also, while the Bible is true, certainly there are elements of figurative language and narrative style that pronounce theological messages. Yet, the essence is not fodder for manipulation and disbelief. Besides, a read of history demonstrates that Biblical accounts actually occurred, though described uniquely in Scripture. There are examples in numerous nonsectarian texts *History of Nations* is one example.

Also, many authentic, well researched Catholic texts, articles, commentaries, etc. exist to reinforce the Divine Hand *in all of history*. As mentioned elsewhere and in the bibliography and resources, *Magnificat* is an all-in-one treasure chest and is highly recommended for educators. Content includes the daily Mass, liturgy, prayer, lives of Saints and by their notable hallmarks, such as healing division (January 2022), and enrichment in all subject areas such as history, science, music, and the arts.

For one example, Saint Anthony of the Desert, though a hermit, was a great counselor to clergy, monks and laypeople. In one "Meditation of the Day" (January 17, 2022), Saint Anthony references the transitory nature of one's bodily (temporal) name. He recalls Jacob wrestling with an angel called Israel which means *mind that sees God*. Let just that one sentence truly penetrate, as it upholds all we need to know about the orientation of our our intellect, and, actually, as that should correspond to our senses, appetites, memory, imagination, cognitive ability, and will

St. Anthony goes on to emphasize that the enemies of virtue are always plotting against truth. "For this reason not at one time only did God visit his creatures, but from the beginning there were some who were prepared to come to their own Creator by the law implanted in them, being taught by it to worship their Creator as is right."

## Chapter Nine: The Eternal Age vs Man-Constructed Ages

*All of the foregoing should give teachers pause. History is not merely the recording of people and events but its origins in Our Creator, as manifested in the Word Made Flesh—The Truth; and driven by the Holy Spirit.*

True, man makes his (or her) personal choices, often in opposition to the Word and desired Will of God for the good of His people, but repetitively the telling of history should serve as a beacon, not as the personal self glorification of man and his imprint on the temporal world. Ours is most often a muddy stomping, made even and solidified by the sacrifice of the saints and martyrs and Divine Mercy.

Now, it is not suggested that Catholic teachers preach (let alone screech) history cast in the shadows of evil except for God because that would be the other extreme. Heresies have their roots in worldly absolutes. Still there must be an overarching purpose, and that is most simply stated as guiding children to "know, love, and serve God in this world and be happy with Him for all eternity in the next."

Speaking of including Scripture and Church history, there are other "inclusionary" considerations. Interestingly, in "secular circles" this is being closely vetted as Critical Race Theory (CRT) and differently sexually oriented historical figures are being merged and even monopolizing history content. CRT has reached an apex of controversy. As 1776Unites emphasizes, truth is essential, but care must be taken to be accurate, yet not cherry pick, especially for political reasons. Incidentally, 1776Unites founded by Robert (Bob) Woodson, well-known civil rights activist, offers a wonderful and uplifting Black history curriculum, as of 2021 for high school, but with plans to expand.

Catholic teachers could take a clue from 1776Unites in planning wholesome accounts, perspectives, and analysis of history. Well-formed contextualized history with purpose is better than a timeline of dates and actions that the majority of students will forget the day after a test if not before an assessment. That will likely include several intersections with other time periods, personalities, and events, corresponding with different areas in the world. Recently catholiceducation.org shared "Celebrating the Contributions of Black Catholics

(Catholiceducation.org, March 9, 2022), proving that history should also uplift the highest ideals lived by true followers of Jesus Christ.

Connections with other subjects and team planning can greatly accent the impact.

In one Catholic school in recent years, the language arts teacher included *Animal Farm* for class reading. It so happened to correspond with the government component of the social studies unit at or around the same time. Through collaboration, students were greatly enriched in knowledge and understanding of the modern world against the insightful characterization and conflict revealed in *Animal Farm*. Similar opportunities abound.

Also, like race minorities, Catholics and Catholicism have been sharply rebuked in history classes across the country since the origin of the nation. Not unlike Black students, those who profess their faith may receive bigoted backlash. This occurs in Catholic school wherein families of differing faiths have somehow been impressed with right to challenge figures and tenets of the Faith. Going one step further, most figures in Scripture have been ignored in the public domain, as critics bash what they consider to be misogynistic script, among other dismissive critiques. Yet, the courage of Esther and Ruth are unparalleled in modern times.

Teachers need *not*—should **not**—sugarcoat Scripture or Catholic history and some dastardly characters, but they need to take care to focus on Truth, and like the 1776Unites philosophy be *aspirational*. There will always be "bad actors" and some quite influential; actions conspired by the evil one will continue to the end of this world. Moreover, the devil disrupts fruitful fields, not ones already in ruins or "on his side" anyway. Authentic Catholicism is one of the well tended and prosperous groves and a likely target...always.

*Special Postscript on Holy Scripture (Salvation History) and AD Church History Non Negotiable!*

So, it is worth reemphasizing, it is essential for all teachers to know history, and as best against the backdrop of Scripture (Salvation history) and balanced by Sacred History (Church history). For in the absence of Truth, the story of man is subject to gross distortion (falsehood) both intentionally and ignorantly. Also, by the solo hand of man, the temporal becomes the end objective rather than the eternal. Consider just for the moment that God has wholly known everyone in eternity; others can only partially know a few personally in a span of 100 years or less, and even then often erroneously.

Moreover, discussing Biblical history, it is further critical that all teachers know the Word *as interpreted by Catholic Church* in its most pristine evaluation because even that holy text has not gone unscathed outside the Church but also sadly from within. According to Casey Chalk (*How We Lost the Bible*, Catholic Thing, August 4, 2021,) "The promotion of Biblical interpretations serving secular, liberal political agendas of sex and race is only the latest manifestation of a centuries-old trend." He cites a well worthwhile read: *The Decline and Fall of Sacred Scripture: How the Bible Became a Secular Book* by Scott Hahn and Benjamin Wiker.

In recent decades, "cutting and pasting" selective Scripture has gained momentum, and it does not require scholarly knowledge, as the Bible is so readily "researchable" on the Internet and according to "topics." Two arise in prominence as most frequently quoted or referenced in social justice "sermons:" Matthew 25: 42-46 and Acts 2: 44-45. The former highlights the need for the corporeal works of mercy, and the latter would seem to support a communistic economy. While these two passages feature prominently in Christian activism, neither are anywhere near comprehensive as to the entirety of the Good News or the implications therein. (See "Government through the Ages.")

Of course, we must love our neighbor as ourselves and do all we can to help preserve life — contradictory given that often Christians who insist on taking from the wealthy and giving to the poor are sometimes the same "Christians" who also promote abortion—but adherence to Truth and perfect Love is the adhesive that should hold together that purpose and momentum. For do not the pagans do the same? (Matthew 5:47) Therefore, the Ten Commandments and spiritual works of mercy are critical although one may well precede the other, depending on circumstances. We teach Jesus Christ by example, but we teach no other, let alone ourselves. Too, it is an obviously objective fact that some early Christians lived a type of collectivism, but it would be a serious misunderstanding to confuse that with the role of government. Moreover, many could identify similar Christian communities that live "off the grid" today, but without government enabling or taxpayer support. Who is in authority is always the indicator: God or government? Within these communities, one should explore the nature of relationships, and is God at the center?

Charity—sharing—must be initiated in individuals freely giving their goods. Government, especially distant and centralized government, tends towards supporting bad habits and vice, also becoming increasingly tyrannical. Yet more on that in "Government through the Ages" is also a must subject for all teachers.

Still, teachers must also avoid the trap that "secular" is neutral or unbiased, as noted elsewhere in the Primer. They should readily grasp that simply because the word "history" appears on the front cover of a school text, even if adopted by a curriculum department with dozens of Ph.D.ers, and endorsed by a school board, does not mean that the content is all true or complete. In the worst cases, there is a deliberate effort—an agenda —to move students towards certain conclusions about what has happened in the past or in current events. Even the most solid Catholic history books will include biases, albeit often unintentional, and cannot include every detail or facet of a person, event, or era. (See Researching for Reliability and General Custer)

As a reminder, the *Magnificat* provides monthly lessons on Church Saints and leaders through time and with all types of expertise, in teaching, medicine, mathematics, science, government, philosophy, the arts, and research.

**One point to impress on every student is to know who wrote what, when, how, and why. If they can develop that monitor to ensure custody of their mind over what enters it, they will do well, regardless of their specific textbook. Educators want to form reasonably critical evaluators of "incoming information" against the backdrop of well understood truth. (See Researching for Reliability)**

*The Ultimate Priority and Main Objective in HOW to Teach History*

Every child deserves to know the intimate knowledge of God and His infinite Love, from birth (actually from all time), taught both implicitly and explicitly. Grasping history helps integrate this into the child's being throughout his or her life. Knowing the trajectory of God's creation, in its perfect organization and revelation, from individual, to family, to world and the tempo of human behavior in response to the Creator helps form conscience and foster virtue.

Catholic teachers must also realize that in regard to history, the Church (The Mystical Body of Christ) can never be compartmentalized, let alone separated. However, they will be sorely tempted by well written prose and lofty aspirations of educational professors and philosophers who insist they can impart history and all subject matter in a way that enlightens and inspires children to finally build a Tower of Babel to themselves. The humanistic platform for public education was cast in stone by such pioneers as John Dewey and Horace Mann, but the 1960's brought the notion of conquering even death—at least for the desirables— to the forefront.

In *The Social Ideas of American Educators* by Merle Curti, copyright 1935 and 1959, and reprinted in 1968, education is seen against the backdrop of contemporary history with an emphasis on social progress, the notion as John Dewy commented in 1939, "All social movements involve conflicts which are reflected intellectually in controversies. It would not be a sign of health if such an important social interest as education were not also an area of struggles, practical and theoretical."

Thus, "social studies" became the fixed prism through which to study history yet with the aim of using history to identify and justify addressing societal ills and inspiring man to finally and successfully build that Tower. As Cardinal Sarah so simply but profoundly expresses, this is not possible. The fault lies not in yet to be discovered technology and perfected governance but in ourselves, at the core of fallen man. Virtue can be cultivated in all instruction, emphasizing their redeeming quality

We were not made for this temporal world, as St. Augustine so wonderfully made known in the City of God. So, then, the study of history and its ancillary branches of government, geography, economics, and civics (morality) serves its purpose in only reminding people of their shortcomings, how to avoid disaster to self and others, and aim for a blessed eternal life.

As previously noted, history—HIS Story—exists as a subject for review and study for several reasons, all a consequence of The Fall: 1) It is the inclination of man to look in the "rear view mirror" of time. The past is an unfortunate consciousness of human beings. 2) We have a need to understand, so reflection on the past is one way to analyze human behavior, including trends and patterns, and arrive at some commonly held conclusions often geared for the present and future. 3) Universally, the past is studied to hopefully avoid repeating deadly mistakes and to provide for an ideal future, yet ever mindful that this is a temporal world and suffering and sin are ever present effects of the Fall..

Any review of the past is bound to fail if it does not incorporate the truth that history is but a mirror of the inherent nature of persons in a temporal world. Its study is only useful to demonstrate the inane concept that people can wholly perfect themselves and the world, especially in the absence of God, natural law, and morality. There is no way, anyone, no matter how intelligent or skilled, can ensure a world without temptation, vice, tyranny, illness, and death. As these words are written, there is a T-Shirt being promoted that reads: "Life is Dangerous, Live it Anyway." For the Catholic—and all Christians and persons believing in one God—a more apt T-Shirt might read. "Life is From God, Live it Faithfully."

For in essence what history reflects is repetitive, certain failure when people turn from God and virtue and embrace temporal self-will and vice. There are the familiar patterns of regret, repentance, and return to order that are followed by some prosperity and peace. Yet, because man is obstinate, lulled for some generations, descendants from chaos are prone to repeat the fall from grace, repetitively. Again, this is all about the inherent skewed nature of persons in the temporal world. (Concupiscence)

So, "how" to tech history begins with prayer to the Holy Spirit to reach people personally with truisms.

### *God's Divine Plan vs. Man's Defined Eras and Ages*

History may be viewed through the Eternal Age vs. Constructed Ages, knowing that these popular "subtitles" are arbitrary to some degree and certainly not all encompassing of any particular time period. Also, the material selected to illustrate or justify the overarching theme is subject to the opinions of experts, but this often entails some subjectivity. Expect errors, some unintentional or due to sloppy research, compilation, and publication. Also, new information may arise that alters earlier theories or facts. Yet, there are the social engineers who will attempt to cast or recast a particular important time according to ideology or with another aim in mind. Technology has complicated the process, and resources such as Wikipedia have earned their poor reputation due to hacking and laity revision alone.

For the purposes of continuity though not necessarily agreement, special eras and ages are presented herein with those reminders and parallel to Church history. Numerous sources on Church history are in the bibliography, and an attempt is also made to reconcile basic understanding of events, notables and periods of importance.

Be advised that there are many ways to categorize historical eras and ages, periods, and epochs. Some sites will provide more exhaustive and detailed information while others will be generalized. They can be global or by nation, as well.

The point is not to be exhaustive hereabout but to show the human spirit and how reason (or lack thereof) and Faith (or lack thereof) have triggered discoveries and inventions and thwarted or impeded growth in our relationship with God. How man has viewed himself, his capabilities, the limitations to knowledge, as superior or inferior to God or others, all play out in history for better or worse. How people think has consequences for better or worse.

In fact, non-historians, after reading this chapter, should well understand much better why mankind rises and falls even after lessons should have been learned with the the earliest couple, Adam and Eve and later the Israelites in Egypt or Babylon and beyond.

Therefore, the overall purpose, though, of the manner in which this section is relayed is to serve as a platform and springboard for conscientious teachers to teach the City of God in the city of man with more confidence, commitment, and courage.

That aside, as one investigates known man constructed ages, it will be imperative to distinguish between current information and that which shaped objective Truth. Teachers should also forgive past historians, mindful that they are likely only as dependable as the education they received and their personal ideologies. There is also a certain deliberate "forgetfulness" to advance an ideology or right as "new, more scientific, and progressive" knowing that most people rarely dig further back than their own lives, if that, to verify the veracity of any claimant.

So, this is a mere glimpse of highlighted, more pronounced, examples of life, as it first formed the most basic community of God-man to nations God-global community and in different times and places of the world that best illustrate the extremes of this spectrum. It should be emphasized that regardless if it was only Adam and Eve or billions of people, these "falls from and rises to grace" occur in families and also intermittently across locations, like a class setting. What is concluded is that only by living a virtuous life, striving for sainthood do we at least come close to ideal community life, but that it will always be imperfect while we are in *this* world.

One exceptional and powerful visual presentation of history from both the perspective of salvation and secular history is the *Ascension Press Timeline Bible*. One might even suggest it is a must companion for any history teacher, but any educator will benefit by the incredible work accomplished to enable Catholics to "see" the City of God side by side with the city of man through time from Creation to Revelations. (History beyond the time of Jesus Christ, of course, would always be set by the saints who followed, major AD Church history events and figures of prominence, and benchmark Councils.)

In a nutshell, Jeff Cavins sought to better understand the Bible, and in that process, the Ascension Press Timeline Bible was produced with many wonderful extensions since. Cavins divided the Bible into twelve Periods, seventy key events, and six Covenants. Note that while man makes fickle and changing compacts and contracts, God's bond with man is unbreakable—a Covenant. Yet, Cavins and his associates went further and pictorially depicted secular world history and world powers that corresponded to those twelve periods that cover the early world through the foundation of the Church.

A history teacher should be ecstatic to have such a reference. Moreover with respect to the Covenants, one can glean the general Divine Plan of Our Lord in Salvations History as follows: Adam and Eve represent the holy Covenant of the One Holy Couple; Noah of the One Holy Family; Abraham of the One Holy Tribe; Moses of the One Holy Nation; David of the One Holy Kingdom, and Jesus Christ of the One, Holy, Catholic, and Apostolic Church. It comes full circle with Jesus representing the Bridegroom and the Church the unblemished Bride.

That prefaced, man's plans pale in comparison with major eras and ages, often with world commonality. However, these are shown in parallel to the rise of monotheism and Christianity. While collectively recognized by both secular and religious leaders as benchmarks in time, they are also selected for their illustration of the inherent nature of the person regardless of time, space, environment, government, economics, and so forth. Of course, one can also attribute Church history eras in some way to the secular ones.

Still, the descriptions of history may change "on a dime" thanks to the increasingly divided politics of our world and technology, but it is likely to always remain predictable.

One other note before plunging in: History cannot be compartmentalized although it may seem that is the case here. History includes many different individuals in movement in response to, but also in the absence of, the Holy Spirit to lesser or greater degrees. Keep in mind, that someday, history teachers of today will be scrutinized in later times, so be humble but inquiring; humble yet confident; and charitable but truthful.

Why Ages and Eras? Historians are prone to identify certain periods of time as this or that Era or Age, in the hope of capturing the spirit and main characteristics of that time period. Colorful figures, both evil and saintly, offer an engaging narrative, and some times in history have brought forth these individuals and groups most fascinating or appealing. What is referred to as "progress" or "development" become common benchmarks, too. Finally, some persons, events, and time periods are craftily chosen with an ulterior motive, which can be for good or evil. The wise, discriminating (Yes, sometimes that is an apt word!) well-read teacher will heed those instances in recorded history and current events or chronologies.

Also while helpful on one level, these global monikers (Eras and Ages) may mislead students or fail to project the entirety of a century or more. Moreover, if academia responsible for developing textbooks fixate on a particular issue or propagate to persuade future learners, the genuine lessons of history may be maligned or lost.

One illustrative example (though America has special attention further on), is the Gilded Age (1870-1900) which in some ways masked the insidious rise of internal attacks on marriage, family, religion (particularly Christianity), the dignity of persons, and peace as God intended. So named because all that glitters is not real gold, the moniker, nonetheless, tended to focus students of history on temporal concerns in society and government and primarily economic ones. It would take very insightful and diligent scholars to explore the ironically "gilded" reporting of that time period as recorded by general historians. Indeed, those impressions linger, as many observers of American (and world) events, cite the 1960s as the widely accepted benchmark for the "sexual revolution."

*With specificity to American History*

Yet, branding ages and eras in particular fashion is not the only dilemma that can mislead history teachers. Re identifying key events to "fit a narrative" is becoming increasingly hostile to truth.

One glaring example is the current 1619 Project that has been embraced as credible and within months--not years--not decades—and without legitimate scrutiny ,has already influenced public school instruction. As one noted, this is a thesis in search of evidence. Moreover, it has been easily and largely disproved, but the damage has been done as it led to "critical race theory" also already in American classrooms.

This is just one more revision of what many believe to be a trend to destroy the admirable roots of the American Republic and transform it through education into a more socialistic (i.e. communistic) government and society.

Often, then, history is generalized with underlying factors ignored, discarded, or altered to frame reality into a predetermined ideology. Now, it can be fairly argued that in the interests of promoting the ideals of America, past history texts emphasized only that and these facts or presumptions which glorified the country, downplaying unpleasant facts or ignoring them. Tales of George Washington never telling a lie; Abraham Lincoln's extraordinary integrity; and so forth have had a taint of exaggeration, hyperbole, as well. Reviewing background to the Emancipation Act in recent times, demonstrates how political powers can gloss over the fine but revealing details. Did Lincoln whole heartedly free the slaves, or was there other considerations and priorities. For example would he have issued this Proclamation had the South surrendered first?

Still, one could defend that orientation at least in that it bolstered positivity, while today negativity about all that promotes liberty and faith depresses.

See the Appendix for resources—electronic and printed and persons or organizations knowledge and generally trustworthy. Teachers must be *healthy* skeptics, though, and verify, as even well- intended persons can make mistakes or fall prey to supporting an ideal over substance. Listening becomes a most important skill to hone.

### *The Impact of Progressives (Regressive Radicalization)*

History is being contorted even as these words are typed. There is nothing "new" in this, but the rapidity of distorted Truth would be laughable if not so tragic. Obviously technology has its tentacles in these constant challenges. Yet, how does one teach history in such an acidic and fluid assault on objectivity in favor of ideology? Blatant censorship"justified" by alleged misinformation intruded on the freedom of speech world wide during the pandemic.

The Catholic school teacher should be well aware that Christianity, especially Catholics, are persons non gratis. Moreover, biographies and any history is likely to cast dark shadows on events and persons of Faith. It is not atypical that a text book will raise any atrocity about the Crusades while tamping down the brutality associated with Muslim expansion. These subtle anti Christian biases arise in language arts; math; and science as well. Furthermore, any research project, regardless of subject can fall prey to revisionists, propagandists, and outright enemies of truth if it props their ideologies.

## Chapter Nine: The Eternal Age vs Man-Constructed Ages

Contrast the attacks on police, most of whom perform their duties with exceptional virtue, with the reported "mostly peaceful" protest in the wake of the George Floyd death in contrast to the Capitol Building invasion in January 2021.

The violence, destruction, and even deaths attributed to months long sieges of urban areas were rationalized by mainstream media and political figures. Some even emboldened the renegades by paying bail money! The attempted one-day siege of the Capitol Building, while definitely wrong minded and also ending in death, resulted in excessively condemning responses. So, the matter of communicating history goes beyond the glass half full or empty but what is the motivation of the "reporter" or historian "recorder." Even unwittingly, people will incorporate personal perspective and sometimes obstinately, openly and unapologetically.

Hopefully, the foregoing well establishes why it is essential therefore that Catholic teachers -- regardless of special emphasis or grade level--know history, and even become a collector—by scanning or with **a well balanced** library. Note the bold face, as this is not suggestive of leaning towards the other extreme.

Teachers would provide better content and instruction by intentionally searching for contradictory accounts even when it brings discomfort. Primary sources are excellent because these are often lost over the years but can illuminate "movements," the emergence of trends up or downward, and bring to life individuals and stories that provide the human aspect of history.

Also, ancillary subjects that impact history, such as science and sociology, are ever discovering and reporting new aspects of life and the world, yet often "used" to bolster temporal control over the world rather than Divine Will.

Of some assurance is that this is not a new phenomenon, and it would also be advisable for teachers to realize that such maneuvers have been happening for hundreds, maybe thousands, of years.

(Author's Note: Years ago, I picked up a book, *History of Woman*, written by a man no less, about hundred years ago, whose name escapes me now. Some content was laugh out loud; much is a horror. However, I suspect I cannot locate it, as It is buried away from the grandchildren.)

On the other end of the spectrum are works like *Womenhood and Marriage by* Bernarr MacFadden, published in 1918, also over one hundred years ago! Much of it could have been written today in 2021. Among other statements: "We know that some persons can even distort that great book, the Bible, and make its meaning spacious and erotic."

In her chapter "The Crime of Abortion," the author admits her own ignorance about the embryo, but then notes: It is known now, however, the there is life from the very moment of conception, and that to interfere with the process of development which is going on there is, in truth, to take life, which is, in bald phraseology, to commit murder. MacFadden decries that many would would shrink from even killing a mouse, but not hesitate to deliberately kill their own offspring?

Like today, the author admits that they (mothers) do not term it that way.

MacFadden underscores the dangers of abortion even given the so-called experts, and in its aftermath, mothers suffer consequences in many ways including physically.

So, a primary adjunct in "how to teach history" would be to Identify movements that benefitted mankind, along with influences that demeaned the relationship with God and man. Compare and contrast the good, beautiful, and true with falsehoods, evil and ugliness of time periods. (However, there is rarely a pure account of an historical event or era on either side, so candor is paramount, too.) For example, not all Catholic leaders have been exemplary including Popes and other clergy. Distinguish between the weaknesses of persons and the true Faith.)

Teachers in any any subject should be equipped to to impart objective knowledge that honors Faith from the perspective of critical and challenging developments in human thought and behavior for better or worst. Right reason is illuminated by Faith

However, virtuous teachers will not neglect the stellar saints. Sometimes we perceive them only through the lens of Church teaching, and confine their lives in a statue to be viewed from a pew, but most were excellent students and understood historical events and eras by the light of that Faith. They were frequent movers of history, too.

Educators must be confidently knowledgable to dismantle illusionary nouveau thinking with respect to social interaction and achievement. They must futuristically, prepare students to identify signs of socialist deterioration, always marked by pride, self will and self reliance, the diminishment of virtue and the evil acceptance of vice.

In another section, reliable research techniques are detailed, so this will not be a rehash, but the general rule is verify, verify, verify.

## *Developmentally Studying History*

Developmentally Appropriate History Curriculum and Instruction
History in Word Developmentally

Of course, teachers should "Be Not Afraid" but paradoxically" Be Very Afraid," but not in an excitable or panicked manner. What they may prudently fear is the exponentially explosive and intrusive way "education" is eroding the innocence of even toddlers. Fortunately, Catholic Schools are increasingly aware of what used to be "safe" venues. Most recently, for example, more Catholic schools have ceased book fair contracts with Scholastic Books. One of these schools is not even particularly "orthodox" Catholic. They are scrutinizing other book vendors more, as well.

Why? Authors with a bent to secularized, humanistic themes such as same sex relations, Wicca, and the like are breezily promoted to Faith communities. It is easy to suspect, intentionally. Moreover, those who disagree with these irreversible "imprints" are labeled bigoted, intolerant fanatics. Wise educators do not care a whit. Sticks and stones may break some bones, but words cannot hurt. Insults to THE Word, however, could cause irreparable damage to your child's authentic understanding of God's goodness and plan for him or her and the world.

(Author's Note: I have been blessed with a daughter-in-law who has ensured that her son and daughter "hear" the Word integrated throughout their studies. They learn the facts, and will do so appropriately as they age, but what is not permitted is the perverted ideology of modern times. The tints and smokescreens are undeliverables; progressive propaganda—actually outright lies—are nonnegotiable. As my grandson chants timelines that reconcile in history, he also hears Scriptural milestones that places them in perspective of truth. My granddaughter is listening along with him.)

Now, one should not be naïve and think that even those children well educated will never hear anything contrary to objective truth and human events as they occurred. This includes some of the very regrettable sins of even those most faithful to God through time. However, it is all about "timing" and "context." It is, in the final analysis about the formation of conscience, consciousness; and conscientiousness. Being alert to the "red flags" of deceit or the glossing over of essential matters is the underpinning of successful education. It is not so teaching children what to think but *how* to think—how to reason by the illumination of faith. This is no easy task, and even parents who have been fantastic homeschoolers will admit that their grown children do not always walk the path laid out. Still, they have more hope of redemption than the child who was misled from the gate.

So, how does this look? Herein, will be some developmental guides and resources for parents starting even at birth.

**0-2:**

Reading to children in the womb is a great exercise to build that practice once out of the womb. One need not pay attention to the books though never read themes containing seeds of disorder or confusion. Young parents today walk a minefield, as even the small hardback toddler books must be viewed for overt and subtle messaging and images that they do not want your baby to "see" or "hear." As Mickey Mouse's ears turn red, there is not much left to trust.

With respect to history, from the youngest age through preschool, children learn about their neighborhoods and community. They are introduced to basic safety guidance and manners; respect for authority and symbols that guide behavior; and they are often visitors to special forums like museums and historic sites, often with siblings or other family members. Without expressed permission, they will see and hear things that will baffle and challenge parents in seemingly innocuous public spaces.

One family reported multiple incidents as West Hollywood transformed into a Mecca for persons experiencing and acting upon same sex attraction despite an explosion of deadly AIDS in the mid '80s. Their children saw everything from affection between two members of the same sex to cross dressing to flagrant body piercings, and this family had to navigate a firestorm of potential imprints on their children's minds. While that family relocated as soon as feasible, there is literally no safe spaces today.

On a positive note, there are wonderful, virtue filled children's books that focus on family life in reflection of the City of God—Scripture and Sacred Tradition. Make sure that your home environment depicts model family life after the Holy Family, and there are ample examples of nature, arts and architecture, and historic sites that uphold the beauty of Creation. Include sources of archeology, a most noble profession, and what that field has had to offer. Even small children can appreciate how the natural shapes in nature have influenced man's inventiveness, imagination, and creativity. Teach them early that even the fork and spoon are basic articles of technology— manmade tools to help us live more efficiently and comfortably. There is nothing wrong with that! Start young with the value of money even in small change, and the responsibility even toddlers should learn in the rightful and conservative use of resources, including energy.

There are dozens of daily opportunities to teach about rightful relationships with God, self, and neighbor. Small acts, like walking to the store, impress the benefits of exercise while simultaneously teaching that a vehicle using gas is not only sometimes unnecessary but wasteful. Share stories about the past that illustrate the absolute joy that adults and children in previous times experienced in the absence of modern conveniences

Additionally, ample opportunities abound to show even the youngest how historically people lived by doing some of their tasks, as well. How much better will they appreciate butter on their toast if they have churned the butter and baked the bread. Growing a vegetable garden may introduce them to the healthiest foods—neither processed nor artificially preserved. If there is a hen house— fresh eggs—great! The texture is a bit different, but people rave about the flavor. Again, at the same time, share some "history"—including nonfiction tales of homesteading, like *Little House on The Prairie.* A very young child may not understand words, but pictures tell a thousand of them, and you are getting into the habit of integrated education. By the way thrift stores and used bookstores are great treasure troves for these.

Always, of course, young children's minds need direction to consciousness about our loving Father in Heaven. Scripture can bring alive many of these concepts, too. How great is our God who feeds his children—not the local supermarket!

**Preschool/Kindergarten:**

Developmentally, teachers may have two challenges, as a teacher but as a parent. This may be particularly challenging, especially for the working parent who may be a teacher. They are often made to feel guilty, and they have a truly hard road if there is realistically no choice. First, teachers are great resources for other teachers to locate the right learning environment. If possible, utilize trusted Catholic family members. If neither of those are options, teachers should seek authentically Catholic preschools, many of which now offer the Catechesis of the

## Chapter Nine: The Eternal Age vs Man-Constructed Ages

Good Shepherd, which signals a hands-on educational environment. Tuition may be discouraging, but children grow quickly. Still teachers, particularly Catholic teachers should confidently seek tuition assistance. They can and do almost always "pay back" later!

This may well be the most critical decision, though, and even "trusted" sites have their hiccups. One trusted Catholic preschool that allowed a book about alternative lifestyles into its shelf. It was a battle to remove it, and some parents were astonished that this was the case. Of course, children may well see two persons of the same sex with children. This may be in their own families! How many are now divided over this? Still, that is no excuse for "normalizing" same sex relations as though they are just different but equal "human relations." They are not, bluntly, they are not.

So, from the gate, this is the point that some teachers may decide to homeschool first and enter a contracted position later. Either way, a parent-teacher will need to know what to expect for this age group.

Children of this age know the basics of catechism, or should. They were created by God to know, love, and serve Him and be with Him someday forever in Heaven. Still, do not underestimate a young child's ability to recognize their own misbehavior or treating others uncharitably or unjustly. They often have a keen sense of "right and wrong" though the Church does not hold young children accountable for serious sin until the "age of reason" usually around seven or eight years old.

There is temptation to rebel against respect and obedience by self, others, occasion, and the devil. However, there is a reestablishment of peace and order when even a small child shows awareness of offending God or neighbor and shows genuine contrition and serves some consequence. Certainly, all of this can be taught—but more likely illustrated—daily.

As for those gnarly areas, Theology of the Body has been developed even for the young in simple references to creation and sex—male and female. Still, life is full of surprises, and questions about the body may arise. Teachers will hopefully have savvy superiors with a "plan" and frequently proposed questions and answers. Of course, the parents are the primary educators, so they are in this loop, too.

How should teachers acknowledge the thorny matters? Are there any books for young children who have already experienced this? Certainly, there are resources, but for the most part, teachers must determine when and how to broach this topic, depending on their unique situation and the school curriculum. Focusing on the beauty of God's creation and plan for one male-one female and family and sharing books and as many social settings that reinforce this is most beneficial.

There will be times, though, that an unavoidable and uncomfortable circumstance may arise. Teachers may feel conflicted because of family situations in which there are members in same sex attraction relationships. Courage/EncourageRC has a plethora of guiding resources. No other group in over forty years, comes close to their fidelity to the faith in a loving manner. Furthermore teachers should be aware of any organization, even in parishes or as promoted by some clergy, that undermines truth or plants doubt, confusion, and disordered thinking on this topic.

Fortunately, though, at this age, lessons likely revolve around home and neighborhood. Like with toddlers, this is a great age to do many hands-on activities and surround them with healthy arts and architecture, simple reading, including the Proverbs, art, music, and, of course the Ten Commandments and the basic laws of civil societies. Money awareness...value...of its use can be done through simple purchases, and the notion of savings introduced. Basic geography is another reasonable area to start exploring, particularly with globes and other reality based points of reference. Where does the sun "rise" and "set."

As for history, many settings instruct on "community" in this age group—neighborhoods and the like, but there are some wonderful narrative history stories that can provide even small children a sense of the past in instructional and inviting ways. Church history most certainly has its place in preschool. While not promoting much in the way of video presentations, there are Holy Heroes, and other short clips that bring alive early saints and events that even young children can appreciate.

There are several ways to impart the meaning of history and how individuals contribute to the well being of self, family, and neighbor and therefore to a treasured past, joyful present, and prosperous future.

One, teachers are great at creating bulletin boards. They may show student's histories; another may record "major" events in the classroom setting; a third might demonstrate the positive influence of the classroom "history" on the entire family, neighborhood, or school. Perhaps, students may share their family's ties to historic events, as genealogy is so popular.

Two, personal family histories in the way of narrative writing or story book creation are a great way to introduce concepts relating to that subject area. A classroom "newspaper" can be simply developed even in a kindergarten classroom.

Three, field trips to local historical sites or virtually in the age of pandemic.

Teachers may include instruction that shows timeline, sequence, cause and effect, relationships between virtuous behavior and happy outcomes or the opposite. Everyday incidents offer myriad opportunities.

**Primary Grades (1-3)**

With rare exception, public school is now off limits to any teacher (or parent) seeking to ensure that he or she is not indoctrinating innocent children with falsehoods, and worse, evil. This is not to despair the many teachers who are heroically attempting to live asChristian and somehow model that to their students. Yet, the tide is now against them, and, at best, they will look more like tepid cowards than models to exemplify. Teachers are mandated to teach certain materials; they are legally bound to identify children according to the "gender of his or her choice." They must navigate even bathroom passes to accommodate what has become nothing short of ludicrous, but dangerous, policies and practices. Moreover, no teacher should be commanded to call a young boy (by birth DNS) by a girl's pronoun. Do not insist that a girl now identifying as a boy is sent to the boy's bathroom. Do not thrust silly LGBTQ "bios" in lesson plans and mandate special heroes by their sexual orientation.

Mary Rice Hasson, J.D. and Theresa Farnan, Ph.D. co-authored the chilling *Get Out Now: Why You Should Pull Your Child from Public Schools Before It's Too Late,* Regnery Gateway, 2018, but one wonders how many heeded this alarm bell. Incredibly, the clarion call has only grown more urgent in recent years. This is a must read for any parent or teacher of Catholic school age children.

Preschool, Kindergarten, or Primary teachers may wonder why they need to know history in order to teach, including their level of "social studies"? though that term is used loosely for common identity rather than as a preference.

All teachers of all children, including parents are instilling in their children (students) necessary knowledge about citizenship, first in the family (the foundation of government), then the neighborhood, followed by community(its). "Lessons learned" applies to the youngest amongst us, as does familiarity with fundamental economic (fiscal literacy), the cause and effects of behavior, the impact of climate and geography on movement and life in general, and the virtues—principles— that guide living with others, starting with prudence but including justice, temperance, and fortitude. Of course, faith, hope, and charity should be interwoven into the concept of good governance leads to bountiful history.

Even the youngest among us can grasp the Commandments and, particularly the two main Commandments to love God with your whole heart, soul, and mind and to love your neighbor as yourself.

As a teacher of any age, it will be vital to understand history is the landscape of man's risings and fallings; peaceful living emphasizes God and virtue; law and order reign in conscientious times; disorder and chaos are symptoms of a society absent good; war has its roots in evil. More than that, a knowledgeable and capable Catholic educator will understand the slippery slope upon which we now coast. Still, focus on the order of nature and benefits of healthy hierarchy.

In "Beyond Spoiled: Introducing the 'Squishy Generation'" John Horvat (The Imaginative Conservative 3/8/2021) addresses the hyper pampered youth of our day whose parents either from fractured home lives themselves or otherwise wounded, cushion their children through any and every trial or threat of suffering. Even the Spanish daily, "El Mundo" decried the disastrous effects of this upbringing on children."

One would argue that this phenomenon in the midst of all our other troubling signs portends an historical age that will more resemble "The Hysterical Age," wherein and whereby society implodes while those more evil intended rise to brutal power and control. It is imperative that all families recognize the signs of cushy parenting and caretakers in every setting avoid enabling self pity and foster character building.

Children as young as seven or eight in major homeschooling programs are already learning general time periods in US and world history and relaying some information to Catholic history.

Projects may become more complex, like the building of a fort or church; recreating in costume, food, and environment a particular past place or event.

While avoiding stereotypes, definitely portray the reality of history. It is okay for young children to realize that "Thanksgivings" in the past might have featured eel or fish, rather than a twenty pound Butterball deep fried in the back yard.

Pen pals may be another idea. Many decades ago, a Colorado woman began writing to a German girl, before, during, and after World War II. While some of the content of the letters—such as the German girl referencing Hitler as "our great and glorious leader," would be more suitable for an older audience that could grasp the chilling implication of Nazi propaganda, many of the letters spoke of everyday life. Of course, at the time, they were merely current correspondence. Today, they are historic.

Simple maps and discussions on why a particular region prospered in a specific way due to geographical features or suffered decline for the same reasons help incorporate history and provide opportunities for even very young minds to contemplate how neighbors best get along or experience conflicts.

*Special Note: Primary Catechesis*

These students are approaching major Sacramental preparation. Their catechetical formation is more complex and increasingly involves their actions towards others and community. The concept of sin, or offending God and neighbor, is impressed. Here a Catholic school teacher can expand on neighbor, neighborhood, and community, but history will become a component of intentional instruction. Prayerfully, teachers will be assigned by their knowledge and love of the Sacraments, as well as other subject areas. Not all teachers are best suited for these critical "stages," and that is perfectly fine! In fact, fortunate is the school that has a the teaching order on staff.

## *Intermediate (4-8). (Note: May be 4-5 in some schools)*

Fourth and Fifth grades often study local (state) and early US history though many students who are homeschooled may be geared to cycles of learning. Also, some may either remain in a particular subject like math or progress quicker depending on individual challenges and strengths.

Too, youth of this age are developing more awareness in relationships and gaining greater understanding and making connections about the world in general and people in the news.

## *High School (9-12)*

History must be taught in correlation to Church history, and this is not more evident than when students enter what is traditionally

## Chapter Nine: The Eternal Age vs Man-Constructed Ages

called high school. If the foundation has been carefully laid for the study of history, and the basic facts of world and American history presented, students at this juncture can accomplish deeper dives.

At this point, they should be able to identify eras and ages, as specifically named periods of reference to how people have responded to events and trends in thought. The major ones are included at the close of Chapter Eight.

Teachers of all subjects and age groups should be well versed, as well, as the very concept of community relies on knowledge of past communities, globally and over time. Herein, those intentional public school exercises about "diversity, tolerance, and cultural awareness," flow naturally into the most fundamental concepts. However, etymology and expanded lessons on word and concept meaning are crucial.

Furthermore, it is essential that teachers avoid "clumping" when addressing the three major world races: Caucasian, Negroid, and Asian. (Parenthetically, "Negroid" is likely to cause discomfort so teachers should consult with administration. though simply sanitizing history as it was identified should be avoided.)Those of Polish, Irish, Norwegian, Italian, Russian, etc. descent are as varied within their individual identities, customs, and experiences, as are those from the continents of Africa or Asia. See what happens when gathering together a Mexican with someone from Venezuela; a Korean with a Japanese; a Nigerian with an Ethiopian.

Cardinal Arinze has often lamented that people assume that Africa is a country, and he has to remind them that it is a continent with varied countries, often vastly different. (Footnote: )

There is also a big difference between the American Black person whose family has been in North America for generations and someone who has just immigrated from, say, Haiti.

So, all aspects of history are necessary to know and understand correlated to events: government, civics, economics, philosophy, religion, art and architecture, language, community.

Again, tough topics will be raised, perhaps by students and sourced through the homes. Catholic teachers should not be derailed, but neither should they hide truth in the boxcar either. This is when and where excellent teachers can shine by being in tune with current events and trends and knowing their students.

## HISTORY IN WORD—A CURRICULUM SAMPLE

### GENERAL OUTLINE THAT CAN BE DEVELOPMENTALLY ADJUSTED

History in Word
(What do we know by the all-knowing God)

*Background on the concept and reality of history —how only the sacred, integrated with the secular, produces lasting fruit from knowing history. The study of history must have as its primary objective that road map to guide us away from disaster and damnation and towards holiness and Heaven.*

I. Prehistory. (Genesis)
   A. Defined
   B. Scientific Discovery vs. the Unknown
      1. Compatible, Contradictory, and Controversial
      2. Merging knowledge with Faith
         a. Lucy vs Eve—and what happened to Adam?
      3. Mystery ever Present
   C. Resolution through the Soul
      1. True Primate and True Man (True Man and True God)
         (We believe that Jesus Christ was true God and true man, so it is understandable to also believe that at one time, man, who was animal primate, was conceived by the Holy Spirit to be imbued with a soul.

In other words, the breath of God entered into man(kind), sometimes referred to as homo sapiens.

A woman, named Eve, came from him, known as Adam. Yet, they rebelled in a special land known as Eden (Paradise), some believe Mesopotamia. Expelled, they wandered as gatherers and hunters, eventually farmers and herders, and later in civilizations.

From them came the generations of God's children. How this occurred exactly remains a mystery to be revealed by God in His way and time. So, in the meantime, scientists make educated conjectures and theories. Only one fact needs to be acknowledged as truth: No child of God descended from a soulless ape.

To put this in context: All things are possible with God, such as the Immaculate Conception and the Perfect Conception, whereby Jesus Christ, Son of God, entered humanity through the purest vessel and by the Holy Trinity.

II. History
    A. Written Communication Aside the Written Word
    B. A Map of the World through Time
        1. Pangaea Theory
    C. Timeline of History (The World and as Described Scripturally)
    D. Parallel Couple, Family, Tribe, Nation, Kingdom with the World Societies
    E. Ancient Civilizations. (Note Classical or Liberal Arts Pedagogy is most fitting)
        1. The River Civilizations (Egypt, Mesopotamia, Indus, Huang)

2. Ancient Greece
3. Ancient Rome
4. Africa
5. Asia
6. The Americas
7. Elsewhere

III. Major Periods of Transformation
    A. Arising civilizations
    B. Movements of Knowledge and Thought
        1. Law and Order
        2. Government vs. the Individual
            a. Early Codes and Charters
            b. Cycles of freedom vs. slavery; democracy vs. dictatorship
        3. Belief systems
            a. Polytheistic
                i. gods of the spirit world; gods of nature
            b. Monotheistic
                i. God of Abraham; God (Holy Trinity—Jesus Christ); Mohammed
            c. Atheism and Agnostic
            d. Trends over the centuries
            e. Modern beliefs a Return to Ancient Times
        4. Economy
    C. The Influence of Tyrants through the Ages
        1. Early civilization empires, dynasties, caliphates
    D. The Movements of Victory over Despotism
        1. The Intervention of God
    E. Modern Times-Ageless Falsehoods

IV. Revelation vs. Realism
    A. Timeline of Scripture (Presence of God in History) vs. Human Action

B.  Major Events corresponding to Saints

V.  Changing Knowledge; Unchanging Truth

Lesson Activities: Read-Discuss; Reinforce or Investigate; Parallel to Salvation or Catholic History; ***Prehistory*** 5, 000 years ago…

Reading # 1.

In one way, there is no such thing as "pre" history, but from the perspective of sheer human understanding, it references the time before the tools and language to record people and events although there are numerous clues discovered by archeologists and anthropologists. They indicate an evolving person, both physically and mentally, although this should not be confused with Darwinism or the notion that we will eventually become super-brains with perfect hearts and utopian societies.

Also, though scientists have discovered wonderful clues about the advancement of people, technologically and into civilizations, only God knows the whole, true story. Now, some teachers even in Catholic settings will likely encounter The Big BangTheory and the notion that we could not have possibly descended from Adam and Eve.

Note the following Q and A in an Adult Faith Formation bulletin (July 2021): Did we really originate from one single human pair? Paraphrased: Scientists are attentively studying the human DNA and have concluded that the human race did originate from two person somewhere in eastern Africa. Scriptural evidence is found in Genesis but also reaffirmed in the Old and New Testaments. The book of Tobit: (8:6) "You made Adam and gave him Eve his wife as a helper and support. From them the race of mankind has sprung. Acts of the Apostles (17:26) "God hath made of one, all mankind, to dwell upon the whole face of the earth.)

To be certain, science has also seemed to have unearthed evidence of human like creatures (hominids) in multiple locations—many in Africa—over thousand of years, but that does not mean that all of these "branches" were infused with souls. We do not know, exactly. That is why people call this prehistory—a mixture of real science discovery but also speculation.

Still, depending on curriculum, even in Catholic schools, this will be a topic. Generally, one way to address the "Smithsonian Summation" is by asserting that none of God's children, persons of body and soul, were descended from soulless apes. By the way, otherwise that would also indicate that the Incarnate Word was so descendent. At some juncture, in some way, our first parents were infused with souls before pro-generating.

How this was accomplished exactly, we do not know. How other branches, whether more human like or not, sprang up and may have died out, we do not know. How human like beings covered the Earth, we do not know. Scientist earnestly seek evidence but are understandably limited

In fact, it gets seven stickier with the Tower of Babel and the Great Flood—the likes of which are recorded in other cultures' history. How was the world repopulated? Even written history fails to illuminate human knowledge . Then again, is it important to know? For we do not understand even written history's phenomenon, especially as recorded by eye witnesses in the Bible. Still, will grasping every nuance of our lives draw closer to God? Not likely, given all the miracles people have witnessed through time. So we adhere to Faith.

Reading # 2

What is prehistory? Is there even such a thing? Technically prehistory is that period in human awareness of our existence, to the best of our understanding, based on artifacts, remains, and other signs of intelligent life since the dawn of mankind prior to formal written language that recorded such life. Of course, science must be respected in

# Chapter Nine: The Eternal Age vs Man-Constructed Ages

that there are many reliable tools to determine how more advanced beings existed, progressed, and eventually settled into communities.

Yet, while discovery is an ever-wonderful adventure, there are still many unknowns. When people from all different background and beliefs can agree on facts about the past, an incredible story emerges about human development. Still there are many unknowns despite our best efforts and technology. We still have contradictions and controversies. We still grapple with the juxtaposition of faith and purely secular foundations. Mystery is ever present. What are these?

This text will treat prehistory from a solid Catholic viewpoint, even while conceding that certain sources, such as the Bible, may not be interpreted literally. Yet, it is hoped by the end of this section that the reader will emerge as more understanding and even accepting of the premise presented. While prehistory predates human written documentation, ever present has been the Word which would enter history in about 1 AD (The Year of Our Lord)—the Word made Flesh who dwelt among us.

One highly recommended resource for the following is Edward Sri and Curtis Martin's *The Real Story—Understanding the Big Picture of the Bible*. It is so simple but comprehensively clarifies Sacred History in relationship to Secular History. The former is supernatural--omniscient, omnipotent, and omnipresent. God is the all-knowing, all-powerful, immortal and eternal historian. The latter may be infused with or inspired by the Holy Spirit depending on the persons writing the text, but frequently the work is not presented as such. The book will serve as a guide though other knowledge and sources will be interspersed.

*The Birth of the People of God*

Genesis 2:4b-9, 15-17 At the time when the Lord God made the earth and the heavens—while as yet there was no field shrub on earth and no grass of the field had sprouted, for the Lord God had sent no rain upon the earth and there was no man to till the soil, but a stream was welling up out of the earth and was watering all the surface of the ground—the Lord God formed man out of the clay of the ground and blew into his nostrils the breath of life, and so man became a living being.

Then the Lord God planted a garden in Eden, in the east, and he placed there the man whom he had formed. Out of the ground the Lord God made various trees grow that were delightful to look at and good for food, with the tree of life in the middle of the garden and the tree of knowledge of good and evil.

The Lord God then took the man and settled him in the garden of Eden, to cultivate and care for it. The Lord God gave man this order: "You are free to eat from any of the trees of the garden except the tree of knowledge of good and evil. From that tree you shall not eat; the moment you eat from it you are surely doomed to die.

Now, most people know the story—the history—from that point, and that Eve was formed from the rib of Adam; the serpent entered the scene and tempted them to disobedience and consequently expulsion from the Garden of Eden.

It is generally at this juncture, though, that many people turn to Smithsonian history and raise hands in questions and contentions. (We set aside the metaphorical nature of this story.) What about all those discoveries about hominids—what about Lucy? Didn't archeologists find remains of human life in different eras hundreds of thousands of years ago and in so many different places?

What is interesting is that even sides like "23 and Me" will reference Africa as the original ancestral birthplace for most seekers of DNA roots.

Nonetheless, no one can claim exact knowledge, especially with respect to species that may well have been human-like—but not our ancestral parents.

Yet, here is the matter in capsule format from two perspectives, one more spiritually oriented than the other. One, I do not attempt to understand all the nuances of human like beings who likely lived who really knows so long ago. I do appreciate those who continue to "dig" and examine long ago buried beings and their living quarters and utensils, signs of customs and beliefs. I only know and believe that regardless of the species that existed then, I am not a descendent of a soulless ape. Let me repeat that a different way. My original ancestor, dating back hundreds of generations was created in the image of God and had a soul.

Two, along that thread of thinking is this—which admittedly requires faith to embrace. At some juncture there may well have been a true primate or primates. The first children of God, though, Adam and Eve, may have been true primate, but they were also true man. This is, just as Jesus Christ, born of the Immaculate Conception, the Virgin Mary, conceived by the Holy Spirit, was true man and true God.

However one perceives through the prism of faith and knowledge, God created the universe and all that it is in it.

## Another Stumbling Block

Ironically, the greater stumbling block and an understandable one is: From Adam and Eve who was born; how did they cooperate in procreation; where did they go; and how did such multiple couples or tribes migrate and populate the Earth.

Science informs us that man began as hunters and gatherers until he mastered the environment, including such phenomenon as fire and primitive technology using materials of the earth. At some point, people became capable of domesticating plants and animals, and the Age of Agriculture followed. This led to civilizations with cities; government (monarchial in leadership); formal religion (polytheistic) with "priests" closely aligned with kings and rulers; social class structure; job specialization with its accompanying economy and trade; formal written language although often crude and more pictorial; public works; and arts and architecture often with religious themes and functions.

Yet, how this all evolved, no one can say exactly. Sri/Martin's book does provide valuable context though not exact answers.

We can surmise that the descendants of Cain who was sent away as a nomad multiplied, but whose offspring turned away from God. These may well have been most of the inhabitants of Sumer, the earliest civilization on record—though by no means the first settled people, as there were stages of development and tribes. Nomads continued to constitute some portion of the population as well.

For the sake of this text, the focus will be not on the how, but the why. Throughout, God is the Creator. It bears repeating…an all knowing, all powerful; all present; immortal and eternal deity. Also, this text will acknowledge the presence of evil in a being known as satan—lucifer, and his legions of bad angels. Between them, the now disordered world, and the interior turmoil of individuals in the crippled conscience, the rise and fall of civilizations can hardly be surprising.

## Back to Genesis

Genesis 1:27—God created man in his image in the divine image he created him male and female he created them. Then let us (Holy Trinity) make man in our image. Within this tells of relationship, and that requires "rules" of engagement, so to speak. People throughout the ages have always attempted to buck the rules, yes? So, it was from the beginning of Original Sin. It is the ultimate class of consciousness vs. self-consciousness, and awareness and focus on self, rather than God. This would portend the disasters of human relations amongst themselves and opposed to God for thousands of years to this very day.

After exile, Adam and Eve may well have settled in what is known as the "fertile plain" between the Tigris and Euphrates. In what Sri/Martin reference as "A Tale of Two Cities" (which could well be metaphorical for the city of man and the City of God), Adam's genealogy has been simplified to two lines by two sons of Adam: Cain and Seth.

To summarize: Seth lives in God's blessing and his family calls upon the name of the Lord and worships the one true God, walking with Him. Cain lives in God's curse and his family names a city after itself and turns away from the Lord. Cain's family practices polygamy, vengeance, violence, murder and pride. (At least the polygamy does explain some of the population explosion at that time.)

Sadly, the line of Seth did not remain faithful through the generations, and, as a result by their fall, we know that the Flood wiped out the entire Earth except for Noah, his family, including his sons Shem, Ham, and Japheth, and creatures predestined by God to continue. So, Noah then becomes the new Adam and tiller of the soil.

Of course, we know the story does not end well there because Noah "falls from grace." Moreover, it is more than his disgrace, and Ham became complicit and by descent his son Canaan (Gen.9). Now, this is where matters become tricky, but this underscores the grave sexual sins that have toppled whole civilizations, and it seems we do not learn our lesson.

The sin of Ham, in capsulized form, is that he slept with his mother while Noah was intoxicated. Canaan was the fruit of this incestuous, rebellious act. Consequently, not unlike Seth and Cain, we again witness a split between "the city of man" and "the City of God." Shem's descendants will include the Patriarchs of Israel: Abraham, Isaac, and Jacob. The descendants of Ham will include many of Israel's enemies: Egypt, Canaan, Assyria, Babel, Philistines, Jebusites, Amorites, Sodom, and Gomorrah.

It is suggested that the descendants of Japheth formed the maritime nations with their own clans and language

Geographically, Shem's family is located in Mesopotamia, Syria, and Arabia. Ham's people are situated in North Africa. Japheth's family is prominent in the Indo-European regions.

Accordingly, the world is repopulated.

Hopefully, this does help one to understand the nature of the civilizations that arose from those various areas, including the Bible's account of pride and rebellion with the Tower of Babel (a ziggurat to pagan gods of Babylonia), and the subsequent depraved end to such places as Sodom and Gomorrah. To the east, the Medes, Persians, and Hindus will emerge, along with the Mongol power.

Teachers would best focus on the mysterious unknown with an attitude of Faith in that basic tenet above. Certainly, there was a progression in the way people joined together, from the First Couple, to Families, to Tribes, to Towns, to City States, to Civilizations and Nations. Accompanying all of this was the Presence of God, especially to people of the Old and New Testament, to Moses and the Israelites.

More importantly, early history is best viewed in how God influenced man, and man grew in knowledge and understanding with God's plan being revealed even in 2021. There is more than ample material to examine and analyze as to the growth of the human mind and spirit (religion); community relations; and the emergence of language, law, land improvement, government, public works, art and architecture, craft and craftsmanship, trade, and so forth.

From the profound but most basic discovery and taming of fire to the development of the nuclear bomb, people have shown increasing understanding of the world's elements while simultaneously demonstrating innate weaknesses. You can bet your last cave club that the first people to master fire also saw it as both a means of protection and a weapon.

Two culprits: political and technological.

So, conclusively, Catholic school teachers, regardless of setting, grade level, or subject—home, pod, hybrid, Catholic school, or even charter or public, must know history; it will be a major asset because no history is complete without Catholic Church (ie universal Christian) history that embodies God's story and thousands of years of public revelation as contained in Holy Scripture and embodied in Sacred Tradition.

Moreover, as one learns about the earliest philosophers, like Socrates, Plato, and Aristotle and various religious beliefs, coupled by political responsiveness, the 21st Century challenges become clearer and more understandable. They also become tackle able.

Reading Number 3 and Organize along Ascension Press Bible Timeline

Early Civilization

It might be helpful, here, to stop and consider what (and who) exactly rose to power and the continuous rise and fall of various civilizations, all of which were polytheistic until God called Abram from Ur, renaming him Abraham, forming the Covenant with His people. From him his sons Isaac and Jacob would result in more "splits" but eventually lead to the coming of the Messiah and the New Covenant.

Of special note, this text is not including the pre-civilization periods for a couple of reasons, alluded to earlier. One, such "history" does not illuminate the major thesis of this work which is focused on the "city of man" vs. "The City of God." Two, despite exceptional research and findings, we still do not know all about some species that have been discovered and studied in relationship to God's children. That other human like species dwelled on the Earth tens of thousands of years ago is not open to dispute, per se, but would be a deflection more than an assistance here. For more information, in this era, the reader might want to read Christopher Dawson's "The Age of the Gods—A Study in the Origins of Culture in Prehistoric Europe and the Ancient East."

Also, though the early river civilizations had some form of written communication, it was still in crude and cumbersome format, and not easily translated into other areas of the world. The Indus Valley "writing" has not been successfully decoded. Moreover, much of the earliest written communication was at least partially constructed with symbols and pictures.

Early Civilizations of Man

SUMER
(The Covenant with Abraham)
EGYPT
INDUS VALLEY
HUANG VALLEY
MESOAMERICA
GREECE
ROME
(The Messiah and the New Covenant)
THE EMERGENCE OF ISLAM
OTHER—Asia, Mongols
Separate Chapters: Europe and Christendom; Reformation; Renaissance; Scientific Discovery; Enlightenment; Discovery of America.

THE MODERN CIVILIZATIONS
Industrial Age; The Rise of the Machine Age; The Rise of World Conflict; The Rise Fascism and Communism; Continuing World Tension; The Fall of Modern Civilization.

Reading # 4

ERAS. (Geological—Other). NOTE: Different approaches and curriculum focus on history differently.

The four main ERAS are, from oldest to youngest: **PreCambrian**, **Palaeozoic**, **Mesozoic** and **Cenozoic**. Periods are a finer subdivision in the geological time scale. These eras may be an optional reading and dependent on a particular grade level curriculum.

LEADERSHIP. (Also in government)
*Atttibutes*:
Submission to God in authentic Truth and Live

# Chapter Nine: The Eternal Age vs Man-Constructed Ages

Not faultless or without imperfections...subject to temptation by weakened human nature

Yet capable of virtue—ongoing persistent, pervasive self awareness of wrongdoing (sin) with appropriate contrition and reparation.

Prayerful ..

Seeks good of others

Knowledgeable in temporal and supernatural matters

Wise in associates, counselors, and underlings; priorities of action; and a vision, albeit earth bound but enabling a pathway to eternal life

## TOOLS, LESSON(S) AND GENERAL RESOURCES AND MATERIALS—ETERNAL AGE VS MAN CONSTRUCTED

**TOOLS:** This chapter has numerous timelines and a couple of ways to look at history.

*Primary Lesson*: All history is God's story. Man's perspective is the recorded known events and documents or artifacts supporting event descriptions of man's interface with his environment at any given time or place. The supernatural provides the invisible reality that must be accepted by Faith though often there is supporting evidence, as in miracles.

Study one story in history and evaluate the people, place, and event against Catholicism. Develop a two column graphic template headed on one side with natural (temporal) characteristics. Head the other: Christian influences. Evaluate the impact of Christian influences on the persons and situation for the better or worst.

**RESOURCES**: Numerous history texts: Catholic Textbook Project; Phillip Campbell's *The Catholic Educator's Guide to Teaching History* along with his four- part series, "The Story of Civilization"; Schola Rosa. And other homeschool curriculum; Edward Sri: *The Real Story*; Father Kucer; Ascension Press Bible Timeline; James Hitchcock *The History of The Catholic Church* (Other books on Church history in the Appendix Bibliography Section)

# Chapter Ten

## GOVERNMENT THROUGH TIME
## (IMPACT ON AND BY CATHOLICISM)

*"Thus Plato begins **The Laws** his political treatise par excellence, with the old Athenian stranger asking his two interlocutors: "Tell me gentlemen, to whom do you give the credit for establishing your codes of law: Is it a god, or a man?" Cleinias' response is very determined: "A god, sir, a god—and that's the honey truth." (The Imaginative Conservative, Thomas Jefferson and the Declaration of Independence: The Power of a Free People by Ross Lence (Note to self: verify footnote)*

## CATHOLIC TEACHER AS CITIZEN

Whether a preschool or college educator, teachers need to know the concept of government and how that is influences by (religion) Faith—Catholicism—and how it permeates every community, from family to the world, from the classroom to national policies, to international effects. In the absence of understanding "government" and how that has expressed itself through time and space and most notably since public revelation and Jesus Christ in history, false governance can emerge and strangle Truth and Love.

In *Eternal Age vs. Man Constructed Ages* "theology of history" is pronounced, echoing Christopher Dawson's highly acclaimed *The Judgment of the Nations,* in which there is theological interpretation of historical events in relation to God's purposes. Furthermore, while Dawson understood St. Augustine's conflict between the City of God and the City of Man, he also forecast "the times" as either leading to renewal or disaster. (*The Judgment of the Nations, 1942,* reprinted by the Catholic University America Press)

Moreover, he focussed on the root causes and the creator of evil rather than evil's creatures (i.e. Hitler). He also concluded that political or economic responses were insufficient, mere worldly remedies. For him, this was a spiritual war down to individual souls. A student of history, he saw that the Christian Western Civilization had offered spiritual dynamics in its activism for genuine spiritual freedom, following the Greek city-states which acknowledged "freedom" but in political terms. For him, absent the presence of God, or maybe more aptly stated, absent the fully free pursuit of the good, true and beautiful, nations would devolve into warfare and mutual destruction.

Yet the modern "liberal" movement (not to be confused with classical liberalism) subverted Christianity and with a broken compass, so to speak, led the world in progressiveness, not of good, but evil. He noted that Europe was in the hands of planners, social engineers, and others, who depended on human forces in the absence of God, let alone Christianity. Moreover, totalitarianism was the cover for an ensnaring bureaucratic state, a greater loss of individual spiritual awareness and growth. Even almost a century ago, "dreams of humanitarian utopias (are) once again exercising their deceitful power." (Introduction)

The way forward would include the vital task of classical education (the pure liberal tradition), and cited prophetic voices like Pope Leo XIII in his "the Pope and the People" denouncing false liberalism. There is nothing "new" in this, but Dawson went further and distinguished between the time of St. Augustine and "vicious autocrats" like Nero and Domitian. He claimed that the "fundamental Augustine principles of the Two Loves and the Two Cities retain their validity, but have assumed a new form in these times." (Pg 8). He explained, that today, there is a deliberate attempt to "unify and energize" human society from its lower depths. In other words, in the time of Rome, despots persecuted Christians were by perverted pagans; today it is a perversion of humanitarian optimism. Nero never tried to be a saint, never claimed to be one, and did not present himself as messianic. Dawson seems to have perceived the Fall of Rome as an external disaster, while the spiritual catastrophe of modern times strikes directly at the moral foundations of our society. (Pg 10).

## Chapter Ten: Government through Time

Viewing government today in any place of the world, including the Republic of the United States of America, Dawson might have wept. There are all types of wiggle words, terms, and maneuvers to appear democratic, but only the "d" is in common with the reality of despotism. Worse, the enemy steals and coops the vocabulary of the just, including justice, charity, and even morality. This has led us far away from our destiny. Dawson insisted that there must be a development of a human and Christian civilization. Yet, how?

We have been pummeled with the concept of "separation of Church of State" to the point of mute acceptance, as if there is no other way. Yet, the "cause of God and the cause of man are one." (Pg22). We must re address the old theological conflicts, though, including the division between the East and West; division between Catholic and Protestant; and divisions within Protestantism. The rift Martin Luther initiated may be the most difficult as he basically dethroned God by negating the Holy Eucharist, the Real Presence of Jesus Christ, Who will come to judge the living and the Dead. Further he may well have laid the family under the executioner's ax by diminishing the role of the Blessed Mother and Heaven's intersection with humanity. Finally, his perception of the role of natural law and the state lent fuel for deadly separation. We either believe that Jesus Christ is King and therefore Ruler, still present, or we…do not. There is much more in Dawson's treatise and well worth a thorough reading, but for now, suffice to say that the knowledgeable and faithful Catholic educator can be instrumental in guiding students both in their vocations but also their ultimate destiny, to be saints and live forever with God.

It all starts with Catholic teachers identifying as Catholic citizens.

Catholic citizenship, regardless of government model, is vital to the common good, and every educator is responsible for being a healthy citizen, knowing how that expresses itself, and actually acting upon that responsibility in accountable ways.

Still starting with a shared understanding of government itself is helpful, especially in view of relativism which has distorted the purpose and operations of healthy government.

What is government; what different types of government have been prevalent in history; who were the first "governors"? How did the institution of the Church on Earth impact governance—for individuals, families, and societies at large. Is there an ideal government"? What are the hallmarks of wise government, or conversely evil governance? How does a particular form of government influence interpersonal relations, the law, justice, and the individual? Why does good governance always permit the individual pursuit of the good, true, and beautiful for a blessed eternity? How involved is God…Is He political?

These are among the questions Catholic educators should ask and seek answers that will help in the building of the Kingdom of God, the ultimate objective of any and all lessons.

First, what are the hallmarks of good Catholic citizenship? How does a teacher know he or she is acting responsibly in that regard? Some of what will follow may be painful for teachers who have always believed they were "good" people in the political realm, on either side of the aisle. Moreover, several societal developments have pushed a few controversial issues to the forefront and have caused great division even in Catholic schools. The fallout has been disastrous at times, and it is not due to a difference of outlook alone, but also how matters have been addressed. However, there are also times that no matter the goodwill and best efforts of faithful Catholics, pushback will occur.

A repeated refrain of this Primer is that Catholic educators must know their Faith, and it is never more true in how they behave in the public arena which often spills into the classroom and school setting. Yet, the following is the Golden Rule:

***Nothing contrary to Sacred Law or Natural Law is permissible to support in any way, financially, personally, or by public acclaim or advocacy.***

During the 1992 Presidential election season, Bill Clinton visited Ontario, California. Many pro-life supporters peacefully held signs and moved through the crowds displaying them. They were jeered with not just a few yelling, "He is *our* President." The message was clear. These attendees supported not just Bill Clinton but his promised pro-abortion agenda, among other questionable positions. Catholics, including teachers, were actually mixed in their support. Some justified voting for Clinton because of all the other good he would do although, candidly some actually also supported abortion.

By the time Obama entered office, the country was already in the tens of millions of abortions since 1972. Matters had worsened in the Democrat Party besides. Soon, the United States was a country that promoted not just abortion but same sex "marriage," disordered immigration, anti law enforcement laws, and a host of other problems that failed the common good by definition of the wisest and most prudent in the Church, dating back to its inception These include such outstanding minds as St. Thomas Aquinas, Pope Pius's (multiple), Archbishop Fulton Sheen, and numerous writers, commentators, and clergy in the United States at the time.

Yet, astonishingly, there were Catholic faculty lounges gushing for pro-abortion candidates and appealing personalities like Obama. One school secretary lamented that she felt alienated by these teachers, and nothing she said dissuaded them.

Now, this Primer is not a "bash" Democrats or persons within that party line, and there are many Republicans and Independents who espouse the same or have advanced evil in the name of "rights." Evil by any umbrella name is evil. Moreover, the Catholic educator must understand his or her duty as a citizen in one of the last standing Republics by knowledge of government (by "secular" and sacred standards); identifying and defining the strands of citizenship; and acting as good citizens in private and public domains and most critically in the classroom.

<u>However, an upfront exception</u>: It is not the business or duty of any teacher to promote personal opinion about any candidate. For one thing, people can be deceived, and for another, it muddles effective instruction, especially if the lesson is on government. How many reading this last sentence can think of someone for whom they voted who seemed to be an outstanding candidate only to flip or weaken positions

after being elected or otherwise fall from grace. Also, unless it is a higher level classroom—high school or college—any particular proposed law or proposition would likely require extensive research to teach with respect to pros and cons although some are obviously gravely sinful.

Still, best to stick to the basics of good citizenship objectives for this world and the next. Focus on consistent attributes a good government and leadership possesses; warning signs of sinful government involvement; characteristics of healthy candidates (virtues); and how to discern objectivity and truthfulness in political (or government) communication; and what constitutes a government that adheres to its limited role but still advances the common good and promotes virtuous citizens.

Finally, Catholic teachers cannot assume they can walk the fence. Abortion is a foundational issue, as is the sanctity of Holy Matrimony and the sexual integrity of the human being, including assigned sex from conception. The innocence of children should be paramount, but particularly all students deserve protection from insidious ideas that can forever imprint on their memories regrettable and negatively influencing experiences or instruction, Moreover, no amount of good intentions and focus on the corporeal works of mercy in theoretical compensation can nullify fidelity to truth in these other matters. While corporal works of mercy are essential, merely working in a soup kitchen five evenings a week does not cancel promoting any sin.

However, there are also teachers who "lord" their sanctity over others—this does not include teachers perceived to be so—but actually verbally and openly so, especially in a way that directly maligns the ignorant or confused. Some children seated in those classrooms come from troubled homes, and maybe extended families that live ruinous lives. Furthermore, there have been candidates in accord with Catholic teaching, who are otherwise unqualified to serve. These are often individual situations that require the best of living the cardinal virtues.

So, if reading this, any teacher or possible teacher who does not think he or she can refrain from personal contrary opinion, especially that opposed to the Church, or is entering the field to teach from a soapbox, perhaps some time with a spiritual director would be advisable. Past wounds may be impeding a wholesome vision of this vocation, or it is simply not an environment in which to pursue employment.

Having decided that Catholic teaching fits, there is still more to be done as good citizens. One is obvious: growth in sanctity and wisdom. For teachers seeking models, there are many. With respect to political activity, In *Political Science from a Catholic Perspective* Father Peter Kucer describes the lives of seven holy persons and saints who positively engaged in this realm, over time, although there are many more. This selection seems oriented towards different areas of political activity that promoted the common good of society.

They are:

- St. Thomas More (1478-1535) who declared "I am the King's good servant, but God's first" before his execution;
- St. Louis IX (1214-1270) who may have inspired St. Thomas Aquinas to say that an ideal king is one "who makes a whole province rejoice in peace, who restrains violence, preserves justice, and arranges by his laws and precepts what is to be done by men;
- St. Henry II and his wife St. Cunigunde (975-1040) who sought peace and unity while giving generously to the Church;
- Blessed Charles of Austria (1887-1992) of whom Pope John Paul II commented that as a Christian statesman, he conceived of his office as a holy service to his people and strove for peace;
- Otto Von Hapsburg (1912-2011), Blessed Charles' son which demonstrates the power of strong leader role figures in the family;
- And Father Jose Maria Arizmendiarrieta who was instrumental in the founding of the multi billion dollar Mondragon Corporation while instilling in its operations the principles of just distribution of property and resources.

Catholic educators may well pursue studying these and others more closely and sharing with students that Catholic ethics are expected and doable.

More contemporary examples like St. Pope John Paul II, Cardinal Sarah, Cardinal Burke, and Father Frank Pavone come immediately to mind. Notable figures like Steven Mosher (Population Research Institute), Jennifer Roback (The Ruth Institute), and Brian Burch (Catholic Votes) are just a few of the many the laity working diligently to transform political reality into genuine common good. (See resources)

Finally, now, you could be that solid Catholic teacher who inspires students to grow in virtue, discern appropriate vocations, and contribute to society in a way that provides for many in this terrestrial world but also leads them body and soul to the City of God.

## *From the Beginning*

Now, this section will delve into a general historical perspective; a Faith viewpoint; and comparison and contrast of governmental matrixes that tend towards man driven or God directed and the outcomes of these.

Government at its root meaning is "steering." Extending that to an analogy, any government, then, must have several components: a solid vehicle, mechanically and physically; ample room; an origin and a destination; and, obviously, an excellent driver. Also, clearly evident, not all the passengers can drive the car, at least not simultaneously. (The exception being the dual steering found in driving school vehicles.). More on this later.

Moreover, moving forward in this section with coverage of the many aspects of governance—"secular" (or irreligious) and sacred—it should be emphasized first all government starts with self. Even if the world was destroyed and only one person remained, that person would be his or her own "governor." Returning to the woe of Adam and Eve, it was their individual choices that led to their exclusion form the Garden of Eden. Furthermore, they knew it was not God's authority that resulted in this deprivation but their own disobedience and rejection of good. It was their senses which drew to the apple—their passion or appetite that savored the potential of eating that apple—and their intellect that contorted their will to rationalize that taking and eating that apple was a good they deserved that God was denying them. So, the soul relinquished its sovereignty to the body, and the rest is history, as they say.

God gifted us with body and soul. The body is the original visible territory of existence. The body enables the soul, in cooperation with the senses, appetites, intellect, and will, to achieve foremost perfect adoration of the Creator, but then to cooperate with the Creator in ruling creatures and other living matter. Thus individual dignity and respect is due every body and as it embodies a unique soul! Further on, is the exploration of politics (from the word city) that defines and sets forth a more complex system of governance that is beyond any one individual, as we live in community.

Suffice to say for now that those who forfeit wise governance of their bodies can collectively and in increasingly sized populations also forfeit their authentic freedom. As will be demonstrated and explored, teachers and students alike need to understand that the most horrible types of government always originate in the individuals of that society. Evil leaderships arises from indifference of the good, complicity, or fear, or all three. Indifference is a consequence of self getting; complicity involves a significant degree of accord with the evil; and fear is the end result for even for those who opposed the evil. However, among the ranks of the scared faithful can still arise extraordinary fortitude and memorable acts of self sacrifice.

## *The Foundation of Leadership; Individual Integrity and Fundamental Family*

Who were the first leaders? For Catholics (and all Christians and Jews), God is and has always been *the* Authority. He is the Author of Life. He was most certainly the authority in the Garden of Eden, the origin of mankind. There were animals of all kinds and one, then two persons: Adam and Eve. All was well, and God was the provider of goods knowledge, and understanding. All was available to Adam and Eve except for the fruit from the tree of knowledge of good and evil. At some point, temptation entered the Garden. Why we are not told but we know how this chapter ends. Adam and Even fell prey to temptation, and, after disobeying, they were cast from Paradise to fend and toil in a place we call Earth.

Now, it is helpful to pause at this juncture and distinguish between the fundamental law of God and civic law. God's law was broken, but His response was not legalistic punishment as we find through worldly court systems. His response was just and actually based on mercy. Had God not closed Paradise to Adam and Eve, they might well have compounded their sin and eaten from the Tree of Life and never have had to opportunity to repent and revert to Truth and Love. So God actually "steered" Adam and Eve toward opportunity. Teachers should consider these concepts when discussing law and even rules and consequences within their homes or classrooms. The ultimate objective of justice is for good. (A contemporary analogy may help. A young teen is told not to associate with those promoting transsexuality, but he does anyway and begins to pursue sex change. Would the parents be abusive to send their son to distant rural relatives, or should they just let him make a permanent, irreversible alteration of his being?)

Thereafter came the family, and it is presumed that Adam and Eve governed their sons though not exactly how that was imparted to them through God or grace is not revealed. We do know that murder (Cain and Abel) fractured and dissolved the unity of the first family as Cain was exiled. Moreover, the world then became a place of contention and more tension. Again, unlike public government, God's governance shows significant distinctions.

First He afforded Adam and Eve an opportunity to care for themselves, albeit working for their bread. That, by the way, was also the first "economy," the meaning of which references household (finances). Yet, God continued in His Perfect leadership role by certainly outlining the way they should live, but also granting free will. His was not a totalitarian regime. Nor was it a commune with a local food bank by the Gate to Paradise. It must also be accepted that Abel and Cain's occupations, one with animals and the other with produce were appropriate and good. It was just the effect of Original Sin that included weakness and proneness to temptation and sin, the darkness of conscience, that bettered Cain.

Again, though, God demonstrated his Authority by permitting free will, and natural consequences followed. Can people imagine in our own governments behaved similarly instead of trying to "fix" everything and make all things "equal" in their own estimation.

*From the One Couple and First Family Onward…*

As historians, we learned that prehistory indicates a nomadic and primitive existence of creatures generally referenced as hominids, human like beings. The governance found in these roaming families or small tribes likely consisted of the strongest and fittest leading the others, for better or worse. As towns and then city-states, and finally civilizations grew, governance became more complex and conflicted. In Salvation history, one also notes fluctuating but ever present and often increasing tensions between people and those overseeing their lives in some form of governance, from the One Holy Couple, to One Holy Family, to One Holy Tribe, to One Holy Nation, to One Holy Kingdom, to One Holy Catholic and Apostolic Church (See Ascension Press Timeline Bible). So, there are parallels between the sheer terrestrial and God fearing populations, and that within God's chosen people, life was not spiritual paradise.

It was the crafty, the skilled, the physically and mentally superior who tended to become rulers. Interwoven into early governments—most often monarchial but some oligarchical —was the embedding of rule under various powers of nature or multiple gods, and by the deified echelon. The populace believed that their king, pharaoh, priest was ordained by the gods (or were gods) to rule their lives in all areas: religion, economy, social strata; education; arts; public works; communication and even war and peace. Now, it is imperative to acknowledge that the notion of a person claiming power by the authority of God still emerges in the 21st Century. How many running for office might claim that they were called by God? And did not the former Governor of New York, ousted for egregious behavior, just declare that God is not finished with him yet? Rulers in totalitarian regimes do likewise. More on that topic further on.

Still, what distinguishes the earliest pagan forms of government from more modern versions is that there was a fundamental collective acceptance of these rulers and the hierarchy of power; formal education was lacking for most, as they strived to survive and thrive in their respective fields of labor; and they knew no other existence. Travel, trade, and increase of leisure time through technology (in its broadest interpretation) would contribute to more contemplation, self will, curiosity about others, and a sense of upward mobility. Ensuing temptations to jealousy, envy, greed, and pride would fuel what still keeps mankind in the throes of discontent and warfare.

*In Salvation History*

Now, Christians know the story of Noah, but the best lesson to be derived from it is that horrible self governance was at the root of this all-disastrous Flood, but one man and his family were saved by keeping allegiance with God. Note, though, Divine intervention. Yes, God provides free will and He permits (wo)man to self govern, but the big caveat is His ultimate judgment balanced with mercy. Only He, Who exists in the Present, knows all. Obviously, not all the details of the Flood are known, and one could argue that proof in fine detail is unnecessary for all that occurred in this time frame. Much still baffles historians and theologians, as so many have sought to pinpoint the time and location of the Ark, among other areas of inquisitiveness.

Yet, addressing *only* governance, people followed their own instincts and impulses. They did not listen nor follow reason and Truth. The story of Noah is the story of each of us in that all governance starts with self, regardless of who are our temporal leaders. What can also be assumed is that families — whole families—fostered rebellion against God at this juncture because Noah's family was spared. This goes to the heart of the need for strong family leadership, again, regardless of public rulers.

There should be a pause here to permit that foundational truth settle. Two people turned from God and lost Paradise, but one man and his family Noah were saved by obedience. Later we know that the Holy Family would save eternity.

Abraham, a descendent of Noah, was called to lead his family and eventually those whose numbers were like the stars in heaven. Here, too, is the ultimate primacy of God's authority for increasing population: self, family, tribe. Humility and obedience are the root virtues that enable such acknowledge and acceptance, as well. Note the parallels in worldly government that only crudely modeled the Divine Government and often was itself cruel and demanding if not murderous. The essential difference in the success of any government was always the degree of allegiance to Truth and Love.

Then there is the concept of Covenant established by God the Father with Abraham, father of the Israel Nation. (See The Eternal Age vs. Man Constructed Ages.) This was not a pact, a charter, a constitution but an integration of the Divine into the lives of man intricately, wholly, and holy. This was the establishment of God as the superior Authority over all of mankind and his actions and existence. Other city states and eventually nations only managed a basic decree, albeit some with laws codes like Hammurabi (1760 BC).

Astonishingly, though, and one can only accept the human nature is so fickle and fallible that time and again, the Jews permitted themselves to fall into disobedience, rebellion, paganism and all types of offenses against their Creator. It was only when the chosen people confessed their sins, repented, and reaffirmed God as their overarching "Governor" that they were freed to pursue that Faith and prosperity.

How many remain perplexed by the plight of Moses and God's people wandering the desert for 40 years? As would be in the time of Christ, these chosen people were give so many miracles, such astonishing Divine Intervention, ample food and water. What was asked in return? Allegiance to the Commandments which were in themselves a way for good living!

Then, the people demanded kings...just like their pagan neighbors. They just had to have a visible ruler upon whom they could depend. Previously revealed truth had to be taken on trust; Faith was insufficient. Hope rested with the belly, and supernatural Love questionable. Our Lord obliged, and there were good and bad kings. However, even the better ones like David and Solomon, erred...sinned.

In the meanwhile, one can witness all types of governments throughout the early world though still autocratic in nature, some more brutal than others. We see that the Greeks (Athens) and Romans (Republic), in particular, experimented with various forms of representative or democratic models, but that these are often erratic or short-lived and subject to human excesses and faults beyond individual selfishness.

Fast forward to the time of Jesus Christ, and we witness an unfolding revelation about God's authority and governance that will later influence the concept of government in unique ways.

## Enter the Church

Politics which engines government is a faulty scaffold—not a ladder to Heaven though some politicians have done a better job than others to develop "rungs." Still, overall, earthly governments are generally individuals ruling masses, not the Mass ruling the soul. This is true even in so called democracies and republics. They always tend towards oligarchical or dictatorial regimes eventually.

## Chapter Ten: Government through Time

Church history is replete with the errors of man to merge temporal governance with the eternal kingdom (See Eternal Kingdom vs. Global Power). Even in the best of times, during the Middle Ages, when the Church seemed to dominate civilization, there were cracks beneath the veneer. Always there has been and always there will be tension between mankind here and God…everywhere. We still have not accepted that we live in a fallen world.

In a Public Discourse essay (February 17, 2022), John von Heyking does an admirable job in reviewing Veronica Ogle's 2022 book: "Politics and the Earthly City in Augustine's City of God." In it the claim arises that politics can only be improved by personal responses to grace, which is the antithesis of worldly politics that seeks to grapple and transform with whole populations. Especially today, one sees that global uber arch that drives the thinking and behavior of people. COVID 19 brought this to prominent reality. Yet, Jesus Christ always encountered individuals while he decried the Pharisees. Even when feeding the thousands, His count was such that there was an abundance of left overs, speaking to His knowledge of everyone's needs and beyond to eternity. Moreover, Jesus refused to engage with the government of His earthly sojourn. "Render unto Cesar what is Cesar's and unto God what is God's" exposing the compromise of many Jewish leaders with Roman economics and currency. Jesus Christ was all about the Kingdom of God.

Still, Catholic educators must know Church history in addition to earlier salvation history to best grasp how prudent government always relied on Truth. As or when rulers departed from God in prayer, thoughts, words, and actions, trouble and ruin always followed. Yet, even in the best of times, an uneasy relationship between Church and State often caused great disputes and even war. One would think after hundreds of years, man would understand that government of the people always entails the individual right and responsibility to pursue the good, true, and beautiful, and that government exists to secure the people in that freely chosen path.

Nonetheless, many great Saints and writings have poured forth over the past 2,000 years to steer persons to what St. Thomas Aquinas would call the "eternal law", the Divine governance of all created things." This should not be confused with natural law which is more of an internal embedded inclination towards good and avoidance of evil. Yet, due to concupiscence (law of sin), passion can and does rule over intellect and the appetite. Add to that negative social pressures and confusion can erase natural law in souls. (*Thomas Aquinas in Fifty Pages, A Quick Layman's Guide to Thomism* Taylor R. Marshall, Ph.D.)

Such a simple concept, but so evident in government throughout history and today. So often acceptable government is misinterpreted to be the "parent," "the indulger", "the fixer", "the social justice arbitrator," and the "utopian seeker," among many inappropriate roles.

**Models of Government through Time**

As covered elsewhere, all prudent rule begins with self, and absent individual, prudent self "steering," no external government can operate successfully. A rotten core cannot be mended by an external skin, no matter how tough.

No course on government can be compatible with Truth in the absence of ageless knowledge that includes the glimmer of it even in Aristotle's philosophy. Moreover, all government descends from fundamental principles that are either aligned with the city of man or the City of God in various degrees. Still, no manmade government, no matter how it strives to imitate the City of God can be the City of God. Politics, the art of forming and delivering government by men is thwarted with all the failings of individuals in their weaknesses by Original Sin. Even King David and King Solomon tripped, badly! The best we can hope for is one that best adheres to Good as has been revealed by God.

Furthermore, any government is merely the footman for its leadership. As alluded to in The Eternal Age vs Man Constructed Ages, regardless of location in space or time, groups of persons striving to live together and attain security if not prosperity demonstrate the following predictable course. A government is formed, often by powerful individuals or groups; it tends toward conquest, interiorally and exteriorly. It depends on support for its goals or power to suppress opposition. Often certain rulers are capable of great success in their aims. However, power does corrupt, and if the government is based on the absence of good, it may do great damage, but, at some point, it will collapse. What follows may or may not be good, so the cycle continues. Yet, also at the root of a government's failure are all the deadly sins, and if these have influenced the majority of citizens and residents in some way, evil will most surely follow. Moreover, the most empowered and virtuous ruler cannot stop the mob. Ask Moses.

The popular saying is that those who do not know history are doomed to repeat it. Better stated, those who will revise or bury instructive history for personal gain, in addition to a population of least resistance or one more concerned with their "stomachs" (Letters of St. Paul) will bring about the ruin of bodies and souls.

The primary models through time have been monarchial (sole rule, sometimes two, as in Sparta Greece), oligarchical (a few), and democracy (rule by the many directly or representatively). None are perfect; all have succeed or failed at various periods in history. Some governments have naturally fostered great saints or been influenced by such; others by their nature have done likewise but more in the prominence of martyrs. Some single rulers have been outstanding leaders; "democracies" have led millions to their ruin. Again, it all goes back to the heart and soul of individuals .

## STRANDS OF GOVERNMENT AND CHURCH INFLUENCE IN THE CLASSROOM

Even teachers whose subject differs will benefit by having a solid background in government, understanding its meaning and purpose; knowing the history of government; distinguishing the basic models of governance including between monarchies under Divine authority and those ruled by autocrats; and tracing the rise and fall of governments, particularly those that have the hallmarks of either being under God or ruled by atheists (and in between). Some of what follows may seem condescending, and some teachers will skip over it—"Already know that." Yet, if for no other reason that building resources for students or children K-12 and beyond, what is included here may be some snappy and helpful resources.

As previously covered, the "strands" of government include authority; structure and process; laws; citizenship (rights and responsibilities); immigration; commerce and currency; culture; construction and maintenance; treaties and defense; taxation.

So, though Catholic teachers will live in depth the ideals of citizenship more than specifically teach in these areas, but in concept, "citizenship" is cultivated — or incultured — in all classrooms. Studying the role of citizenship and how it should express itself will be incorporated throughout the day. The wise teacher will learn about what this looks like, sounds like, acts like in numerous situations and be prepared to apply the virtue lessons as opportunities arise.

What is an effective Catholic school teacher to do, from setting classroom rules to addressing government?

Basically, there is always the rule of order in any environment, and one that emphasizes God's order. The pillars that uphold this order are always virtues as revealed by God, the Father in the Ten Commandments, Jesus Christ as the Incarnate Word made Flesh, and the Holy Spirit by His fruits. This was in some way known to many great minds, even those distant from the Chosen People or Christianity. Much of what is good is woven in many philosophies; sadly, what is evil has also been enforced by subverting healthy philosophy (love of wisdom).

Of course, there will be numerous situations to model good authority and the duties of classroom citizens to follow directions for their good and the common good of the class environment.

Yet, other aspects will present themselves. consider the enrollment of a new student, as one example. While not an "immigration" issue, per se, it is still a wonderful opportunity to demonstrate how to greet a "stranger" and make sure he or she is welcome and is confident in becoming a member of the class.

Then there is the "elephant in the room," and that is not the Republican one, but the devolvement of our society over the past 150 years which has negatively influenced families and therefore numerous generations of children. The parents of the children being taught, maybe even your own, are descendants of that decline.

Reilly in *America on Trial* carries the reader through the founding of the United States of America and why it was a great nation. The use of the word "was" is intentional because contrary philosophy has soiled its documents and brought its promise to near ruin.

## *Special Note on Culture*

As culture and government are so intertwined and though culture will be reviewed historically, it is still helpful to view its meaning and evolution in the context of government. In representative government, how a people interprets their culture has a direct impact on who they choose as their leaders and for what purpose. This is most evident in 2021.

Culture has never been more fragmented globally or nationally as today, as so many nations, including the United States of America, grapple with that which identifies their citizens and what is important in daily life, in the way of shared views, customs and traditions, language, literature and drama, faith (or the absence of religion), community precepts and principles, public expression, and even architecture.

There is even disagreement, or better stated, multiple views on the ideal of an international or global culture.

In the United States, people were culturally united for "freedom and equality" (Father Kucer) while acknowledging the richness of various ethnic and racial differences. Faith, although diverse in specific beliefs, once shared commonality in a moral code based on the Ten Commandments and Natural Law. The widely acceptable language was

English; patriotism was touted as a virtue; public decency was upheld; and despite outlier political visions, the Republic was revered. The government mirrored those shared values and expressions. At one time, a public figure caught in scandal of any major type resulted in that person's resignation. Although one would be naive to think there were not some "backroom" deals and voting shenanigans, those vices were at least publicly denounced. Together, Americans survived two world wars, and even the Vietnam War did not completely unravel that shared culture though it most likely was a catalyst for what the country is experiencing today.

Bluntly, there is no longer a shared culture, even state by state. The United States of America is in name only. Large city-states rule even in major, national elections with rural areas disadvantaged and underrepresented by sheer numbers. Even the majority of county votes failed to sway for the Republican President (Trump) in 2021. Moreover, within the major urban areas, questions arose as to who was voting and how. Regardless, there is a significant gap in cultural identity between urban and rural residents and within regions of the country.

Furthermore, major conflicts over issues like abortion, basic rights, climate change, education (including history), language, and even citizenship are going to continue to fissure cultural identity.

We have basically three cultural paradigms existing concurrently: counter-culture; cancel culture; and coop-culture. The last is the hope for resolving our mutual, cohesive ties, but that cooperation cannot include some fundamental difference.

Yet, it is worth a revisit to clarify that from which we have departed so disastrously. It is also paramount for a Catholic teacher if we hope to return to our roots. However, this can never be taught "politically" but as philosophy of good governance because politics involves groups, even parties, and there are bad seeds in all.

Also, as much as possible, good governance starts in the home must must be evident in classroom without surrendering authority. Children can learn that the most effective governance is of oneself by

Chapter Ten: Government through Time

watching adults. Understandable, workable rules complement the principles of good governance such as open prayer to God for His will; honoring free speech, sharing of goods, respecting privacy and personal property, and so forth.

That stated…developmentally:

## **Preschool and K:**

Even the youngest child can grasp basic concepts such as rightful use of freedom; the value of virtues; the fundamental order of authority; and that which is true, good, and beautiful from that which is deceitful, bad, and ugly. Most importantly, what they register at this young age will most likely help form a lifetime foundation. While being prudent, teachers can access some excellent guides, and not shy away from the truth just because the students are so little. They can focus on the positive and instill that scaffold of healthy governance that will serve as a guide and comparative for them going forward. Teachers are laying that foundation and the orientation for thinking years in the future. So, here is government for these tots:

**Family under God** is the cornerstone building block for all governance, and, any government outside Divine authority and the family should respect and honor that. The obvious first government in the Holy Trinity, albeit it may be the only realistic one whereby three Persons can agree unanimously on anything. Teachers can instruct with that caveat. Still, the Holy Trinity is the ideal. (Later students will learn in politics about ideal models of government, but that temporal, manmade structures are always flawed and so fall short of perfection.)

Incidentally, the subject of gender may be raised by colleagues, administrators, or parents. Trust that some parents will question anything that they perceive is racist, sexist, or imperialistic. There are some simple but great resources on the Holy Trinity, but we know that God the

Father is spirit and encompasses (wo)man. That all three are male-referenced connotes ideal masculinity which is perfect Love. We do NOT understand this, and we do not need to grasp that entirely but to trust God.

Also there is the human face of the Holy Trinity in the ***Holy Family.*** There we can explicitly portray an ideal family as headed by a man and a woman committed to knowing, loving, and serving God, and being cooperative in creation, also known as procreation. Children can appreciate this. Four year olds gravitate towards books "Angels in the Water," where the development of a baby in the womb under the loving auspices of his or her Guardian Angel is wonderfully told. Underscore the virtuous lives of Mary and Joseph, again, models for motherhood and fatherhood, ideal femininity and masculinity. Share that St. Joseph, father of Jesus, has no speaking role in all of Holy Scripture. Ideal masculinity is humble and obedient.

Here, a classroom teacher will be appropriately sensitive to any child who may not have a mother or father. Perhaps you have students who have suffered trauma by a parent. Widowhood is a possibility. Divorce is highly prevalent as is the introduction of stepparents. Though Catholic schools are wary about the enrollment of children in a same sex relationship (or even single parents with that orientation), there is also that possibility. What do teachers do? That depends on the student's age, but prayerfully, the teacher has been well and faithfully coached.

Neighbors might present another challenge, as students (children) may well be socializing with children of different faiths, cultures, and political leanings, some of which may be opposed to Catholicism. Young children are very quick at picking up "relational disturbances" in their environment; they may overhear their parents talking; maybe the neighbor says something awry or acts in a way contrary to the child's home. Even homeschool educators are quite aware of this.

Suffice to note here, that parents and children should be reassured that none of us is perfect. You may even be a teacher who was reared in a single parent home, or maybe your marriage ended poorly. (See

Teacher in God's Light.) So you know, first-hand how feeling outside that bubble of idealism can hurt. It will be paramount to present to even young children what God wants for us may not be our reality, but it is one that leads to perfect happiness, and we can all desire that as much as possible on Earth. That their lives may not reflect that ideal does not mean they cannot or should not seek it for themselves in the future.

Children should also be taught that there is Our Blessed Mother Mary and St. Joseph who are always nearby to provide exceptional parental love. The Holy Family is everyone's ideal, and all children should look to them for that perfect example throughout life.

Moreover, living in a less that ideal home does not mean that they lack love and care. After all, their parent is sending them to a Catholic school, and hopefully one that is uncompromisingly loving but uncompromisingly truthful.

Still, there is no way around the Truth, and that is that the *ideal* family, as ordained by God, is a vocation (calling), one headed by a male father and female woman in a unitive and procreative life long marriage, with **all** its members, including children, striving to be saints and governed as if already in the City of God.

## **Primary (1st-3rd)**

Teachers will echo — review — earlier understanding as family as the central government. For older children, though, a couple of other concepts, particularly those pertaining to community. Increasingly they may provide more complex examples of government, from the neighborhood, to towns, cities, states, and nations. It is not unusual for many homeschool programs to at least touch on previous civilizations and the rise and fall of empires and how the Catholic Church played a role.

Teachers need not delve deeply, but this is a good age to present the different general forms of government, and which are the most conducive to natural law and Divine authority.

They can:
- Emphasize the need for discerning wise leaders and leadership. Use everyday examples and stories that illustrate those characters who are God fearing and loving and wise in contrast to rulers who may be guilty of any or all of the deadly sins. Animal stories are excellent vehicles.
- Work with colleagues to develop numerous activities that compare and contrast; predict outcomes; show cause and effect in simple lessons.
- Study neighborhoods, communities, towns, and cities (local)
- Invite faithful Catholic speakers who may hold office or civic leadership. Focus on the positive but do not neglect the truth.
- Build healthy citizenship in students and instill in them to this lifelong duty. Show examples of good citizenship, as well as justice.

Note that many homeschool programs, classical and Catholic study world and U.S. history in a spiraling approach. Students will be introduced to Greek philosophers, the Roman Republic, and basic principles of United States history. So, the more well rounded a Catholic teacher, even for younger students, the better able to gauge how to develop lesson plans with both hindsight and foresight.

Local state governments are studied, usually from fourth grade, but they may be topical. Definitely teachers may visit the bibliography for trusted sources on history and geography. Beware of revisionist history which also tends to distort impressions of legitimate and ideal government. While students do not need to know the details of the controversial 1619 project, an adult teacher should. By the way 1776Unites, CAAP, and Heritage Foundation offer excellent responses to the theory raised in this project now being mandated in many public schools.

**Intermediate (**Fourth and Fifth Grades). In some settings, this includes 6th grade)

Depending on location and type of schooling, students will likely add more detail to previously learned governments around the world and through time. United States history will most likely be the focus in fifth grade.

Catholic school teachers should know the Declaration of Independence and the Constitution. A brief bulleted overview of "America on Trial" is included in this chapter at the end to better inform even the general introductory political science student. Again, it is strongly advised that all teachers have a clear idea of our background as a country and what has worked or not throughout history. Wonderfully, some Popes have been astute in this area, St. John Paul II being one, and check the wisdom of the Encyclicals for sound Catholic perspectives on government.

**Intermediate** Sixth through Eighth Grades (NOTE: In some settings considered Junior or Middle School)

Catholic schools often follow public school subject guidelines, so teachers will likely discover that sixth and seventh grade focus more deeply on world history and therefore world government. Some publishers are more objective than others, even more knowledgeable. In the chapter whereby teachers grow antennae for that which is anti Catholic or overly secularized humanism, it is easy to conclude that ignorance of the truth has gradually rendered our country deaf, dumb, and blind to ageless principles rooted in natural law and Divine authority.

For example, Islam and its influence in governance is often treated with kid gloves, emphasizing times and incidents of "tolerance" while the rise of Western Christianity is deemed as absolutism and persecutory. Hinduism and Buddhism and other Eastern philosophies receive gentle treatment as well with the image of Buddha gazing benevolently over a courtyard. Now, this is not to say that Christians (Catholics) were sinless or blameless or that Muslims are all terrorists and Buddhists are all godless (though Buddhism does not profess a belief in God.)

However, as a Catholic school teacher it is imperative to know and believe that Christianity in its purest understanding offers the best possible foundation for governance and one that upholds individual liberty to do good. Moreover, civilizations that are not Christian or anti-Christian can and often reign terror on people.

Some excellent selections include "Animal Farm" which if studied with collaborating Literature and History teachers can implant a healthy distrust of persons seeking power at the expense of freedom and rights.

## **High School** 9th - 12th grades typically

In high school, students will likely study all of history in a deeper way, particularly the United States. Political science is frequently offered as a separate course. Current events, world affairs, and the concept of global cooperation will be explored.

This is an opportunity, perhaps the last one, to instill in students the indisputable good effects of Catholicism well known and lived. These years will also lend themselves to ensuring that students understand such concepts as inquiry, investigation, verification, and clarification with respect to the world around them and at a distance.

What sources may they reference? How will they be able to detect falsehood or propaganda? Who may they trust in government implicitly or only reservedly? How can they embrace idealism without surrendering their reason illuminated by Faith?

Many temptations arise in this stage of development and through college. Freedom promises to attack that which was instilled in youth from a very early age. Peers and crafty educators can sway opinion even in educated and solidly reared Catholics. These young minds are prey.

Catholic teachers have the foremost duty to ensure that students, regardless of the subject, recall their true roots. As in middle school, English and Literature teachers will encounter book selections for which some students are not prepared, depending on the Archdiocese or school district. Most home school programs have a prepared list of classics, and another source is available in this text. However, a teacher's library will need continuous updating. Those antennae are critical with respect to what students digest, especially if some of the reading is mandatory.

Science is another subject that may appear far afield of government, but think again. Climate change and all the theories that impact government in the 21st century must be addressed. Genetic engineering, biological understanding of the human body and gender, even life development related to abortion, should be understood factually and in light of Church teaching.

Math may seem exempt except that government often uses statistics to advance itself and its policies.

Even the arts cannot be ignored. How have tyrannical rulers used the arts, including music, drama, and paintings or drawings to implant a way of thinking well of an otherwise dictatorship?

Technology? Today, Big tech is being accused of influencing governments around the world and swaying the population to accept a basically anti-Christ form of government, or at least one that largely relies on carefully prepared analysis of how the populace must behave. Cyber attacks may be imminent.

Nothing will substitute for knowing the Catholic faith and being watchful. Students should know news sources that pass the indoctrination test, but are well balanced. Better are specific lessons that teach them to build their *antennae*. That way whether they are in an environment that permits forbidden sites, by explicit instruct on disguising language or deceptive approaches, they will more likely detect truth or falsehood and make rightful discernments.

Students as young as twelve can learn how to detect subjectivity in news reporting, starting with the headlines and leads. Moreover, they should be exposed to some of the offenders to objective, well rounded news reporting.

Teachers may model how to develop personal library of primary sources, too. Students with guidance can then more aptly determine how history has a way of changing players but not predictable outcomes. For example atheistic totalitarianism always starts with a proclamation of justice, especially for the poor or working class, but unchecked always leads to enslavement and the stripping of not just rights but the very dignity of persons. Whether such governance is called fascism, communism, socialism, democratic socialism, etc., they all share common traits, including the appeal to those who desire a temporal utopia and Heaven, too.

By being well informed and pre warned, teachers are naturally more confident, and courageous.

## INTERSECTING MAN'S LAW WITH NATURAL LAW (The Individual vs. the State)

As previously discussed, governance—the concept of steering a people towards healthy community living—had its origin in the eternal Holy Trinity. It is only (wo)man's ignorance and pride that have interfered or derailed peoples. At the root are the seven deadly sins—bluntly—and the remedy is always virtue and the fruits of the Holy Spirit.

Also, various peoples have had a glimmer of truth and discovery through time and around the world with various degrees of understanding about supernatural or mysterious power and how we are to react, adapt or impact those realities. Original sin's effects have left many blind to authentic truth and love. Moreover, even those civilizations that were most benefitted from the first monotheistic Covenant between God and His chosen people to Christians have often stumbled, badly. Again, from Satan, self, and the world, arise temptation.

# Chapter Ten: Government through Time

## TOOLS, LESSON(S) AND GENERAL RESOURCES AND MATERIALS—GOVERNMENT THROUGH TIME

### TOOLS:

References like the Constitution and other government library materials for quick reference; templates and timelines (Thinking Maps).

### LESSONS:

LESSON ACTIVITY

Create TYPED strips for research and discussion from the following. THIS IS ADULT STUDENT-TEACHER ORIENTED. Pertinent citations are limited by space. However, all teachers, but particularly history and government teachers are urged to read these texts cover to cover, among others.

**From *America on Trial: A Defense of the Founding*** Robert R. Reilly (Ignatius Press). Student Teachers should read and reflect on the excerpt themes which date back to Greek and Roman times.

- ➢ Aristotle and Aquinas, as the thread of thought—reason—are surprisingly comparative. Aquinas reflecting Aristotle, notes that the essential character of sin or vice is its irrationality. The Catholic Church holds that sin is an offense against reason. (31) *Respond to: Marriage between persons of the same sex is nonsense.*
- ➢ Socrates and political philosophy: In heaven there is laid up a patter of it (the ideal city) which he who desires may behold, and beholding may set his own house in order. (32). *How does this reasoning reflect the life of a Christian?*
- ➢ To pagan Rome, nothing is more shattering than the revelation that man's soul is drawn not only to the good but goodness itself which is God. True home is not in the polis but the City

of God. Socrates' "city in speech" finds its true location and reality in Augustine's City of God. *How does this similarity of thought reinforce that God penetrates our very minds with Truth.*

➢ Pope Benedict XVI warned, Whenever politics tries to be redemptive, it is promising too much. Where it wishes to do the work of God it becomes not divine but demonic. (Man's self deification) (54). *Nancy Pelosi alluded to the "divinity" in all persons when praising the misnamed Marriage Act. How is this an example of Pope Benedict's concern?*

➢ Augustine acknowledged man's equality as the foundation for the requirement for his consent in how he is governed. Consent, however, must operate with the dictates of natural law. (61). *Again, we see threads through historical philosophy that remain immutable. Explain or demonstrate one way, you, as a teacher can relay this to students even in Primary grades?*

➢ Pope Paul III's 1537 Encyclical on the Enslavement and Education of Indians, called demonic those who denied the full humanity of the Indians. (62). 1839, Pope Gregory reiterated teaching against slavery *Supremo Apostolates*—reference to the inhuman slave trade (63) *Research other similar Encyclicals. How do past Encyclicals dispute the argument that Christianity ignored and even endorsed slavery?*

➢ Three main types of law: divine, natural, human—human must be infused with both divine and natural law in accord with reason. (88) *Discuss the order of priority with Divine first. How do the other types correspond?*

➢ What touches all, must be approved by all. Roman maxim Taken form Code of Justian 5, 59, 5,2-3) most influential in the Middle Ages (91) *Discuss how this relates to the premise that power is granted government by the people's consent?*

➢ Pope John XXII: 1320s—What God established at the very beginning in an ideal state of nature is not common possession but individual property. (103). *Contrast that to a modern Church*

# Chapter Ten: Government through Time 349

> statement that borders on collectivism. *Distinguish between stewardship and ownership.*
> 
> ➤ In Middle Ages the sword of the church and state served one truth. *Describe how this looked.* (127)
> 
> ➤ Luther translated Romans 3:28 to read that "man becomes justified by faith alone"…the word "alone does not appear in the original Greek. (141). *There are numerous distortions of Scripture over time that have led to heresy and schism. Reflect on the importance of adding one word; the omission of a word or verse; and the hyper focus on only a few Biblical references to the exclusion of others.*
> 
> ➤ Divorced from natural and eternal law, legal positivism is anchored in will. Once the state absorbs religion and no longer has a moral reference point outside itself, it becomes pure power. Getting close to Machiavelli. (150). *Identify two ways this is occurring today.*
> 
> ➤ Another form of absolutism arose in the late 16th Century—the Divine Right of Kings (196). In 1628 Parliament forced Charles I to accept the Petition of Rights. Charles dissolved Parliament the next year, sowing seeds for the English Civil War. (2030). *Are there similar events in US government today? Cite one.*
> 
> ➤ Sidney echoing Cicero, Aquinas, Suarez and Bellarmine: "That which is not just, is not Law, and that which is not Law, ought not to be obeyed." "There can be no peace, where there is no justice; nor any justice if the government instituted for the good of a nation be turned to its ruin." (222). *How has the modern slogan "No justice, no peace" chanted by several riotous group—even mobs—been incorrectly appropriated from this thought?*
> 
> ➤ Founders used the same language as Hooker, Bellarmine, Suarez, Sidney, Locke—of natural law traditions reaching back to Aquinas, Cicero, and Aristotle. *Study a philosopher mentioned in this excerpt. Explain his understanding of natural law*
> 
> ➤ 1772—James Mason speaking within the tradition developed in the Middle Ages: All acts of legislature apparently contrary

to natural right and justice are, in our laws and must be in the nature of things, considered as void. The laws of nature are the laws of God, whose authority can be superseded by no power on earth. Our legislature must not obstruct our obedience to Him from whose punishments they cannot protect us. All human constitutions which contradict His (God's) laws, we are in conscience bound to disobey. (257). *Were you aware of these founding principles? If not, to what do you attribute that ignorance?*

➤ The violence of the Revolution (French) was entirely what must be expected when people attempt to deny the reality of original sin and to take their destiny into their own hands. The events of the Terror were literally satanic, re enacting the revolt of the fallen angels, and displaying what ensues when human beings reject the idea of authority, and imagine themselves capable of discovering a new form of government in the freedom from government. —Sir Roger Scruton (279). *How are radical thinkers today denying original sin? Cite three examples.*

➤ John Dewey (1859-1952) looked forward to a time that schools would be managed on a psychological basis as great factories based on chemical and physical science. He criticized the founders in that natural rights and natural liberties "exist only in the kingdom of mythological social zoology." (326). *How did Dewey contribute to the moral deterioration of public education? Describe one eventual outcome.*

➤ Barack Obama in *The Audacity of Hope* rejected the idea that the Constitution incorporated absolute truths. (327) *Note the word "incorporated" which implies that the founders did not enshrine natural law either. Discuss: If that were the case, which it is not, how does that also then contort the concept of "hope"?*

➤ Ratzinger (Pope Benedict XVI) The denial of truth of natural law leads to the "tyranny of unreason." It last the ground floor for what St. Pope John Paul II called "totalitarian democracy." (328). *Trace the pattern of this thinking from the time of Aristotle.*

## Chapter Ten: Government through Time

Lesson Two: Read the following excerpts. How is Dietrich Von Hildebrand's battle like the ones persons of Faith are confronting today? Are there any modern spins? How is language may be used to disguise evil intent?

**FROM DIETRICH VON HILDEBRAND — MY BATTLE AGAINST HITLER—FAITH, TRUTH, AND DEFIANCE IN THE SHADOW OF THE THIRD REICH. (2014, Crown Publishing)**

**Objective: Identify the rise of Fascism; Compare it to modern movements; Analyze the Role of Church in Relations to State and Individual Accountability**

Permeating through this book which includes both Hildebrand's memoirs and some of his essays, is the absolute inflexible position that there can be no compromise with evil regimes, and Nazism and Bolshevism are cut from the same cloth: Both are collective totalitarian government paradigms, excluding God, extinguishing the person—individual child of God, and promoting the concept of the masses in an impossible endeavor to produce a utopia, heaven on earth. The consequences are catastrophic, and the Catholic Church and its clergy and laity cannot in any way endorse even those aspects that appear beneficial because they are an illusion to attract the naive and corruptible.

Note: Von Hildebrand's perspective on "nationalism"—as opposed to patriotism—and marked by militarism and "racism" in reference to the supposed superior Arianism or perfect race, not to be generally applied to today's meaning. Incidentally, this comparison and contrast—patriotism vs. nationalism— would be a great student lesson.

Below are some quotes from the book, but the brevity of them in this Primer does not do the work justice. A simple Internet search shows that the book is available. Some libraries may carry it. Also, visit archive.org for this and other enriching material.

1933: "The deification of the state is an old error—found in Sparta—while nationalism is a product of the modern era, above all a creation of the French Revolution. Both rest on classical dangers in human nature. Racism, by contrast, is a completely artificial, far-fetched, stupid theory with no organic basis in human nature. (46). *NOTE: In the former the state was to be glorified; in Hitler's time, the Fatherland was used to evoke singular loyalty.)*

"Yet it was clear to me that I could not longer teach in a National Socialist country because I was convinced I would be forced to" make compromises, and that I would either have to be silent about the injustices that would come or else risk the concentration camp. (52). *Compare this to teaching in government schools today. Though there are no concentration camps, per se, economic and social deprivation are common.*

Just fourteen days after Hitler's seize of power, the German bishops lifted the excommunication that previously had been attached to membership in the National Socialist Party, including both the SA and the SS. Franz van Papen was working zealously for a Concordat between German and the Holy See. The conclusion of the Concordat…it must have given Catholics throughout German the impression that the Vatican was withdrawing its rejection of National Socialism and of racism—as if it were possible to be a Catholic and a Nazi at the same time. (69). *Compare to the controversy about excommunication of contemporary American politicians.*

Von Hildebrand could be quite expressive remarking in one conversation to the Provincial (of the German Dominicans and prior of the monastery in Berlin) who claimed "that ….Above all he (Hitler) keeps speaking abut God. I answered, "Hitler is so stupid that he does not even know what the word 'God' means; when he uses the word, in no way does it mean that he is professing the true God.." (70). *Do not our leaders assert they are devout Catholics while supporting evil like abortion? What might Von Hildebrand say or write today about Biden or Pelosi?*

RE Monsignor Kaas"s telegram offering Hitler best wishes on his birthday, Von Hildebrand notes, "What a disastrous and undignified way to ingratiate himself with Hitler…There was no reason to hope

## Chapter Ten: Government through Time 353

that a congratulatory telegram would alter Hitler's stance toward the Church or secure greater freedom for Catholics, or that one could somehow convince him not to encroach on the life of the Church, on Catholic schools, etc.... let alone gain for the Church an exemption from the Nazi policy of Gleichschaltung. (74-75) *Again, in what way do our Catholic leaders emulate Monsignor Kaas?*

But as soon as Pope Pius XI saw that Hitler was not respecting the terms of the Concordat, but was trying to enslave the Church in Germany, he raised his voice in the magnificent encyclical Mit brennender Sorge (With Burning Anxiety). He did not speak in a conciliatory spirit, but he condemned with holy authority, like St. Gregory VII. (Terrible persecution of the Church followed.) (81) *Discuss: Was this too little, too late?*

Note: Given the paradoxical events of our day, in the absence of absolute truth and objective morals, Von Hildebrand related: I heard that a school teacher who had been fired for drinking but who was a fervent member of the Nazi Party had been appointed Minister of Culture in Bavaria. (86) *Identify top tier politicians. Recently, there was a controversy about one who oversaw nuclear waste disposal. Are our times the same or worse?*

Regrettably, it is so easy to influence even many well-meaning people with slogans, such as "enemy of the workers," "brutal dictator," etc (136). *Explore today's often repeated labels and slogans and examples of impact such as censorship.*

From the so-called journalistic truce, Austria still asserted its independence and did not wish to be Nazified. ...yet its leaders wrongly thought one could live in peaceful coexistence with Hitler, and that through concessions one could induce him to greater friendliness. (Fundamental error of all, except Italy, in that they did not grasp the spirit of a totalitarian state.)(214). *Identify the "spirit" or a totalitarian state, and discuss if there can ever be a truce with it.*

Von Hildebrand discusses what he calls a monstrosity of a book, Hudal's book in which the author tried to demonstrate that National Socialism and Catholicism were in principle entirely compatible. The author tried to claim 95% agreement or at least harmony, while only

5% needed modification. This book was published after the encyclical (With Burning Anxiety and that persecution of the Church was already in full swing. Ironically the book failed in Germany because the Nazis did not deem it sufficiently orthodox. (226). *Note the Baptized Catholic politicians who attempt to politicalize Jesus Christ in similar ways. Cite five examples in recent years.*

Von Hildebrand notes that we must never get used to sin. He asserts that those who habitually consort with the morally perverted will slowly become poisoned themselves. (260-261). *Discuss this timeless advice.*

People generally remain indignant only for a short while. After a certain time, a person tends to to become weary of disapprobation, even if the deed that occasioned his revulsion goes unpunished and the sin continues to cry to heaven. He later notes that Christians can never succumb to embittered attitude of hatred and must remain compassionate towards those who have gone astray, (262). *Do you know people who have been numbed by the deterioration of society or basically thrown up their hands and "go along"? Have you? How can Catholics not grown weary and remain loving? Describe one recent experience when that could have been demonstrated.*

The Danger of Quietism (Der Christliche Standesamt, March 10, 1935). Hildebrand addresses the danger of "quietism" which challenges Catholics to take their faith outside the church sanctuary and into public life, especially when public life has been taken over by criminals. (279) *This is happening today. Research an article that promotes separation of church and state by "permitting" worship inside a Church but not lived in the public square.*

All Catholics must fight for Christ in the political sphere with full personal commitment, representing (in season and out of season) the claims of the kingdom of God, and thus, implicitly, those of morality and the natural law. (281). Von Hildebrand emphasized that persons have the right to expect governments afford them the freedom to be good. This is regardless of: "Naturally, the Christian rejects every form of earthly messianism and remains ever aware of 'how great is heaven and how small the earth.'" Catholics have an obligation to carry the spirit of Christ into this domain (politics) (282) *What should that look like today?*

"A person belongs to it (community) only insofar as he is a citizen; but his membership in the state does not constitute the totality of his being. His final destiny transcends the sphere of the state by fare: he is created by God, destined by God, and belongs 'totally' to God alone. He is moreover, primarily destined to be a member of the Mystical Body of Christ, and only secondarily to be a citizen of the state." (288). *Relate this to The City of God. Distinguish between state citizenship and heavenly citizenship. What is never permitted; what is always desirable? Where is compatibility?*

The National socialists leaders frequently declared that there was no objective right or wrong but only what is right and useful for the German people. (295) *Did you think the absence of objective truth emerged only in recent times? How does that perspective harm education?*

"The fate of states, nations, and peoples as such is incomparably less important than the eternal salvation of a single immortal soul." (297). *Consider this powerful statement. What does it indicate for the Faithful Catholic teacher?*

"Even the noble unbeliever knows that marriage primarily concerns the ultimate form of communion in love between two persons and the coming into existence of a new human being out of this most intimate, loving union. For the Christian, this ultimate community of love is an image of the unity between Christ and His Church, and therefore a Sacrament." (303) *Do you think Von Hildebrand would be astonished at the irreverent state of marriage today? Could he have foreseen this incredible devolvement of the purest union between man and woman?*

Hildebrand references the religious vacuum in all those who have allowed themselves to be influenced in any way by the National Socialist movement, whether they defend it with apologetic zeal or hesitantly and tepidly approve of its so-called 'positive aspects.' The result of this litmus test cannot be altered merely by a visit to a church, no matter how fervent; nor by reception of the Sacraments, no matter how frequent; nor by any profession of allegiance to the Church, no matter how emphatic. (304). *Write a dialogue between Von Hildebrand and a self proclaimed, pro abort politician on this matter.*

LESSON # 3.

Review the following and discuss. Where is there agreement; disagreement? How can knowledge of Salvation History and Church History support "Virtuous Self government according to Divine Revelation, but in submission to His Divine Will"?

GOVERNMENT STARTS WITH SELF and acknowledgment of God

Recent events boldface the urgency of addressing "governance"—as it must exist in the individual, the family, the neighborhood, the town, the city, the county, the state, the region, and nation. It all begins with "self"—Lacking rightful self governance, there is no hope for an overarching government that will serve the people.

Similar to seeing a piece of fruit or vegetable that may look edible on the exterior, once squeezed, a person knows it is rotten from the inside, so it is with government. Some nations may appear to be democratic and good, but peer closer, and it is all a shell.

Yet, beyond the individual, governance must be embraced in sound philosophy. Regrettably, even the concept of philosophy has been hijacked by devious minds. As mentioned, philosophy literally means love of wisdom (addressed in another chapter), but if those who ponder the origin of life, its meaning, and its destination, are not "lovers of wisdom" but skiers of wisdom or, worse, agents of the diabolical, we need to identify their exposition as such. From the perspective of governance, a close look at that distinction is mandatory.

Many people seek wisdom, but for lack of knowledge misunderstand it and veer off course. Certainly, no wisdom can be discovered apart from God. One might call these otherwise earnest pursuers as quaesitorosophers (other possibilities). Their conclusions will miss the

## Chapter Ten: Government through Time

mark in some way, but there will likely be elements or figures of truth. The third possibility can be difficult to ascertain, as one would need to know the heart and soul of the one developing a philosophy. Yet, we know that not all "crafters" are well intended. Some like Machiavelli were ruthless in their discourse that touted temporal power and how to attain it.

Those who intentionally ignore or dismiss God, Divine Authority, and Natural Law with incorporation of morality, are truly Odiumosophers—haters of wisdom. They must be called such, so that the innocent are not deluded into lumping them among philosophers. Also, there would be the ongoing danger of relativism within our contemplation of wisdom—Truth.

From this angle, the thinkers through the ages may be viewed through a clearer lens and perceived with all their wrong directions and poor conclusions. Always, one finds that the mere "seeker" or the odious mind can be detected based on …simply…God's revelation and His Covenants with human beings since Adam and Eve. Moreover, another "tell" emerges, and that is when a seeker relies on sources of knowledge apart from God. We witness this daily in the 21st Century, whereby people turn to the oddest expertise in the most contradictory persons. Without mentioning names, per se, in recent years a young teenage girl rose to celebrity status as a defender of the environment based on her enhanced visibility and supposed grasp of climate change. Truly, she became a modern day goddess for millions.

In our currently blind world, others without any credibility have gained hero status or have been emulated solely on their publicized intersection with current events. Thus, we have seen hardened criminals and those who could not overcome their circumstances surpass the truly gifted and sacrificially giving among us. The sinners have become saints, and the saints have been stoned.

There is no wisdom.

Yet, educators will also need to be equipped to wisely navigate in instruction, so as not to break the weakest reeds. Many if not most children of this age have not been steered in wisdom. While it is true that God's law is impressed upon their heart, that may well be clouded by parental rearing and societal messaging that focuses on falsehoods.

Furthermore, despite error, some thinkers have struck veins of truth, and those would be noted. There is wheat among the chaff.

What follows will be a table that illustrates the most famous thinkers from Adam and Eve until today, and how their conclusions fall into "wisdom", "foolishness," and "falsehood." Note that a the "foolish" may also be false but the thinker's intent was to arrive at truth. Understanding this will also help educators understand that they, too, may fall into similar error regarding matters of Faith. Our imaginations and memories are often culprits (Rippenger…Introduction…)

Always, the refrain must be "Turn to God; Trust in God." Even without "understanding," teachers cannot go wrong following the real script.

LESSON FOUR Article Reviews and Discussion

Choose for future reading the abundance of articles and books related to the Polis of Man vs. the Polis of God

See Father Peter Samuel Kucer, STD, MSA (holyapostles.edu): *Politician and Sanctity*

**Another Activity** developed to educate and prompt lesson ideas
SURVEY ON CAPITALISM AND COMMUNISM
Read the following statements and mark as CA for Capitalism, CO for Communism, B for both, N for neither
1. Asserts that the person is born to serve the state.
2. Believes all people should be employed.
3. Is always based in Christianity.
4. Upholds the individual entrepreneur.
5. Is atheistic.
6. Redistributes wealth

Chapter Ten: Government through Time         359

7. Respects the class system but that there should be opportunity to rise in society.
8. Relies on the free market.
9. Property and businesses owned by the government
10. Can lead to monopolistic greed

(1: CO; 2: B; 3: N; 4: CA; 5: CO; 6: CO; 7: CA; 8: CA; 9: CO; 10: CA)

## RESOURCES

Rev. Peter Kucer *Political Science through the Catholic Perspective*
Christopher Dawson "Judgment of the Nations"
Archbishop Chaput: *Rendering Unto Caesar*

Catholic Vote (and The Loop); Population Research Institute; The Public Discourse; The Imaginative Conservative; Crisis Magazine; American Society for the Defense of Tradition, Family and Property; LifeSite News; Ruth Institute; Students for Life; Convention of States (COS) although not Catholic

Other: archive.org and ducksters.com (not Catholic)

# Chapter Eleven

## RELATING SECULARISM THE CATHOLIC WAY

### *How Secularism became "Sick"ularism and other Language Manipulation*

While flushing out this Primer section, it became clearer that language, overall, has been abused to such an extent that people utter words and phrases in the absence of original meaning and purpose. Though this section will emphasize that the constant reference to "secularism" has lost its compass, there are numerous other contexts distorted by manipulated meanings.

One example arose in a protest against a Florida law protecting innocent children from being bombarded with intensely sexual content. A group strolled the state capitol shouting "Gay, gay, gay." (March 7, 2022)

Gay--another word stolen, contorted, and compromised for ideological purposes. However, given some original meaning, perhaps "gay" is appropriate for those acting out same sex behavior. Though its meaning leaned towards a positive connotation as early as the 12th century--full of joy or mirth-- "gay" may well suit this lifestyle given that it may also relate to Old High German, "gahi" meaning impulsive. Also, gay also was meant as "wanton, lewd, lascivious" (late 12th century, as a surname, Philippus de Gay). One source claims that the word "gay" by the 1890s had an overall tinge of promiscuity--a gay house was a brothel. (Data Lounge). This all makes for some very interesting implications. NO--same sex, trans sex, and other topics for mature audiences and guidance, including parents , do not belong in K or Primary. Educators may feel empowered to offer parents insights, but they have no right to intrude in family business and children's consciousness in these matters alone in their innocence, excepting extraordinary and rare situations. Even then, parents must be notified first and foremost.

Many other such instances could be equally noted and studied. The lesson activity at the end of this section will explore etymology, cultural context, and how the devils disciples have cunningly maneuvered evil to appear either benign or good by the use of language. They who "own" Merriam-Webster dictionaries (and others), steer the communication and therefore the direction of society. Still, currently, the incessant focus on secularism utilized in so many written and oral commentaries, in public debate, and in the media requires attention to what it truly means in 2023 and what it does not.

Secularism is so pronounced especially as the uber directional in global society—not just American— it must be viewed as its own entity and obstacle to Catholic teaching and freedom of religion. In particular, in the field of education, **the concept of secularism has been so deeply embedded, it has become an accepted "belief system" all of its own with atheistic, anti-Christian tentacles**. How could a nation like the United States whose Constitution forbids the hindering or advancing of any belief system insist on implanting Antichristianity. For it is one thing to deny someone free will (even in abortion) and another to criminalize and confiscate property (i.e. taxes) from opponents to this obvious murder of life and who genuinely believe that complicity, even compelled, is a grave offense.

Yet, this did not occur overnight. The stealthiness of the enemy was truly brilliant, but then Lucifer was God's brightest angel in the beginning.

At one time, if anyone communicated that an idea was "secular," most would interpret that to mean it was a non sectarian concept, an idea free from any ties to particular dogma, evidence of "separation of church and state." However, aside from morally neutral opinions, like what flavor of ice cream to serve in the school cafeteria, that was a nonstarter from the beginning. There is no worthy idea about life that does not have as its genesis some belief about the supernatural, that which may not be provable by natural or clinically scientific observation and experimentation. Particularly in a school setting, the exclusion of any expression of faith is tantamount to establishing the Antichrist

## Chapter Eleven: Relating Secularism the Catholic Way

because he is the prince of nihilism, the accuser against truth, the devil in every locker ready to fill the vacuum left by the nothing.

Predictably, what has evolved is more than that folly of neutrality, but increasing diabolical environments that forbid religious freedom and the opportunities to pursue truth, do good, and relish beauty.

In his *Degenerate Moderns*, Michael E. Jones fully and painfully exposes (literally) the creepy progression—actually regression—of embraced church reformists (Luther), social scientists (Mead), psychiatrists (Freud), sex research (Kinsey), and artists (Picasso) as agents of this devolvement that was predestined given the settings empty of God's acknowledged presence. In other words, evil slowly but surely overtook the "empty space" left by "secularism."

We have been pummeled with the reality that we live in a secular world replete with pluralistic beliefs, some of which deny absolute, objective truth and even centuries held moral codes. Furthermore, we have moved beyond "relativism," to "psychosis" because there is no more "debate," but irrational absolutes.

Yet, it is worse than a simple acknowledgment that people are in different places on their Faith journey, and often not on the same path. The faithful of a 2,000+ year religion are now commanded to capitulate to the most base of these antichrist belief systems, a humanistic, agnostic (at best), collectivistic perceptive of governance, economy, and community. It is insufficient to simply live differently and according to sincerely held beliefs about God, natural law, and Divine authority, people are significantly penalized if they do not quell and submerge those beliefs to accommodate basically pagans, pantheists, and atheists. Many have lost occupations, life long investments, and public esteem.

Moreover, it does not matter that anyone has any intention of compelling others to share his or her beliefs. It does not matter that the minority are respected by the Constitution with respect to expression of religion, and that government is prohibited from establishing one religion—yet, in effect—it has. That one societal religion is not "secularism" but "satanism."

Herein, the argument will be made that 1. The persecution of Christians, especially Catholics, is real and threatening; 2. Human-based and Church history actually support the Christian (Catholic) paradigm of authority, natural law, and the Constitution of the United States; and 3. No person may call him or herself a Catholic teacher who does not with conviction, commitment, and courage defend the Faith as the one true way to the City of God and eternal unity and relationship with the Blessed Trinity.

## What is secularism; when and from where did it arise; and how has it numbed the missionary spirit of the Church

Secularism is a term that references a separation of religion from civic affairs and the state. However, It arouses a negative connotation as being anti Church, even atheism. Over the past century, even longer, in the United States, the spirit of secularism has increasingly eroded all public, and even private, recognition of God and His laws and order. Ironically, it was God's revelation to mankind, first through Israel and then through the Second Person of the Holy Trinity, Jesus Christ that eventually led to the counter movement, often referred to by the misleadingly benign sounding "secularism."

Prior to monotheism, though, many classic civilizations were hardly so "obliging" in permitting residents to be religiously neutral. Even in Egyptian history and shards of truth in ancient Greece and Rome, the rise of community in city-states and then civilizations were under the rule of those believed to be gods or god-like. *Government was under the auspices of deity in some form, and those civilizations that made their gods at the center of government, economics, and civil life, were more successful.* So, then there was no reason to establish the concept of secularism, nor would these deified rulers even conceived of such a contradictory license. People had no choice; they knew from birth their place in their respective societies; and there were severe consequences for those who resisted or rebelled, with little sympathy from the public.

This included civilizations East and West which are covered in a different section: (See Unmasking the Religions of the World for Truth and Error.)

It is important to boldface the fact that **none of these pagan governments ever had any inkling to smooth the egos of those who did not believe**.

Then entered God, first as he appeared to the Jewish nation, as the Origin of Life, the Supreme Truth; the Author of History; the Eternal Lord. God gave the world basic commands and expectations that Jewish leaders later so manipulated as to discourage and burden the people. Those who should have reflected the Face of God instead disfigured that Holy Image and faith eroded; people betrayed God; and they were led into captivity.

It is the never ending story!

Still, truth could not be extinguished any more than God's mercy could be exhausted.

Meanwhile, in other civilizations, God permitted truths to permeate philosophy giving credence to the fact that God will illuminate any genuine truth seekers regardless of their location in time or space and whether or not they are believers.

One critical discovery was the concept of "self-evident" truth, a word we find in our own Declaration of Independence.

Then Jesus Christ, Second Person of the Holy Trinity, entered human history as True God and True Man. As so many figures beforehand have established, either Jesus was the Son of God or He was a liar, a fraud. He could not be both. The late Archbishop Fulton Sheen's *The Life of Jesus Christ* is a masterpiece at establishing Jesus Christ as the Son of God. Yet, there are others. Equally important are all the writing from Sacred Scripture and the early Church Fathers, saints, and other holy persons that establish, explain, elaborate on Truth without detracting or diminishing its full potency. The devil was displeased and had to combat this truth and love from the beginning but with increased persecution of Catholics, in particular.

Other competing understandings of life and after death experience, the notions of good and evil, consequences for living in vice rather than virtue, and how we are to act in community were all affected by these various perspectives. Many of these were Eastern in such systems of Buddhism (not a religion, actually) and all its factions; Hinduism (and its varying sects), and such offshoots as Zoroastrianism. In the 600s, Islam, considered by many to be actually a heretic belief, erupted and would change the world in many ways. The Reformation would be incredibly destructive and usher in the rationale for "secularism."

Even so, there was some commonality it how a person was to conduct him or herself towards self and others. There was a basic morality code. Sure in some cultures, thievery and assault (or killing) was justified as opposed to Christians who acknowledged extenuating circumstances but always called such acts inherently evil. (These distinctions would later complicate or muddle credibility about right and wrong.)

Western Civilization arose and eventually the Church and State were intertwined, but not without some controversy. Which had ultimate authority, especially as royal rulers would contend that they were anointed by God, not unlike Saul, David, or Solomon? How did the Pope's election by the Holy Spirit respond? Where was the legitimate divisions in law, economy, and living the Faith? It went back and forth, with eventually establishing that kings had their rightful place in the governance of people in everyday life of the State and by laws, but the Pope was the ultimate voice for the Faith and appointment of Bishops and clerical roles. What followed is crucial:

*At all times, though, the state was to be subservient to the Church (the Mystical Body of Christ—the Magisterium) in matters of immortal health of souls, beginning with life in the temporal world. In other words, as Thomas Aquinas asserted, the Church cannot anticipate every legal remedy or way a society can be constructed for the health and prosperity of its citizens, so a State government is necessary. Also, the Church cannot prescribe every remedy or penalty in regards to any group (city, state, nation) when laws are violated. Even temporal justice could differ in various cultures, evangelized or not. Yet, at all times, the State was to be subservient to natural law and Divine Will in its exercise of authority.*

*The bottom line, then, was that the State would serve the Church—absolute, objective Truth—for the betterment of its subjects or citizens and their ultimate salvation.*

As is easily detected today, the opposite has occurred whereby the modern State insists that religion bow to its edicts and judgments, no matter how vile or counter to that absolute Truth and dangerous to multitudes of souls. Christians, and especially Catholics are now proclaimed enemies even as the currently sworn in President and Speaker of the House (2022) claim themselves Catholic. Only the devil could succeed in such a ridiculous but evidently successful ruse. Yet, that is not the extent of blindness in this nation.

Consider also all the other glaring and even boasted contradictions that counter the assumed "necessity" of secularism to merely neutralize differences of belief. During the March to Life (2022), Busboys and Poets, a pro abortion establishment, cancelled "last minute" a reservation made months in advance by the Democrats for Life. So, a restaurant can refuse to serve a group that merely wanted lunch, but a baker and florist lose their livelihoods and life long investment, not because they refuse to serve those with differing beliefs, in general, but that they cannot directly use their vocation for an event that compromises their conscience (mediate.com).

Then while the DOJ intentionally exceeds its authority in pursuing parents concerned about their children's education, numerous interstate attacks on Catholics and their property are virtually ignored. This is not secularism; this is "sick"ularism. It is the height of spiritual depravity which often fosters irrational intellectual reactivity.

## *History Proves Absolute Truth*

The ultimate irony may be that history proves absolute Truth and that the Catholic Church—The Mystical Body of Christ—literally embodies that Truth. What follows is the pristine view of original Christianity, now inherent in Catholicism, not the aberrations, betrayals, and conflicts that shadow its history. It is a given that human beings, even those who have risen to great spiritual heights, may be felled by temptations of the self, world, and or devil. There also may be only a small remnant, as well. A Jesus posed though knowing the answer, "When the Son of Man comes, will he find faith on the earth?" (Luke 18:8).

The integrity of the fullness of Faith discovered in the unchanging Magisterium of the Church remains. As Jesus promised, "The gates of hell shall not prevail against it." (Matthew 16:18).

How is this known? History proves it!

Catholic educators, including parents, would greatly benefit by a parallel study of history, side by side, as man recorded it, and as revealed in Salvation History, much through Sacred Scripture and other holy testimony and writing. The intervention of the Divine is easily recognizable and intense in some eras. (See The Eternal Age vs. Man Constructed Ages)

In fact, it can easily be demonstrated that all history is God's story though humans often distort, omit, embellish to boost human power over the Divine or propagate human endeavors towards an illusionary utopia instead of the reality of eternal life with God.

### Catholic Teachers Must be Catholic Authority Figures!

Many wonderful people become teachers, persons impassioned about imparting knowledge and skills to young people to enable them to be productive and contented contributors to society.

They are often empathetic, exceptionally generous, self sacrificing, diligent, and competent in their array of subject knowledge and methodology for delivery instruction. Yet, another reality must be acknowledged.

Those in Catholic schools most often have been baptized and reared in the Faith to one degree or another, fully or partially, faithfully or in error. That is just a fact. Moreover, Catholic schools now employ nonCatholics as there are certain areas of expertise that may not bring forth a Catholic, such as in the arts, music, or technology. Some of these teachers work well in a Catholic environment, respecting the

Faith; others have been known to exhibit their hostility and openly combat administration and pastors! In the latter situations, it is not unusual that fellow Catholic colleagues will defend the nonCatholic teacher. It's a mess.

Homeschooling parents, already know this, and the quagmire of compromised Catholic education is most often the primary reason for homeschooling. Ditto for some pods and hybrids. Catholic teachers seeking greater understanding of the Faith, might be upset by this. Maybe they have dear friends who disagree with Catholicism, but love their students. Then, candidly, those step children of "sick"ularism: notions of "tolerance," "nonjudgment," and "diversity" and misconstrued "compassion" rear their ugly head. Acceptance is confused as love; openness is embraced as evangelizing (ecumenism); debating as truth-seeking. Here is the news. The Truth has already been discovered and made known. He is Jesus Christ as revealed in the Catholic Church.

No argument, but the contention stands. No one can call him or herself a Catholic school teacher who does not embrace the totality of the Church's teaching and understand that the Truth is superlative to all the humanistic ideologies that threaten the Faith of those with whom they are charged to teach. As stated elsewhere, each individual is responsible for the students in his or her care. If teachers, in any way, mislead them in the Faith, they will answer to the final Judge, and there is no Supreme Court in Heaven.

Now, it must be interjected that this is not about a genuine misunderstanding or conveyance of what is believed to be true. That has happened and will continue to occur. Teachers are imperfect; they have faults and defects of personality. However, that is why this Primer was developed. There should be few such incidents with the Truth and all the resources.

Also, fellow faithful teachers will need to voice that truth on occasion even at the risk of being alienated or mocked. Many years ago, a young Catholic teacher joked at a Pastor lunch about the Holy Spirit being "her"—ignorantly based on wisdom being a "she" Later, another teacher pulled her aside and inquired about the remark, gently chiding her. This other much more knowledgeable teacher patiently explained the fallacy, and the receptive teacher was more careful in the future and more determined to seek solid knowledge of the Faith.

Then Catholic Archdiocese and Catholic Schools offices would help their teachers by professional development that specifies the dangers of secularism. This should include the history of this movement, starting with countering the current propagandized definition of secularism: religious skepticism or indifference; the view that religious considerations should be excluded from civil affairs or public education; exclusive attention to the present life and its duties, and the relegation of all considerations regarding a future life to a secondary place; the system of the secularists; the ignoring or exclusion of religious duties, in structure, or considerations.

Moreover, by some historical reference, they can place the term in context. The original understanding was its reference "living in the world, not belonging to a religious order" (c 1300), also from Old French (secular) "belonging to the state", Late Latin seculars: worldly, of an age, occurring once in an age, span of time, lifetime, generation, breed. All well and fine for the religious. *However, the overwhelming majority of people do live in the world and still must be given the freedom to live their Faith, openly and without prejudice.*

Administrators should also show how the interpretation has evolved from denotation of separation from "eternal life" to one that rejects the Divine, the ethereal, by which humanism, naturalism, and attention to only this life has entered into culture, civics, education, and government. Something—no some spirit will fill the vacuum. People will never cease pondering the universe, and in particular the origin, purpose, and destination of being. History—both man recorded and salvation revealed— proves this!

If there is not all "hands on deck" in the realm of Catholic education, the worst may occur.

In the United States (but globally), due to evil influencers, Americans have traveled from varying and strict sects that had to provide each other respect and religious freedom to what is now essentially an agnostic, at best, and atheistic, at worse, nation. Perhaps in what anyone can call a departure from reality, a form of psychosis, or schizophrenia, numerous powerful leaders profess a religion they do not live in public and one wonders even in private.

Regardless, the facade is extremely thin; the transparency all revealing.

Thus, you have persons like Congressman Nadler declaring that "the will of God" is not a consideration in legislation.

How far mankind had fallen from the knotty arguments of who oversees government: the king or the Church, and does a monarch have a say in Church matters to "every persons is his or her own ruler, and there is no Church." Cynically, one might even assert that using only the pronouns "his" and "her" is insufficiently "secular" by today's definitions.

For many millennium, God was recognized, at times multiple gods, but always *divinity*—the unknown God, the supernatural figure(s), the forces over human life— was acknowledged and respected. The earliest civilizations were ruled in cooperation with the priests or other religious figures of that particular society. In many cases, those deemed spokesperson for the divine were held in high esteem, even feared by authoritative figures, including kings.

Certainly mere mortals seeking conquest made their own devil's bargains, and some ruthlessly ignored or subjugated religion to their narcissistic personalities. They continue to do so, but currently, it is the devil they encounter and seemingly accept. In that vein, unless explicitly and urgently refuted, man will be overtaken by self, the world, and the devil.

## TOOLS, LESSON(S) AND GENERAL RESOURCES AND MATERIALS—RELATING SECULARISM

Book of Word Etymology (preferably prior to 2000)

**TOOLS:** A dictionary and book on etymology pre 2001 if possible. Do NOT rely on the Internet to define words; build a list of trusted commentators and sites for current issues and matters related to culture. Cross Curriculum will have a "Marian-Wexford" Dictionary.

**LESSONS:**

*Primary Lesson*: The Deception of Separation of Church and State

**Activity Lesson**: Words Matter
Objective: Students will identify several words that have been redefined, applied and manipulated to stealthily transform civilization over the past two centuries. They will explain how changing meaning undermines understanding of past and current events and contemporary thinking and behavior in a way that steers government and culture; They will give examples of usage in three centuries if possible.

Materials Needed: Handouts with excerpts from a book on word etymology; list of words to be studied: secularism, tolerance, diversity equality, judgment, discrimination, racism, deportation
Seven articles that contain the above vocabulary as used in the past; seven contemporary articles that use the words today in their updated meaning.

Procedure: Brief presentation on etymology and its important in understanding language and how, in turn, language drives human understanding and behavior.

Seven Pairs (or individual): One partner has the older version; the other the article showing the most recent usage. A work activity sheet that focuses on the word meaning by context and then implication will be completed and then shared with each other as partners and then whole group.

(NOTE: Other words may be added for larger groups, such as social justice, immigrant, progressive, misogynist, and so forth)
Pg 210

**RESOURCES**: The Catholic Thing; Catholic World Report; Public Discourse; St. Thomas Aquinas; Epoch Times (this is non Catholic and promotes Falon Gong, an Eastern religion.)

# Chapter Twelve

## THE ETERNAL KINGDOM VS THE TEMPORAL GLOBE

*The Triumph of the City of God over Global Powers*

### Primer Conclusion

*Consider this temporal life span as you would a single grain of sand against the eternity composed of all the grains of sand in the world, the solar system, the galaxy and the universe, plus one ad infinitum.*

*Consider a personal and immediate encounter with Jesus Christ following temporal death. Immediately, every soul knows its state. Moreover, for those who have such difficulty anticipating God's judgment as arbitrary, excessive, or unmerciful, while the opportunity still exists, ponder this: If the self has been the dominant recipient of the person's attention, it is then an identical polar* **force** *of God. What happens when two magnets of the same polar force draw near each other? They repel each other…naturally. In short, a person who has not followed God's Commandments and lived a life of debacle and shame cannot draw near to God. It is literally a physical impossibility…barring an exceptional shaft of Divine Grace by another's prayers and sacrifices. Yet, people should not presume that this will intercede for eternal punishment..*

As these words are typed, Ukraine has been invaded, and the typical apocalyptic panic has set in. Now, the old saying is that "Just because you are paranoid does not mean that you do not have anything to be paranoid about." The world *is* a mess. Global tensions are at a height. Bad actors possess many threatening nations. The Antichrist is real.

Yet, every age has had to face threats with some era more peaceful than others. However, it does not matter—in some ways—what will happen to the world tomorrow but what will be the destination of anyone's soul. To be ill prepared is the greatest tragedy because none of us knows the hour or day, except our Heavenly Father. That means staying the course, and for Catholic teachers, planning for next week even if it looks dim.

On September 11, 2001, as schools had recently begun a new year, the Twin Towers were hit in a horrific attack on American soil. School systems had to decide how to communicate that to students even as they grappled with the unknown. Could other assaults be imminent and from where and for whom would they be targeted? In at least one school, teachers argued about the practicality of keeping students in the classroom or sending them home. Most determined that students would fare far better in school, learning, that sitting in front of a TV watching a continuous loop of the attack.

The point is that life goes on…until it does not. As previous sections have hopefully emphasized, Catholic educators are living in vocation, and, in some respects that is 24/7 with respect to building the Kingdom of God. And, candidly, nuclear war is not the greatest threat. The attack on Faith, worldwide and by some very wealthy sinister plotters may be far more dangerous, as it has eternal consequences.

Now, this is neither conspiracy theory nor is there an intention to determine, let alone establish, what others reference as the Great Reset. Simply, it is well established that mega billionaires in this country and around the globe exert enormous influence in governments and the economy, and their mission is not Christian. In fact, it may well be cooperation with the Antichrist.

Moreover, it all comes down to one single reality: Will Catholics strive for the eternal kingdom even if it means the ultimate sacrifice? Will Catholic educators emphasize the reality of the eternal kingdom even if it means they are limited to where and when they can teach? Will they stay the course even if threatened? Already, many have been denied catechesis and the dwindling Catholic schools—despite the recent bump—testify to their weakened and vulnerable state. Couple that with the probability that teacher education programs are found mostly in irreligious colleges and universities, and the reality of propagandized teachers increases—though they may themselves be unaware of such indoctrination.

## Chapter Twelve: The Eternal Kingdom vs. the Temporal Globe 377

There is a crisis, and the sooner that is recognized the better. Faith is on life support in many places, and people are increasingly blinded to the severity of the situation. Yet, satan is ever clever. He knows that minimizing the threat while promoting temporal prosperity and the false confidence that there is an eternal Paradise in the end, regardless, has led millions to eternal damnation—self damnation—when finally encountering indisputable Truth.

Even now, there are persons reading this and scoffing at the rigidity and extremeness of this outlook. Moreover, they will cite numerous writings and quote Catholic scholars and those at high as the seat of Peter to counter any pessimism about the future of souls. Decision makers who read this section first may well toss the entire Primer in a bottom drawer if not the trash can. It will not change facts, objective and absolute Truth, or Perfect Justice for those who reject Divine Mercy—which is not a "get our of jail free card" but an invitation to travel the Boardwalk to heaven rather than Mediterranean Avenue to Hell, or Purgatory at worst.

Reason and Faith substantiate this premise. Yet there is ample evidence to support Reason, alone. So, herein, three points to present the case:

One, history, including the entrance of Jesus Christ, True God and True Man into human history although eternal.

Two, science with all its wonders but inexplicable mystery such as Pi, infinity, laws of nature in relationship to Natural Law, and composition of the universe. The Blessed Mother's miracles, including apparitions, render proof.

Three, all the gifts of intelligent but faith filled persons who recorded Sacred Scripture, oversaw the recognition and implantation of Sacred Tradition, and appeared throughout history at pivotal, if not critical, moments to save mankind and the world. But not absent the need for repentance, contrition, penance, and resolve to live in accord with Natural Law and under Divine Authority.

Throughout this Primer, but most notably in the chapter on The Eternal Age vs. Man Constructed Ages, a few historical truths and patterns emerge. Man is fickle, subject to temptation, and even when living in a perfect environment (Garden of Eden), victim to self will. People are doubters who quickly forget the lessons passed down generationally and require continuous reassurances. They are too easily overcome by the enticement; they surrender for immediate relief when suffering or confronting the threat of deprivation. Some call this human nature. It is actually the triple negative of immediate gratification, expression of pride, and blind presumption.

Take any Biblical story—any—and in the background will be either an heroic or a sad tale of man's triumph over evil or the consequences of succumbing to evil. Moreover, there are stories of rekindling of Faith and persons who "rent their garments" and show true sorrow for having failed to love God and rebuild.

True, history is also about those who seemingly never knew God and developed animistic, paganistic, or atheistic belief systems. Even with monotheism, disruption occurred. In the aftermath of God's Covenant with Israel, Jew splintered into various factions. Islam arose from quasi Christian teachings. During the Reformation and in its aftermath, hundreds—thousands—of denominations and non denomination "churches" sprang up. Still, regardless, history asserts that the Catholic Church has never altered essential dogma—the Magisterium is intact after 2,000 years on the recorded promise of Jesus Christ that hell would not prevail against her gates. That is fact.

The sciences, including philosophy, attest to the supernatural though so many have been frustrated attempting to unknot and understand that which is simply beyond human comprehension. Note though that the unknown is still acknowledged. Amazingly, students of the greatest thinkers discover that for every genuinely wise Reasoner, there is someone to dispute, contort, or return arguments to man based intelligence.

It is as though there is an intellectual amnesia or intentional avoidance of truth. Even miracles fail to rouse the conscience. Over 70,000 people witnessed the sun dance at Fatima over a hundred years ago. Some atheists converted, but many others managed to dispute their own eyes and attribute the phenomenon to mass hysteria or hypnosis.

Finally, there are the persons of Faith over thousands of years that lend solid credibility to life after death and that there is eternal happiness or rage. The exact nature of Hell, especially for each individual, has not been entirely revealed although Souls from Purgatory give testimony to a particular fire. For those who assume they are going to Heaven because they perceive themselves "good" people, err for several reasons: Scripture, Saints, and Jesus Christ.

*The Flame of Love* is one such riveting composite of these experiences that come with a warning to repent and turn back to God. They are lent credibility by medicine and science in that these witnesses were on the brink of dead or had been declared dead. Their testimony bares the soul's worst vices, a public confession of sloth, lust, greed, anger, and other vices.

**Contrasted with the World**

Then, look at the world and what it offers? The United Nations is neither "united" nor truly "national"; this corrupt body seeks to rule over individuals on a global scale, and again, there is solid evidence to their failure. All those well sounding organizations, like Save Our Children are funded by a relatively few uber wealthy who have deliberately intentionally set up a network of philanthropic groups to appear giving. They are fronts.

There is no utopia on Earth, and one can put stock in the fact that Heaven has a wall—it is in the Bible.

Yet, most importantly, for the Catholic teacher, it is not a matter of preaching "brim and firestone"—which rarely evokes genuine love but rather fear and anxiety. Still, it is imperative that in informing the mind and body, the soul is also properly and fully enlightened. Jesus spoke of love and mercy; He followed with the impression that the time is always of the essence because thereafter justice (and judgment) follows.

So definitely teachers must stress that it is love God seeks, but with specificity in lessons on what and how that looks and feels, as the class pursues history, science, the arts, and so forth. Lessons to compare and contrast living and nonliving things in relationship to the soul are helpful. Why did the plant die? Perhaps there was no sun…or no water. Perhaps an enemy insect or fungus destroyed it. Can anyone resurrect a dead plant. No. Is it good for anything…compost for the soil, but Jesus warned about dead salt—good for nothing. (Scripture citations).

*Signs of universal Utopia*

A brief history of utopias is covered in *The Story of Utopias* (Mumford, 1922). For the most part, it is an intriguing look at the attempts to create utopia multiple times, but in just reading about St. Thomas More's work in that area, it is evident that the author is a non Christian.

The good news is that there is a utopia; the bad news is that it is not in this world. And, one has to strive for that citizenship in the City of God.

Cultivating the virtue of prudence is a nonnegotiable for educators, and particularly Catholic educators. Of what or whom should humans fear? No one or anything. Yet, neither can anyone be blind to the real threat of Big Tech, huge global conglomerates, shrewd foreign multi billionaires bent on the accumulation of more power and wealth, or the ignorant public that has been cultivated via public education for several decades.

The argument regarding global community is strong, but we have individual national identities for a reason. While people should not all look alike, neither should countries. There is something noble and enriching about individuals, states, regions, and so forth.

Yet, neither can someone be so anxious or hyper focused on one type of enemy that he or she neglects truth, as well as the fact that sometimes, we are our own worse enemies. While credible persons and organizations have unmasked devious and sinister plotting, there has also has been sage caution about the reality of a world conspiracy to "enslave the masses."

Most likely, what is unfolding is the natural consequences of wide spread rebellion against natural law and Divine authority. Millions are blind, and the clever arise to take advantage of the weaker. It may not be an organized effort, as much as wolves gathering from different corners of the world into a pack. And, the devil is happy to oblige by his manipulation of consciences and events to make certain the environment is ripe for take over.

What do we know? Population Research Institute which has studied China and the world for the past three decades and even prior under the umbrella of Human Life International, another group savvy about world affairs has repeatedly warned of the intent of China to dominate the world. Even previous skeptics are arriving at that conclusion. Moreover, there is collusion with other powers to control people through reproductive policies and laws, euthanasia, climate regulations, and so-called rights that are actually depressing individual liberty, including the freedom of religion, speech, media and corralling whole groups of people.

The United Nations—study its history and how its power has not quelled the evils of abortion or even war.

*Catholic World Report* has noted events and persons. In fact, the Catholic Church may well be compromised at the highest levels. Let us not forget the warnings at Fatima and other apparitions. Read Cardinal Zen or Archbishop Vigano , the latter both vigorously defended and critiqued. Papal Encyclicals of the past century identify the hall marks—horn marks of the devil in many human affairs. It is a horror to contemplate and faithful Catholics are well advised to avoid "personalizing" the trend, as the Church is still in Jesus Christ's domain.

*Epoch Times* though a secular news source with open ties to Eastern philosphy knows well the evil of communism. *American Spectator* has been a bell ringer for the decline in America, and there are numerous other publications and sources to bold face reality. *Catholic Vote* has boldly emerged as a faithful and thorough reporter on politics and government.

Of course COVID 19 only added gas to the fires of global tyranny.

Yet, science is being abused at all levels and everywhere to manipulate the human body and even infect it such as with the pandemic of 2020. The white lab coat has been donned by the modern tyrants.

However, there are also, unfortunately, some who either exaggerate or utilize false narratives to scare people, and red flags must be raised on any skeptical charges. The boogey man is not under every bed, and not everyone is the enemy. Much of the time, it is the ignorant and graceless that promote or prop the evil few with too much power.

The resolution lays in our absolute trust in God and knowing He is ever close and always accessible for "consultation and consolation." Indeed, as this manuscript draft was being prepared for initial submission, as it happens, on the Feast of the Annunciation, this was made abundantly crystal clear in morning prayer and reading—no more than thirty minutes in total. In every single one, there was holy communication to advise and elicit the perfect consent to God, as our Superior Authority. The first is a reminder that the world is passing away, but we are not, and eternity awaits those who also say "yes" to God. The second, which just happened to be next in reading, to accept that a "sword will pierce our hearts" by way of tribulation and suffering because Mary's "yes" was to the entire life of Jesus, not just the Incarnation. Moreover, any "glory" by humans does not last. The third, provides spiritual direction to move away from self, considering our own faults and sins and recognize the other.

In *Magnificat*, two gems for the Catholic teacher: "The Grace of Mary's Yes" by Father Garrigou-Lagrange, the late Dominican theologian and theology doctoral adviser of the future Saint John Paul II. Father brings up a frequent point of confusion that people have because they place God in temporal time. God is in the present, and as clarified here, …"that God has efficaciously willed and infallibly foreseen everything that will happen in the course of time. So while God—

## Chapter Twelve: The Eternal Kingdom vs. the Temporal Globe

from all eternity—gave Mary grace to move her consent, He always knew that she would freely and most heartedly utter her "Fiat."

Then there was the reminder for humor in "The Zucchini of Life" by Therese Obagi, a Catholic wife and homeschooling mother, that special thanks should be given for being helpless at times, not being able to attend to all that needs to be done. Amid a day of chaos, in one very brief moment with her precious four-year-old daughter with a wayward vegetable, in the bedroom no less, Obagi was able to laugh, when her daughter dropped a zucchini over her shoulder and into her lap, uttering, "This is the zucchini of heaven."

Praying for much humor in the lives of Catholic school teachers, at home or in the classroom!

*The Imitation of Christ* (Chapter 6, 2 On the Joy of a Good Conscience): Those who love God will glory in tribulation for their only joy is to glory in the Cross of Jesus Chris, Our Lord. The glory given and received by humans last but a little while and is usually followed by sadness. The glory of good persons is in their own consciences, not in the praise of others. The happiness of the good is in God and of God and their joy is in the truth.

*Introduction to the Devout* Life, the third part, #36 "We Must Preserve a Just and Reasonable Mind," by St. Francis de Sales: We rigorously demand our own rights, but want others to be considerate in insisting on theirs…We complain easily about our neighbors, but none of them must complain about us. (St. Francis de Sales continues on the "two weights" (and two hearts) the first most advantageous to self; the other critical of others.

And, then, Avila Institute's daily treasure, this one from the loving soul of Anthony Lilles. (Reprinted with author's permission on 3/25/2022 via email). There is no more fitting conclusion of Teaching the City of God in the City of Man than this. Thank you Sacred Heart of Jesus and the most Immaculate Heart of Mother Mary.

*The solemnity of Annunciation—the great mystery of Gabriel announcing to Mary that she would be the Mother of "the Son of God"—opens a new pathway for our anxious world today.*

*To embark on this journey, the Church invites us to consecrate ourselves to Jesus through her — and so we place ourselves as well as our communities and even our nations in her heart. It is within the act of faith that she made that we too will receive Jesus until His reign extends through us as well.*

*In the angelic greeting, a new sovereignty is revealed, an authority to govern. The legitimacy of this authority is not rooted in earthly powers but instead in the fulfillment of a divine promise that does not pass away. Unlike any kingdom of this world, this kingdom rests not on the temporary peace that comes through conquest of an enemy. Instead, the "yes" of a woman to God's promise has brought a new kind of peace. The conception of Jesus in the womb of Mary introduces into this passing world a new order and legitimacy in human affairs that will never pass:*

*Then the angel said to her: Do not be afraid, Mary, for you have found favor with God. Behold, you will conceive in your womb, and bear a son, and you shall name him Jesus. He will be great and will be called Son of the Most High, and the Lord God will give him the throne of David his father, and he will rule over the house of Jacob forever, and of his kingdom there will be no end. (Luke 1:30-33)*

*Mary's openness to the blessings of God chart a way forward for humanity toward an eternal sacred order before which the exigencies of each historical moment must yield. Not by forced subjection or brutality, but by love, this is a trail of humility and fearlessness on which the Son of the Most High leads us. Consecrating ourselves to Jesus through Mary expresses the commitment to follow this pathway. To set one's existence under a power and authority not of this world is to open oneself to what is primordial, an order of things more powerful than the disorder of the present moment. This new kingdom is not in competition with what passes away but rescues everything that is noble and true about our lives from every threatening evil. Rooted in a mystery that transcends time, all earthly kingdoms fall and rise before this throne, and Mary who is the first to receive this into her heart is also the one who helps us sing with her, "He has cast down the mighty from their thrones and has lifted up the lowly."*

*Unlike the kingdom announced by Gabriel, the kingdoms of this passing world come to an end. This is because we tend, as individuals and communities, away from humility before the truth of our situation. Yet great humility is called for since the common good often eludes our grasp. We do not understand what really binds us together and we are weak in the face of our own avarice. Without humility before a reference point that transcends our own desires, the foundation on which we build our communities lacks the solidity of truth and, over time, fails to bear the weight of human existence.*

*At the brink of a world war, today's earthly kingdoms seek salvation by technological force. It is presumed that developments in economic and military capabilities through advances in technology can build and protect a better humanity. Indeed, tremendous wealth, honor, and control have been realized through technological advancement.*

*Yet there is a caveat. When nations or businesses rely on the power of technology to coerce or manipulate, it is at the expense of their own legitimacy and so they fall. The legitimacy of any institution rests on the degree to which it protects human dignity and freedom. Such things that flow from our divine image and likeness do not pass even when we act against them. When we betray them, they testify against us because we betray ourselves. This is true of our own acts of freedom .... it is also true of our institutions and businesses. Whether our own tent cities or new refugee camps, we have lived to see that new ways to nudge, shame, and coerce into compliance do not yield a cohesive society or world peace. The opposite is true. The more limits imposed on human dignity, the more out of control the discord becomes. This is as true for nations as it is for neighborhoods, dinner tables, and hearts.*

*The Annunciation opens humanity to the kingdom of heaven, a kingdom all about saving human dignity from dehumanizing powers. Only under the rule of Christ can human freedom finally find room to unfold and disclose its full potential – not just for individuals but also in the societies we form together. This is because the throne of this kingdom does not rest on coercion or manipulation but on love and love alone. Yet this love is hidden, disguised in poverty, rejection, and humility.*

*To consecrate ourselves to Jesus through Mary is to choose this pathway even when it may seem that the powerful and mighty of this world are in control. It is to live by faith that the reality of the God who saves us is ever greater and more present – more real to the human reality than what seems conventional, comfortable, and convenient. Mary opened the heart of humanity to this truth. Thus, we entrust worldly powers to the Lord through her until our own hearts sing, "He who is mighty has done great things."*

So, Catholic educators…in conclusion "prayer and sacrifice" is the ultimate answer to all that ails the world and the ultimate lessons for successful teaching.

## TOOLS, LESSON(S) AND GENERAL RESOURCES AND MATERIALS—THE ETERNAL KINGDOM

**TOOLS:** Place handy visuals in eyesight around work space that remind you of the City of God. These may be Scripture; pictures, and brief wise sayings.

**LESSONS:**
Primary Lesson: The Illusion of UtopiaResources
Choose and conduct readings with discussion questions about the folly of temporal utopias. These activities may include "compare and contrast" as Cummings did in his book; focus on the leaders of these foolish concepts, describing their backgrounds, and belief (or lack of belief ) in God; misleading promises of utopians; encyclicals that address utopian ideology.

Lesson #2

Review an article in a leading, contemporary periodical, blog, or website of a trusted Catholic source that addresses the conflicts of the world with the ultimate destiny of men. Among possible sources are:

*Catholic World Report*; Cardinal Zen and and Sarah; Epoch Times (with Catholic balance); Population Research Institute; Pope Pius IX, X, XI, XII Encyclicals and writings; Pope Leo XIII; St. Pope John Paul II . With some caution, commentary of Archbishop Vigano may be included, but Catholic teachers should understand the broad "appeal and

## Chapter Twelve: The Eternal Kingdom vs. the Temporal Globe

dissent" that surrounds him. Speaking of which, there are many sites that are "orthodox"—considered ultra traditional. Teachers should be broad readers but also discern what would be advantageous to share in class. Consulting with superiors is highly recommended if there is any doubt.

**RESOURCES:**

Books
*Judgment of the Nations* by Christopher Dawson
*The End of the Present World and the Mysteries of the Future Life,* Father Charles Arminjon (1824-1885), translated by Susan Conroy and Peter McEnerny, Sophia Institute Press, 2008.
*The Flame of Love: The Spiritual Diary of Elizabeth Kindelmann,* Queens of Peace Media 2020

# APPENDIX

## BIBLIOGRAPHY AND RESOURCES

Any source or resource may now or in the future veer from Truth and Charity. These are listed as those that have benefitted authentic Catholic education in some manner, but there may be errors in reasoning, fact checking, and reporting.

Some are secular but still underscore the good, true, and beautiful in a particular way.

*This is by no means an exhaustive list. Catholic educators are encouraged to explore sources that will most benefit them. News sources are emerging daily. Look for them.*

*A personal note: Catholic educators have never had more ample and faith filled resources, referrals, and materials by which to impart authentic Catholicism and within all areas of education. However, they are gently advised to **"prioritize and pace"** reading, listening, viewing, and studying these materials. Growing in the Faith is a lifelong journey, that requires reflection, respite, and even recreation. However also budget some time to visit used bookstores, as a recent Public Discourse writer exclaimed. Therein you will find affordable books and hidden treasures. Some surprises will delight; others horrify, but in all it will be so worthwhile.*

## **PRIMER CHAPTER RESOURCES AND REFERENCES**

Special Note: There is a complete list of books/publishers, articles, websites; visual organizations/associations, apostolates, credible Catholic spokespersons (clergy and laity) who are writers or communicators, and further educational opportunities. However, following each Primer chapter there are sources and resources specifically geared to the topic.

Also, it is critical to underscore that educators must read with a desire for Truth, be aware of the faults of any person, including experts, and discern. Note the numerous resources that are wholly public and not identified as Catholic, Christian, Jewish, or Islam—hesitating to use the word secular.

Some sources listed under a particularly topic may well also apply to others in the Primer

## APOSTOLATES, ASSOCIATIONS/ORGANIZATIONS

Alphabetically listed with code of "C" for Catholic; "P" or Political

The American Society for the Defense of Tradition, Family, and Property (TFP) (C)
Avila Institute (C)
CAAP (formerly the Coalition of African American Pastors, now Coalition of Americans for Action and Principles) (P)
CatholicsComeHome.org (C)
Catholic Culture (C)
Catholic League (C)
Catholicscientists org. (Society of Catholic Scientists) (C)

- The 16-volume Dictionary of Scientific Biography, editor-in-chief Charles C. Gillespie (Charles Scribner's Sons, 1970-1980). For a description of this work see https://en.wikipedia.org/wiki/Dictionary_of_Scientific_Biography#Dictionary_of_Scientific_Biography
- The 15-volume Catholic Encyclopedia (Robert Appleton Company, 1913). For a description of this work see https://en.wikipedia.org/wiki/Catholic_Encyclopedia
- Christianity and the Leaders of Modern Science, Karl Alois Kneller, translated from German by T.B. Kettle (B. Herder, 1911). This book has an index of scientists' names at the back.

Appendix 391

> The scanned full text is available here: https://archive.org/stream/christianitylead00knelrich#page/n7/mode/2up

Catholic Vote (C)
CERC (Catholic Education Resource Center); Catholic School Playbook (C)
Church Militant (C): **(This source draws criticism even from orthodox Catholics for its perceived unnecessary emphasis on *only* what is troubling in the Church, using combative descriptors, and its reporting and speculation about the integrity of some Catholic media and spokespersons. However, the investigative quality of information gathering has gained a good reputation over the years, and where are others do not delve. Its nuggets of objective fact finding and bold disclosures by inside sources, render this a reference worth including. Besides it is a site Catholic teachers will likely encounter, or have brought to their attention.)**
Convention of States (P)
Courage/Encourage:(C) Enormous, reliable Resources for anything related to same sex and other sexual-oriented issues with personal testimonies and credible research
Daily Catholic Wisdom (C)
Dynamic Catholic (C)
Edify (C)
EWTN (C)
Heritage Foundation
Hillsdale College (online)
Human Life International (C)
Ignatius Press (C)
Institute of Catholic Liberal Education (ICLE) (C)
Lepanto Institute (C)
Lion and the Ox Catholic Education (C)
National Catholic Education Association (with attentive antennae) (C)

Peace Hill Press: <u>The Story of the World, History for the Classical Child</u>—Susan Wise Bauer's three volume work. While not "Christian" per se, the narrative tales and rich detail add to overall engagement in these various time periods.
Population Research Institute (C)

Priests for Life (C) (Father Frank Pavone) (C) **NOTE: Father Pavone, Executive Director was laicized recently reportedly for profane language used in communication and disobedience to his Bishop. Moreover, Father Pavone's ardent political efforts and support of one major politician in recent years, Donald Trump, has led to further criticism, regardless of the former President's incredibly influential support for pro life. The state of the organization (PFL) may be in flux, but teachers can certainly glean the enormous good this priest and organization has accomplished and advise students to make distinctions between person who may act contrary to (a) virtue and those who are merely courageous. Employ those skills discussed in *Research for Reliability*.**

The Public Discourse (formerly Witherspoon)
Religious Life Institute (C)
Return to Order (C)
The Ruth Institute
Sophia Institute (C)
Students for Life
Voice of the Family (C)
Women of Grace (C)
Women for Faith and Family (co founder the late Helen Hull Hitchcock)
1776Unites—An organization dedicated to truth about Black history; it does not conceal harsh facts but places them in context.

Appendix

## PERIODICALS AND NEWSPAPERS; BLOGS; INTERNET SITES; PODCASTS

Alphabetically listed (Noted as CF for Catholic Faith, C for Christian, O for other religion, P for political or S for "secular" meaning non or irreligious)
Aleteia (CF)
Public Discourse (formerly Witherspoon (C)
The American Spectator (S)
Catholic Answers (CF)
Catholic Brain (com) (CF)
Catholic 365.com
The Catholic Thing (CF)
Catholic World Report (CF)
Bushman, Douglas, *Understanding the Hierarchy of Truths,* Catholic World Report, March 30, 2022
CNA (Catholic News Agency)
Crisis Magazine (CF)
Daily Catholic Wisdom (CF)
The Epoch Times (O)
First Things (CF)
Just Facts (P)
Heritage The Daily Signal (various articles) (C)
Hillsdale College (free online courses) (C)
Homiletic and Pastoral Review (CF)
The Imaginative Conservative (P)
    Arberry, Glenn, *Truthfulness Not Optional,* Imaginative Conservative, February 2, 2022
Imprimis (CF) under Hillsdale College
Lighthouse Media (C)
Magnificat (CF) A wonderful periodical to subscribe to…filled with daily Mass and other readings, wonderful Saints' stories, replete with historical references; meditations by reliable Catholic voices and saints

The Remnant Newspaper (CF) (While some criticize this publication for its extremism, it is helpful to include it as a resource and use it in contrast with those spokespersons and publications on the polar opposite, like National Catholic Report and the Jesuit American Magazine. We cannot turn a blind eye to the wide array of information, all claiming to be Catholic without some barometer of Truth, but we must all agree that the most innocent, naive, and ignorant, may and will fall pray to material under the banner of Catholic, regardless. Educators must learn to develop antennae through solid catechetical formation, to, intern, impart skills to their students to do likewise and separate the the folly from the Faith.)

Tobet org (Theology of the Body)

## **PUBLISHERS**

*Some of these are also "sites" or offer other mediums of communication than books*
Ascension Press: Includes the Great Bible Adventure, a newly formatted timeline, DVDs, and Epic (a history series.) Some of this is on an adult level, but there is also a teen version of the timeline. The Augustine Institute
Catholic Textbook Project (C)
Dynamic Catholic
Enroute Books (C)
Ignatius Press (C) Father Joseph Fessio, SJ just announced a *K-8 Word of Life* religious education series and The *Word of Life* student book club to counter anti-Christian ones in the public square.
Lion and the Ox Catholic Education
Religious Life Institute (C)
Return to Order (C)
The Ruth Institute
Sophia Institute (C)
Tan Books and Publishers (C)
Women of Grace—an organization and source of publications

Appendix

## **AUTHORS/COMMENTATORS/COMMUNICATORS**

Alphabetically listed with "D" for deceased. NOTE: There are dozens of outstanding authors, commentators, and communicators. To be finalized is "Cross Curriculum" to accompany the Primer and offer ongoing recommendations. One helpful way to recognize a faithful Catholic is how he or she is perceived by other faithful Catholics, yet considering someone be miss the mark at times—err—but their overall body of work is commendable.

Thomas Aquinas (D) — All Church Early Fathers and Doctors
Mother Angelica (D)
Cardinal Arinze
St. Augustine (D0
Dan Burke
Archbishop Charles Chaput. (Also see under Books, Government
Ronda Chervin (Taming the Lion Within) (C) but others
G.K. Chesterton (D0
Dorothy Day (Although some of her life is shrouded in controversy, she was an amazing convert) (D)
Christopher Dawson (D)
Father Groschel (D)
Father John Hardon (D)
Scott and Kimberly Hahn
Dietrich and Alice Von Hildebrand (D)
Thomas Kempis (Imitation of Christ) (D)
Peter Kreeft
Very Rev. Peter Kucer
C.S.Lewis
Anthony Lilles
Michael D. O'Brien
Father Chad Ripperger
Cardinal Sarah
Archbishop Fulton Sheen (D)
Edward Sri

Father Peter Stravinskas
Popes: Pope Leo XIII, Popes Pius IX, X, XI, XII; Pope Benedict
Saints (St. Augustine, St. Francis deSales, St. Pope John II) St. Therese of Liseaux, St. Faustina-Divine Mercy Diary)
Dr. Paul Thigpen
J.R.R. Tolkien
Katie Warner (Children's books)
Father Sebastian White

## **BOOKS** (CITED AND RECOMMENDED): *Teaching the City of God to and in the City of Man*

*Resources for "Teaching the City of God in the City of Man" may be listed related to respective sections. There are, again, literally thousands of worthwhile books, too many to list. Vet and Prioritize!*

### *AMERICA. (United States)*

*America* by D'Souza
*America on Trial* (Reilly)
*Catholic Textbook Project (Venture)*
*Death of a Nation* D'Souza
*Growth of the American Republic (Volume II) 1942.* Oxford University Press Samuel Eliot
Morrison and Henry Steele Commagee

Land of Hope, An Invitation to the Great American Story, Wilfred M. McClay—Also History
*Patriots and Pioneers* (Tan)
*The Story of Civilization Volume IV—The History of the United States*, Phillip Campbell Tan Publishers 2019
*The Church in America St. John Paul II*

# Appendix

## CURRENT EVENTS AND SOCIAL ISSUES

*A Mother's Ordeal,* Steven Mosher
*The Field of Social Work*
*Conserving Marriage and Family*

## EDUCATION

*CERC (Catholic Education Resource Center)*
*Credible Catholic (and coursework for teachers): Father Spitzer*—Credible Catholic's Certificate in Contemporary Apologetics
*Holy See's Teaching on Catholic Schools (Father Michael Miller)*
*School Playbook*
*Hillsdale College* (Multiple Courses On line by Donation)
*MisEducation of the Negro* by Woodson

## HISTORY (Also See America-United States)

Biblical Figures including Ruth and Queen Esther
*The Age of Innocence*
*The Bible As History*
*Black Catholics (Notable Black Catholics in Church History)*
*Catholic Textbook Project*
*God, History, and Historians*

**The Bible as History** Werner Keller 1956 secular
**Walking the Bible: A Journey by Land through the Five Books of Moses** Bruce Feiler 2001 Secular

<u>**History of the Catholic Church**</u> for Catholic and Parochial and High Schools by the Brothers of Mary, Third edition published in 1919.

**Very Rev. Peter S. Kucer, MSA, and series of En Route books** including *The History of the Catholic Church, Western Civilization, Eastern Civilization, Prophetic Literature, Historic Books,* etc.

**Tan**—(more high school oriented): **Christ the King, Lord of History** Anne W. Carroll; Workbook Belinda T. Mooney. Tan now offers homeschooling guidance and many resources.

*Left to Tell* (contemporary autobiographical)
*The Outline of History HG Wells Volume I and II*
*The Nazis and the Occult*
*The Naked Communist*
*The Devil and Karl Marx (Kenger)*
*Can it Happen Here?*
*The Epic of America James Truslow Adams, Little, Brown, and Company 1931*
*Parish School (NCEA)*

Peace Hill Press: <u>The Story of the World, History for the Classical Child</u>—Susan Wise Bauer's three volume work. While not "Christian" per se, the narrative tales and rich detail add to overall engagement in these various time periods.

*Progress and Religion by Charles Dawson*

*The Story of the World (with caveat) Bauer*

*The Story of Civilization (four volumes) Phillip Campbell, Tan Publishers: The Ancient World (2014); The Medieval World (2017); and The Making of the Modern World (2018; other under America.* NOTE: *This series is accompanied by other materials including timelines, CD.s, Activities, and Assessments.*

*Mystery In History* (Protestant but with some valuable timelines and a comparative viewpoint subject to analysis and evaluation)

*Up From Slavery Booker T. Washington*
*Western Civilization from Prehistoric Times to the Protestant Reformation – Father Kucer*
*Western Civilization from the Renaissance to Modern Times - Father Kucer*

## *CURRICULUM*

Catholic Homeschool—Numerous curriculum and instructional guides. Many parents have discovered that they must research, consult, and collaborate with other homeschool parents to determine the "best" fit for their children. However, it is not unusual to have a mix of sources depending on the strengths and weaknesses of each offering with respect to individual children.

History in Word is intended to be a comprehensive middle school (6th-8th grade curriculum) for Catholic schools. It was conceived by an experience of instruction that primarily relied on secular texts, such as Pearson and Prentiss Hall. Moreover, in two archdioceses (at least), the Catholic Textbook Project, while praiseworthy, was not determined to be adequate to teach the full range of objectives from prehistory and the dawn of civilization to modern times.

Since beginning this project in the spring of 2019, there have been some fantastic discoveries of similar efforts to ensure that our children are learning about His Story—Salvation History—and as impacted and intersected by recorded secular history and world events. Even so, there is no specific emphasis on reaching younger students (11-14) in a comprehensive way that includes fully engaging plans and activities. Perhaps some are also working towards this goal, even as I write, and as the need is evident in some of my discoveries. Yet in the meantime, this project will move forward.

## GOVERNMENT/Political Science (Including Economy)

Agricultural Problems and the Gilded Age Politics
*Democracy in America* (Tocquville)
Magruder, Frank Abbott. *American Government (with a Consideration of the Problems of Democracy)*. Allyn and Bacon 1927.
*Basic Issues of American Democracy*
Kucer, Peter. *Political Science from a Catholic Perspective* (St. Louis: En Route, 2015).
*Understanding the Constitution*—Heritage foundation
Archbishop Charles Chaput, *Render Unto Caesar: Servicing the Nation by Living Our Catholic Beliefs in Political Life* Image, 2009.
Greany, Michael D., and Dawn Brown, *The Greater Reset: Reclaiming Personal Sovereignty Under Natural Law*, Tan Books, 2022.

## MILITARY and LEADERSHIP

## SAINTS (Biographies, Works)

*The Autobiography of Fulton J. Sheen*

## SCIENCE

Giglio, Louie, *Indescribable—100 Devotions About God & Science,* Passion Publishing, 2017 (Though not Catholic, this little read aloud brings science and God, our Creator, together in an instructional and inspirational way. Though noted for children and youth, persons of all ages will delight in the awesome facts contained in this little book.)

## RELIGION (Note: Subdivisions of Apologetics; Cathechism; Scripture; Devotional; Faith and Morals; Prayer)

*(Encyclicals could be placed in several places)* Encyclicals categorized by topic and subtopics: Labor, Government, Social Justice (i.e. slavery)

## APOLOGETICS

Kucer, MSA, Peter S. *Apologetics, Witnessing to a Defense of Faith.* (St. Louis: En Route Books, 2018).
*Apologetics and Catholic Doctrine,* the most Rev M. Sheehan DD, 1955, M.H. Gill and Son, Ltd.
*Apologia Pro Vita Sua,* John Henry Cardinal Newman, Image 1956
*Catholic Apologetics Today, Answer to Modern Critics,* Father William G. Most, Tan Books and Publishers, 1984
*Catholic Truth for Youth* Robert Fox
*Confessions and City of God* St. Augustine
*The Treasury of Catholic Wisdom (a Catholic library in miniature),* Father John A. Hardon, Ignatius Press, 1987 (fourth edition)

## BIBLE (SCRIPTURE)

NOTE: Numerous Bibles have been produced, and the Catholic educator will want a full library of authentic translations and presentations of Holy Scripture which also reveals Salvation History.

*Always Inspired; Why Bible Believing Christians Need the Catholic Church,* Basil Christoper Butler, Sophia Institute, 1960
*You Can Understand the Bible,* Peter Kreeft, Ignatius
*The Real Story—Understanding the Big Picture of the Bible,* Edward Sri and Curtis Martin, Dynamic Catholic, 2012.
    This simple to follow but comprehensive book demonstrates God's narrative of the story of man and the drawing of his people culminating in the coming of Jesus Christ and the establishment of His Church. Readers can quickly grasp the very first struggle between good and evil, the tensions between mankind pursing the city of man (utopia) and the City of God (heaven) from the Fall to and through ancient civilizations.

*The Story of the Bible, Volume I and II,* Tan Books and Publishers, 2015; *Story of the Bible, Old Testament*

Dynamic Catholic: Edward Sri and Curtis Martin: <u>The Real Story: Understanding the Big Picture of the Bible.</u> This simple to follow but comprehensive book demonstrates God's narrative of the story of man and the drawing of his people culminating in the coming of Jesus Christ and the establishment of His Church. Readers can quickly grasp the very first struggle between good and evil, the tensions between mankind pursing the city of man (utopia) and the City of God (heaven) from the Fall to and through ancient civilizations.

## *CATECHISM*

*Baltimore Catechism,* Tan Books and Publishers
*Catholic Answers* Rev. Peter Stravinskas, Our Sunday Visitor
*The Church's Confessions of —a Catholic Adult Faith Catechism, Ignatius, 1987 (originally German Bishop Conference)*
*The Deposit of Faith—What the Catholic Church Really Believes, (Jesus Teaching Divine Revelation in His Body, the Church)* Eugene Kevance, Ph.D., 2004, Author House
*Catholic Catechism (related to Scripture)*
*The Catholic Catechism,* Father John A. Hardon, S.J, 1974, Double Day
*The Questions and Answers one Catholic Catechism,* Father John A. Hardon, S.J., Image, 1981

## *CULTURE AND SOCIAL*

*Degenerate Moderns (Modernity as Rationalized Sexual Behavior);* E. Michael Jones, Fidelity Press, 2012

**Father Chad Ripperger (among others, "Introduction to the Science of Mental Health"—three volumes)**

Appendix

## *FAITH AND MORALS*

Thompson, Edward Healy, MA, *The Life and Glories of St. Joseph,* Tan Books originally in 1888. (Often one thinks of female teachers, but there are many men who are called this a vocation of Catholic education. That which forms them well in their manhood will portend their effectiveness as teachers, and no one is a better model than St. Joseph. Pope Pius IX declared St. Joseph the Patron of the Universal Church (December 8, 1870)

*A Map of Life*
*Avoiding Bitterness and Suffering*
*A Refutation of Moral Relativism Peter Kreeft*
*Dark Night of the Soul, St. John of the Cross*
*Dressing with Dignity, Colleen Hammond*
*The Exorcist*
*Feminine Free and Faithful,* Ronda Chervin
*The Guide to Healing the Family Tree,* Dr. Kenneth McCall
*The Catholic Guide to Depression*
*Introduction to the Science of Mental Health Father Chad Ripperger*
*How to Resist Temptation*
*A Doctor at Calvary*
*The Antichrist Micelli*
*The Face of God*
*The Day Christ was Born Bishop*

## The Church and Modern Society Bishop Ireland. (Vols. 1 and 2)

*God as Father and Priests as Fathers, Brothers....*
*Finding God's Will for You*
*Keys to the Kingdom* Cronin
*The Church and Modern Society Volumes I an II Bishop John Ireland*
*Man's Religion*
*Inside the Atheist Mind*

*The Christian Aetheis* Father Groeschel
*Christ the King (with Workbook)* Belinda Mooney
*The Passion* Dr. Paul Thigpen
*Religion of the New World*
*The Salvation Controversy* Akin
*The Word Made Flesh*
*Truth and Tolerance by Cardinal Ratzinger Pope Benedict XVI*

## WORLD

*The China Threat*
*Bully of Asia (and update).* Seven Mosher
Archbishop Charles Chaput, *Stranger in a Strange Land: Living the Catholic Faith in a Post Christian World* , Ignatius, 2019

## CHRISTIAN AND CATHOLIC

Archbishop Chaput, *Things Worth Dying For: Thoughts on a Life Worth Living*, Ignatius, 2022
*Catholic for a Reason (Hahn and Suprenant)*
Tan—(more high school oriented): *Christ the King, Lord of History* Anne W. Carroll; Workbook Belinda T. Mooney
*The Everlasting Man.* Chesterton
*Screwtape Letter, Proposes Toast* C.S. Lewis
    *Miracles*
*Arise from Darkness Other* Groeschel
*Stumbling Blocks, Stepping Stones*
*Evangelical is not Enough*
*Behold the Man (Male Spirituality)*
*Forty Reasons I Am Catholic* Peter Kreeft
*Image of the Man*
*Last Call,* Ronda Chervin
*Made for More,* Martin

# Appendix

*Rome Sweet Home* Scott Hahn
*The Sermons of St. Francis de Sales*
*The Scandal of the Scandals*
*The Third Millennium Woman (with caveat)* Patricia Hershwitzky
*The Spiritual Life* St. Theophan the Recluse
*Thomas Aquinas in 50 Pages (A Quick Layman's Guide to Thomism),* Taylor R. Marshall, Ph.D. 2013
*The Father They Wish to Have by Anyamele*
*Rediscovering Catholicism (Dynamic Catholic)*
*Did Adam and Eve have Belly Buttons (Pinto)*
*Born Fundamentalist; Born Again Catholic (Currie)*

## DEVOTION and THE MIRACULOUS; SAINTS

*Ann Catherine Emmerich (three volumes)*
*Apparitions of the Modern Saints*
*City of God Agreda*
*The Diary of St. Faustina*
*The Contemplative Challenge of St. John of the Cross*
*Imitation of Christ (Thomas Kempis*
*Introduction to the Devout Life, St. Francis de Sales*
*The Saints that Moved the World*
*The Books of Infinite Love.*
*The Pilgrim Way*
*Dominican Saints*
*Gaitly: The One Thing is Three*
*30 Days to Morning Glory; You Did it to Me*
*Living the Mystery of Merciful Love*
*The Life of St. Joseph As Seen by the Mystics,* Dr. Paul Thigpen, Tan Books, an excellent perspective of attainable holy matrimony.

## *FAMILY AND MATRIMONY*

Anderson, Ryan T., *Truth Overruled: The Future of Marriage and Religious Freedom,* Regnery Publishing, 2015 (The Catholic Church recognizes exceptional voices of reason in all areas of life including ethics, law and the authentic Common Good. Anderson founded the online essay forum, Public Discourse, formerly and also known as the the Witherspoon Institute.)

*The Catholic Marriage Manual* Rev. George A. Kelly, Random House, 1958
*Good and True Media*
*Good News about Sex and Marriage,* Christopher West, Servant Books
Edward Sri's books
*When Harry Became Sally,* Ryan Anderson, Books Encounter, 2018

*Special The Eucharist/Sacraments*

*The Miracles of the Eucharist*
*The Eucharist Miracles of the World*
*The Blessed Eucharist*
*This is My Body, This is My Blood* Bob and Penny Lord
*The Eucharistic Adoration*
*The Mystery of the RedemptionLamb's Supper* (Scott Hahn)
*Jewish Roots of the Eucharist* (Brant Pitre)
*True Devotion to Mary*
*The Secret of the Rosary*
*Marian Devotions (Father Kucer)*
*St. Joseph (See Father Calloway's Consecration) Cite other books.*
*Forty Dreams of St. John Bosco*
*The Life and Glories of St. Joseph*
*Padre Pio Man of Hope*
*The Last Mass of Padre Pio*
*St. Michael and the Angels*
*Enthronement of the Sacred Heart*

Appendix

## *PRAYERS*

*Prayers for You*
*Prayers for Priests*
*Flame of Love*
*Participate in 33 Day Devotions, hopefully as a faculty staff.*

OTHER Sources: (Note: These are not all Catholic but provide some wonderful perspective on common moral objectives, objective truth, and common goals to develop a virtuous life as conscientious citizen)

www.ingramcontent.com/pod-product-compliance
Lightning Source LLC
Chambersburg PA
CBHW050849160426
43194CB00011B/2081